BUSINESS LAW IN GERMANY

BUSINESS LAW IN GERMANY

HANS-CHRISTIAN ACKERMANN
DR. MICHAEL RATH
(EDITORS)

HANS-CHRISTIAN ACKERMANN, DR. STEFAN ALTENSCHMIDT,
SILVIA C. BAUER, RÜDIGER BONNMANN, INGO ERBERICH,
DR. ULRIKE FREIGANG, DR. MICHAEL FRITZSCHE,
DR. FRANZ-RUDOLF GROSS, DR. HANS-GEORG HAHN,
DR. RICHARD HAPP, DR. STEFANIE HELLMICH, DR. HELMUT JANSSEN,
DR. THOMAS KAPP, DR. ROLF KOBABE, DR. THOMAS KUHNLE,
CLAUDIA LEYENDECKER, DR. DETLEF MÄDER, ACHIM MEIER,
DR. ALEXANDER MÖNNIG, ULF-DIETER PAPE, DR. MICHAEL RATH,
DR. WULFF-AXEL SCHMIDT, DR. VOLKER SCHNEIDER,
ULRICH SIEGEMUND, DR. HOLGER STAPPERT, VOLKER STEIMLE,
DR. DETLEV STOECKER, THOMAS WEIDLICH, REINHARD WILLEMSEN,
JUTTA WITTLER, DR. ANGELIKA YATES

GLP
German Law Publishers
www.germanlawpublishers.com

ISBN 978-3-941389-15-1

The Deutsche Nationalbibliothek lists this publication in the Deutsche Nationalbibliografie; detailed bibliographic data are available on the Internet at http://dnb.de.

Typesetting: le-tex publishing services GmbH, Leipzig
Printing and binding: Beltz Bad Langensalza GmbH, Neustädter Straße 1–4, 99947 Bad Langensalza

PREFACE

Dear Reader!

The Federal Republic of Germany is the largest European economy and the fourth largest economy in the world in real terms, behind the United States, China and Japan. Furthermore, Germany still ranks as the world's second largest exporter. Its major trading partners include France, the United States, the United Kingdom, Italy and the Netherlands. All of the 500 largest companies in the world and in total about 45,000 foreign companies are present in Germany. According to a BBC poll of March 2011 Germany is the most popular country for foreign investment.

Doing business in Germany therefore still offers many lucrative business opportunities for foreign and domestic investors. This book is intended to serve as an introduction to the legal and tax regime which is applicable whilst doing business in Germany. The basic principles outlined in this book are intended to provide an idea of how many alternatives there are to efficiently structure a company with its business seat in Germany.

Our special thanks go to our Luther colleagues in the secretariat and marketing bureau. Furthermore, we thank our co-authors for their contributions and their excellent cooperation.

Please do not hesitate to contact us and any other author if you have any questions or comments. It would be our pleasure to answer your questions regarding the German jurisdiction and market.

This publication reflects legislation current as of April 2012.

Enjoy reading!

Yours sincerely,

Hans-Christian Ackermann Dr. Michael Rath

CONTENTS

CHAPTER 1
LEGAL FORMS OF DOING BUSINESS IN GERMANY

THOMAS WEIDLICH, LL.M.
DR. ANGELIKA YATES

German law offers a broad variety of legal forms which may be used for doing business. There have been some significant new developments in recent years, including a comprehensive reform of German company law, the so-called Company Law Reform 2008. All business vehicles are subject to registration requirements with the Commercial Register at the local District Court at the place of operation of the business respectively the registered office.

Keeping all basic information on the business entity in electronic form, the Commercial Register is publicly available to anybody interested in the legal details of the owner and managers of a business.[1]

In Germany, foreign investors might start a business either through a "dependent" structure (a branch or representative office of the foreign entity) or through an independent German legal entity (a corporation or partnership).

The following provides a brief overview of the main features of the different German business vehicles – including the legal form of the European Public Company (*Societas Europaea*) and the proposed European Private Company (*Societas Privata Europaea*) – to identify which vehicle might fit best the needs of a potential investor.[2]

1 Electronic Federal Gazette: http://www.unternehmensregister.de;
Commercial Register: http://www.handelsregister.de.

2 An overview and a more comprehensive introduction to German company law in English is provided by Wirth / Arnold / Morshäuser / Green, Corporate Law in Germany, 2nd ed. 2010; Wendler / Tremml / Buecker, Key Aspects of German Business Law. A practical Manual, 4th ed. 2008; du Plessis et. al., German Corporate Governance in International and European Context, 2007.

A. Representative Offices

Foreign entities exploring the German market for the first time will often consider the establishment of a "representative office" (*Repräsentanz*). German law makes no specific provision for a representative office, but as in many other jurisdictions it is accepted practice in Germany.

Opening a representative office is regarded as a first step when venturing into a new market and is often used as an opportunity to evaluate the local market conditions. This can be achieved by simply seconding an employee to Germany and arranging for the employee to explore the local market from a German situated office. Also, it is possible to engage an independent agent who generates business and might also be entitled to conclude contracts (*Handelsvertreter*) on behalf of the foreign entity. Such a structure must be considered carefully in order to avoid creating a permanent establishment (*Betriebsstätte*) in Germany as this could have adverse tax effects.[3] Furthermore, in the event that the representative office is actively involved in the business operations itself, it is considered to be a dependent branch (*unselbstständige Zweigstelle*).

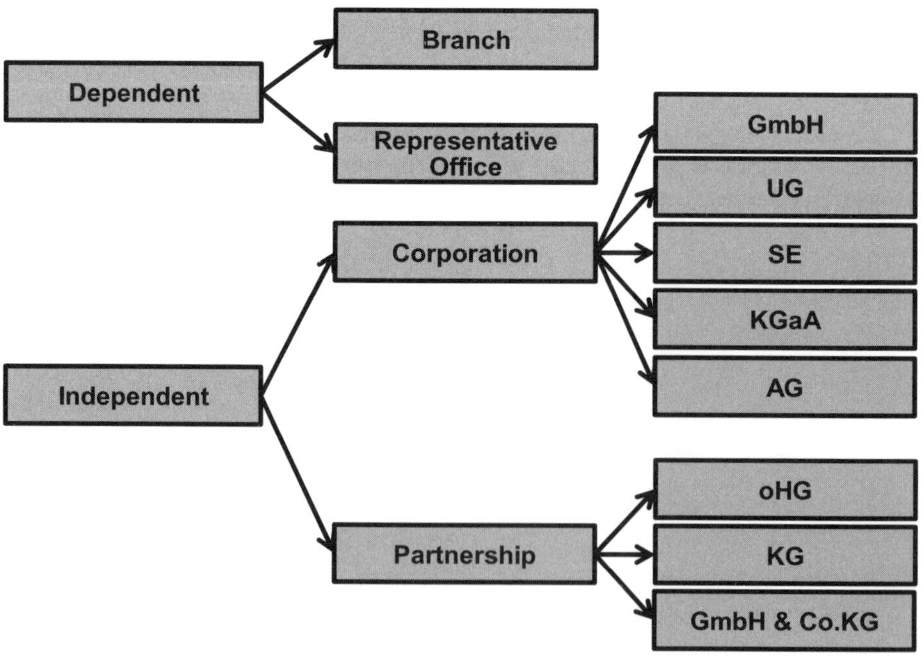

3 For prerequisites and implications of a permanent establishment, please refer to the chapter "Taxation in Germany".

B. Branch

Foreign companies who do not wish to set up a new business vehicle or who are not yet sure about the sustainability of their involvement and commitment to the local market can simply establish a branch office (*Niederlassung*). Opening a branch office may have certain tax advantages compared to a corporation.[4] A branch office can be established as an independent branch office (*selbstständige Zweigniederlassung*) or as a dependent branch office (*unselbstständige Zweigstelle*).

However, even an independent branch has no separate legal entity status and, therefore, is regarded as an integral part of the foreign company. A branch may engage in business activities independently, but the foreign company is liable for the business transactions concluded by the branch. The relationships with the branch's customers and business partners are generally subject to German law. Furthermore, it has to be kept in mind that a branch not only makes the foreign company subject to German jurisdiction, but also creates a permanent establishment for tax purposes. The foreign company owns all assets and incurs all liabilities and debts deriving from the branch's operations. Consequently, the foreign company is also the contractual partner for customers and business partners of the German branch. However, claims can be brought up in German courts at the location of the branch.

At the organizational level, the branch is to a certain extent independent from the foreign company and usually has the following attributes:

- Management with freedom to act according to its own judgment (i. e. with full power of attorney and power to contract);
- Its own capital resources and bank account;
- Separate accounting;
- A branch office can use its own name affix; the name of the foreign company must appear including its legal designation (for example: XY Ltd., branch office, Berlin).

Before commencing its business operations, the independent branch office has to register with the Commercial Register[5] and with the local Trade Office of the municipality where the branch office is to be located.[6] For some business sectors, a permit or authorization may be required.[7]

4 Please refer to the chapter "Taxation in Germany".

5 Sects. 13 (1)–13 g (1) HGB (*Handelsgesetzbuch* – Commercial Code).

6 Sec. 14 (1) GewO (*Gewerbeordnung* – Trade Licensing Act).

7 Restricted sectors are, for example restaurant business (*Gaststättengewerbe*) or gambling activities (*Spielhallengewerbe*).

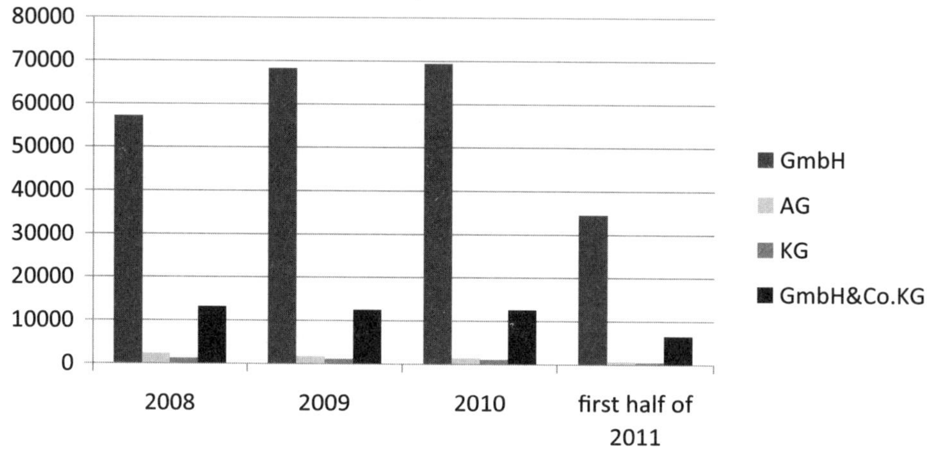

Whereas the Trade Office only requests basic information about the branch name, its owner, representatives and type of business, the application for registration with the Commercial Register must also include details of the relevant foreign company such as its legal form, place of incorporation, principal place of business, share capital and the names of its officers and directors. The application must be accompanied by certified copies of the Certificate of Incorporation and Articles of Association of the foreign corporation and must be signed by the directors of the foreign company. A notary public must certify the signatures of the directors. The certifying notary may be a foreign notary, in which case, however, the notary's certificate must then be legalized, unless this requirement has been waived pursuant to a bilateral treaty. This means that the authenticity of the notary's certificate (i. e. the competence of the notary public and the authenticity of the signature) has to be confirmed by the embassy of the foreign country. In most countries, the legalization can be done by way of an Apostille under the Hague Convention.[8] The registration procedure can be quite time-consuming, especially where translations of the relevant documents are required.[9]

A dependent branch office is dependent on the head office in every respect. Its operations are unified and the only difference is that the branch office is in a different

8 Hague Convention dated 5th October 1961 "Abolishing the Requirements for Legalization for Foreign Public Documents". The Convention is in force since 14 January 1965 and has been ratified by 102 contracting states (as of 19 September 2011). The Apostille is a simplified form of authenticity. The certification of the document by a notary public and the legalization by the embassy are not required for authenticity. The competent authority only has to issue an Apostille, which replaces the legalization in all countries which signed the Hague Convention.

9 Due to harmonized EC law, documentation requirements for EU companies have been reduced and are fairly modest now. Non-European companies have to provide extensive evidence as to their existence, incorporation and authorized officers.

location to the head office. The dependent branch office does not have to be registered with the Commercial Register, but with the local Trade Office.[10]

The choice between doing business in Germany through a branch or through a separate German legal entity is mostly tax-driven. Leaving aside tax considerations, a branch is the suitable business vehicle if the business conducted in Germany is unlikely to have any substantial size and/or the foreign company does not have a long-term commitment to setting up business in Germany.

If a sustainable medium for long-term investment is sought, a potential investor should consider setting up an independent German business vehicle.

C. Corporations

German law allows the establishment of three major forms of corporations (*Kapitalgesellschaften*): the *GmbH* (*Gesellschaft mit beschränkter Haftung* – limited liability company); the AG (*Aktiengesellschaft* – stock corporation); and the rarely used KGaA (*Kommanditgesellschaft auf Aktien* – partnership limited by shares). Since October 2004, an investor can also use an European Public Company (*Societas Europaea* or *SE*) as a business vehicle in Germany. A new European Private Company (*Societas Privata Europaea* or SPE) has also been proposed, but is not yet available under European and German law.

D. GmbH

The GmbH[11] is the corporate entity most commonly used in Germany and can be set up for any legally permissible purpose.[12] According to official statistics, there are presently about one million GmbHs established in Germany.[13] The graph below shows the number of GmbHs compared to the number of other corporations and partnerships.[14]

---

10 Sec. 14 (1) GewO.

11 For an overview in English translation, see also Muller, The GmbH: A Guide to the German Limited Liability Company, 2006; Jungmann / Sartoro, German GmbH Law, 2011.

12 Sec. 1 GmbHG (*Gesetz betreffend die Gesellschaft mit beschränkter Haftung* – German Limited Liability Companies Act); For an English translation of the relevant provisions of the GmbHG please refer to Wirth / Arnold / Morshäuser / Greene, Corporate Law in Germany, 2nd ed. 2010 (Part 2, pp. 231 et seq.).

13 Kornblum, Bundesweite Rechtstatsachen zum Handels- und Gesellschaftsrecht, GmbHR 2011, pp. 692 et seq.

14 Ibid.

The number of incorporations of a GmbH is constantly increasing. The graph below shows the number of incorporations of new companies within the last year.[15]

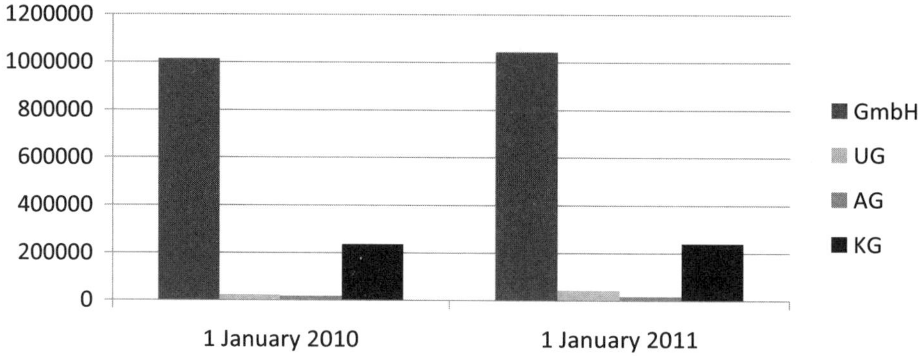

Each year, more than 50,000 GmbHs are incorporated in Germany. Within the first six months of 2011, more than 30,000 GmbHs were incorporated by entrepreneurs. The structure of a GmbH is best described as a private company limited by shares. It is designed for closely held businesses (an IPO is not possible) with a clear and stable shareholder structure. A GmbH provides full liability protection to its shareholders in that they are generally only liable up to the maximum amount of their capital contribution.

In 2008, the German Limited Liability Companies Act (*GmbHG*) underwent its most comprehensive reform since it came into force 110 years ago. After years of discussion, the Act on the Modernization of the Limited Liability Companies Act (*MoMiG*) was passed, the relevant amendments taking effect from 1st November 2008.[16] The main objective of the Corporate Law Reform 2008 was to achieve greater flexibility and deregulation in order to make the German GmbH more attractive and competitive in the international market, as well as to address certain areas of misuse.

15 For more details, please refer to the homepage of the Federal Statistical Office (*Statistisches Bundesamt*): http://www.destatis.de (*Gewerbeanzeigen* – business notifications).

16 For an overview concerning the modernization of the GmbHG refer to: Busch, Überblick über die Neuerungen ab November 2008 im Bereich des Handels- und Registerrechts nach dem "Gesetz zur Modernisierung des GmbH-Rechts und zur Bekämpfung von Missbräuchen (MoMiG) vom 23.10.2008" (http://www.ghr.nrw.de).

I. Advantages of a GmbH

The reasons for the popularity of the GmbH and its main advantages compared with the other legal forms available in Germany are as follows:

- The formation of a GmbH is quite simple;
- Relatively low minimum share capital of EUR 25,000.00 is required;
- The Articles of Association (*Gesellschaftsvertrag*) of a GmbH can be easily adapted to the requirements of the shareholders, granting far-reaching autonomy to its owners;
- A GmbH is not subject to as many strict legislative regulations as an AG or the SE; and
- The shareholders of a GmbH may issue binding instructions or directions to the Managing Directors (*Geschäftsführer*) and can thereby exercise direct influence on the GmbH's management.

The highest corporate body of a GmbH is the shareholders' meeting (*Gesellschafterversammlung*) which determines the objectives of the company and may give instructions to the Managing Directors. A GmbH must have at least one Managing Director who represents the company externally. If a GmbH has 500 or more employees, a supervisory board (*Aufsichtsrat*) has to be installed which will then exercise certain monitoring functions; alternatively, an advisory board (*Beirat*) may be established voluntarily.

II. Incorporation and Registration

A GmbH is formed by the founding shareholder(s) executing a Deed of Formation and Articles of Association (*Gesellschaftsvertrag*) before a German notary public.[17] A GmbH can be set up with only one shareholder and is not restricted to a maximum number. Foreign individuals, partnerships or corporations may become shareholders of a GmbH. A representative of the founding shareholder(s) acting under power of attorney (which also must be certified by a notary public) may execute the Deed of Formation and the Articles of Association.[18] As a result of the Corporate Law Reform 2008, a model document for incorporation has been introduced to accelerate the formation and registration process. However, this model document can only be used by a model-document GmbH (*Musterprotokoll-GmbH*), which consists of no more than three shareholders and one Managing Director.[19] The statutory share capital of the model-document GmbH must be contributed in cash. The founding shareholders

---

17 Other than through formation (*Gründung*), a GmbH may also come into existence through conversion (*Umwandlung*) of another legal entity; for more details please refer to the chapter "Conversion".

18 Sec. 2 (2) GmbHG.

19 Sec. 2 (1a) GmbHG.

are not allowed to deviate from the model document. This means that the standard procedure may not be suitable in all instances. The model document for incorporation is divided into different parts and replaces the Articles of Association as well as the shareholders' list. The model document sets out the name, registered office and object(s) of the GmbH as well as provisions about the statutory share capital. Furthermore, the model document sets out provisions for the appointment of the Managing Director. Further amendments to the Articles of Association and/or the appointment of additional Managing Directors may be carried out at any time once the GmbH has been formed and registered with the local Commercial Register. Notary costs incurred in connection with the formation of a model company are also likely to be lower if the standard incorporation procedure is used.[20]

The notary fees for the incorporation of a standard GmbH with a share capital of EUR 25,000 are as follows (in total approx. EUR 500):

- Notarization of Articles of Association: EUR 168.00 and if the company has only one shareholder (*Ein-Mann-GmbH*) the fee is only EUR 84.00;[21]
- Notarization of appointment of Managing Director/certification of shareholders' meeting: EUR 168.00;[22]
- Drafting of application form for Commercial Register and notarization of signatures of the Managing Directors: EUR 42.00;[23]
- Costs for the notice in the Federal Gazette: around EUR 100;[24]
- Filing of shareholders' list: approx. EUR 13.00.[25]

Immediately after notarization of the Deed of Formation and Articles of Association, but prior to filing the application for registration with the Commercial Register, the GmbH must open a bank account. Cash contributions to the share capital must be deposited in said account prior to filing for registration. In addition to other registration documents, the Commercial Register may request that bank statements be submitted to confirm that the cash contributions were in fact deposited into the company's bank account. The Managing Director(s) must certify to the Commercial Register that the said cash contribution is still at the company's disposal at the date of filing the application.[26]

---

20 According to Sec. 41d KostO (*Kostenordnung* – Law on Costs in Affairs of Voluntary Jurisdiction), the transaction value (*Geschäftswert*) of EUR 25,000.00 does not apply for the incorporation of a model-document GmbH which results in lower notary fees.

21 Sec. 32 (1), Sec. 36 (1), (2) KostO as well as Appendix to Sec. 32 KostO.

22 Sec. 32 (1), Sec. 47 KostO as well as Appendix to Sec. 32 KostO.

23 Sec. 32 (1), Sec. 38 (2) No. 7, Sec. 145 (1) KostO as well as Appendix to Sec. 32 KostO.

24 For more information, please refer to the homepage of Electronic Federal Gazette: http://www.ebundesanzeiger.de.

25 Sec. 30, Sec. 32 (1), Sec. 147 (2) KostO as well as Appendix to Sec. 32 KostO.

26 Sec. 8 (2) GmbHG.

The application for the registration of a GmbH needs to be signed by all Managing Directors in person before a notary public, who must certify their signatures and instruct them about their duties as Managing Directors vis-à-vis the German courts. Certification and instruction by German consulates abroad is possible.[27]

III. Step Plan: Incorporation of a GmbH

1. Preparation of incorporation documents:

   - Articles of Association (*Gesellschaftsvertrag*)
   - Power of attorney to be issued by foreign company to proxy (see step 3.)
   - Deed of Incorporation
   - List of shareholders
   - Application letter to the Commercial Register

2. Obtaining approval from the local Chamber of Commerce regarding the proposed name of NewCo.
3. Signing of power of attorney before notary public authorizing proxy to incorporate NewCo.

   <u>Note:</u> Foreign companies often appoint a proxy to act on their behalf in the incorporation process based on a power of attorney.
   Signature by the duly authorized representative of the foreign company under the power of attorney must be certified by a notary public and apostilled (if required). A notarial confirmation regarding the authorization of the signatory acting on behalf of the foreign company or other evidence will also be required (e.g. Company Secretary Certification, Board Resolution etc.).

4. Notarization of the Deed of Incorporation (by proxy) before a German notary public, including:

   - Articles of Association
   - Appointment of Managing Director(s)

5. Opening of a bank account in Germany for NewCo by the duly authorized managing director of NewCo
6. Payment of the share capital into the bank account of NewCo.

   <u>Note:</u> The minimum share capital for a German GmbH is EUR 25,000.00. In such case, at least EUR 12,500.00 must be paid initially into the bank account.

---

27 Sec. 10 (1) No.1 KonsularG (*Konsulargesetz* – German Act on Consular Officials, Their Tasks and Competencies).

7. Forwarding to the notary public a copy of the statement of account, evidencing that the share capital has been credited to NewCo's bank account.
8. Signing the application letter to the Commercial Register by all Managing Directors before a notary public.

   Note: The notary public will instruct the Managing Directors regarding their duties. The signature under the application letter must be certified by a notary public and apostilled (if required).

9. Signing the shareholders' list by NewCo's managing directors.
10. Filing the application for entry of NewCo with the competent Commercial Register (will be done by the acting German notary public).
11. Entry of NewCo in the Commercial Register (approx. 1–2 weeks after filing the application form).

IV. Liability Prior to Registration

Following notarization of the Deed of Formation and the Articles of Association, the company will exist as a so-called "Company in Formation" (*Vorgesellschaft*) and may commence business. Once the company has been registered with the Commercial Register it becomes a separate legal entity.[28]

Rights and liabilities arising from preregistration activities are legally the rights and liabilities of the Company in Formation, but only to the extent that the Managing Director(s) are acting within the authority vested in them by the Articles of Association or by shareholders' resolutions. The Managing Director(s) and the Company in Formation remain jointly and severally liable to creditors for any liabilities incurred prior to registration of the GmbH with the Commercial Register.[29] To the extent that the shareholders have consented to business activities prior to registration, they are also liable for the debts of the Company in Formation.[30] Upon registration of the GmbH, all rights and obligations of the Managing Directors assumed prior to registration are assigned by law to the GmbH and the Managing Directors no longer have any personal liability in respect of these.

Although a GmbH may commence business prior to its registration, its net assets, as of the date of registration, must not be less than the amount of its registered share capital. If this is the case (for example as a result of losses incurred prior to the registration of the GmbH), the shareholders will be liable for the shortfall between the amount of the registered share capital and the net assets as of the date of registration.

28 Sec. 11 (1) GmbHG.
29 Sec. 11 (2) GmbHG.
30 BGH (*Bundesgerichtshof* – Federal Supreme Court), published in BGHZ 134, 333 et seq.

V. Limited Liability of Shareholders

Once registered in the Commercial Register, only the GmbH itself is liable for its debts. The liability of the shareholders is limited to their capital contribution. Courts will pierce the "corporate veil", i. e. the limited liability status, only on very rare occasions. The mere fact that a shareholder is permanently and comprehensively controlling the GmbH, will not result in the piercing of the corporate veil. A controlling shareholder will only be liable for a loss suffered by the GmbH if he or she willfully acts contrary to the best interests of the GmbH and to the detriment of its creditors and does not respect the integrity and independence of the GmbH.[31] In particular, a shareholder might forfeit the protection of the limited liability shield if the shareholder intentionally abuses his controlling position to the disadvantage of the GmbH or its creditors.

VI. Articles of Association

Depending on the degree of flexibility desired by the shareholders, the Articles of Association may be formulated in short form setting out only minimum mandatory provisions regarding purpose, name, registered office, registered share capital, nominal value of each share assumed by the shareholders, representation and management of the GmbH.[32] The Articles of Association may, on the other hand, constitute a comprehensive document including detailed provisions on shareholders' rights and obligations, classes of shares and restrictions on the transfer of shares.[33]

A GmbH may be formed for any lawful purpose which has to be stated in the Articles of Association. No doctrine of ultra vires exists under German law.[34] A GmbH may therefore enter into binding obligations with third parties, which may not necessarily relate to its corporate purpose, in which case, however, the Managing Director(s) may be liable for damages which such obligations cause to the GmbH.

A GmbH may also use any name including a fictional name provided that no risk exists of confusing the name with any other corporation within the same local area and that the name is not misleading. It should be noted, however, that registration officials remain cautious regarding the use of the words "International" and "Germany" in a corporation's name if no substantial international business actually exists

---

31 "Trihotel"-decision of the BGH, NJW 2007, 2689 et seq.; decision of the BGH, NJW 1994, 1801 et seq.

32 Sec. 3 (1) GmbHG.

33 In addition, the rights and duties of shareholders may be set out in a separate shareholders' agreement (see below).

34 A duly authorized Managing Director has comprehensive authority vis-à-vis third parties and can in principle represent the GmbH in any matter, i. e. a GmbH can in general not act beyond its power.

or if the corporation only conducts local business rather than business throughout Germany. Before filing the documents for incorporation with the Commercial Register, the name of the GmbH should be reviewed by the local Chamber of Industry and Commerce. The competent District Court for the Commercial Register usually follows the decision of the Chamber of Industry and Commerce as to whether a name is confusing or misleading.

German corporation law is federal law; from a legal perspective this means that there is no advantage if the corporation is registered in a particular German state.[35] Tax advantages may, however, arise if a GmbH is registered in a particular city because trade tax rates are determined by municipalities and consequently vary from location to location.[36]

When an independent branch (*selbstständige Zweigniederlassung*) is set up, the branch has to be registered with the respective local Commercial Register. The main registered office shall be the place where the GmbH operates its business or where its management is located. The registered office must be within Germany.[37]

As a result of the Corporate Law Reform 2008, it is no longer essential for the place of the management (*Verwaltungssitz*) of the company to be the same as the registered office, and it can be located anywhere within Germany and even abroad, e.g. the place of management can be located in Berlin or London and the registered office can be in Cologne. If the place of management is moved to another location, the Articles of Association do not have to be amended. This distinction between the place of management and the registered office also means that foreign shareholders can manage their subsidiaries registered in Germany from a head office outside of Germany and German corporations with a worldwide operating business can run their foreign investments – with a few exceptions – in the familiar legal form of a GmbH. Within the EU, existing foreign corporations can be merged into a GmbH, which is registered with a Commercial Register in Germany, but which is managed and operated at the location of the transferring foreign entity abroad.

VII. Share Capital

The minimum share capital of a GmbH is EUR 25,000.00 with the exception of a special form of a GmbH (the so-called "Small GmbH") described below. The shareholders are free to divide the share capital into any number of shares. The min-

35 In practical terms, local registration courts do not always follow the same administrative procedures and the incorporation or subsequent changes to the articles of a GmbH may be more difficult or lengthy at some locations in Germany compared to other places.

36 For more details please refer to the chapter "Taxation in Germany".

37 Sec. 4a GmbHG.

imum nominal amount of a single share is EUR 1.00.[38] Shares may be issued in any nominal amount which is divisible by EUR 1.00 and any shareholder can subscribe for several shares with different nominal amounts (as part of the Corporate Law Reform 2008, the previous minimum nominal value of EUR 100.00 was abolished).

The GmbH is not required to issue share certificates or to maintain a share register. The ownership of the shares is documented only in the incorporation deed and any subsequent transfers will be documented in notarial transfer deeds and the shareholders' list. Upon incorporation and each subsequent transfer or division of shares, the Managing Directors or the involved notary public must submit an up-dated list of shareholders to the Commercial Register. If the Managing Directors or an acting notary public do not comply with their obligations of reporting changes to the shareholders' list, claims for damages may be raised against them.[39]

VIII. Contribution and Maintenance of Capital

Contributions to the share capital may be made in cash or in kind. For contributions in kind, the Articles of Association must set out the specific form of the contribution as well as the amount of the nominal value of the shares. The shareholders must provide a report on the valuation of the contribution in kind and, if the contribution in kind is a business to be transferred to the GmbH, the financial results of the business for the previous two years. The contribution in kind must ultimately be worth at least as much as the corresponding nominal value of shares issued, and the Commercial Register will want to see documents evidencing this (in practice, expert valuations are often submitted). The contributing shareholder must pay any shortfall in cash.

In the case of a cash contribution, at least 25 % of each nominal share and in total at least 50 % of the minimum share capital must be paid up in cash at the time of filing for registration of the GmbH.

The legislation governing the GmbH contains several provisions designed to ensure that the share capital of a GmbH is fully paid up and maintained. A GmbH is generally not authorized to make any payments or grant any other benefits to shareholders which would reduce the net assets of the corporation below the stated amount of its registered share capital.[40] If such payments or benefits are made to the shareholders violating the capital maintenance rules, the respective shareholders are obliged to repay the received contributions and the Managing Directors of the company, being responsible for the unlawful contributions, can be held liable for any damages sustained by the company.

---

38 Sec. 5 (2) GmbHG.

39 Sec. 40 (3) GmbHG establishes a liability of the Managing Directors towards affected shareholders and creditors.

40 Sec. 30 GmbHG.

IX. Transfer of Shares

The purchase and transfer of a share in a GmbH requires notarial form.[41] Without notarization, a purchase contract concerning shares in a GmbH is null and void. However, if the share transfer is performed in accordance with the notarial form, the lack of notarization of the underlying contractual obligation to transfer (i. e. the share purchase agreement) is cured.[42] Due to high notarial fees before German notaries in the past, it used to be rather common to notarize larger M&A transactions outside Germany, in particular in Switzerland (and especially in Basel). This practice was based on a decision of the Federal Court recognizing foreign notarizations if they were equivalent to notarization in Germany (which was subsequently confirmed for certain Swiss notaries also by various regional courts in Germany).[43] However, this practice is seen less often in recent years since the fees for German notaries have been capped at approximately EUR 60,000.00 for a single transaction.

Shares in a GmbH are, in principle, freely transferable. However, the Articles of Association may provide that other requirements must also be met (for example, consent of the other shareholders, preemption rights).[44] In order for the acquirer to exercise the rights of a shareholder vis-à-vis the company (i. e. the voting rights), an updated shareholders' list must be filed with the commercial register.[45]

It is not yet clear whether a foreign reorganization of the shareholders of a German GmbH (i. e. a merger) will trigger the automatic transfer of the shares in a German GmbH (i. e. by way of universal succession) or whether the German statutory formalities also have to be satisfied. Since there are no binding court rulings available and the law does not provide sufficient guidance, it is recommended that the GmbH shares are also in addition transferred by way of a notarized transfer deed in the course of the reorganization abroad, when implementing any foreign reorganization which may have an impact on the shareholder structure of a GmbH.

X. Managing Directors

A GmbH is managed and legally represented by its Managing Director(s) in all legal transactions in and out of court.[46] Although a GmbH must have at least one Managing Director, there is no maximum number and it is possible for it to have as many as it likes. When a GmbH has no Managing Director and becomes "leaderless" (*füh-*

---

41 Sec. 15 (3), (4) GmbHG.
42 Sec. 15 (4) sentence 2 GmbHG.
43 BGH, BGHZ 80, 76 et seq.
44 Sec. 15 (5) GmbHG.
45 Sec. 16 (1) GmbHG.
46 Sec. 35 (1) GmbHG.

rungslos), the shareholders are appointed by law to represent the GmbH and receive notices until a new Managing Director has been appointed.[47] A Managing Director does not need to be a shareholder or a German resident.[48] Only an individual (but not a corporate entity) may be appointed as Managing Director.

In the absence of any restrictions, each appointed Managing Director may act for and bind the GmbH vis-à-vis third parties. Any restrictions on the authority of the Managing Director(s) to bind the GmbH which are set out in the Articles of Association, in a shareholders' resolution or in the service contract of the Managing Director (particularly any requirement to obtain the approval of the shareholders prior to entering into certain transactions) do not affect the Managing Director's ability to bind the GmbH.[49] The breach by the Managing Director of any of the aforementioned restrictions may subsequently, however, give rise to a claim for damages by the GmbH against the Managing Director.[50]

If only one Managing Director is appointed, he/she is the sole representative of the GmbH. If more than one Managing Director is appointed, generally, they will represent the GmbH jointly. The shareholders may, however, grant one or several Managing Directors the right to either:

- Represent the GmbH individually; or
- Represent the GmbH jointly with one or more other Managing Directors or an authorized officer (*Prokurist*) who will be a representative of the company with a general power of attorney.

The power of representation of each Managing Director and each authorized officer must be registered with the Commercial Register and is binding in relation to third parties.

The Managing Directors must manage the company's business with the due care of a prudent business person.[51] Additional specific obligations can be found in the GmbHG and in other statues, or may be imposed by the Articles of Association or the service contract. Further, the shareholders – acting by a simple majority resolution – can give binding instructions to the Managing Directors which they have to obey unconditionally unless the instructions are unlawful. Managing Directors who are in breach of their duties are jointly and severally liable for any damages sustained by the company. In particular, Managing Director(s) may not disclose trade

47 Sec. 35 (1) cl. 2 GmbHG.
48 For further details regarding the immigration procedures of a non-EU resident, please refer to the chapter "Employment Law").
49 Sec. 37 (2) GmbHG.
50 Sects. 37 (1), 43 (2) GmbHG.
51 Sec. 43 (1) GmbHG.

secrets of the GmbH, must file for bankruptcy if the GmbH is overindebted or insolvent,[52] must call a shareholders' meeting if more than half of the stated share capital is lost,[53] must ensure that the GmbH keeps proper records,[54] must submit tax returns on behalf of the GmbH when due,[55] and must ensure that the shareholders' list is updated.[56]

A Managing Director of a GmbH can be held personally liable for any damage resulting e.g. from an incorrect list of shareholders. A Managing Director should therefore always carefully review the current list of shareholders which is filed with the Commercial Register. Concerning the general duty to run the GmbH's business in a prudent manner, the German courts have acknowledged that Managing Directors may make mistakes when taking business decisions and have granted a broad scope of discretion in this context ("business judgment rule").[57] However, the GmbH management may not have a personal interest in the matter, must act in good faith and is obliged to take decisions on an informed basis and if necessary based on appropriate external advice to avoid liability.

XI. Supervisory Board

Contrary to a German stock corporation (AG), a GmbH, as a rule, does not need to have a supervisory board. However, a GmbH may voluntarily establish a supervisory board consisting of "non-executive" members.[58] However, if a GmbH has more than 500 (and less than 2,000) employees, the installation of a supervisory board is mandatory and 1/3 of its members must be employees' representatives.[59] If the (regular) number of employees of the company exceeds 2,000, half of the members of the supervisory board must be employees' representatives.[60] Employees of companies controlled by or integrated into the GmbH also count towards these thresholds.[61] The Employee Participation Act (*DrittelbG*) and the Co-Determination Act (*MitbestG*)

52 Sec. 15a (1) InsO (*Insolvenzordnung* – Insolvency Code).
53 Sec. 49 (3) GmbHG.
54 Sec. 41, 42 GmbHG.
55 Sec. 34 AO (*Abgabenordnung* – General Tax Code).
56 Sec. 40 (1) GmbHG.
57 BGH, published in BGHZ 135, 244 et seq. ("ARAG").
58 If the optional supervisory board not only has an advisory role, but also carries out monitoring responsibilities, most of the relevant provisions for a supervisory board of an AG apply, Sec. 52 GmbHG.
59 Sec. 1 (1) No. 3, Sec. 4 (1) DrittelbG (*Gesetz über die Drittelbeteiligung der Arbeitnehmer im Aufsichtsrat* – Employee Participation Act).
60 Sec. 1 (1) No. 1, Sec. 7 (1) No. 1 MitbestG (*Gesetz über die Mitbestimmung der Arbeitnehmer* – Co-Determination Act).
61 Sec. 5 MitbestG.

contain further provisions regarding membership, qualification requirements, election procedure and competencies of the supervisory board.[62]
Where there is the voluntary establishment of a supervisory board, the functions of the supervisory board may be stipulated in the Articles of Association. The basic function of the supervisory board is to supervise the management of the company and it may also be assigned the right of appointment and removal of the Managing Directors, adoption of the annual financial statements and calling of shareholders' meetings.

XII. Shareholders and Shareholders' List

The shareholders of a GmbH are subject to various rights and duties. The most important of which are as follows:

- Voting rights and other rights to participate in the shareholders' meeting;
- The right to participate in the profits of the company;
- Rights to any surplus upon liquidation;
- The right to obtain information;
- The duty to pay their contributions;
- A fiduciary duty toward the company and other shareholders.

The Articles of Association or a separate shareholders' agreement often contain more specific provisions with respect to shareholders' rights. The advantage of a shareholders' agreement is that it does not have to be published with the commercial register and hence its provisions can be kept confidential.

Only a person who is actually registered in the list of shareholders will be considered by the company to be a shareholder. The acquirer of GmbH shares may generally rely on the accuracy of the list of shareholders if no objection has been raised to a false entry during the last three years.[63] It is possible to acquire GmbH shares in good faith from a registered shareholder even if the list of shareholders subsequently turns out to be incorrect.

The shareholders exercise their powers in relation to the GmbH by passing resolutions in a general meeting (or by circular resolution). The shareholders' meeting is the ultimate decision-making body of the GmbH. The Articles of Association often contain specific rules of procedure and majority requirements for certain decisions. A shareholder will generally have one vote per one Euro of share capital. The Articles of Association may, however, provide otherwise.

---

62 Sec. 4 et seq. DrittelbestG; Sec. 6 et seq. MitbestG.

63 Sec. 16 (3) GmbHG.

Shareholders' resolutions must be approved by a simple majority (i. e. more than 50 % of the votes cast) unless mandatory law or the Articles of Association require a higher majority and/or the consent of certain shareholders to be obtained. Shareholder resolutions amending the Articles of Association must be notarized.[64]

For example, amendments to the Articles of Association require a special majority (75 % of the votes cast). This majority requirement may only be increased, and not decreased, by the Articles of Association.[65] German law requires the consent of certain shareholders, or indeed all of them, when the obligations of some or all of the shareholders are to be increased, and in this case it will only be possible to make such a change with the consent of those shareholders whose rights will be affected.[66]

Shareholders have the right to inspect the books and records of the GmbH and to be informed about the company's affairs.[67] This right of information is generally unrestricted, but must not be misused, for example, to benefit a competing business.[68] Managing Directors, upon a shareholders' resolution, may refuse to provide information to a shareholder if there is a likelihood that the requested information will be used for improper purposes, thereby causing substantial harm to the company.[69] The affected shareholder may bring a court action against such a decision.[70]

Each shareholder owes a duty of loyalty to the company as well as to the other shareholders. This duty is not expressly stipulated by statutory law and its exact scope depends on the structure of the company; for example, when there are only two shareholders of a GmbH, they normally owe each other a higher degree of consideration than the shareholders in a GmbH with many shareholders. German courts have recognized fiduciary duties in various areas, such as the exercise of voting rights[71] or the right to give instructions in a group of companies.[72] Although shareholders are, as a general rule, not prohibited from competing with the GmbH, under certain circumstances their fiduciary duty may impose such a restriction. This does not mean, however, that the shareholder should place the interests of the GmbH above his/her own in each case, but it does place some limits on the extent to which a shareholder may pursue his/her own interests to the detriment of the company.

---

64 Sec. 53 (2) GmbHG.
65 Sec. 53 (2) GmbHG.
66 Sec. 35 BGB (*Bürgerliches Gesetzbuch* – German Civil Code).
67 Sec. 51a (1) GmbHG.
68 BGH, published in BGHZ 135, 48 et seq., BGHZ 152, 339 et seq.
69 Sec. 51a (2) GmbHG.
70 Sec. 51b GmbHG; Sec. 132 AktG (*Aktiengesetz* – Stock Corporation Act).
71 BGH, published in BHGZ 65, 15 et seq.
72 BGH, published in BGHZ 89, 162 et seq.

XIII. Ongoing Accounting Obligations and Disclosure Requirements

A GmbH must keep accounting records and prepare annual financial statements in accordance with the provisions of the German Commercial Code (*HGB*) which lays down detailed requirements as to the form and content of the annual financial statements.[73] Furthermore, medium-sized and large corporations must have their annual financial statements audited. Relevant criteria are the number of employees, turnover and the balance sheet total.[74] A company is considered a medium-sized corporation when at least two of the following thresholds are passed: the number of employees calculated on an annual average exceeds 50 (but not 250); the turnover for the last twelve months exceeds EUR 9,680,000.00 (but is less than EUR 38,500,000.00); and the balance sheet total for the last two business years exceeds EUR 4,840,000.00 (but is less than EUR 19,250,000.00). A company is considered to be a large corporation if it accesses an organized market through securities issued by the company or if two of the respective higher thresholds (in brackets above) are surpassed or if it has applied for authorization for trading on a regulated market. The (audited) annual financial statements must be filed with the electronic Federal Gazette within twelve months of the end of each financial year.[75] Penalties may be imposed on the Managing Directors and the GmbH itself if these disclosure obligations are not observed.[76]

However, German corporations are not obliged to lodge an annual confirmation or update of their registered details (also known as "annual returns" in other jurisdictions) with the Commercial Register. Only actual changes relating to the registered information (e.g. registered office, Articles of Association, registered share capital, etc.) must be notified and registered.

E. "Unternehmergesellschaft (haftungsbeschränkt)" or "Small GmbH"

The Corporate Law Reform 2008 introduced the so-called "Small GmbH" (*Unternehmergesellschaft (haftungsbeschränkt)*) as a new type of GmbH in response to foreign entities entering the German market.[77] It can be set up quickly and does not

73 Sec. 238 et seq. HGB (*Handelsgesetzbuch* – Commercial Code).

74 Sec. 267 HGB.

75 Sec. 325 (1) HGB.

76 Sec. 331 et seq. HGB.

77 Since November 2008, approx. 45,000 UGs have been formed; refer to Kornblum, Bundesweite Rechtstatsachen zum Handels- und Gesellschaftsrecht, GmbHR 2011, 692 et seq.

require a minimum capital. A Small GmbH only differs from a "proper" GmbH in relation to three major points:[78]

- The Small GmbH is not subject to the statutory minimum capital of EUR 25,000.00 applicable to a "normal" GmbH. The Small GmbH may therefore be incorporated with a statutory share capital of EUR 1.00;
- The application for the registration of a Small GmbH is only allowed if the share capital is fully contributed. Contributions to the share capital may be only made in cash, not in kind. A Small GmbH must allocate one quarter of its annual profits to its capital reserves. This obligation ceases only after the shareholders have either converted such capital reserves into statutory share capital or increased the statutory share capital by additional contributions to at least an amount equal to the statutory minimum share capital required for a "proper" GmbH (i. e. EUR 25,000.00);
- Finally, the Small GmbH must indicate its status as a Small GmbH in its company name which therefore reads "*Unternehmergesellschaft* (*haftungsbeschränkt*)" or "UG (*haftungsbeschränkt*)". Only after the shareholders have increased the share capital to the statutory minimum of EUR 25,000.00 can the suffix for a Small GmbH be dropped and replaced with the usual suffix "GmbH".

F. Shelf Companies

Companies formed by service providers without prior business operations, so called shelf companies, are used sometimes to avoid the time-consuming formation of a GmbH. This is legally permissible, but the Federal Court considers the acquisition of the shares of a shelf company identical to the formation of a new GmbH from an economic point of view, and hence the provisions in the GmbHG regarding the raising of the registered share capital apply.[79] As a consequence, the Managing Directors of the newly acquired shelf company must confirm with the commercial register that the share capital is still at their free disposal.[80]

G. Aktiengesellschaft (AG)

The stock corporation AG (*Aktiengesellschaft*)[81] is the corporate form adopted by many of Germany's largest corporations and the vast majority of listed companies. It is also

78 Sec. 5a GmbHG.

79 BGH in BGHZ 117, 323 et seq.; BGHZ 153, 158 et seq.

80 Sec. 8 (2) GmbHG.

81 For an overview in English with the translation of the relevant provisions of the AktG please refer to Wirth / Arnold / Morshäuser / Greene, Corporate Law in Germany, 2nd ed. 2010 (Part 2, pp. 294 et. seq.); Schneider / Heidenhain, The German Stock Corporation Act. Bilingual Edition with an Introduction to the Law, 2nd ed. 2000.

used by some of the major publicly held US corporations for their German subsidiaries, for example Ford AG (the German subsidiary of Ford) and Esso AG (the German subsidiary of Exxon), as well as by other foreign investors (e.g. Fiat or Nestlé).

I. Structure of an AG

The AG is the German legal form which is most comparable to a public limited liability company in Anglo-Saxon jurisdictions. The principal advantage of an AG is that, unlike a GmbH, the shares of an AG may be transferred with relative ease and can be listed on a stock exchange. However, some closely held businesses have also adopted this corporate form due to the arguably higher market reputation which an AG has and the fact that the management of an AG is not bound by the directions of shareholders.

An AG is subject to extensive legal regulation. Because most of the applicable regulations are mandatory, little flexibility exists to adapt the Articles of Association to include specific shareholder requirements. Certain standards regarding the Articles of Association of a listed AG have also developed in practice, and these will need to be applied if the shares of an AG are subsequently listed on a stock exchange.

An AG has a registered share capital (*Grundkapital*) divided into shares.[82] It has three corporate bodies: General Meeting (*Hauptversammlung*); Supervisory Board (*Aufsichtsrat*); and Management Board (*Vorstand*). A German AG is accordingly characterized by its two-tier system of management and supervisory board, contrary to the one-tier board in France, Switzerland and many Anglo-Saxon jurisdictions. An important feature of an AG is the independence of the Management Board in relation to the day-to-day management of the AG. The members of the Management Board are appointed by the Supervisory Board, which is mandatory for an AG, rather than by the shareholders. In addition, and in contrast to a GmbH, neither the shareholders nor the Supervisory Board may issue binding directions to the Management Board.

Furthermore, the members of the Management Board can only be dismissed during their term of office for good cause. As a result, neither the shareholders nor the Supervisory Board have direct influence on the management of the AG.

II. Incorporation and Registration

An AG may be established by one or several shareholders.[83] The formation procedure of an AG is similar to a GmbH. In particular, it requires notarization of the

---

82 Sec. 1 AktG.
83 Sec. 2 AktG.

Articles of Association and subscription for the initial shares by its founding shareholder(s).[84] The founding shareholder(s) then must appoint the first Supervisory Board and the first auditor of the company. Such appointments must be notarized.[85] The first Supervisory Board appoints the first Management Board. The founding shareholder(s) must prepare a written formation report which must state all relevant details concerning the establishment of the AG. The Management Board and Supervisory Board will then scrutinize the foundation procedure and in particular circumstances (e.g. where members of the Management Board or the Supervisory Board take up shares or where shares are issued against contributions in kind) the formation report must be audited by an independent auditor.

The formation of the AG must be registered with the Commercial Register and the application for registration must be signed before a notary public by all founding shareholders, as well as by the initial members of the Management Board and the Supervisory Board. Upon registration the AG exists as a separate legal entity.[86] Persons acting for and on behalf of the AG prior to registration will be personally liable for any debts incurred.[87]

III. Step Plan: Incorporation of an AG

1. Preparation of Incorporation documents:

   - Articles of Association (*Gesellschaftsvertrag*)
   - Deed of incorporation
   - Minutes of the first meeting of the Supervisory Board
   - Appointment of a formation auditor who prepares a formation audit report which is required if a member of the Management Board is one of the promoters (according to Sec. 33 (3) AktG, the formation audit report may be issued by a notary public).
   - Formation report (by the promoters or the members of the Management Board and Supervisory Board)
   - Calculation of the costs of formation of the NewCo
   - Power of Attorney (if required)
   - Application letter to the commercial register

2. Obtaining approval from the local Chamber of Commerce regarding the envisaged name of NewCo

84 Sects. 23, 29 AktG.

85 Sec. 30 (1) AktG.

86 Sec. 41 (1) sentence 1 AktG.

87 Sec. 41 (1) sentence 2 AktG.

3. Signing of

   - Calculation of the cost of formation of the NewCo
   - Formation report
   - Appointment of the formation auditor (notary public)
   - Power of Attorney

   Note: Foreign companies often appoint a proxy to act on their behalf in the incorporation process based on a power of attorney.
   Signature by the duly authorized representative of a foreign company under the power of attorney must be certified by a notary public and apostilled (if required). A notarial confirmation regarding the authorization of the signatory acting on behalf of foreign company or other evidence will also be required.

4. Notarization of the deed of incorporation (by proxy) before a German Notary Public, including:

   - Articles of Association
   - Appointment of the first members of Supervisory Board
   - Appointment of the first Management Board by the Supervisory Board
   - Appointment of the auditor of financial statements for the first financial year

5. Opening of a bank account in Germany for NewCo by duly authorized member(s) of the Management Board of NewCo
6. Payment of the share capital into the bank account of the NewCo.

   Note: The minimum share capital for a German AG is EUR 50,000.00. In such a case, at least EUR 25,000.00 has to be paid into the bank account.

7. Formation audit reports and first meeting of the Supervisory Board
8. Forwarding to the notary public a copy of the statement of account, evidencing that the share capital has been credited to NewCo's bank account.
9. Signing the application letter to the Commercial Register by all promoters, all members of the Supervisory Board and the Management Board before a notary public. Signature on the application letter must be certified by a notary public and apostilled (if required).
10. Filing the application for entry of NewCo with the competent Commercial Register (will be done by the acting German notary public).
11. Entry of NewCo in the Commercial Register (approx. 1–2 weeks after filing the application form).

The Corporate Law Reform 2008 made it possible for an AG (just as for a GmbH) to move its management within Germany and also abroad, irrespective of the company's official registered seat with a Commercial Register in Germany.

IV. Limited Liability of Shareholders

As is the case with the GmbH, upon registration with the Commercial Register, only the AG will be liable for its debts and the liability of its shareholders shall be limited to their respective capital contribution. Arguably, the principles developed by the courts regarding the piercing of the corporate veil of a GmbH (cf. above) also apply to an AG. However, since the shareholders do not have the same power of influence over the management of an AG, such cases rarely arise in practice.

V. Articles of Association

The minimum contents of the Articles of Association are prescribed by the German Stock Corporation Act (*Aktiengesetz*), which regulates the AG, and include:[88]

- The company's name and registered seat;
- The object(s) of the company;
- The amount and division of the company's share capital;
- The type of shares (bearer shares or registered shares); number of the members of the Management Board or the rules for determining such number.

The Articles of Association may regulate other issues, but can only deviate from the provisions of the AktG where this is expressly permitted by law.[89] Since only few and limited deviations are permissible, there is very little flexibility in drafting the Articles of Association of an AG. The objective of this strict regime is to protect existing and future shareholders by having a fixed framework of rules.

VI. Shares and Share Capital

An AG must have a registered share capital of at least EUR 50,000.00.[90] Shares may be issued either with a par value (*Nennbetragsaktien*) of at least EUR 1.00 per share or multiples thereof,[91] or without a par value (*Stückaktien*).[92] Shares may not be is-

88 Sec. 23 (3) AktG.
89 Sec. 23 (5) AktG.
90 Sec. 7 AktG.
91 Sec. 8 (2) AktG.
92 Sec. 8 (3) AktG.

sued for an amount below their par value.[93] However, shares may be issued for a higher amount than their par value;[94] in this case, the AG receives a premium beyond the required registered share capital which is allocated to the capital reserves.[95]

German law further distinguishes between bearer shares (i. e. shares where the name of the owner is not registered in the share register of the AG – bearer shares are the vast majority) and registered shares (i. e. where the name of the owner has been registered in the AG's share register – registered shares are rather rare).[96] The Articles of Association must specify the type of shares that may be issued. Bearer shares may not be issued unless they are fully paid up. Traditionally, most AGs only issue bearer shares. However, this seems to have changed in recent years and publicly traded companies have begun to introduce registered shares as this gives them an overview of the current shareholders. The transferability of bearer shares may not be restricted, whereas the Articles of Association may provide that registered shares can only be transferred with the consent of the Management Board.

Furthermore, shares may be issued as ordinary shares or as preferred shares (*Vorzugsaktien*) which are similar to but not identical with "preference shares" in many common law jurisdictions. The latter may be issued with or without voting rights.[97] The holders of preferred shares are entitled to preferred dividends, usually calculated as a fixed percentage of the nominal value of the preferred shares (a mere link to the annual profits earned by the AG is not allowed). Shares with multiple voting rights are not permitted.[98]

VII. Contribution and Maintenance of Capital

Contributions to the share capital may be made in cash or, if permitted by the Articles of Association, also in kind. As with a GmbH, the value of a non-cash contribution must be at least equal to the share capital to which it relates. Certain procedures must be followed in order to safeguard this principle (i. e. formation report of the founding shareholders, audit of the formation report by an auditor and examination by the courts). Generally contributions in kind must be fully made upon incorporation although if the contribution in kind involves the transfer of a particular asset, such a transfer must be made any time up to the expiry of the period ending five years from the date of registration of the AG with the Commercial Register.

93 Sec. 9 (1) AktG.
94 Sec. 9 (2) AktG.
95 Sec. 272 (2) No. 1 HGB.
96 Sec. 10 (1) AktG.
97 Sec. 12 (1), Sec. 129 et seq. AktG.
98 Sec. 12 (2) AktG.

If shares are issued for cash, at least 25 % of the par value of each share (plus the full amount of any premium) must be paid up prior to filing for registration of the AG with the Commercial Register.[99] This amount has to be paid unconditionally and at the free disposal of the Management Board.[100]

As with a GmbH, the legislation governing an AG is designed to ensure that the share capital is paid up and maintained. The rules applying to an AG are in fact even stricter in this respect. Contributions may generally not be repaid to shareholders, irrespective of whether this would reduce the net assets of the AG below its registered share capital.

VIII. Transfer of Shares

Shares in an AG are transferable with relative ease. Unlike the transfer of shares in a GmbH, a transfer of shares in an AG does not require a notarized transfer deed. The parties only need to agree on the transfer of title, which does not require a specific form. The transfer of bearer shares normally invites the handing over of the respective share certificates, and similarly in the case of registered shares if they are transferred by way of endorsement.[101] Restrictions on the transfer of registered shares (but not on the transfer of bearer shares) may be imposed in the Articles of Association.[102]

IX. Notification Requirements

Any direct or indirect shareholding in an unlisted AG exceeding 25 % of the registered share capital must be notified by the relevant shareholder to the AG in writing.[103] The same notification requirement applies again if the shareholding exceeds 50 % of the registered share capital or the voting rights. Without proper notification, the shareholder rights attached to such shares will be suspended. If the shareholding falls below these thresholds, the same notification requirements also apply.

In the case of a listed AG, shareholders must notify any direct or indirect shareholding exceeding (or falling below) 3, 5, 10, 15, 20, 25, 50 or 75 % of the voting rights to the AG and the German authority supervising listed entities (*Bundesanstalt für Finanzdienstleistungsaufsicht, BaFin*). The notification shall be immediately, and at the latest four trading days after changes within the percentage of voting rights come

---

99 Sec. 36a (1) AktG.
100 Sects. 36 (2), 54 (3) AktG.
101 Sec. 68 (1) AktG.
102 Sec. 68 (2) sentence 1 AktG.
103 Sec. 20 (1) AktG.

to the shareholder's' knowledge or he should, in ordinary circumstances, have reasonably become aware of the fact that his voting rights exceeded or fell below the above mentioned percentages.[104] If the shareholder does not notify the AG and/or the BaFin within the specified period, the notification shall be deemed not properly carried out, even if the delay was not caused by the shareholder. The legal consequence of such a default is that the shareholder is not able to exercise his rights until notification is made.[105]

X. Management Board

The Management Board bears the sole responsibility for managing the day-to-day business of the AG.[106] In contrast to a GmbH, neither the shareholders nor the Supervisory Board members may issue binding directions to the Management Board regarding the management of the AG. The general meeting has a say in the management of an AG only if the Management Board has requested such a decision.[107] However, the Management Board requires the consent of the Supervisory Board for certain transactions.[108] In practice, the shareholder structure normally determines how independently the Management Board can act. A majority shareholder will usually insert his influence on the Supervisory Board and thereby also on the management of an AG.

Stock corporations with more than EUR 3,000,000.00 in share capital must have a Management Board of at least two persons, unless the Articles of Association provide otherwise. Only individuals may be appointed to the Management Board.[109]

An AG with more than 2,000 employees must have a so-called Industrial Relations Director (*Arbeitsdirektor*) as a member of the Management Board holding responsibility for employment and social affairs.[110]

Members of the Management Board are appointed by the Supervisory Board. Shareholders may not direct the Supervisory Board as to who should be appointed as a member of the Management Board. Shareholders' agreements on the composition of the Management Board are therefore not enforceable. In practice, however, informal consultations usually occur between the Supervisory Board and the major shareholder(s) regarding the appointment of the members of the Management Board and usu-

104 Sec. 21 (1, 1a) WpHG (*Gesetz über den Wertpapierhandel* – German Securities Trading Act).
105 Sec. 28 WpHG.
106 Sec. 76 (1) AktG.
107 Sec. 119 (2) AktG.
108 Sec. 111 (4) sentence 2 AktG.
109 There is no requirement as for German citizenship or residence, i. e. the entire board may consist of non-Germans.
110 Sec. 33 MitbestG.

ally the Supervisory Board will only appoint members who are acceptable to majority shareholder(s). Members of the Management Board are appointed for a maximum term of five years, although this term can be renewed for further periods of up to five years. Once such an appointment is made, however, it can only be revoked for good cause by a resolution of the Supervisory Board.[111]

The manner in which the members of the Management Board may legally represent the AG must be expressly set forth in the Articles of Association (individually, jointly, etc.). The powers of the members of the Management Board are limited by the Articles of Association or by the Supervisory Board by stipulating that certain matters require the consent of the Supervisory Board or the shareholders in General Meeting. Such limitations do not, however, affect the validity of the actions of the Management Board vis-à-vis third parties.[112]

The members of the Management Board must apply the due care of a prudent and conscientious manager in managing the company.[113] If they breach their duties, the members of the Management Board are jointly and severally liable for any damages sustained by the company. The liability of the members of the Management Board imposed under the AktG is quite strict. In particular, the burden of proof lies with the members of the Management Board who must prove that they complied with their duties.[114] However, German courts have applied the so-called "business judgement rule" which means that the members of the Management Board are not liable where they could reasonably assume (based on an appropriate level of information and after obtaining external advice) that they were acting in the best interests of the company.[115]

XI. Supervisory Board

An AG must have a Supervisory Board. If the AG has over 500 (but less than 2,000) employees or if the AG has less than 500 employees but was registered prior to 10th August 1994 and is not family-owned, 1/3 of the members of the Supervisory Board must be employees' representatives. If the AG has more than 2,000 employees, half of the members of the Supervisory Board must be employees' representatives.[116]

The function of the Supervisory Board is to supervise and advise the Management Board. If there are no employees' representatives on the Supervisory Board, all mem-

111 Sec. 84 (3) AktG which also gives some examples for good cause: gross breach of duty, inability to properly manage the company or a vote of no-confidence passed by the General Meeting.

112 Sec. 82 (1) AktG.

113 Sec. 93 (1) AktG.

114 Sec. 93 (2) AktG.

115 BGHZ 135, 244 et. seq. "ARAG", now incorporated also in Sec. 93 (1) sentence 2 AktG.

116 Sects. 1 (1), 4 (1) DrittbG; SSects. 1 (1), 7 (1) No. 1 MitbestG.

bers of the Supervisory Board are appointed by a simple majority vote of the shareholders, unless the Articles of Association provide that a particular shareholder may appoint one or more members of the Supervisory Board. If the AG has more than 2,000 employees (with 50 % of the members of the Supervisory Board being employees' representatives), the Chairman of the Supervisory Board who is elected by the members of the Supervisory Board, has a casting vote in the event of a tie.[117] The voting procedure set forth in the relevant legislation is designed in such a way that the Chairman may not be elected to the Supervisory Board against the wishes of the shareholders' representatives. This procedure, together with the Chairman's casting vote, ensures that the ultimate decisions of the Supervisory Board rest with the shareholders' representatives. Members of the Supervisory Board are appointed for a maximum term of five years.[118]

Members of the Supervisory Board may be dismissed:[119]

- By a court ruling, for good cause, upon the initiative of the other members of the Supervisory Board;
- By a 75 % majority of votes in a General Meeting (only applies to shareholders' representatives);
- By the appointing shareholder, if a specific right to appoint is set out in the Articles of Association (only applies to the representative of the appointing shareholder).

The main functions of the Supervisory Board are as follows:

- Appointment and dismissal of the members of the Management Board;
- Supervision of the Management Board,
- Involving the examination of both legal and commercial aspects of Management Board actions;
- Representation of the AG in its dealings with the Management Board;
- Representation of the AG (together with the Management Board) in litigation relating to the validity of shareholders' resolutions;
- Consent to major business decisions of the Management Board as required by the Articles of Association or by the Supervisory Board (e.g. by internal rules of the Management Board issued by the Supervisory Board or by individual resolutions on a case by case basis);
- Review and approval of the annual financial statements.

117 Sec. 29 (2) MitbestG.
118 Sec. 102 (1) AktG.
119 Sec. 103 (3) AktG.

The members of the Supervisory Board must apply the same due care as the members of the Management Board and in case of a breach of their duties may also be liable for any damages sustained by the company. In particular, the members of the Supervisory Board must not disclose any confidential information regarding the company and its affairs. Along with tightening corporate governance standards, Supervisory Boards are increasingly under scrutiny for (not) pursuing liability claims against the Management Board.

XII. Shareholders

The shareholders of the AG exercise their powers by passing shareholders' resolutions in General Meetings.[120] An AG must hold its annual general meeting within the first eight months after the end of every financial year in order to conduct routine business. During such annual general meetings, the annual financial statements of the previous financial year will be laid before the shareholders and the shareholders will pass resolutions relating to dividend payments and the exoneration of the members of the Management Board and the Supervisory Board with respect to their actions in the previous financial year.

The Management Board is entitled (and in certain cases obliged) to convene extraordinary general meetings, although the Supervisory Board may also call such extraordinary general meetings in certain circumstances. Furthermore, shareholders holding at least 5 % of the registered share capital may require the convocation of a General Meeting.[121] The Articles of Association may, in addition, grant the power to call General Meetings to other persons, for example, to majority shareholders. The calling of a General Meeting of an AG is subject to quite onerous notice requirements.

Shareholders' resolutions require a simple majority (more than 50 % of the votes cast) unless mandatory law or the Articles of Association require a greater majority. For example, a 75 % majority of the votes cast is required for any amendments to the Articles of Association, increases or decreases in share capital, control agreements with other companies (i. e. agreements whereby a corporation submits itself to the control of another or agrees to transfer its profits), the transfer of all assets and the change of corporate form. Furthermore, the AktG requires the consent of certain shareholders whenever their rights are affected by certain measures of the company.

120 Sec. 118 (1) AktG.
121 Sec. 122 (1) AktG.

Most shareholder rights in an AG are mandatory and stipulated in the AktG. Shareholders may defend their rights and bring an action against the AG if their rights are violated.[122]

As mentioned above, the shareholders decide on the distribution of profits in General Meetings. The shareholders are, however, bound by the annual financial statements prepared by the Management Board and approved by the Supervisory Board; such decisions may therefore not deviate from the profits stated in said financial statements.

In making their decisions, shareholders of an AG have a duty of loyalty to the company, but due to the capitalistic structure of the AG, in principle not to the other shareholders.[123] Similar to a GmbH, the shareholders of an AG must be treated equally under equal circumstances.[124]

XIII. Ongoing Accounting Obligations and Disclosure Requirements

An AG must keep accounting records and prepare annual financial statements in accordance with the provisions of the German Commercial Code which lay down detailed requirements as to the form and content of the annual financial statements. Furthermore, medium-sized and large corporations must have their annual financial statements audited. The (audited) annual financial statements must be filed with the Commercial Register within twelve months of the end of each financial year.[125]

H. KGaA

The partnership limited by shares (*Kommanditgesellschaft auf Aktien, KGaA*) is a form of a corporation which is not used very often in Germany.[126]

The KGaA is a hybrid structure that combines the features of a limited partnership with those of an AG. The KGaA must have at least one general partner who is personally liable for all debts and liabilities of the KGaA.[127] Corporations with limited

---

122 BGH, published in BGHZ 90, 92 et. seq.; BGHZ 110, 323 et seq.

123 The German courts have recently also recognized fiduciary duties amongst AG shareholders in particular circumstances, e.g. no use of a veto right if this would endanger the existence of the company; BGH, published in BGHZ 129, 136 et seq.

124 Sec. 53a AktG; BGHZ 71, 40 et seq.

125 The same applies for the GmbH, see above section "GmbH".

126 See statistics above in section "GmbH". One of the most prominent examples is Henkel KGaA.

127 Sec. 278 (1) AktG.

liability can act as the general partner of a KGaA, e.g. a GmbH & Co. KG. This means that it is possible for investors to be completely shielded from any liability. The KGaA is similar to the very popular partnership structure of a GmbH & Co. KG.[128] Apart from the general partner, there can be an unlimited number of capital investors (*Kommanditaktionäre* or limited shareholders) who hold shares in a KGaA. The limited shareholders are protected from any personal liability as long as they have properly made their relevant capital contribution.[129]

Although legally treated like an AG, as a corporation with separate legal entity status, the internal management of a KGaA is more comparable to that of a KG (i. e. a limited partnership). The provisions governing the KG in particular also apply to the relationship between the general partner(s) and the limited shareholders and to the representation of the KGaA vis-à-vis third parties.[130] This means that the KGaA is managed and legally represented by the general partner(s), who are personally liable for all debts and liabilities of the KGaA.[131] The limited shareholders have more or less the same legal rights and obligations as shareholders in an AG.

The shares are freely transferable. It is also possible for the shares of a public KGaA to be listed. Due to this extraordinary hybrid structure and the lack of precise legal provisions regarding its internal management, a potential investor willing to choose the KGaA as an investment vehicle is likely to face some difficulties (but will also receive the benefits or certain specific advantages) when compared to the traditionally used forms of corporation. Furthermore, due to the limited number of corporations which have been established as a KGaA, only very few court rulings which relate to the operation of the KGaA exist. This leaves uncertainty regarding a number of legal issues in relation to the operation of this form of corporation. However, a KGaA has the same ongoing accounting and disclosure obligations as an AG.

Any investor who is contemplating using a KGaA as an investment vehicle should be aware that this rarely used form will not only trigger additional incorporation costs but that there will also be higher tax compliance costs.[132] Therefore, the KGaA will normally only be considered as the appropriate vehicle to carry out business, if:

- It is possible to attract a large number of limited shareholders via a public offering, (avoiding the control rights applicable to shareholders of an AG);
- A preferred tax treatment can be achieved (e.g. in an acquisition scenario).

---

128 See below section "GmbH & Co. KG".

129 Sec. 278 (1) AktG.

130 Sec. 278 (2) AktG.

131 Sects. 164, 170 HGB.

132 For more details see chapter "Taxation in Germany".

I. European Public Company

Since December 2004, it has been possible to form an European Public Company, also-called "*Societas Europaea*" or abbreviated "SE", as a legal entity in Germany. The provisions that govern the SE in Germany are based on an EU Regulation[133] that has been implemented by German national law.[134] Even though the provisions of the EU Regulation directly apply in each of the EU Member States, the EU Regulation has left some room for the EU Member States to adopt supplemental legislation.[135] Accordingly, there are slightly different provisions which relate to the operation of the SE in various European jurisdictions, and this means that the choice of Member State in which the SE is incorporated is likely to make a difference for foreign investors planning to invest in Europe via an SE.

The SE has become increasingly popular in recent years. As of September 2011 approximately 900 SEs have been set up Europe-wide and more than 250 have been established in Germany, despite the fact that the German SE is based on the very complex concept of an AG.[136] Popular examples are Allianz SE, BASF SE, Bilfinger Berger SE, BP Europe SE, Fresenius SE, MAN Diesel SE and Porsche SE. An SE comes with a number of advantages in running a group of companies, compared to the traditional German company forms. As explained below, the SE offers more flexibility as to how the Supervisory Board is constituted. Another common major reason why German firms have adopted this legal form is that employee participation can be negotiated and therefore be less rigid.[137] Furthermore, the SE brings a European corporate identity to a company.

The features of a German SE are very similar to those of an AG. However, like any SE (regardless of the EU Member State in which it is incorporated), the German SE must have a link to at least two Member States of the EU.[138] Therefore, a mere German business operation cannot be conducted through an SE.

---

133 Council Regulation (EC) No. 2157/2001 dated 8 October 2001 of the Statute for a European Company (SE).

134 German Act for Introduction of the European Company (*Gesetz zur Einführung der Europäischen Gesellschaft (SEEG)*), which consists of two parts: German Act implementing the Council Regulation (EC) No. 2571/2001 (*Gesetz zur Ausführung der Verordnung (EG) Nr. 2157/2001 (SEAG)*) and German Act regarding transposing the Directive regulations regarding the involvement of employees in SEs (*Gesetz über die Beteiligung der Arbeitnehmer in einer Europäischen Gesellschaft (SEBG)*).

135 According to Art. 10 Council Regulation No. 2157/2001 the SE shall be treated in every EU Member State as if it were a public limited-liability company formed in accordance with the law of the Member State in which it has its registered office.

136 For more details please refer to European Trade Union Institute (ETUI): http://ecdb.worker-participation.eu.

137 Art. 1 (4) Council Regulation (EC) No. 2157/2001; Council Directive 2001/86/EC of 8 October 2011 supplementing the Statute for a European company with regard to the involvement of employees.

138 Art. 2 (1) Council Regulation (EC) No. 2157/2001.

I. Formation and Registration

The German SE can only be formed in one of the following four ways:[139]

- The merger of two or more existing public companies (including existing SE) based in different EU Member States into a newly formed SE;
- At least two existing corporations (including existing SE) based in different EU Member States setting up a holding SE;
- At least two existing corporations or other legal entities (including an existing SE) based in different EU Member States forming a subsidiary SE; or
- By transforming an existing stock corporation based in an EU Member State into an SE (the existing stock corporation must have had a subsidiary in a different EU Member State for at least two years).

Upon formation, the SE must be registered with the relevant Commercial Register in the state where it has its registered office and the registration of an SE must be disclosed for information purposes in the Official Journal of the EU. The SE is entitled to relocate not only its principal place of management but also its registered office to another EU Member State. The transfer of the registered office of an SE does not result in the winding up of the SE or in the creation of a new legal person. This therefore leaves a degree of flexibility for future development and could be one of the main reasons for choosing an SE. However, it has to be considered that upon relocation of the registered address the national law of the other EU Member State applies.

II. Minimum Share Capital

The capital of an SE shall be expressed in Euro and the SE must have a minimum share capital of EUR 120,000.00. This specified minimum capital is imperative and must be fixed in the Articles of Association of the SE. Where a Member State requires higher capital for companies carrying out certain types of activity, the same requirement will also apply to an SE with its registered office in that Member State, e.g. the minimum capital of an investment stock corporation in Germany (*Investmentaktiengesellschaft, InvAG*) is EUR 300,000.00.

III. Management

The major difference between the internal structure of a German SE and an AG is that the German SE may choose to have a one-tier board system (Administration Board) rather than the otherwise mandatory two-tier board system of an AG (Man-

139 For more details please refer to the homepage of Societas Europaea: http://www.societaseurpaea.eu.

agement Board and Supervisory Board).[140] As a result, the German SE may have only one administrative body that is responsible for the management of the company. The German legislation provides that the (one-tier) Administration Board may then appoint certain persons who will be responsible for the day-to-day business and the management of the SE, including its legal representation.[141] Such persons may or may not be members of the Administration Board.[142] The Administration Board of a German SE is likely to consist of executive and non-executive members, which is more similar to the one-tier board system applied in Anglo-Saxon jurisdictions.

IV. Employees' Participation Rights

The EU Regulation does not set out specific requirements regarding the participation of employees' representatives on the Supervisory Board or Administration Board of the SE. The employees' participation rights are regulated in the Council Directive 2001/86/EC. The Council Directive provides for a complex negotiation model. In a nutshell, a negotiation committee consisting of employees' representatives (*Besonderes Verhandlungsgremium*)[143] must negotiate in good faith with representatives of the founding companies' management in order to reach a decision as to whether or not and, if so, to what extent, employees' representatives will be included in the administration of the SE.[144] In the event that no agreement can be reached, the highest level of employees' participation currently existing in the founding companies (usually the German AG) must be maintained within the SE (the so-called "before/after principle"). However, if none of the founding companies had employees' participation rights immediately prior to forming the SE, the SE may avoid employee participation, even if the relevant thresholds of employee headcounts are likely to be exceeded in the future.

J. European Private Company

In June 2008, the EU Commission presented a proposal for a Regulation on a European Private Company, also called the *Societas Privata Europaea* or abbreviated "SPE" (the "SPE Regulation").[145]

140 Art. 38 (b) Council Regulation (EC) No. 2157/2001.
141 Sec: 40 SEAG.
142 Sec. 40 (1) SEAG.
143 Art. 3 (2) Council Directive 2001/86/EC.
144 Art. 4 (1) Council Directive 2001/86/EC.
145 For more details please refer to the website of Societas Privata Europaea: http://www.europeanprivatecompany.eu.

Although this proposal has been generally welcomed by the Committee of Legal Affairs of the European Parliament, a number of amendments were suggested in March 2009. This has created uncertainty regarding some specific details of the proposed SPE Regulation. The next steps to be taken and the final implementation date for the proposed SPE are therefore not clear and remain to be seen.

The main aim of the SPE is to reduce compliance costs for the creation and operation of businesses in different EU Member States arising from the disparities between national company laws.

Under the current proposal, the SPE will be a private company limited by shares with a minimum share capital of EUR 1.00.[146] The European Parliament has, however, suggested an amendment which means that the EUR 1.00 minimum capital shall only be sufficient for SPEs whose executive management signs a solvency certificate; otherwise the minimum share capital shall be EUR 8,000.00.[147]

The SPE's main features will be comparable to those of the German GmbH and most other national private companies available within the EU. Like an SE, the creation of an SPE will be subject to a cross-border requirement, but this cross-border component will be more flexible and broader.[148] This means that the component can be satisfied by evidence of a cross-border business intention or corporate object, or an objective to be significantly active in different EU Member States, as long as this can be demonstrated by the SPE within two years of registration. Each SPE has to be registered in the EU Member State in which it has its registered office in a register designated by the applicable national law.[149] Under the proposed SPE Regulation, shareholders should have the power to determine the management structure of the SPE in the Articles of Association of the company, i. e. whether the SPE will have a single director or several directors, a one-tier or a two-tier board system etc.[150] It is envisaged that, as a general principle, the rules regarding the participation of employees in the Member State in which the SPE has its registered office should apply.[151] If more than 500 employees of the SPE are working in another Member State (or states) which provide more accommodating rules regarding the participation of employees, special provisions of the proposal on SPE Regulation should also be applied.[152] These special rules are very similar to the SE rules regarding the participation of employees.

---

146 Art. 19 Proposal for a Council Regulation on a European private company dated 27 June 2008.

147 For more details please refer to http://www.europeanprivatecompany.eu/news/.

148 Art. 3 (3) Proposal for a Council Regulation on a European private company dated 27 June 2008.

149 Art. 10 (1) Proposal for a Council Regulation on a European private company dated 27 June 2008.

150 Art. 27 (3, 4) Proposal for a Council Regulation on a European private company dated 27 June 2008.

151 Art. 35 (1) Proposal for a Council Regulation on a European private company dated 27 June 2008.

152 Art. 25 (1a) Proposal for a Council Regulation on a European private company dated 27 June 2008.

K. Other National European Corporations

Due to various landmark decisions of the European Court of Justice,[153] it is also possible for foreign corporations incorporated in a Member State of the EU to relocate their principal place of management, immediately after their incorporation, to Germany provided that the respective EU jurisdiction allows and respects the expatriation of the corporation.

For instance, a UK company with limited liability duly incorporated and registered in England with a management located in Germany will be recognized as a legal entity in Germany and allowed to carry out its business from and in Germany without facing any restrictions. (With respect to companies incorporated in the USA, for example, which relocate to Germany, the same principles apply, based on a German American bilateral agreement).[154]

Whether a foreign (shelf) company is a feasible alternative to a German corporation for a company considering the establishment of a business in Germany depends upon a number of aspects which should be carefully considered. Apart from questions regarding the company's acceptance by German customers and its reputation in the market, the tax and accounting implications of forming a foreign company located in Germany should also be carefully assessed.

L. Partnerships

Partnerships (*Personengesellschaften*) are available as general partnership (*Offene Handelsgesellschaft*, *oHG*) and limited partnership (*Kommanditgesellschaft*, *KG*).

The only major difference between the two forms is the liability of the partners. While all partners of an oHG face unlimited liability for the partnership's debts and liabilities,[155] a KG consists of at least one general partner with unlimited personal liability and one or more limited partners which are only liable with their subscribed and registered partnership contribution.[156] A partnership has a quasi-legal entity status, i. e. it can enter into contractual relationships, own assets and incur liabilities in its own name and on its own behalf.[157]

153 ECJ. Judgment of 9.3.99, "Centros", 999 [ECR] I-1459. Judgment of 5.11.02, "Überseering", 2002 [ECR] I-9919; Judgment of 30.9.03, "Inspire Art", 2003 [ECR], I-10155.

154 Treaty of Friendship, Commerce and Navigation between the United States of America and the Federal Republic of Germany of 29 October 1954 (Art. XXV V 2).

155 Sec. 128 HGB.

156 Sec. 161 (1) HGB.

157 Sects. 124 (1), 161 (2) HGB.

The major reasons for investors using a partnership instead of a corporate structure are:

- Greater flexibility in tailoring the internal affairs to the individual needs of the partners;
- Possible tax advantages;
- Fewer publication requirements (the partnership agreement need not be filed with the Commercial Register);
- More possibilities to dissolve a partnership and to distribute its capital to the partners;
- Direct management by the (general) partners.

Against this background, partnership structures are commonly used for smaller and family owned businesses or for certain fund structures.

I. Formation and Registration

At least two partners are required to set up a partnership. Possible partners (general as well as limited partners) of a German partnership can be individuals, German or foreign corporations or other partnerships.

The formation of a partnership requires the execution of a partnership agreement. While it is possible to have an oral partnership agreement, it is more common and preferable for it to be in writing (although the partnership agreement does not need to be notarized or filed). The partnership must then be registered with the relevant Commercial Register.[158] To achieve liability protection for the limited partners of the KG and for the KG to become legally effective, the amount of the subscribed partnership contribution must be properly registered with the Commercial Register.[159] If the KG commences its business activities prior to its registration, all partners including the limited partners are, in principle, fully liable for any obligations arising from such pre-registration dealings. The liability of the limited partners will only become limited when both the KG and the subscribed partnership contribution are registered with the Commercial Register.[160]

II. Transfer of Partnership Interest

The transfer of any partnership interest as a limited or general partner requires an agreement (written or oral) between the transferor and the transferee together with

---

158 Sec. 106 (1) HGB.
159 Sects. 171 (1), 172 (1) HGB.
160 Sec. 176 (1) HGB.

the consent of all other partners unless the partnership agreement provides otherwise. The partnership agreement may also impose certain restrictions relating to the transfer of a partnership interest. The change of partners must be registered with the Commercial Register, although this is not a requirement for the effectiveness of the transfer.

III. Management

The partners may, in principle, freely agree upon their rights and obligations in the partnership agreement.

However, limited partners in a KG are excluded by law from managing the partnership.[161] It is therefore only possible for a limited power of attorney to be granted in favor of a limited partner (i. e. for certain types of transactions only). The management responsibility is assumed by the general partner(s) of a partnership (oHG and KG). However, it is possible in some instances to restrict a general partner from managing the partnership.[162] If the general partner is a corporation, it will be the management of such corporation (rather than the general partner) which therefore manages and legally represents the partnership.

The limited partners have certain information rights. In particular, they are entitled to request a written copy of the financial statements of the KG, as well as to inspect the records and accounts of the KG in order to verify that the financial statements are correct.[163] The partners can make decisions on the affairs of the partnership through partnership resolutions. Partnership resolutions must generally be passed unanimously. Although the partnership agreement may modify this principle, there are certain key matters (fundamental issues relating to the partnership) which by law require the unanimous resolution of all partners. The position of partners who acquire only a minority interest in a partnership is, therefore, slightly stronger than it would be in a GmbH or AG.

IV. Ongoing Accounting Obligations and Disclosure Requirements

A KG must keep accounting records and prepare annual financial statements in accordance with the provisions of the German Commercial Code (*HGB*) which lay down detailed requirements as to the form and content of the annual financial statements. Unless at least one general partner is a natural person, a medium-sized or

161 Sec. 170 HGB.
162 Sects. 125, 161 (2) HGB
163 Sec. 166 (1) HGB.

large KG[164] must have its annual financial statements audited. Subject to the same exception (one general partner being a natural person), the (audited) annual financial statements must be filed with the Commercial Register within twelve months of the end of each financial year. Any actual changes relating to the registered information (e.g. registered office, registered partnership contribution etc.) must also be notified to the Commercial Register.

M. GmbH & Co. KG

A popular way of achieving the advantages of a partnership structure (i. e. better tax treatment), whilst shielding the partners from the risk of unlimited personal liability, is to appoint a corporation (generally a GmbH) as the sole general partner of the KG, thereby forming a so-called GmbH & Co. KG. Usually, the limited partner(s) also hold all shares in the GmbH which acts as the general partner. The result of this structure is that the limited partner(s) are not only holding all of the interests in the KG directly and indirectly via the GmbH, but that they are also controlling the partnership via their shareholding of the GmbH even though they are excluded from managing the KG directly.

Due to the similarities of this structure with a corporation, a number of statutory provisions otherwise only applying to corporations are also applicable to a GmbH & Co. KG. For example, a GmbH & Co. KG must provide the same information on its letterhead as a GmbH.[165] As in a GmbH, its management must apply for insolvency in case of illiquidity or overindebtedness.[166] However, there is no comprehensive set of provisions governing this legal form and in practice the Articles of Association should be carefully drafted to provide a suitable framework for this legal structure.

N. UG & Co. KG

The formation of a UG (*haftungsbeschränkt*) & Co. KG can be an interesting alternative for holding companies as this has the form of a German limited partnership (i. e. a GmbH & Co. KG). While the holding company still benefits from the corporate shield which will be created, as the general partner (in this case the newly introduced "Small GmbH") will still have limited liability, less share capital will be required to form the holding company. The Small GmbH must, however, receive remuneration for assuming the role of general partner.

---

164 For criteria please refer to section "GmbH (Ongoing Accounting Obligations and Disclosure Requirements)".

165 Sec. 125a HGB.

166 Sec. 15a (1) sentence 2 InsO.

O. Overview of the different types of Corporations and Partnerships

	Gesellschaft mit beschränkter Haftung (GmbH)	Unternehmer-gesellschaft (UG; "Small GmbH")	Aktiengesellschaft (AG)	Societas Europaea (SE)	GmbH & Co. KG**
Incorporation and Registration Costs	Approx. EUR 600.00 to EUR 1,000.00 *	Approx. EUR 600.00 to EUR 1,000.00 *	Approx. EUR 1,000.00 to EUR 1,500.00 *	Depends on type of formation (merger, conversion etc).	Approx. EUR 1,000.00 to EUR 1,500.00 * (including incorporation of general partner GmbH)
Duration of Incorporation and Registration	1 to 2 weeks	1 to 2 weeks	2 to 4 weeks	Depends on type of formation (merger, conversion etc) – usually fairly lengthy process (several months).	2 to 4 weeks (including establishment of general partner GmbH)
Minimum Number of Shareholders	One	One	One	One	Two
Formal Requirements of Incorporation	Notarization of deed of incorporation and registration with commercial register.	Notarization of deed of incorporation and registration with commercial register.	Notarization of deed of incorporation and registration with commercial register.	Notarization of formation documents (merger, conversion etc.) and registration with commercial register.	Execution of partnership agreement (notarization only required with respect to incorporation of general partner GmbH) and registration with commercial register.
Minimum Share Capital	EUR 25,000.00	EUR 1.00	EUR 50,000.00	EUR 120,000.00	No minimum partnership contribution required (but minimum share capital for the general partner GmbH).

	Gesellschaft mit beschränkter Haftung (GmbH)	**Unternehmergesellschaft (UG; "Small GmbH")**	**Aktiengesellschaft (AG)**	**Societas Europaea (SE)**	**GmbH & Co. KG****
Capital Contribution (Cash)	25 percent of the nominal value of each share (but at least half of the minimum share capital EUR 12,500.00).	100 percent of the nominal value of the shares.	25 percent of the registered share capital (minimum € 12,500.00) plus full amount of any premium.	25 percent of the registered share capital (minimum EUR 30,000.00) plus full amount of any premium.	No minimum payment requirements for KG (other than for general partner GmbH). However, if the contribution is not fully paid in, the limited partner is personally liable up to the subscribed amount.
Capital Contribution (in kind)	100 percent of the nominal value of the shares; documents evidencing value of the contributed assets are required (e.g. valuation report). Any shortfall must be paid in cash.	Initial share capital must be contributed in cash. Thereafter, same as GmbH.	100 percent of the nominal value of the shares; documents evidencing value of the contributed assets are required (e.g. valuation report). Any shortfall must be paid in cash.	See AG.	100 percent of the nominal value of the partnership contribution. No evidence of value of contributed assets required. However, if the fair market value of the contributed assets is below the nominal value of the partnership contribution, the limited partner is personally liable up to the shortfall amount.
Maintenance of Capital	Payments to shareholders which would reduce the company's net assets below its registered share capital are not allowed.	See GmbH.	Prohibition on: – repayment of capital to shareholders; and – financial assistance for acquisition of its own shares.	See AG.	No specific restrictions apply. However, the limited partner is personally liable up to the subscribed amount if his contribution is paid back to him.

	Gesellschaft mit beschränkter Haftung (GmbH)	Unternehmergesellschaft (UG; "Small GmbH")	Aktiengesellschaft (AG)	Societas Europaea (SE)	GmbH & Co. KG**
Management	Generally one tier structure with minimum of one Managing Director. Supervisory Board only required if more than 500 employees. Participation of employees: – if more than 500 employees 1/3; – if more than 2,000 employees 1/2 of the members of the Supervisory Board must be employees' representatives.	See GmbH	Two-tier structure: Management Board and Supervisory Board required. Participation of employees: – if more than 500 employees 1/3; – if more than 2,000 employees 1/2 of the members of the Supervisory Board must be employees' representatives.	One or two tier structure. Employees' participation rights depend on outcome of negotiation procedure or "before/ after principle".	The general partner GmbH manages the partnership.
Directors' Liability	The directors are liable for breach of their managing duties.	See GmbH	The directors are liable for breach of their managing duties.	See AG	The general partner GmbH is liable for breach of its managing duties.
Shareholders' Liability	Limited to capital contribution.	See GmbH	See GmbH	See GmbH	Unlimited liability of the general partner GmbH; liability of the limited partners is limited to their (paidup) partnership contribution.

	Gesellschaft mit beschränkter Haftung (GmbH)	**Unternehmergesellschaft (UG; "Small GmbH")**	**Aktiengesellschaft (AG)**	**Societas Europaea (SE)**	**GmbH & Co. KG****
Transfer of Shares	Notarized transfer deed required.	See GmbH	Transfer agreement. No notarization required.	See AG	Transfer of the interest in the KG requires the consent of all partners. Notarization required if shares in the general partner GmbH are also transferred.
Costs of Share Transfer	Notary fees depending on the purchase price.	See GmbH	No notary fees incurred.	See AG	Transfer of interest in the KG does not incur notary fees.
Mobility within EU	Registered office must remain in Germany. Relocation of registered office results in the dissolution of the company. However, relocation of principle place of administration allowed within EU.	See GmbH	Registered office must remain in Germany. Relocation of registered office results in the dissolution of the company. However, relocation of principle place of administration allowed within EU.	Relocation of the registered office and the principle place of administration is possible within EU.	Registered office and principle place of administration must remain in Germany. Relocation results in the dissolution of the KG.
Cross-border merger within EU	Can participate in cross-border mergers pursuant to Sects. 122a et seq. German Transformation Act.	See GmbH	See GmbH	Can participate in cross-border mergers pursuant to Sects. 122a et seq. German Transformation Act (prevailing view) and SE Regulation.	Can participate in cross-border mergers (as absorbing entity "import merger") based on SEVIC case of the European Court of Justice.
Taxation	Taxable in Germany (corporation tax and trade tax).	See GmbH	Taxable in Germany (corporation tax and trade tax).	See AG	Partnership is only subject to trade tax. Profits are taxed at the level of the partners.

* not including legal fees
** with respect to the general partner GmbH we also refer to the information contained in the first column

P. Conversion

The German Transformation Act (*UmwG*) sets out several restructuring options, including in relation to the conversion of a legal form (*Formwechsel*). Nearly all types of entities, including partnerships (*oHG*, *KG*) and corporations (*GmbH*, *AG*, *KGaA*), can be converted into another legal form under the German Transformation Act.[167]

For a conversion to be effected, a notarized resolution of the partners/shareholders of the converting entity must be passed by a special majority of at least 75 %.[168] The conversion must be registered with the Commercial Register and will become effective immediately upon registration. The entity in its new legal form will generally be able to keep its existing business name, but must add a suffix indicating its new legal form.[169]

The registration of the new legal form has the following effects:[170]

- The converting entity continues to exist but under the new legal form;
- The partners/shareholders of the converting entity now keep their interest in the entity in accordance with the law applicable to the new legal form.

Since the EU Cross-Border Merger Directive[171] has been implemented into the national law of most EU Member States, it is now also possible to convert a corporation from one EU Member State into a corporation operated in accordance with the laws of another EU Member State (i. e. a UK Limited into a German GmbH). Such a "cross-border conversion" can be achieved by the existing entity (e.g. UK Limited) setting up a subsidiary in the target legal form (e.g. German GmbH) and then carrying out a cross-border downstream merger between the parent UK Limited and the subsidiary German GmbH.[172] As a result, all assets and liabilities of the UK Limited will be assumed by the German GmbH and the UK Limited will be automatically dissolved. The German GmbH will continue to exist with the same shareholder structure as the dissolved UK Limited. The process of a cross-border merger is rather complex since two national laws (here English law and German

---

167 Sec. 191 UmwG (*Umwandlungsgesetz* – Transformation Act).

168 Sec. 193 UmwG.

169 Sec. 198 UmwG.

170 Sec. 202 UmwG.

171 For more details please refer to the website of European Commission: http://ec.europa.eu/internal_market/company/mergers/index_en.htm.

172 National legislation implementing the EU Cross-Border Merger Directory may contain additional requirements. For example, UK law does not allow a merger with a newly established foreign company without prior business operations.

law) and two national registration proceedings will apply in parallel. It will also be important to ensure that there are no adverse tax consequences as a result of the merger, i. e. as a result of disclosing hidden reserves.

Thomas Weidlich, LL.M. (Hull)
thomas.weidlich@luther-lawfirm.com

Dr. Angelika Yates
angelika.yates@luther-lawfirm.com

CHAPTER 2
TAXATION IN GERMANY

DR. ULRICH SIEGEMUND

Germany is a high tax country although tax rates have come down during recent years for corporations and for individuals.

The tax rates for corporations were reduced from 33–41 % to 23–33 % by the 2008 Business Tax Reform. The reduction of the rates was accompanied by measures to broaden the tax base, e.g. the introduction of new interest deduction limitation rules and new loss trafficking rules. Further, transfer pricing rules and their application have become a focus of the tax authorities in the recent years.

Double taxation is avoided by the so-called part-income system. Corporations are paying taxes at rates lower than individuals. Dividends distributed to individuals are only subject to reduced rates which ensure that the income of corporations is not taxed two times (part-income system). Dividends paid to a shareholder who is a corporation are in principle tax exempt (participation exemption). Similar rules apply to capital gains from the sale of shares in companies by corporate or individual shareholders.

A. Corporations

I. General

German corporations (i. e. AG, GmbH and KGaA) and foreign corporations which are tax residents in Germany are subject to German Corporate Income Tax (*Körperschaftsteuer*, *CIT*), plus a solidarity surcharge on their worldwide income (unlimited tax liability). A corporation is tax resident in Germany if it has its legal seat in Germany or if it is effectively managed and controlled in Germany. The place of effective management and control is defined as the place where the management is making day-to-day decisions of a certain importance.

Corporations not tax resident in Germany are subject to CIT plus a solidarity surcharge on their German source income (limited tax liability). Corporations are also subject to Trade Tax on income (*Gewerbesteuer*, *TT*).

II. Tax Rates

CIT is levied at a rate of 15 %. Additionally, a solidarity surcharge, which was introduced after the German reunification to meet the financial needs of the East German states, is levied at a rate of 5.5 % of the actual CIT burden. The combined rate of CIT and solidarity surcharge therefore is 15.875 %. Neither CIT nor the solidarity surcharge or Trade Tax are tax deductible.

B. Partnerships

Both general and limited partnerships (OHG and KG) are treated as transparent for the purposes of German CIT and IIT (*Einkommensteuer*, Individual Income Tax). Income derived by a partnership is allocated to its partners, and each partner is subject to CIT or IIT (plus solidarity surcharge) on the partner's proportional share of income at the partner's individual tax rate, regardless of whether the income is retained in the partnership or withdrawn by the partners. Withdrawals of income by the partners are therefore tax neutral. Whether the partners are subject to CIT or IIT on their income share will depend on whether the partner is a corporation or an individual. The German tax system does not provide for a "check the box"-option for partnerships to be taxed as a corporation. Partnerships engaged in commercial activities are also subject to TT (cf. below).

C. Permanent Establishments (Branches)

I. General

Non-resident corporations or individuals who derive income from a permanent establishment located in Germany are subject to limited CIT or IIT liability in relation to such income. Under most of the German tax treaties with other countries a permanent establishment is defined as a fixed place of business from which business activities, in excess of mere auxiliary activities such as storage of goods or procuring of information, are carried out. A permanent establishment is also created by a dependent agent who has the authority to conclude contracts in the name and on behalf of the foreign principal.

II. Tax Rates

Income derived from a German permanent establishment by a foreign corporation is subject to CIT at a rate of 15 % plus solidarity surcharge. Progressive IIT rates (plus solidarity surcharge) apply to foreign individuals. Furthermore, the income is subject to TT.

III. Individuals

Please refer to the chapter "Employment Law" for further information.

D. Trade Tax

I. General

Any income derived from business activities carried out through a fixed place of business in Germany is subject to TT, irrespective of the form in which the business is carried out (e.g. sole proprietorship, partnership or corporation). TT is a municipal tax, the assessment rate of which is set by the municipalities. TT qualifies as a non-deductible expense for CIT purposes. Partnerships are not treated as transparent for TT purposes and are therefore themselves subject to TT on their trade income.

II. Tax Rates

Because the assessment rate for TT is determined by the municipalities, tax rates vary from municipality to municipality and therefore depend on where the business is located. Effective TT rates generally range from 7 % to 17.2 %. A minimum TT rate of 7 % was introduced to close down municipal TT havens. If a business has permanent establishments in several municipalities, trade income is allocated to those municipalities according to the salaries paid to the employees working in the permanent establishments of the respective municipalities. Individuals conducting a business as sole traders or through a partnership are granted a partial tax credit for TT on their personal income tax liability to avoid or at least reduce the extra tax burden suffered by an individual on business income due to being subject to individual IIT and TT.

E. Losses

CIT and IIT losses may either be offset against income in the same year or may be carried back to the previous tax year (up to a maximum of EUR 511,500). CIT and IIT losses can also be carried forward without limitation as to time or amount; although there are restrictions on the utilization of the loss carry forwards in any given year. Loss carry forwards may be fully offset against income of up to EUR 1,000,000.00. For income in excess of this amount, the utilization of loss carry forwards is limited to 60 %, i. e. the remaining 40 % of the income in excess of EUR 1,000,000.00 is subject to tax, even if additional loss carry forwards are available (so-called minimum taxation). The remainder of the loss can be carried forward in future years.

TT losses may not be carried back, but may be carried forward under the same conditions as CIT and IIT losses.

Further restrictions on the use of losses apply in certain circumstances if more than 25 % of the shares in a loss-making corporation are transferred or if the corporation is merged (cf. below).

F. Taxable Income

I. Income for CIT Purposes

The basis for determining the taxable income for CIT purposes is the income shown in the German GAAP commercial profit and loss statement to which certain adjustments will be made. The principal differences result from non-deductible items such as CIT, TT and solidarity surcharge, hidden dividend distributions, 30 % of entertainment expenses and 50 % of the compensation paid to members of a Supervisory Board, and from the different tax treatment of self-created intangible assets, provisions for contingent losses, liabilities and provisions for long term obligations exceeding one year, pension and anniversary provisions, provisions for maintenance and write-downs in value.

Except for capital gains derived from the sale of shares in corporations, the German CIT system does not distinguish between regular trade income and income derived from the sale of assets. German source capital gains are calculated as the difference between the current book value of an asset and the proceeds received, and are in principle subject to CIT at the regular rate. The taxation of capital gains from the sale of certain fixed assets (i. e. land and buildings) can be deferred under certain conditions by deducting them from the acquisition cost or the cost of production of replacing assets (roll-over relief) or by setting-up a tax-free reserve.

Capital gains derived from the sale of shares in a German or foreign corporation are generally tax exempt, irrespective of the amount of shareholding or the period for which the shares were held prior to the sale. However, in the same way as dividends, 5 % of the tax-exempt capital gain will be treated as a non-deductible expense and will thus in effect be subject to tax.

The tax exemption does not apply to the extent that tax effective write-downs in the value of the shares have been claimed in earlier years and have not been recaptured in the meantime and the exemption does not apply to shares held as trading stock by banks or financial institutions. Further, the exemption does not apply if the shares in the corporation have been issued in exchange for the contribution of business assets at a value below fair market value under the German Transformation Tax Act (*Umwandlungssteuergesetz, UmwStG*) prior to 2007 or after 2006 if in the latter case these shares are sold within a period of seven years after the contribution. Losses incurred in connection with the sale of shares in corporations are non-deductible. Write-downs in value on the shares are not accepted for tax purposes.

Dividends received from a German or foreign corporation are generally exempt from CIT, except dividends on shares held as current assets by financial institutions. However, in the same way as capital gains, 5 % of the tax-exempt dividend will be treated as a non-deductible expense and will thus in effect be subject to CIT. Actual expenses incurred in connection with the shareholding in a corporation are fully tax deductible.

Income derived from permanent establishments located in treaty countries is exempt from CIT under most German tax treaties. Tax credits are available for tax on income derived from permanent establishments in non-treaty countries.

II. Income for Individual Income Tax Purposes

Please refer to the chapter "Employment Law" for further information.

III. Income for TT Purposes

The assessment basis for TT is calculated by making various adjustments to the income subject to CIT (or ITT, if applicable). The most important examples of this are the increase of the CIT basis by adding back 25 % of interest on debts and on a deemed interest portion included in certain other expenses (annuities, payments to the silent partner, leasing and rent payments for movable and immovable assets, license payments). The add-back applies as far as the sum of EUR 100,000 is exceeded for such kinds of payments. Other add-back items are the dividends from German or foreign corporations for which certain holding and activity requirements are not fulfilled. The profit shares from German or foreign partnerships are deducted from the TT basis as well as income from real estate for businesses not performing actively but just holding real estate assets.

G. Withholding Taxes

I. Dividends

Dividends distributed by a German corporation are subject to withholding tax (WHT) at a rate of 25 % (plus 5.5 % solidarity surcharge). However, there is a potential refund of a part or all of the WHT for non-resident corporations. Where distributions are made to EU corporate shareholders the WHT is, upon application, reduced to zero if the EU entity directly has held at least 10 % of the share capital of the German corporation for an uninterrupted period of at least 12 months at the time of the dividend distribution. A refund is possible if, after the distribution, the 12 month period is met. For distributions to foreign non-EU shareholders, the double tax treaties with the respective countries usually provide for WHT reductions to 5 %, 10 % or 15 % if certain holding requirements are fulfilled. For corporate non-treaty country shareholders having sufficient substance WHT is reduced to 15 % (plus 5.5 % solidarity surcharge).

In order to benefit from a WHT reduction under a treaty or under EU rules, the recipient must meet substance requirements[1] that have been significantly tightened, effective 2007 and again changed in 2011. Those rules apply to withholding tax on dividends and to other withholding taxes. The substance test needs very careful consideration and is, for instance, often not met in the case of dividends paid to foreign holding companies. The purpose of the substance requirements is to avoid the interposition of a company in order to benefit from double taxation treaties or other tax reductions. The amended rules have been interpreted by the Federal Ministry of Finance by a letter dated 24 January 2012.

Treaty or EU directive benefits according to this rule are restricted

- for shareholders of the foreign recipient who would not be entitled to the same benefits, if they derived the income directly rather than through the interposed company and
- as far as the income generated is deemed to be bad income.

Gross income of the foreign company is good income

- as far as it is resulting from its own business activities or
- with respect to bad income of the foreign entity there are economic or other relevant reasons for the interposition of the recipient and it participates in general commerce with business infrastructure adequate for the purpose of its business.

---

1 Sec. 50d (3) EStG (*Einkommensteuergesetz* – Income Tax Act).

By the following example the Ministry illustrates its interpretation of the new wording of the law: The foreign company's shareholders do not benefit from any reduction rule (they are resident outside the EU and not in a Treaty country). 80 % of the income of the foreign company is not resulting from own business activity. For 60 % of this income (60 % of 80 % = 48 % of the income of the company) the interposition of the foreign company had good economic reason and it runs sufficient business operations. 20 % plus 48 % = 68 % of the payments subject to German withholding tax are benefiting from the reduction rule.

Since the percentage of good income may change from year to year it is important to know which year is the basis for the calculation. For the refund of tax withheld the year of the payment is decisive. When applying for an exemption certificate the income test is done on the basis of the previous year. If an exemption certificate is available the tax authorities hold that the foreign company has to give notice to the tax office, if the percentage of good income has significantly reduced.

An exemption from the substance requirements applies, if the recipient or ultimate parent of the recipient is a stock listed company or an investment company comparable to an investment stock corporation according to the German Investment Act and all companies including the intermediaries are entitled to the same level of withholding tax relief as the recipient of the payments.

Good active income includes arm's length fees for services rendered to group companies and dividends and interest income from EU subsidiaries actively managed by the company. Subsidiaries are actively managed for this purpose, if the shareholder actually takes and enforces decisions regarding the subsidiaries' businesses. The shareholder must take long-term leadership decisions of fundamental importance. Single business functions – e.g. granting loans, exploit licenses – do not suffice. Bad income is, for example, income from activities not carried out in the country of residence of the shareholder, income related to functions outsourced to other group companies or to third parties (law firms, consultancy firms), or dividends from subsidiaries that are not actively managed.

If the substance requirements cannot be complied with by the direct shareholder the test can still be met by the indirect shareholder. If the shareholder at this level is another EU company eligible under the EU Parent Subsidiary Directive and meets the substance requirements, the 0 % rate applies. If the shareholder at this level is a non-EU company and meets the substance requirements or is an individual benefiting from a German treaty, the respective treaty rate applies (e.g. 5 %, 10 % or 15 %). If the shareholder at this level is a company in a non-treaty country, the domestic rate applies.

Even if there are no plans to distribute dividends, it is recommended that the German subsidiary of an international group apply for an exemption certificate since it may happen in a tax audit that excess payments to shareholders or other related parties are treated as deemed dividends and become subject to dividend withholding tax. If an exemption certificate is available, withholding tax is not an issue. If it is not available, withholding tax has to be first paid to the tax office and thereafter a refund has to be applied for.

II. Interest

Interest is not subject to withholding tax except interest on certain profit participating loans. Interest and all other kinds of capital income paid to individuals are basically taxed at a standardized tax rate of 25 % plus solidarity surcharge. The tax is levied as a withholding tax (*Abgeltungssteuer*). In the case of interest payments made to non-residents, there is no necessity to withhold the standardized tax. However, the residency outside Germany must be proved by a certificate of exemption from the German Federal Tax Office which has to be applied for.

III. Royalties

Royalties, e.g. for the use of patents, know-how and other intellectual property rights, are only subject to WHT if paid to a non-resident. The WHT rate amounts to 20 % and, in the case of payments to non-resident corporations 15 % (plus 5.5 % solidarity surcharge). However, reductions of, or exemptions from, WHT are available under most German double tax treaties and the EU Interest and Royalties Directive. Substance rules as described above also apply to withholding taxes on royalties.

IV. Wage Tax

Employers are responsible for withholding wage tax (plus solidarity surcharge) from wages and salaries paid to employees. This also applies to salaries paid to employees by third parties, e.g. the top level group entity. If the parent company grants stock to its German employees, wage tax has to be withheld on behalf of the employee.

H. Tax Consolidation

Tax consolidation is available for CIT and TT purposes under the tax group (*Organschaft*) concept. Such tax group exists where one or more German corporations are financially integrated into (i. e. the majority of the shares or the voting rights in the German corporation are held by) the business of a German parent corporation or an active partnership or a German branch of a foreign enterprise and have concluded a profit and loss absorption lasting a minimum of five years with the parent so that the profits and losses generated by the integrated companies will be allocated to and aggregated with the profits or losses of the parent for tax purposes.

I. Administration

I. Filing of Tax Returns

The tax year in Germany is the calendar year. While companies may have business years deviating from the calendar year, the change of the business year from the calendar year to a different period requires the prior approval of the Tax Authorities. CIT and TT returns must be filed annually. The general filing deadline is five months after the end of the tax year under assessment, i. e. 31th May 2012 for business years ending in the year 2011. An automatic extension of 7 months is granted for tax returns prepared by a tax advisor. Further extensions may be granted upon application, but this requires specific grounds.

II. Payment of Taxes

Quarterly CIT and TT prepayments have to be made and these will be assessed by the tax authorities based on the taxable income of the prior year or, for newly established businesses, based on a forecast from the taxpayer.

III. Tax Audits

All substantial business operations are subject to full scale, on-site tax field audits on a more or less continuous basis. Annual taxes will normally be assessed subject to review, based on the tax returns filed by the taxpayer, and final assessments will only be issued after a tax field audit has been carried out. The tax authorities may, in the course of a tax field audit, request access to the EDP system of the taxpayer which enables them to apply their own review tools to the EDP system. Additionally, special audits reviewing VAT, wage tax or social security contributions take place.

J. Anti-Avoidance Rules

I. General

The German tax system operates under the principle of "substance over form" and places particular emphasis on the economic background and intention of transactions and structures. Agreements, even if legally invalid, are taken into account for tax purposes to the extent that the parties in fact observe the economic effects of such agreements. The General Tax Code contains provisions according to which tax laws may not be avoided by the abuse of legal structures. The Income Tax Act (*Einkommensteuergesetz, EStG*) contains an express provision against treaty shopping.

II. CFC Legislation

Germany has extensive CFC legislation under which income created by passive foreign subsidiaries in low tax countries can be attributed to the German shareholder and subjected to German tax. For subsidiaries in EU countries, those rules have been amended taking into consideration EU non-discrimination rules.

K. Transfer Pricing

I. General Transfer Pricing Rules

Inter-company pricing between affiliated companies must be on an arm's length basis to be accepted for tax purposes. The German Ministry of Finance (*Bundesfinanzministerium*) has issued a Decree-Law regarding the Determination and Documentation of Profits[2]; which provides principles on how to determine arm's length prices. In addition numerous administrative principles have been published by the Ministry[3]; which have to be considered by taxpayers having international activity. Inter-company pricing is pursued particularly vigorously by the German tax authorities where multinational groups are involved. Charges for goods and services to a German enterprise by a foreign affiliate (and vice versa) will be adjusted, if they are not in line with the arm's length principle. The adjustment impacts the basis for German CIT and TTI.

---

2 *Gewinnabgrenzungsaufzeichnungsverordnung* dated 28th October 2003.

3 Principles for the Examination of Cost-Sharing Arrangements between Internationally Related Enterprises of 30th December 1999 (*Grundsätze für die Prüfung der Einkunftsabgrenzung durch Umlageverträge zwischen international verbundenen Unternehmen*); Administration Principles for the Examination of the Allocation of Business Property and Income of Permanent Establishments of Internationally Operating Enterprises of 24th December 1999, 20th November 2000 and 25th August 2009 (*Grundsätze der Verwaltung für die Prüfung der Aufteilung des Betriebsvermögens und der Einkünfte bei Betriebsstätten international tätiger Unternehmen*); Principles for the Examination of Income Allocation between Internationally Related Enterprises in Cases of Employee Secondments of 9th November 2001 (*Grundsätze für die Prüfung der Einkunftsabgrenzung zwischen international verbundenen Unternehmen in Fällen der Arbeitnehmerentsendung*); and Principles for the Examination of Income Allocation between Related Parties with Cross-border Business Relations with Respect to Determination and Cooperation Duties, Adjustments and Mutual Agreement and EU Arbitration Procedures ("Procedural Principles") of 12 April 2005 (*Grundsätze für die Prüfung der Einkunftsabgrenzung zwischen nahestehenden Personen mit grenzüberschreitenden Geschäftsbeziehungen in Bezug auf Ermittlungs- und Mitwirkungspflichten, Berichtigungen sowie auf Verständigungs- und EU-Schiedsverfahren*).

II. Transfer Pricing Methods

German tax authorities mainly require taxpayers to use the comparable uncontrolled price (CUP) method, the resale price method and the cost-plus method to determine arm's length prices. Sec. 1 of the Foreign Tax Act[4] clearly states that these three traditional methods should be used, with a preference for the CUP method.

Germany has not implemented the OECD Transfer Pricing Guidelines into national law, which is why these guidelines cannot be applied directly in transfer pricing negotiations but can be used for interpretation purposes only. Profit-oriented methods, such as the comparable profit method, profit split method and transactional net margin method are only used and accepted to recalculate and support transfer prices determined using traditional transactional methods.

III. Transfer of a Function

According to the German Foreign Tax Act and the Decree-Law regarding the Transfer of Functions, the transfer of functions covers all tangible and intangible assets, chances, risks and other benefits which are connected to the function transferred. Three different cases are possible:

- The domestic function is entirely given up and relocated with its profit potential abroad;
- Simply a part of the function is transferred abroad;
- Transfer of risks and opportunities, leaving a limited profile domestically connected with an increase of risks and opportunities abroad.

If no limitation on performing the function domestically is observed within the first five years after the relocation, it is not considered as a transfer of functions (so-called duplication of a function).

A function is defined as an organic part of the German business (not a separable part of a business operation – *Teilbetrieb* – necessary). As such, functions are considered among other activities in relation to production, assembly, quality control, organization, transport, after-sales services etc.

When a German entity transfers its production to another foreign affiliated entity without also transferring the marketing and sales activities, a relevant transfer of a function is given.

---

4 Sec. 1 AStG (*Außensteuergesetz* – German Foreign Tax Act).

In general, the entire function is evaluated as one "transfer package". Evaluation of each asset separately is an exception and allowed if no material intangibles are transferred or any transferred material intangibles can be exactly identified and the sum of the chosen transfer prices is at arm's-length. An intangible is material if it is required by the function and its price makes up more than 25 % of the price for the entire package. The price is at arm's-length between the difference in the company value of the transferring entity before and after the transfer and the difference in the company value of the receiving entity after and before the transfer. The evaluation should be based on future earnings outlooks. If it was carried out incorporating significant uncertainties, the tax authorities may conduct a price adjustment.

IV. Documentation of Transfer Prices

Transfer pricing documentation in cases of cross-border transactions with related parties is required by German law.[5] At least two types of documentation are required:

- Documentation of the facts and circumstances; and
- Documentation of the arm's length nature of the cross-border transactions.

This documentation is required for normal transactions and for extraordinary transactions. The differentiation between these two kinds of transactions affects the deadline for submission of such documentation (see below).

Extraordinary transactions include, in particular, but not exclusively, the conclusion or modification of long-term agreements with a material influence on the taxpayer's income in Germany, transfer of assets in the case of a restructuring, transfer of functions, transfer and surrender of the use and benefit of assets and advantages related to changes of functions and risks in the company (such as changes from dealer to commission agent, from manufacturer to extended work bench or from an independent research and development unit to a contract research and development division), and transactions concerning material changes in business strategy with respect to transfer pricing and the conclusion of cost-sharing agreements.

The period of time between the transactions and the compilation of the documentation should not be too long. Documentation prepared too much later might not be accepted in cases of recurring losses or might be treated as insufficient. Insufficient documentation could trigger an estimation of income plus penalties.

The documentation of facts and circumstances and the documentation of the arm's length nature of cross-border transactions are normally requested for purposes of tax

5 Sec. 90 AO (Abgabenordnung – German General Tax Act)

field audits. At the request of the tax field auditors, both types of documentation must be submitted within 60 days in the case of normal cross-border transactions and within 30 days in the case of extraordinary transactions. Failure to meet these deadlines is punished with a fine.

The German tax administration has a right to receive all documents in German. German taxpayers can apply for an exemption from this obligation either prior to the preparation of the documentation or after the documentation has been requested, at the latest. In most cases, documents in English may be accepted; other languages are normally not accepted by the tax authorities.

If such documentation cannot be provided, the tax authorities can make an income adjustment based on estimates and penalties can be imposed.

V. Mutual Understanding Procedures

Mutual Understanding Procedures in many cases are the only way to avoid double taxation, if the German authorities increase the income of the German taxpayer under transfer pricing rules. Germany's tax treaties, which mostly follow the OECD Model Tax Convention, contain clauses allowing mutual understanding procedures. Mutual understanding procedures are also possible under the EU Arbitration Convention which has been implemented into national law and which takes precedence over German tax law. Mutual understanding procedures are very burdensome to both the tax authorities and taxpayers and both sides, in many cases, come to agreements which avoid those procedures.

L. Interest Deductibility Restrictions

Interest deduction is limited under interest barrier rules (*Zinsschranke*). The new rules replaced the thin capitalization rules back in 2008. A decree on the application of the earnings stripping rule was published on 4th July 2008 by the Federal Ministry of Finance.

The rules apply to any compensation which is paid in connection with the lending of money including compensation for profit-participating loans, yields on typical silent partnership agreements, profit-sharing bonds and yields on participation rights. The interest barrier applies irrespective of whether the lender is a shareholder or a third party, irrespective of the term of the loan and irrespective of whether or not a security is granted. The interest barrier also applies to all businesses which are German taxpayers, regardless of their legal form.

The rule stipulates that a taxpayer will only be able to immediately deduct net interest expenses (interest expense less interest income) up to 30 % of the income before interest, taxes, depreciation and amortization (EBITDA). The EBITDA is calculated according to tax rules, so that, for instance, the EBITDA of corporations is increased by the addition of hidden distributions and reduced by tax exempt dividends and capital gains. Tax groups (*Organschaften*) are treated as one business.

The limitation does not apply, if one of the following exemptions is met:

- Net interest expense is less than EUR 3,000,000. If this threshold is exceeded, the full amount, rather than only the exceeding amount, is subject to the 30 % restriction. There is no general allowance of EUR 3,000,000;
- The taxpayer is not part of a corporate group (non-group affiliation);
- The equity ratio of the borrower is at least equal to or higher than the equity ratio of the whole group, with a tolerance of 2 percentage points being allowed (escape clause in the event of group affiliation). The equity ratio is the balance sheet equity divided by the balance sheet total.

Whether a business belongs to a group and the determination of the equity for the purposes of the calculation of the equity ratio of the business and of the group is, as a rule, determined based on IFRS financial accounting. The local GAAP of an EU member state or US-GAAP may be accepted as a basis for these issues, if certain requirements are met.

In determining the equity ratio, the figures originating from IFRS, local GAAP or US-GAAP are subject to a number of specific adjustments for tax purposes.

In the case of a corporation, the exemption for non-group affiliation and the escape clause are subject to the additional requirement that the corporation is not borrowing funds from shareholders to a harmful extent. Shareholder debt is tainting if more than 10 % of the entity's net interest expense accrues to substantial shareholders (holding more than 25 % of the shares in the corporation paying tax in Germany) or to a person that is related to such a shareholder.

For the escape clause, even interest on third party loans can be tainting, if – subject to the 10 % rule – the third party has recourse to a substantial shareholder or to a related party. Shareholder financing and security granted between members of the consolidated group are, in turn, disregarded for this test.

The escape clause requires that not only the German entity in question undergoes this shareholder financing test, but so does each and every world-wide member of the group. Therefore, the escape clause requires proof which can be burdensome to obtain, especially for larger groups of companies.

Non-deductible interest expenses can be carried forward and be deducted in future years in compliance with the 30 % EBITDA rule.

Interest carry forwards will be lost in the event of harmful shareholder changes, as defined in the loss trafficking rules.

M. Loss Trafficking Rules (Change-of-Ownership Rules)

Under the loss trafficking rules, any carry forwards of tax losses (corporate income tax and trade tax) will be completely forfeited if more than 50 % of the shares or voting rights in any company are directly or indirectly transferred to an acquiring shareholder or a group of acquiring shareholders within 5 years.

In the case of a direct or indirect transfer of more than 25 %, but not more than 50 % of the shares, within the 5-year period, the carry forwards of tax losses will be forfeited proportionally. Capital increases and decreases might also be treated as transfers of shares, resulting in the forfeiture of the carry forwards of tax losses, if there is an effect on the proportion of shares owned by an existing shareholder.

Several shareholders may be regarded as one shareholder if they are deemed to have aligned interests. The rules also apply if a change in shareholding takes place at an upper-tier level within a group structure.

According to the tax authorities, certain transactions such as a merger or a contribution in kind into the loss company or the acquisition of own shares might also be treated as transfers of shares, resulting in the forfeiture of the carry forwards if there is an effect on the proportion of shares owned by an existing shareholder. Also, agreements on voting rights (e.g. waiver of voting rights) might be regarded as a harmful transaction and could lead to a (proportional or complete) forfeiture of the losses.

There is a relief for certain intra group transactions. If the transferring entity and the entity receiving the shares are directly or indirectly 100 % held by the same shareholder, the loss trafficking rules do not apply.

Further, there is a hidden reserve escape from the loss trafficking rules. Unused tax losses survive a share transfer to the extent that they are compensated by domestic hidden reserves (inherent capital gains). These hidden reserves must lie in business assets of the loss corporation being subject to German taxation. This escape can even apply to transactions with third parties.

Hidden reserves are the difference between the fair market value of the transferred shares and the respective portion of the company's tax equity to the extent allocable to German business assets. On share transfers of more than 50 %, the total tax equity is compared with the fair market value of all shares. If the equity of the loss company is negative, hidden reserves are defined as the difference between the (full or proportionate) fair market value of the business and the (full or proportionate) equity of the company.

Another relief from the strict loss trafficking rules had been enacted for cases in which the shareholder change is part of a plan to avoid insolvency or over-indebtedness under strict requirements. The EU Commission holds that those rules are an offence against EU rules. As a result those rules are not applicable. According to a new law enacted on December 14th, 2011 the relief rule will become valid again if the resolution of the EU Commission is abregated by the European Court of Justice.

N. Other Taxes

I. Value Added Tax

Value Added Tax (*Umsatzsteuer*, VAT) is currently levied on the supply of goods and services in Germany at a rate of 19 %. A reduced rate of 7 % applies to certain goods and services including the delivery of books, certain food items and taxi services within city limits.

The German VAT system is governed by EU law. Any entrepreneur supplying goods or services in Germany is liable for VAT, regardless of legal form and nationality. VAT charged to an entrepreneur for goods supplied or services rendered by another entrepreneur may be claimed as input VAT, with some restrictions.

The entrepreneur has to file quarterly or, if VAT due in the previous year exceeded Euro 7,500, monthly preliminary VAT returns as well as annual VAT returns.

For VAT purposes, fiscal groups can exist meaning that several companies can be treated as one entrepreneur.

II. Real Estate Transfer Tax

Real Estate Transfer Tax (*Grunderwerbsteuer*, RETT) is levied on the sale and transfer of real estate located in Germany and on certain other transactions deemed to be a transfer of real estate, such as the transfer of at least 95 % of the shares in a company owning real estate to one purchaser or a group of related purchasers or the complete or almost complete change of the partners in a partnership owning real estate. A complete or almost complete change of partners occurs if, within a period of 5 years, at least 95 % of the partnership interest is transferred to one or several new partners. The tax rate is set by each of the 16 German federal states. It amounts to 3.5 %–5 %. The basis for RETT is the consideration paid for the real estate or, in certain situations, a special assessed tax value of the real estate.

Institutional real estate investors usually tend to structure a real estate acquisition as a share deal in order to avoid RETT. Depending on whether the real property is held by a partnership or a corporation, this can be done by making sure the seller of a partnership keeps 5.1 % of the partnership interest for at least five years or the seller of a corporation sells 94.9 % of the shares to one purchaser and keeps 5.1 % or sells it to a third party.

III. Inheritance and Gift Tax

Inheritance and Gift Tax (*Erbschaftsteuer*) is levied on the transfer of property by gift or by inheritance. Where neither the donor/decedent nor the beneficiary is a German resident, taxation is limited to property located in Germany. The tax rates vary from 7 % to 50 %, depending on the degree of family relation and on the value of the property. Tax allowances are available for spouses and children, and for the transfer of business assets and shares in corporations resident in the European Economic Area.

Citizens of a foreign country being unlimited taxpayers in Germany, e.g. due to having a place of residence in Germany are fully subject to this tax even if they plan to stay in Germany for a limited period of time. There are only very few Double Tax Treaties for inheritance and gift tax in place with other countries, e.g. with Switzerland, USA and France. This can hit expatriate workers and their families very severely.

Dr. Ulrich Siegemund
ulrich.siegemund@luther-lawfirm.com

CHAPTER 3
MERGERS AND ACQUISITIONS

DR. THOMAS KUHNLE

The catch-all term "mergers and acquisitions" (M&A) covers all kinds of corporate consolidations including the acquisition of a business or a company in whole or in part, management buy-outs, management buy-ins, initial public offerings (IPO), joint ventures and other cooperations, as well as all transactions relating to such acquisitions, such as pre-sales and post-completion restructurings. In the following, the typical features and procedures of M&A transactions, particularly with respect to cross border transactions, will be outlined.

A. General Aspects

While the decision on the sale or acquisition of a business is frequently driven by many different objectives (external growth, changes in the field of business, financial issues, etc.), the actual deal structure is often shaped by the financing of the transaction as well as tax issues. As these issues have to be handled as the case arises, the following description will concentrate on the main types of transactions under German law.

In Germany, there are no laws relating specifically to the acquisition of businesses. The key German law governing business transactions and combinations, depending on the structure of the business combination, consists of the following legislation:

Civil Code (*Bürgerliches Gesetzbuch, BGB*); Commercial Code (*Handelsgesetzbuch, HGB*); Limited Liability Company Law (*GmbH-Gesetz, GmbHG*); Stock Corporation Act (*Aktiengesetz, AktG*); Reorganisation Act (*Umwandlungsgesetz, UmwG*); Takeover Act (*Wertpapiererwerbs- und Übernahmegesetz, WpÜG*); Securities Trading Act (*Wertpapierhandelsgesetz, WpHG*); Act Against Restrictions on Competition (*Gesetz gegen Wettbewerbsbeschränkungen, GWB*); Securities Prospectus Act (*Wertpapierprospektgesetz, WpPG*); Insolvency Order (*Insolvenzordnung, InsO*); Co-Determination Act (*Gesetz über die Mitbestimmung der Arbeitnehmer, MitbestG*); Works Constitution Act (*Betriebsverfassungsgesetz, BetrVG*); One-Third-Participation Act (*Drittelbeteiligungsgesetz, DrittelbG*).

The German Limited Liability Company Law has been reformed by new legislation (Gesetz zur Modernisierung des GmbH-Rechts und zur Bekämpfung von Missbräuchen, MoMiG) on 1st November, 2008. These changes will influence transactions in which German limited liability companies are involved (e.g. due diligence, share and purchase agreement, financing etc.). However, even for these transactions there will be no fundamental structural modifications in M&A transactions and therefore in the following narrative, reference is made only when appropriate.

The existing legal provisions on the sale of individual rights and assets do not cover the specifics of the sale of a business as a collectivity of rights and assets. Therefore, the parties ordinarily agree on their own set of rules.

In contrast to many other legal systems, German law has one characteristic which has a considerable impact on the structuring of transactions under German law: the legal transfer of assets/participations comprises two separate legal acts: an agreement under the law of obligations (= sale and purchase agreement, *Verpflichtungsgeschäft*) in which the parties agree on the commitment to transfer the relevant assets/participations, and a further agreement in rem (= transfer agreement, *Verfügungsgeschäft*) for the change in ownership of the assets/participations sold. However, both agreements are normally incorporated in one document.

The distinction between "*Verpflichtungsgeschäft*" and "*Verfügungsgeschäft*" has to be considered irrespective of the structure of the transaction as Asset or Share Deal.

B. Deal Structure of Asset Deals

When a business is sold in an asset deal (in whole or in part), the purchaser acquires individual assets that in aggregate make up the business sold. This kind of deal structure is often used if the purchaser is not interested in acquiring the whole business or if certain risks have been identified which the purchaser does not wish to take on. To a certain extent, an asset deal enables the purchaser to "cherry pick".

The following aspects should be highlighted with respect to national asset deals:

I. Sale and Transfer of Individual Assets

With respect to the sale and transfer of individual assets and liabilities, the parties especially have to consider the following:

Sale and transfer agreement: as a number of individual assets and (possibly) liabilities are sold and transferred, the sale and transfer agreement must specifically describe and define the assets and liabilities being sold. A general description such as "all fixed assets and inventory relating to the business" is not fully sufficient. This requirement can be met by geographical localization of the assets to be transferred (e.g. "all assets located on the real estate named "xy"") or, which is preferable for the sake of clarity for the buyer and the seller, by attaching computer printouts of the assets and liabilities sold, which are often available from the electronic accounting system of the target business. However, the compilation of the relevant data can be time-consuming and should therefore be started early in the process.

Transfer of accounts payable/contracts: the transfer of accounts payable and contracts requires the consent of the respective creditors and contracting parties. This consent may be, and usually is, obtained after the execution of the sale and transfer agreement. In this case, the purchaser has to insist on specific provisions in the event that such consent is not given (e.g., reduction of the purchase price, right of withdrawal, etc.).

Transfer of licenses and permits: as a rule, public licenses and permits relating to the operation of the business (*betriebsbezogene, sachliche Genehmigungen*) may be transferred. On the other hand, licenses and permits relating to a specific person (*personenbezogene Genehmigungen*) cannot as a rule be transferred from the seller to the purchaser; the purchaser has to apply for a new license in order to continue the acquired business.

Further approval requirements: besides the consent requirements mentioned above, there might be – depending on the assets sold – further requirements of approval from third parties (e.g., in the case of a chattel mortgage or if the assets constitute almost the entire property of the seller).

Requirements as to the form of the contracts: the sale and transfer agreement only requires a specific form if assets are sold whose sale and transfer mandatorily requires execution in a specific form (e.g., the sale and transfer of real property requires a notarial deed). Otherwise, for purposes of proof, the written form is advisable.

II. Transfer of Employment

The employment relationships of all employees of the business being sold are transferred automatically to the purchaser pursuant to Sec. 613a of the German Civil Code (*Bürgerliches Gesetzbuch, BGB*). The purchaser assumes all rights and obligations resulting from the employment relationships existing at the time of transfer. However, as employees are free to choose their employer, they have the right to object to their employment relationships being transferred. To enable the employees to exercise this right, the seller or the purchaser must notify the employees of the transfer of the business prior to such transfer. As to the content and the coverage of such notification, there exists extensive case law which has to be considered. The effect of an objection by an employee is that his or her employment relationship is not transferred to the purchaser and remains with the seller. Unless the latter has another position for the employee raising the objection, it may terminate the employment relationship for compelling business reasons. The purchaser is not entitled to terminate employment merely on the grounds of the business transfer. Termination of employment for other reasons, e.g. because of reorganization measures following the transfer of the business, is, however, still possible.

Employees' rights and obligations which are governed by the terms of a collective agreement or by a works agreement form the basis of the employment relationship between the purchaser and the employees and may not be modified to the detriment of the employees for one year from the date of transfer. This does not apply, however, if and to the extent that the purchaser has collective agreements or other works agreements covering the same subject matter, in which case these agreements replace those relating to the transferred business even if they are less favorable.

For further details please refer to the section Industrial Relations and Labor Legislation.

III. Liability of the Purchaser

In principle, the purchaser assumes only the liabilities expressly assigned to it pursuant to the sale and transfer agreement. Under German law, however, there are exceptions with regard to the following liabilities:

Tax law: if the purchaser continues the business operations, it is jointly and severally liable for tax debts which have their sole basis and origin in the acquired business and which arose in the year preceding the transfer of the business. This concerns trade tax and VAT in particular.

Commercial law: if the purchaser continues the acquired business under the former company name, then it assumes joint and several liabilities for all debts of the seller originating from the seller's business operations unless it is – following the parties' application – stated in the Commercial Register that such liability has not been transferred to the purchaser or unless the seller or the purchaser have notified a third party accordingly. However such liability can also be avoided by variation of the former company name.

Employment law: the purchaser is jointly and severally liable for obligations relating to transferred employees that fall due on or up to one year after transfer of the business.

C. Deal Structure of Share Deals

In a share deal, the purchaser acquires the shares in a company that owns a business. As a share deal does not affect the ownership of the company's assets, the purchaser acquires the company with all its assets, receivables, liabilities, obligations (even those it does not know about) and generally public licenses and permits. The possibility for the purchaser to continue the business "as is" may be the decisive argument for carrying out a share deal.

The following aspects should be highlighted with respect to national share deals:

Transfer of interests/shares: since the interests in German partnerships (OHG, KG, GmbH & Co. KG) are not freely transferable, such a transfer always requires the approval of all other partners, unless the partnership agreement provides otherwise. In comparison, shares in a German corporation (GmbH, AG, KGaA) are freely transferable unless otherwise stipulated in the company's bylaws. The bylaws of family-owned GmbHs in particular often stipulate certain transfer restrictions (e.g., approval by the company or by the shareholders' meeting). The bylaws of an AG may only stipulate such restrictions with respect to the transfer of registered shares, while such consent requirements are not allowed for bearer shares.

Requirements as to the form of the contracts: the sale and transfer of interests in a partnership and of shares in an AG does not need to be executed in a specific form; the simple written form of the relevant contracts is sufficient. If an AG has issued share certificates, the shares may be transferred by endorsement (and delivery of the share certificate) or by simple transfer of the right, with title to the share certificate following by law. In contrast, contracts for the sale and transfer of shares in a GmbH must be drawn up in notarized form.

D. Joint Ventures

A joint venture is a commercial arrangement between at least two economically and legally independent partners. The establishment of a joint venture may be prompted by the scale of a project such as the joint financing of an expensive project or the need for special expertise (e.g., technical, marketing or cultural expertise). In particular, when a foreign investor intends to invest in a country with quite different cultural and/or political conditions, a joint venture is often used as the first move into the new market.

A joint venture can be established either by creating a new company or taking on shares in the joint venture company or by agreeing to collaborate on a contractual basis. In the first two cases, the parties become joint shareholders of the joint venture company. Thus, the company's bylaws (*Gesellschaftsverträge*, *Satzungen*) constitute the basis for the rights and duties of the parties as shareholders. However, since bylaws of corporations have to be published in the Commercial Register under German law, the shareholders generally also enter into a separate shareholders' agreement (*Konsortialvertrag*) in order to regulate those rights and duties that are to be kept confidential. Such shareholders' agreements often set out detailed rules on the management of the company and its business (e.g., appointment of the members of management and other corporate bodies, determination of management transactions requiring the prior approval of the shareholders, exercise of voting rights, financing, call options, put options, etc.)

When the parties agree to collaborate on a contractual basis, the cooperation agreement commonly sets forth similar provisions to that of the shareholders' agreement, e.g., the scope and financing of the joint venture, the rights and duties of the participants, the sharing of returns and related costs, the duration of the legal relationship, etc.

E. Typical Procedure in M&A Transactions

Although every M&A transaction is a unique and complex procedure, there is a typical pattern to all such deals. Generally, an M&A Transaction includes the following phases: Preparatory Phase or Pre-Sale Reorganization; Transaction Phase; and Post-Closing Integration Phase.

I. Preparatory Phase/Pre-Sale Reorganization

The Preparatory Phase is probably the most important phase for the success of the transaction.

Ideally, the seller can sell its business "as is" and the potential purchaser is interested in exactly that business. However, often there is a need for a Pre-Sale Reorganization in order to construct the business to be sold (restructuring, carve-out etc.). Such Pre-Sale Reorganization may also be triggered by tax-optimization issues.

During the Preparatory Phase, the seller has to decide whether he intends to sell the business by contacting one or a limited number of potential buyers or through a controlled auction. Controlled auctions are increasingly used even for smaller and midcap transactions to facilitate negotiations with one or more potential buyers at home and abroad, to accelerate the decision-making and to optimize the results for the seller (purchase price, guarantees etc.). In an auction situation it can be beneficial for the seller to perform a legal vendor due diligence to identify issues early in the sale process, allowing it time to solve issues or, at least, to put a positive "spin" on them, as far as possible. A legal vendor due diligence, which will be made available for the potential buyers, can also help to attract bidders who might otherwise be put off by the cost to be incurred early in the process.

If the M&A transaction is not carried out via a controlled auction and the seller has granted exclusivity, the potential purchaser might also request a specific business structure, in order to make a tax-optimized acquisition from his point of view.

II. Transaction Phase

With the Transaction Phase the direct contact between the seller and the potential buyer(s) begins.

F. Information Memorandum

The first contact between the seller and the purchaser may be organized by the parties or by an M&A advisor, such as an investment bank. The M&A advisor normally prepares an information memorandum to inform the potential purchaser about key data of the target business (size, location(s), number of employees, sales markets, etc.).

If there is contact between seller and buyer, the parties will usually sign a non-disclosure agreement which contains sanctions for the breach of the agreement.

G. Letter of Intent

If the parties decide to pursue the transaction further, they usually agree a letter of intent (LoI) or memorandum of understanding (MoU). Primarily, this LoI/MoU confirms the intent of the parties to carry out the contemplated transaction, states the outcome of previous negotiations and defines the further course of the transaction procedure. As the purchaser incurs considerable cost and expense during the subsequent phases, in particular in connection with the due diligence review of the target business, it is in the purchaser's interest to agree on an exclusivity period during which the seller is not allowed to otherwise sell or negotiate the sale of the target business.

No exclusivity will be granted in controlled auctions. In that case the LoI/MoU will contain an even more detailed description of the further transaction procedure, in particular regarding the time and the content for a first indicative and a following binding offer for the business to be acquired. The indicative offer is usually requested before the business can be examined in detail in the subsequent due diligence. The information necessary for such an offer has usually been included in the information memorandum or forms part of the LoI/MoU. In some cases the seller or its M&A advisors may ask for a first indicative offer after having transmitted the information memorandum.

Although the LoI/MoU could be legally binding, the parties normally agree that it shall be a predominantly non-binding document. In any case the LoI/MoU is binding regarding the non-disclosure of information, the regulations as to cost and the sanctions for the breach of the LoI/MoU. However, experience shows that even if the LoI/MoU is intended to be non-binding, it is often difficult to depart from the terms set forth in the LoI/MoU in subsequent negotiations.

H. Due Diligence

The LoI/MoU is usually followed by a due diligence review. A due diligence review is a review of the target's legal, economic, financial, tax, personnel and other affairs, such as environmental, cultural and technological aspects of the business, that is carried out by the purchaser and its advisors. The potential purchaser normally sends a request list for information before starting the due diligence procedure, upon receipt of which the seller prepares or completes an already prepared data room. The data room will be set up physically or in electronic form; the electronic form is more often used in controlled auctions. During the due diligence process the potential buyer(s) is/are usually entitled to ask for further information on open/unclear issues and these questions are answered during the due diligence process by the seller (Q & A session). Questions may also be asked during a presentation by the management of the seller about the business to be sold. The results of the due diligence review are summarized in a due diligence report.

The purpose of a due diligence exercise is, on the one hand, to enable the purchaser to examine the target business to decide whether or not it meets its expectations. On the other hand it enables the purchaser to identify potential risks and/or "Deal Breakers". Furthermore, the due diligence should provide a sound basis for subsequent negotiations, in particular with respect to the determination of the purchase price as well as representations and warranties. Thus, the due diligence is an essential precursor to contractual protection and helps to identify the level and areas of protection needed.

I. Negotiation Phase

If the due diligence has not revealed any "Deal Breakers", it is followed by the negotiation of the specific terms and conditions of the transaction and the preparation of the contractual documents. Unless the bargaining position of the seller is much stronger than that of the purchaser (as is generally the case in controlled auctions), the drafting is normally done by the purchaser.

The negotiation phase is certainly highly sensitive as cross-border mergers are often accompanied by a clash of cultures, languages and management styles. These differences may arise during the negotiations and it is important for the success of the transaction to take these "cultural aspects" into consideration, even for the predominant party.

J. Signing and Closing

The Anglo-Saxon concept pursuant to which the signing of the sale and purchase agreement and the closing or consummation of the transaction traditionally take place at two different points in time is being adopted in Germany to an increasing extent, even though it is not necessary under German law. However, this concept is mandatory in connection with large, complex transactions that require several rounds of approval, including board approval or merger clearance (for details regarding merger clearance, please see the chapter on anti-trust law). In these cases, the sale and purchase agreement is signed when the parties have agreed on all terms and conditions, while closing occurs at a later point in time, usually after all approvals or other conditions precedent have been obtained or fulfilled.

I. Post-Closing Integration Phase

The success of an acquisition is especially dependent on the successful integration of the acquired business into the existing operations of the purchaser. Such integration is normally less complex in a share deal than in an asset deal, since in the latter case every individual asset and liability sold must be transferred and integrated. Moreover, in an asset deal there will be other post-completion matters to attend to, such as administrative matters, insurance, payroll, VAT and pensions.

With respect to representations and warranties, each purchaser is advised to set up a process to monitor any potential warranty claims that arise, so that the deadlines are not missed. If the seller grants certain guarantees as to the amount of equity of the target company, as of the closing date (in a share deal) or the amounts of accounts receivable (in an asset deal), a closing balance sheet or other financial statements must be prepared after the acquisition. Sometimes, the purchaser also decides on post-sales restructuring. This is often performed for tax purposes.

K. Special Features of Cross-Border M&A Transactions

I. Choice of Law

In cross-border transactions it is essential for the parties to choose the law that will govern the contracts. There may be disagreement because both the seller and the purchaser wish the governing law to be the law of their home country, particularly if the parties come from different legal systems.[1]

Although international standards for M&A contracts that have evolved in the Anglo-Saxon world in particular are increasingly being adopted in Germany, a contract governed by German law is still much "shorter" than a contract subject to common law. Since German law has codified many general and abstract rules which take effect unless otherwise stipulated by the parties, there is no need to describe and define every single detail, as is the case in common law contracts, but it is sufficient to make reference to codified legal definitions and codified legal consequences.

According to German international law, the parties are only free to decide on the law governing the sale and purchase agreement, and have no choice regarding the law applicable to the transfer since the transfer of assets/participations is mandatorily governed by the law of the country in which the assets are located or – with respect to participations being sold – in which the company is based. If bearer stocks are to be transferred, the transfer is mandatorily governed by the law of the country in which the stocks are located during the completion of the acquisition.

II. Dispute Resolution

Arbitration clauses are regularly used in German M&A transactions, especially if foreign parties are involved. In addition to the well-known advantages of the arbitration process compared to ordinary courts (confidentiality, special expertise of the arbitrators, shorter duration and higher flexibility of proceedings etc.) the court of arbitration may be conducted in the language agreed by the parties. There is no requirement that proceedings be conducted in German.

1 Please refer to: www.lawmadeingermany.de.

III. Choice of Language for the Negotiations and Documents

Besides the choice of law and dispute resolution, the choice of language is an important issue – even from a psychological perspective. Clearly, if the parties do not ordinarily communicate in the same language, each party will try to ensure that the negotiations are conducted and contracts drafted in their own language. The choice of law and the choice of language are usually interconnected: if the parties wish to regulate their legal relationship in one particular language, there is likely to be some logic to adopting the law of the jurisdiction where that language is spoken, and vice versa. However, the number of transactions negotiated and/or documented in English is increasing and this applies in particular to transactions in the form of controlled auctions where the involvement of foreign investors is common.

So, even though English has become the common language in international transactions, a German seller does not have to agree on using English. Under certain circumstances it could also be advantageous for the foreign investor to waive the usage of the English language for the negotiations and the documents and to accept, in negotiations with a German seller, the German language instead, as this could be seen as a positive signal to the German contractual partner that the foreign investor is not interested in an unfriendly takeover of the German business but is willing to cooperate (particularly if the target is a family-owned business).

IV. Foreign Investment Control

Germany is one of the most open markets world-wide, with very liberal regulations concerning government approval of foreign investments. The acquisition of arms manufacturing companies by non-resident purchasers is traditionally subject to such approval. In addition, since 2009 it has been possible for the Federal government to prohibit the acquisition of a minimum of 25 % of the voting rights in a German company by a foreign investor based outside the EU or EFTA if the acquisition puts public safety and order at risk. As to the scope of application, "utilities and service providers of strategic relevance" are given as an example in the explanatory notes to the legislation. Legal certainty for investors is ensured inasmuch as investors are legally entitled to a clearance certificate if a risk does not exist; this certificate is deemed issued when an examination procedure is not initiated within one month after the – voluntary – submission of an application for approval (the Federal government estimates that not more than 10 such procedures are initiated annually). If an application is not filed, the Federal government may prohibit the takeover ex post within a period of three months. Even if strategically relevant (large) companies in the above sense are acquired, the new rule will not normally lead to a delay if the transactions are planned carefully, given that in such cases, the transactions will probably also be subject to mandatory notification under anti-trust law and both examinations can be carried out simultaneously.

V. Interdisciplinary questions during M&A Transactions

Beyond the questions about the choice of law and the choice of language, there is typically a whole array of economic, legal, technical and social issues to address during M&A transactions. Thus, it is advisable for each party to select an interdisciplinary team of advisors for all phases of the transaction in order to ensure that all relevant issues will be considered. From the seller's point of view, the involvement of an interdisciplinary team is important during the planning phase if the seller is looking to restructure the business up for sale and to address all relevant issues and disclose potential risks relating to the business sold in order to be prepared for the negotiation phase.

VI. Mergers between a German and a Foreign Company

Based on the developments regarding the permissibility of mergers between a German and a foreign company in recent years, especially since the implementation of the EC Merger Directive into the Reorganization Act on 19th April 2007, cross-border transactions within the European Community will become more important in the future. Particularly from a German point of view, lengthy restructurings are no longer necessary in order to merge the business of a foreign investor into a German company, or the business of a German company into a foreign company. The new provisions provide for detailed regulations regarding the procedure, the legal consequences and how such merger becomes effective.

Dr. Thomas Kuhnle
thomas.kuhnle@luther-lawfirm.com

CHAPTER 4
REGULATORY MATTERS

DR. MICHAEL FRITZSCHE

Investors seeking to acquire business in Germany are confronted – in addition to planning and building laws and regulations as well as environmental laws and regulations (see above) – by very few additional public law rules and approval requirements, particularly in relation to business and trade, which are summarized below.

A. Business Regulations

I. General

The admissibility of a business is governed first and foremost by the provisions of the Trade Code (*Gewerbeordnung, GewO*) and special legal regulations such as those set out in the laws relating to foreigners, skilled trades and other lines of business. The trade law provisions are designed to ensure quality and thus, in the first instance, to protect consumers. Trade law also serves the purposes of public safety law and thus also protects the general public against potential dangers arising from such businesses. Trade law underlines the principle of freedom of trade, which also extends to foreign business people, but only where exceptions or restrictions are not set out in the Trade Code.[1] Restrictions on the freedom of trade can arise in notification duties and duties to obtain permits. If a business person does not comply with these duties, penalties will be imposed, e.g. the authority can impose a fine.[2]

II. Notification Duties

Any business is subject to a notification duty under Sec. 14 GewO (*Gewerbeanmeldung*), independent from and in addition to any registration in the commercial register (*Handelsregister*). This duty requires that the commencement of a business (including a branch office or a "permanent establishment"), the relocation of the business, the change of business purpose or extension of its purpose to include addi-

1 Sec. 1 GewO (*Gewerbeordung* – German Trade Code).
2 Sects. 144–148b GewO.

tional or other activities, as well as the abandonment of a business is notified to the public authority responsible for the specific location (e.g. the township or county). This notification is required to allow the authority to monitor the conduct of the business.[3] Furthermore, the notification enables an efficient economic policy as the competent authority thus has notice of the amount and the kind of permanent establishment.[4] Apart from the general notification duty of the Trade Code, other special legal notification duties based on other laws also exist such as, for example, under laws applicable to restaurants, skilled trades, and (fire) arms.

III. Duties to Obtain Permits

A permit must be obtained for special lines of business such as security firms,[5] real estate agencies[6] and other businesses requiring special supervision.[7] The permit is granted to the business person and therefore constitutes a personal license. Previously, a permit could be granted not to a person, but for an installation; said permit is referred to as an installation license. However, the possibility of an installation license according to the Trade Code was abandoned in 1999.[8] Depending on the purpose of the permit, a number of duties are attached to obtaining a permit for the operation of an installation. A permit must therefore be obtained for the construction and operation of installations whose nature or operation potentially constitutes a serious threat to the environment or which can endanger, substantially prejudice or cause material nuisance to the general public or a neighborhood. As opposed to the notification duty, a business requiring a permit may not be conducted until the permit has first been granted.[9] A permit is furthermore not granted until the public authority has examined the matter. The permit does not, however, release the business from the notification duty under the Trade Code. Furthermore, the competent authority can ban a business even after a permit is granted if the business person lacks reliability.[10]

A special permit procedure exists where planning permission is mandatory for installations that have a particular impact on surrounding areas, nature and the countryside. Nuclear plants, alterations to constructions on the banks of waterways and lakes, and installations with especially high rates of emissions, such as landfills, may,

---

3 Martinez, Beck OK GewO, § 14 Tn.1; OVG Münster DÖV 1996, 520; LR GewO/Marcks GewO § 14 Rn 1.

4 BVerwG (*Bundesverwaltungsgericht* – Federal Administrative Court), NJW 1977, 772, 772.

5 Sec. 34 a GewO.

6 Sec. 34 c (1) GewO.

7 Sects. 30–34 e GewO.

8 See the old version of Sects. 16–28 GewO.

9 Sec. 15 (2) 1 GewO; Sydow, Beck OK GewO, § 15, Tn. 12–14.

10 Sec. 35 (1) GewO.

require planning permission. During the permit application procedure, the investor's interests are weighed against the interests of those affected by the project, and these interests are reconciled by issuing collateral provisions and requirements that must be met to obtain approval.

During the planning permission procedure, legal relationships are established not only between the investor and the authority, but also with all parties affected by the project.

In addition to the personal licenses, a number of other notification and approval duties are required by various acts of legislation including the Medical Product Act, the Pharmaceuticals Act, and laws relating to food, drugs and labor regulation.

B. Trade Regulations (Import/Export)

Within the European Union (EU), by its constitutional definition, no trade restrictions are allowed.[11] However, this does not exclude some rare restrictions within the EU, e.g. concerning weapons of mass destruction (*Massenvernichtungswaffen*) and goods which are intended for illegal re-export from the recipient EU-member country. Beyond the EU, though German enterprises principally enjoy freedom of foreign trade, certain national laws and in particular EU directives[12] and regulations may impose special restrictions on sensitive goods listed in an annex to the Foreign Trade Act (*Außenwirtschaftsgesetz*, AWG) and the Military Weapon Control Act (*Kriegswaffenkontrollgesetz*, *KrWaffKontrG*), i. e. the export list (*Ausfuhrliste*) and import list (*Einfuhrliste*).[13] They mainly refer to sensitive goods like weapons, military and nuclear equipment, or goods that may also be used for prohibited purposes ("dual use"), and also for purposes of specific protection, e.g. on wildlife products from protected species. Such controls generally mean that approvals or licenses are needed for exporting and/or importing (and transportation) for certain products (e.g. mass destruction weapons as above), and in particular with respect to specific countries (embargos), and it also means the absolute prohibition of trade.

Furthermore, there may be general requirements (mostly imposed by EU-regulations) for security controls (testing and certification), labeling, packaging, trademarks, documentation etc.

11 Art. 26 and Art. 28–66 TFEU (Treaty on the Functioning of the EU).

12 For example: Directive 79/409/EEC on the conservation of wild birds; Directive 89/398/EEC.

13 The Foreign Trade Act and Military Weapon Control Act were modified, i. e. harmonized in 2011 because of the Directive 2009/43/EC.

Beyond the fact that EU member countries apply a common external tariff to imports from outside the EU, the European Commission has entered into numerous preferential trade agreements with other countries by which import duties are considerably reduced or abolished, or a quota established. Germany is also a member of the World Trade Organization (WTO) and the Organization for Economic Cooperation and Development (OECD) which seek to restrict and limit such trade barriers.

C. Exchange Controls

At present, no exchange control restrictions are in force, although various reporting requirements are in effect for tax purposes.[14] The Euro is freely convertible into foreign currencies. The federal Government can impose, under certain conditions, restrictions on foreign money or loan capital coming into Germany by requiring a cash deposit with the Federal Central Bank (*Deutsche Bundesbank*), if this is not prohibited by existing EU regulations. At present there are no such restrictions in force.

Dr. Michael Fritzsche
michael.fritzsche@luther-lawfirm.com

---

14 http://www.bundesbank.de/download/volkswirtschaft/mba/2001/200107mba_kapitalverkehr.pdf.

CHAPTER 5
ENERGY LAW

DR. HOLGER STAPPERT
FRANZ-RUDOLF GROSS

Due to several law-making initiatives taken by the European Union, the electricity and natural gas markets in Germany are open to competition today. The liberalization process started in the late 1990s, but the new Energy Industry Act 2005 provided for a fundamental change of the legislative framework, implementing two EU Acceleration Directives enacted in 2003. Today, both the electricity and the gas sectors are liberalized, but highly regulated by the numerous provisions of the EnWG and several governmental ordinances. Whereas the EnWG covers the general principles, the ordinances provide for detailed rules on, for instance, access to the networks, network access fees, concession fees, and metering services. In addition, there are ordinances on the general terms and conditions of supply to household customers, on low voltage and low pressure network connection and on network connection of power generation plants. Finally, in order to promote climate protection, there are special laws establishing an emission trading system and encouraging the production of energy from renewable resources.

A. Third Party Access (TPA)

The Energy Industry Act provides for the opening of electricity and gas networks to everyone. Thus, every network operator must offer its network for transmission and distribution of electricity and gas in an adequate, transparent, non-discriminatory manner and according to objective criteria. Network operators at all levels are obliged to cooperate on a large scale in order to guarantee the functioning of the system.[1]

The conditions and methods which regulate TPA to the electricity grid are different from those in the gas sector. TPA to the electricity grid is largely based on the former, well-established system preceding the 2005 reform. In addition to the statutory provisions,[2] the Federal Network Agency has determined binding best practice guidelines. The rules described therein with a view to specific standard situations need to be obeyed by all network operators and electricity suppliers with regard to,

---

1 Sec. 20 (1) EnWG (*Energiewirtschaftsgesetz* – Energy Industry Act).

2 Sec. 20 (1a) EnWG and the corresponding Ordinance on Access to Electricity Grids (*Stromnetzzugangsverordnung*).

for instance, changing the supplier of an end customer or starting or stopping electricity supply of an end customer. Additional guidelines deal with the procurement of balancing energy by the transmission system operator and the cost for balancing energy which grid users have to pay.

In the gas sector, however, today's TPA regime calls for a genuine entry-exit system, for the possibility to trade capacity rights without restrictions, and for effective congestion capacity management.[3] The gas network operators agreed on a cooperation agreement[4] which provides for the details. Accordingly, several networks form a single market area (*Marktgebiet*), each providing for only one virtual trading point. Access to the gas network must then be based on the so-called two-contract model which requires only one contract regarding an entry capacity (from the import point of the market area to the virtual trading point) and another contract regarding an exit capacity (from the virtual trading point to the extraction point of the particular market area). The number of market areas has been narrowed down from initially 19 to only two in Germany, one solely for high calorific value gas (H-gas) and one for H-gas and low calorific value gas (L-gas). Within the latter market area it is possible to convert H-gas to L-gas and vice versa by payment of a respective fee. However, with regard to network access in the gas sector, many binding and complex decisions of the Federal Network Agency exist which deal, for example, with the costs for balancing energy, the converting fee or even details of network access agreements.

B. Network Access Fees

Starting with the 2005 reform and up to the end of 2008, network operators were required to apply for prior approval of their network access fees with the regulatory authorities. In January 2009, however, an incentive regulation ordinance (*Anreizregulierungsverordnung)* came into force, imposing revenue caps on the access fees which network operators are allowed to charge. These revenue caps are determined by calculating the costs incurred (capital expenditures, capex, and operating expenditures, opex) and the results of an efficiency measurement of the respective network operator. Under specific circumstances, the ordinance on the calculation of electricity network access fees (*Stromnetzentgeltverordnung)* allows for individual fees to be agreed with end customers who are characterized by a very high power consumption and capacity demand. End consumers with a consumption of more than 10 GWh and more than 7,000 hours per year will be released from the obligation to pay network access fees. Furthermore, the feed-in of electricity is free of charge. Many de-

3 Sec. 20 (1b) EnWG and the corresponding Ordinance on Access to Gas Grids (*Gasnetzzugangsverordnung*).

4 Agreement on Cooperation according to Sec. 20 (1b) EnWG between Operators of Gas Grids in Germany, dated 30th June 2011 (*Kooperationsvereinbarung*).

tails of the calculation of network fees and the level of revenue caps imposed on the individual operators are controversially discussed among network operators, regulatory authorities and the courts.

C. Network Connection

According to the Energy Industry Act, electricity and gas network operators must offer connection to their networks to end customers and other networks in an adequate, transparent, non-discriminatory manner and according to objective criteria. The details of how to connect end customers to the low voltage and low pressure networks and how the network connection may be used by them are regulated by two ordinances.[5] They cover, inter alia, the liability of network operators for outage and interruption of supply and the fees operators may charge for building a network connection or for reinforcing the grid. In the recent past, industrial customers and electricity network operators often argued about the precise voltage level at which the customer may be connected to the grid, as connection to a higher voltage grid results in lower network access fees.

D. Connection of Power Generation Plants

The details of how to connect power generation plants to the electricity network are determined in an additional ordinance (*Kraftwerks-Netzanschlussverordnung*, Kraft-NAV). This ordinance provides for a procedure from the first connection request of a project developer via a feasibility study and the negotiation and conclusion of a network connection agreement to the realization of a network connection. Furthermore, the KraftNAV contains detailed rules on how to share the costs for the connection between plant and grid operator. Finally, the ordinance provides for a privileged right to feed-in for such plant operators which connect their generation plants until 31st December 2012.

E. Unbundling

In order to enhance transparency and to enable the regulatory authorities to supervise the markets effectively, the Energy Industry Act requires electricity and gas network operators to act independently from energy suppliers and energy generators

5 For the electricity grid: *Niederspannungsanschlussverordnung*, NAV, for the gas grid: *Niederdruckanschlussverordnung*, NDAV.

affiliated with them. Thus, within a vertically integrated energy company, the network has to be operated by a separate legal entity (however, not in separate ownership), and the personnel of the network operator has to be sufficiently separated from the other entities of the group in order to avoid conflicts of interest (legal and management unbundling). However, with regard to distribution system operators and gas storage operators which, in principle, also fall within the scope of the unbundling regulations the requirements are less strict than for transmission system operators. However, these rules do not apply to networks with less than 100,000 customers. The statutory provisions on unbundling of accounts and on informational unbundling, however, need to be observed by all network operators.

F. Closed Distribution Networks

Special rules can apply to local energy networks supplying electricity or gas only within a geographically confined industrial, commercial or shared services site (e. g. airport, industrial site, clinical center) without, however, supplying household customers. Upon request, the competent regulatory authority will declare such a grid to be a closed distribution network.[6] In that case, the provisions on incentive regulation or prior approval of network access fees as well as some reporting obligations will not apply. However, operators of closed distribution networks still have to grant third party access to their grids and to calculate network access fees in an adequate, transparent, non-discriminatory manner and according to objective criteria. Furthermore, the provisions on connection of customers to energy networks continue to apply.

G. Regulatory Authorities

In order to comply with the EU Acceleration Directives, the Energy Industry Act established energy regulatory authorities for the electricity and gas sectors on the federal level (*Bundesnetzagentur* – Federal Network Agency) and on the federal state level (regulatory authorities of the German states), the latter being responsible for networks with less than 100,000 customers provided they do not extend beyond the borders of a federal state. The regulatory authorities are in charge of enforcing the Energy Industry Act including, for instance, electricity and gas network access, incentive regulation of network access fees, unbundling, and network connection with regard to more than 900 electricity network operators and more than 700 gas network operators. In addition, the competition authorities on the federal level (*Bun-*

6 Sec. 110 EnWG.

deskartellamt – Federal Cartel Office) and on the federal state level (competition authorities of the German states) enforce the anti-trust law rules such as the prohibition to restrict competition, the prohibition to abuse market dominance, and the merger control regime. With respect to the energy industry, the competition authorities, in the recent past, have focused in particular on electricity generation, gas prices and long term contracts for the supply of resellers. The Federal Cartel Office is solely responsible for applying mergers control rules in the energy sector.

H. Concessions for Lines

Municipalities are obligated to offer on a contractual and non-discriminatory basis the use of public property for laying and operating lines for the direct supply of energy to end customers within the municipality. Energy companies must in return pay concession fees for this right of way. The amount of fees per kilowatt-hour depends on the number of inhabitants of the municipality. The concession fees are invoiced together with the network access fees which network users have to pay to the network operators. Details, in particular on the calculation of concession fees, are regulated in an ordinance on concession fees (*Konzessionsabgabenverordnung* KAV).

I. Terms and Conditions of Energy Supply Contracts

In principle, energy suppliers and their customers are free to negotiate the terms and conditions of electricity and gas supply contracts, in particular with regard to the partner of the agreement and to the price. However, some restrictions apply. In the recent past, price adjustment clauses have often been challenged by customers in court as they were allegedly non-transparent. Supply contracts between producers, importers, or wholesalers with resellers are subject to the guidelines of the Federal Cartel Office on long term energy supply contracts.

Finally, two ordinances (StromGVV, GasGVV) determine the relationship between energy suppliers and household customers. They cover the terms and conditions, in particular conclusion, content and termination, of such energy supply contracts. These ordinances automatically apply if (a) the utility is a so-called basic supplier (supplier of last resort) and if (b) the end customer asks for a basic supply contract or if the end customer consumes energy without having concluded a written contract. They do not automatically apply to energy supply contracts with commercial and industrial customers. Some provisions of the ordinances are nevertheless sometimes referred to in those contracts.

J. Energy Trading

Germany has an efficient, liquid electricity and gas trading market. OTC trading is common and is mostly performed on the basis of standardized contracts such as the EFET General Agreement or the German Master Agreement. Furthermore, the European Energy Exchange in Leipzig (EEX) provides a market platform for institutionalized trading of energy and related products. However, regulatory changes are likely to occur within the next few years driven by the European Union. Namely, the proposed European Market Infrastructure Regulation (EMIR) on OTC derivatives, central counterparties and trade repositories and an update to the Directive 2004/39/EC (MiFID) will have an impact on the energy trading markets not only in Germany, but also in Europe.

K. Energy from Renewable Resources

The Act regarding the Priority of Energy from Renewable Resources,[7] which has been renewed as of 1st January 2012, provides for the obligation of electricity network operators to connect facilities which produce electricity from renewable resources to their network and to purchase such electricity. In Germany, wind power (onshore and offshore) is currently the most important renewables sector.

The Act guarantees that network operators pay a certain minimum price to the generator of electricity from renewable resources depending on the source of energy fed into the network (wind, solar power, biomass, water, etc.). The network operator is obliged to sell the energy fed in by the producers of renewable energy to the market at the market price. Because the statutory guaranteed tariffs still exceed the market price there will be a gap. Therefore, network operators invoice a certain surcharge to their network customers, i. e. the energy suppliers. They, in turn, pass on this amount to the end consumers supplied by them. As this may cause a heavy burden on businesses which consume much electricity for running their manufacturing processes, the Federal Office of Economics and Export Control (*Bundesamt für Wirtschafts- und Ausfuhrkontrolle)* will grant, upon request, a reduction of the surcharge if the statutory conditions are met.[8]

Apart from selling at statutory tariffs, each producer of electricity from renewable resources may choose to sell the electricity directly to a customer (so called "direct marketing"). In this case the price has to be negotiated between the parties them-

7 *Gesetz für den Vorrang Erneuerbarer Energien*, EEG 2012.
8 Sec. 40 et. seq. EEG 2012.

selves. The statutory tariffs of the EEG will not apply. However, under certain circumstances the network operator has to pay in addition the difference between the market price of the energy and the feed in tariff to the plant operator. The choice between the feed in tariff system and direct marketing may be reversed on a monthly base. However, as of 2013 operators of biogas plants with an installed capacity of more than 750 kW have to opt for the direct marketing system.

L. Combined Heat and Power Generation (CHP, Co-Generation)

The Act on Maintaining, Modernizing and Increasing Combined Heat and Power Generation (*Gesetz für die Erhaltung, die Modernisierung und den Ausbau der Kraft-Wärme-Kopplung)* came into effect on 1st April 2002. Initially, it was to have remained in force until 31st December 2010. However, the respective provision was deleted, and the KWK-ModG is still in force. This Act is to promote the use of CHP stations in Germany. It obligates network operators to connect CHP facilities to their network, to purchase the electricity generated by these, and to pay a certain surcharge in addition to the price agreed between the parties.

M. Cooperation, Mergers & Acquisitions

Cooperation between energy companies and mergers & acquisitions are admissable within the framework of anti-trust law, in particular the merger control regime. Since liberalization of the energy industry started in the late 1990ies, many foreign energy companies and investors have entered the German market, either by establishing subsidiaries or by acquiring existing German utilities. Due to the burden imposed by network regulation, many network operators and integrated utilities try to cooperate in various ways.

Dr. Holger Stappert
holger.stappert@luther-lawfirm.com

Franz-Rudolf Gross
Franz-rudolf.gross@luther-lawfirm.com

CHAPTER 6
DATA PROTECTION AND PRIVACY

SILVIA C. BAUER
DR. STEFANIE HELLMICH, LL.M.

In Germany, the collection, processing and use of personally identifiable data is subject to the German Federal Data Protection Act which is complemented by several specific acts regulating the protection of personal data in particularly sensitive areas such as the telecommunications and media sector, the healthcare sector and the criminal prosecution sector. The Telemedia Act and the Telecommunications Act, for example, contain specific legal requirements in relation to the electronic processing of personal data.

A. Collection, Processing and Use of Personal Data

Basically speaking, the collection, processing or use of personal data is only lawful when a statutory legal basis is available or if the affected data subject has explicitly consented. Such personal data may be collected (a) for the contractual purposes for which the data has been provided, or (b) if the collecting party has a justified interest in collecting, processing and using such data and the affected data subject does not have an overriding legitimate interest in preventing such use. The collection, processing or use of special categories of personal data (such as data on racial origin or health) for a party's own business purpose is only permitted (without the data subject's consent) if it is necessary in order to safeguard vital interests of the data subject or of a third party and if the data subject is physically or legally incapable of giving his consent; if the data in question has clearly been placed in the public domain by the data subject; if it is necessary for the establishment, exercise or defense of legal claims and there are no grounds for believing that the data subject has an overriding legitimate interest in excluding the collection, processing or use; or if it is necessary for conducting scientific research and the scientific interest in carrying out the research project substantially outweighs the data subject's interest in precluding collection and the purpose of the research could not be achieved by other means without unreasonable effort or at all. If there is no applicable statutory provision in relation to the collection, processing or use of personal data, the explicit consent of the affected data subject is required. In order to obtain a valid consent the data subject has to be informed in detail about the purpose for which the data will be collected, processed or used.

B. Transfer of Data Outside EEA

The transfer of personal data to entities located outside the European Economic Area (EEA) (the European Union plus Iceland, Liechtenstein, and Norway) is permitted only if the data subject does not have a legitimate interest in excluding such a transfer. A legitimate interest in excluding a transfer will be recognized if it is clear that an adequate level of data protection cannot be guaranteed by the recipient. The adequacy of the afforded level of protection is to be assessed in the light of all circumstances relating to the data transfer.

In certain cases, however, a data transfer may be permitted irrespective of an adequate level of data protection. This is primarily the case if the consent of the data subject has been given or if the transfer is necessary for the performance of a contract. In addition, public interest, the establishment, exercise or defense of legal claims or the protection of a vital interest of the data subject may justify a transfer, regardless of the level of protection afforded by the recipient to which the data is transferred. In addition, the supervisory authorities may authorize the transfer of personal data if an adequate standard of protection is confirmed under contract or by means of applicable binding corporate rules.

Increasingly, binding corporate rules are being introduced by multinational groups which have their headquarters in Germany in order to facilitate the group-wide transfer of data. Group-wide transfers can result, for example, from the use of employee management software or customer relationship management programs. Due to the complex structure of the supervisory authorities in Germany there has been no uniform approach, so far, to the evaluation of the binding corporate rules introduced. Whilst some authorities consider that such rules demonstrate an adequate standard of protection, others consider that an explicit authorization by the competent supervisory authority is necessary for each transfer.

C. European Standard Contractual Clauses/ Safe Harbor

An adequate level of data protection in case of an onward transfer to an entity located outside the EEA can be ascertained on the basis of the European Standard Contractual Clauses (SCCs) which have been adopted by the European Commission. The European Commission has approved two alternative sets of SCCs for use in transferring personal data to a data "controller" outside the EEA.[1] In 2010 the Commission approved another set of SCCs[2] to be used when transferring data to a "processor", which replaced the former set of 2002. Basically a controller makes decisions about what data to collect and how to use it, while a processor (upon commission) merely performs operations on data only on behalf of the controller and according to its instructions (see below the explanations concerning "data processing upon commission"). Business process outsourcing in a Non-EEA country is a common context for using SCCs to protect employee and customer information or other personal data furnished by a European company.

For controller to controller transfers companies generally may choose between the two sets of SSCs. The 2004 SSCs set is perceived more business-friendly, in particular, concerning litigation, allocation of responsibilities or auditing requirements. For this reason the German supervisory authorities have made some reservations concerning the use of the 2004 SSCs set for employee data.

The concern addressed in the 2010 controller-processor SCCs is that processors (upon commission) increasingly subcontract some of their processing activities (e.g. storage and technical support functions) to third parties. This applies, in particular, to cloud computing scenarios, where several entities might be involved in handling and storing the data. Based on the 2010 SCCs, the company that remains responsible as data controller in Europe therefore needs to approve any proposed subcontracting, and the subcontractor must be contractually bound to the same obligations that apply to the contractor.

Furthermore, the European Commission adopted in 2000 a Decision determining that an arrangement put in place by the US Department of Commerce known as the "safe harbor" provides adequate protection for personal data transferred from the EU to the US. Therefore when data transfers to the US are concerned, participation of the US company in the Safe Harbor program is a further mean of legitimizing such data transfers. Due to criticism concerning enforcement deficits in implementing the safe harbor principles, the German supervisory authorities have ruled in a Decision of 28th/29th April 2010 that German companies have to verify certain minimum requirements of the Safe Harbor certification. These minimum requirements relate, in particular, to the presentation of a certification document, the certification not being more than seven years old, and evidence documenting compliance with information duties.

---

1 Commission Decision (2004/5271) of 27th December 2004, amending Decision 2001/497/EC as regards the introduction of an alternative set of standard contractual clauses for the transfer of personal data to third countries and Commission Decision 2001/497/EC of 15th June 2001.

2 Commission Decision (2010/87/EU) of 5th February 2010 on standard contractual clauses for the transfer of personal data to processors.

D. Supervisory Authorities and Notification Requirements

In Germany, several data protection supervisory authorities exist. Private companies are subject to the supervision of the state where they are located. Similarly, public institutions are subject to the supervision of the state which they belong to. While in some states the supervision of the private and the public sector is done by the same authority, other states had two supervisory authorities until recently. To ensure the independence of the supervisory authorities, these authorities have been integrated and separated from the state ministries of the interior. For federal institutions and companies in the post and the telecommunications sector, the Federal Data Protection Commissioner (*Bundesbeauftragter für Datenschutz*) is the competent supervisory authority. In principle, the responsible state authority has to be notified of all data processing activities in the private sector. However, such notification is generally not required if the controller has appointed a data protection officer (*betrieblicher Datenschutzbeauftragter*). Only if the data processing activities bear a considerable risk of exposure, i. e. if personal data is stored in a certain way for the purpose of transferring it or if it is being provided in connection with an anonymous commercial transfer, will such activities need to be notified.

E. Data Protection Officer

In contrast to other jurisdictions, in Germany private companies are automatically required to appoint a data protection officer if they employ more than 10 employees whose personal data they either collect, process or use. In the case of entities which process or use personal data in the course of their business, a data protection officer has to be appointed irrespective of the number of employees employed. The duties and functions of a data protection officer may be performed by an employee of the respective company (a so-called "internal data protection officer") or by a third party engaged for such purpose (a so-called "external data protection officer").

F. Data Processing upon Commission

A so called data controller processes data for his own purposes under his own responsibility. A company acting as data controller may employ a data processor upon commission (*Auftragsdatenverarbeitung*) for example, an IT service provider or a marketing agency who processes the controller's data under the controller's responsibility. The data controller needs to ensure the legal basis for the processing of the relevant personal data in question and the data processor has to follow the instructions of the data controller when processing the data. A data processing upon commission relationship must be laid down in a written agreement. The written agreement has to contain the minimum requirements determined by law.[3] Such requirements include for example the obligation to check the security measures implemented by the service provider and reporting obligations of the data processor via the data controller. The disclosure of data within a data processing upon commission relationship to a processor located within the EEA is not considered a transfer of data in the legal sense requiring a separate legal basis. Such data disclosure is privileged by law. If the data processor, however, is located outside the EEA such privilege does not apply.

G. Sanctions

Offences against the data protection regulations may attract a fine of up to EUR 300,000.00 or imprisonment of up to two years. The affected data subjects may file a complaint with the supervisory authority and individuals may also make a claim for damages if they can prove actual damage as a result of the unlawful processing of their personal data. In practice, the ability of competitors to apply for an injunction based on the illegal collection, processing or use of personal data in connection with a violation of unfair competition law rules has become increasingly important – the unfair competition law rules impose additional restrictions on the use of personal data in a number of cases and particularly where unsolicited communications are involved.

H. Processing of Employee Data

Recently some companies in Germany have been investigated by national prosecutors in relation to potential breaches of privacy, e. g. watching their employees via a video surveillance system, monitoring phone calls or comparing employees' data with the data of suppliers in order to reveal incidences of corruption and bribery. As a result, some companies have been fined by the supervisory authorities and in 2009 specific provisions for the collection, processing and usage of employees' personal data came into force.[4] Additionally, discussions about a specific, detailed Employees' Data Protection Law taking the interests of employees into account have been revived and the legislator has already published first drafts of such regulations. However, since the drafts are highly disputed, the regulations are not expected to come into force before 2012.

3 Sec. 11 BDSG (*Bundesdatenschutzgesetz* – German Federal Data Protection Act).

4 Sec. 32 BDSG.

Basically, now, the collection, processing and usage of employees' personal data is legally allowed if this is necessary for the decision on the establishment of the employment relationship, or, after it has commenced, for its execution or termination. This includes the collection, processing and usage of the employees' data which is necessary for the performance of the employment relationship, e.g. skill management, payroll. Furthermore, the definition "employee" includes now applicants as well as part-time workers, retired employees, trainees etc.

Beside this, employees' data may only be used for the purpose of uncovering criminal acts, if there are factual indications that the employee has committed such a crime during his employment relationship. Furthermore, the employee has to have no overriding interests in the exclusion of such usage of his data, in particular taking into consideration that the manner and scope of such usage must not be unreasonable compared to the alleged act. It is highly disputed if compliance measures, e.g. for fraud prevention, are allowed under this Law because the wording of the Law forbids such measures. Anyway, in practice, company management has to secure that their companies and the employees comply with the applicable Law. Furthermore, they have to control compliance. If they refrain from the implementation of such measures, they might be liable personally for damages based on such violations. As a consequence, companies have to consider carefully which measures they take e.g. for monitoring the employees' behavior and must check if these measures are proportional.

In daily business, companies have to check if their data processing activities comply with the applicable data protection Law. New technologies, particularly, such as RFID, biometry, GPRS, tachographs and thinking cameras now make it easy for companies to monitor every act of an employee or to locate them easily without their knowledge. In addition, DNA analysis or drug tests can also be used by an employer to obtain a detailed picture of the personality or state of health of a particular employee.

Generally, such activities can only take place with the specific and freely given consent of the employee. Only in exceptional cases might such consent be considered as dispensable, e.g. if the employee is a driver of an armored car and knowledge of the location of the employee is crucial for his security or if monitoring is necessary to verify a well-founded suspicion of criminal activities.

The same applies to the control of e-mails, telephone or internet usage of employees: monitoring of such usage may not only be considered a violation of data protection regulations, but also a violation of the telecommunications secrecy. If a company allows its employees such usage for private purposes, it is for example, not allowed to monitor employees' telephone connections without their explicit prior consent.

As a consequence, as stated above, companies processing employee data need to consider carefully what activities are permitted under the current data protection legislation before starting any data processing in Germany. Furthermore, if a works council exists, detailed advice should be obtained beforehand as the works council may need to be informed or involved and/or a works council agreement (*Betriebsvereinbarung*) may need to be drafted and agreed upon. A works council agreement is considered as an "other legal provision"[5] which can – beside the consent or a provision of the BDSG – legalize the processing and usage of the data. Therefore, companies with a works council have the option of concluding such an agreement on data processing and usage. The works council agreement should outline the data processing and usage in question, the data processed and used, the purposes and potential recipients of the data. This agreement forms in this case the justification for the processing and usage, It is discussed whether a works council agreement may extend the scope of the permissible data processing and use. The German Data Protection Authorities, however, argue that the protection granted by the Law should not be undermined by such an agreement where the individual employee has no possibility for voicing his concern. Therefore, it is recommendable not to reduce the data protection level granted by the Law in order to avoid the works council agreement or part of its regulations being considered illegal.

I. Whistleblowing Hotlines and Ethical Codes

Sec. 301 Sarbanes Oxley (SOX) requires Audit Committees at SOX-regulated companies to establish hotlines for the submission of employees' concerns or complaints regarding questionable accounting or auditing matters to their employer (so-called "Whistleblowing Hotlines"). The US Securities and Exchange Commission (SEC) as well as internationally operating SOX-regulated companies often assume that such hotlines have been made available to all employees, including employees working in the subsidiaries located outside the US, particularly as many non-SOX-regulated companies offer such hotlines to their employees to implement anti-corruption programs or ethical and behavioral codes.

As part of such a hotline, personal data about the notifying employee and the accused person is likely to be processed. Even if such processing is required and allowed in the US, in Germany – and in other European states in which such a hotline may be offered by an employer – compliance with the respective data protection laws has to be ensured. Under German Law no specific binding regulations previously existed, although now the "*Duesseldorfer Kreis*", which is the national coordinating group of the German data protection supervisory authorities, has issued a written guidance (opin-

5 Sec. 4 BDSG.

ion of 20th April 2007). According to this guidance, such a hotline shall only be offered for employees to report concerns relating to specific issues including criminal offences, audit/accounting fraud, banking and bribery issues. Issues related to ethical standards of the company cannot be included. Anonymous whistleblower calls are only allowed on an exceptional basis and generally should be discouraged. Under certain specific circumstances existence of the hotline will need to be notified to the supervisory authority.

Launching such a hotline as well as implementing an ethical code requires detailed consideration of the mandates of SOX, the company's needs and the German data protection law. The works council will also need to be involved.

J. Processing of Data for Marketing Purposes

Incidents of misuse of consumer data have caused the German legislator to enact new regulations for the usage of consumer data for marketing purposes, address selling and advertisement. The new regulations were intended to employ a stricter regime regarding such processing (e.g. the consent of the data subject should be obtained for such usage of his data). Anyway, the proposed changes were subjected to criticism, in particular from the advertising industry and address sellers. As a consequence, the regulations which came into force on 1th September 2009 were ultimately amended to impose a less strict regime than originally suggested.

Under the revised Act, the processing and use of personal data for the purposes of selling addresses and using contact details for marketing will be permitted only if the data subject has declared his explicit consent in writing to such use.[6] In cases where such consent has not been given in writing, the data controller has to confirm the data subject, the consent and its exact content in writing.

However, there are, several exceptions to this basic rule:

- Processing and use of data sets which have been stored by the data controller before 1st September 2009 continues to be governed by the old Law until 31st August 2012. All data collected after 1st September 2009 is governed by the new Law.
- Processing and use of certain personal data of members or a group of persons (information that the data subject is member of the group, name, address, title, academic degree, job, industry, business title and year of birth) summarized in a list is permissible if it is necessary for the purposes of: (a) promoting the data control-

6 Sec. 28 et. seq. BDSG.

ler's own offers if the data controller collected the data directly from the individual or from a public directory; (b) advertising regarding the professional services of an individual using a professional address; or (c) advertising for charitable donations.
- Such listed data may be transferred without the data subject's consent if: (a) information regarding the origin and the recipient of the data is recorded for two years; (b) such information is provided on the data subject upon request; and (c) the advertisement identifies clearly which data controller originally collected the data. The last requirement may create some burdens for companies, e.g. if the data are transferred from one company to another and it is not so easy for the advertising company to determine who collected the data. As a consequence, in cases where companies obtain personal data in lists for advertising purposes, they must ensure that they receive such information from the company which transfers the data.

All alternatives for using data for marketing purposes must outweigh the interests of the data subject, which the data controller has to evaluate by itself before usage or transfer of data for the purposes in question. Furthermore, the data may be used for promoting third-party offers only if the advertisement states the identity of the data controller responsible for the data.

While Sec. 28 BDSG deals basically with the use of data for marketing purposes that were originally collected for legitimate purposes (e.g. in connection with a purchase contract), Sec. 29 BDSG regulates the commercial collection, processing and usage for purposes of the transfer if this serves the activities of advertising, address selling or credit agencies.

Processing and usage of personal data is legally allowed if:

- There are no grounds available for assuming that the data subject has an interest meriting protection in the exclusion of the collection, processing and usage for the purpose in question; or
- The data can be collected from publicly available sources; or
- The data controller would be permitted to publish the data unless the data subject has overriding interests; and
- These activities are, by reference, also subject to the general requirement of consent with the outlined scoped exceptions.

The transfer of data is only allowed if the recipient has sustained a legitimate interest in receipt and knowledge of the data and there are no grounds available for assuming that the data subject has an interest meriting protection in the exclusion of such transfer.

In addition to taking into account the new rules when planning marketing campaigns, sharing listed data or executing third-party promotions, the existing arrangements should be reviewed to evaluate whether there will be a legal basis for transfer and use after the 31st August 2012 which is the compliance deadline for all data.

Furthermore, companies have to keep in mind that in Germany online marketing activities are widely discussed: in particular the German Data Protection Authority from the state of Schleswig-Holstein, the "*Unabhängiges Landesdatenschutzzentrum Schleswig Holstein*" (ULD), called on all companies in Schleswig Holstein to shut down Facebook fan pages and remove the "Like" button from their websites. They are of the opinion that such features violate the German Data Protection Law. The same applies for Google Analytics: In both cases the Authorities stated that the features were not transparent enough and the transfer of data to Facebook or Google should be considered as illegal. While for Google Analytics a solution has been found (e.g. the companies using Google Analytics have to enter into a data processing agreement with Google), the Authorities are still in discussion with Facebook. As a consequence, companies offering German websites for German customers/users should keep an eye on the discussions in order to minimize the risk of sanctions.

K. Data Processing Audit

An increasingly important means to ensure compliance with German data protection regulations is to carry out an audit of the respective data processing activities. A bill has been passed by the legislator in order to establish uniform guidelines for such auditing (Data Processing Auditing Act). These provide that carrying out an audit is optional but, where used, it shall be carried out by an official auditor. The Data Processing Auditing Act also regulates the procedure for the carrying out of such audit as well as the necessary requirements for obtaining an official seal. However, the proceedings have been refused as too formal; therefore, the legislator has delayed the establishment of such guidelines indefinitely. In practice, companies conduct private audits in order to check if they comply with the applicable data protection law and to increase their level of data protection.

Silvia C. Bauer
silvia.c.bauer@luther-lawfirm.com

Dr. Stefanie Hellmich, LL.M.
stefanie.hellmich@luther-lawfirm.com

CHAPTER 7
EMPLOYMENT LAW

HANS-CHRISTIAN ACKERMANN
DR. VOLKER SCHNEIDER

Every entrepreneur who wants to do business in Germany has to know about the special requirements of Employment Law. There is no uniform code of law, like the German Civil Code (BGB). German Employment Law is a mixture of several acts, court decisions and common law. Especially dismissal, works constitution and the social system in Germany are showing the need for an entrepreneur to have knowledge about the characteristics of German Employment Law.

A. Industrial Relations

In Germany, there are two national employer organizations: the Confederation of German Employers (*Bundesvereinigung der Deutschen Arbeitgeberverbände, BDA*) and the Federation of German Industry (*Bundesverband der Deutschen Industrie, BDI*). BDA is the umbrella association of 14 independent employer organizations in the federal states. It represents the interests of its members in social and employment topics towards politics and the media. It gives information and recommendations during the collective bargaining process but does not negotiate with the unions itself. BDI does not deal with social policies but represents the individual sectors of industry in economic and commercial affairs.

The German Trade Union Federation (*Deutscher Gewerkschaftsbund, DGB*) is the major union federation with eight member unions covering workers in all major industries and almost 6.2 million members overall in 2012. DGB does not enter into collective bargaining agreements and does not negotiate with the employers directly; it coordinates union activities and acts on behalf of its members by commenting on political, social and employment issues towards politicians, parties and associations. The biggest single unions are *IG Metall* with almost 2.25 million members in 2012 and *ver.di* with about 2.2 million members in 2012. *Ver.di* is a combination of five formerly independent unions, mainly representing white-collar employees, while IG Metall mainly represents blue-collar employees.

Labor relations operate within a legal framework covered, for the most part, by the German Civil Code (*Bürgerliches Gesetzbuch, BGB*) and several employee protection laws. Collective bargaining is carried out on a national or industry-wide level as well as on a regional or local level. Said agreements apply only to those employers and employees who are members of the respective employer organization or trade union, unless the agreement is declared to be generally binding by the Federal Department for Labor and Social Affairs. A collective bargaining agreement may be declared to be generally binding if the employers bound by the agreement employ fifty percent or more of the employees coming within its sphere of application and if such declaration appears necessary for the public interest.[1] In 2011, 476 collective bargaining agreements, out of a total of approximately 73.000, were declared to be generally binding.[2] The climate of labor relations in Germany is generally calm and stable, with a high degree of cooperation existing between management and trade unions. This becomes obvious by, inter alia, looking at the number of working days affected by strikes: while in Germany between 2000 and 2007 only 5 working days per 1.000 employees were affected by strikes, the respective number of days for Great Britain was 30, for the USA was 32, and for Spain was 173.[3]

B. Works Councils and Co-Determination

German Labor Law provides for two kinds of co-determination, namely co-determination related to the individual works and co-determination related to the whole company. The works constitution envisages the formation of works councils representing the employees and lets them hereby participate in decisions concerning the individual works. Co-determination with regard to the company provides for employees' participation mainly in the supervisory board and so in decisions concerning the planning, organization and management of the company.

Works councils, respectively committees of employee representatives (*Betriebsräte*), may be formed in all plants with five or more employees, upon the request of the employees. Members are elected for four years and need not be union members. The exact number of members of the works council depends on the number of employees in the works.

The rights of the works council, as set forth in the Works Constitution Act (*Betriebsverfassungsgesetz*, *BetrVG*), range from mere information over consultation rights to "real" co-determination rights where a measure cannot be carried out without an agreement with the works council (where no such agreement can be reached, a conciliation board followed by Labor Court procedure can be appealed to for a decision

1 Sec. 5 TVG (*Tarifvertragsgesetz* – Collective Bargaining Act).
2 Report of the Federal Ministry for Labour and Social Affairs (BMAS).
3 Statistics of the Cologne Institute for Economic Reserch (*IW Köln*).

that replaces the failed agreement). Different rights of the works council with regard to co-determination exist with regard to organizational, social, personnel and economic matters.

In relation to social matters, the employer is obligated to negotiate rules with the works council, inter alia, on the order in the works and the conduct of the employees, allocation of working hours, vacation schedules, grievances, technical equipment suitable (not necessarily dedicated) to monitor the employees-safety and welfare matters and methods of payment of remuneration (but not the exact amount or volume). With regard to all these matters, the works council has a right of co-determination where no exhaustive statutory or collective bargaining provision exists unless the latter provides for an explicit exemption. The works council is entitled to enforce its co-determination rights, because it often has a right of initiative equal to the right of the employer.

In relation to personnel matters, the employer requires the approval of the works council to every hiring, classification, re-classification and transfer where the company is normally employing more than 20 employees. The works council may refuse the approval of the measure for certain reasons, but the employer can appeal to the Labor Court to rule in lieu of the works council. Moreover, the works council must be informed prior to the dismissal of any employee, otherwise the dismissal is invalid. If the works council objects to the dismissal, the employee can be dismissed nonetheless but is entitled to claim for continuing employment during the lawsuit.

In relation to economic matters, the employer must inform and consult the works council in companies normally employing more than 20 employees with regard to operational changes which may bear significant disadvantages for the personnel such as closures, cutbacks, relocations, amalgamations and fundamental changes and restructurings. The employer and the works council must, under certain circumstances, negotiate not only such reconciliation of interests (*Interessenausgleich*) but also a social compensation plan (*Sozialplan*) in the case of mass redundancies or major restructuring, in order to compensate employees for the actual and financial disadvantages suffered as a result of the restructuring.

Co-determination with regard to companies is a particular German characteristic in comparison to other European countries and their legal systems.

Its origins lay in the aftermath of the Second World War when the trade unions' intention was to socialize the key industries. After the foundation of the Federal Republic of Germany in 1949, socialization was abandoned in favor of employees' participation in the decision-making. Co-determination was then originally introduced in the iron, steel and coal industries in 1951 and provides for representation of workers on the supervisory board of certain corporations. The most important co-determination laws are the Act on One-Third-Participation (*Drittelbeteiligungsgesetz, DrittelbG*) and the Co-determination Act 1976 (*Mitbestimmungsgesetz, MitbestG*).

The Act on One-Third Participation, which replaced the former Works Constitution Act 1952, provides that all GmbHs, partnerships limited by shares, mutual insurance corporations, cooperative societies and AGs, limited companies, with normally more than 500 employees, as well as all AGs, irrespective of their work force, if registered in the Commercial Register prior to 10th August 1994 and not family-owned, must allow employees to elect one third of the members on the supervisory board.[4]

The Co-determination Act 1976 requires that all AGs, KGaAs-partnerships limited by shares, GmbHs or cooperative societies with normally more than 2,000 employees must give employees equal representation with shareholders on the supervisory board.[5] Employee representatives must include at least one management employee representative. The chairman (usually a representative of the shareholders) has the casting vote in the event of a tie.[6]

The vast majority of all companies subject to the Act on One-Third Participation or the Co-determination Act 1976 have either the legal status of an AG or GmbH, whereas the other companies are seldom.

Co-determination in a so-called "Societas Europaea" (SE) is covered by the Act regarding the Employee's Participation in a European Company (SE-Beteiligungsgesetz, SEBG). Co-determination after transnational mergers is covered by the European Directive of Mergers (Directive 2005/56/EG) and the German Act transacting the Provisions concerning Co-determination after Transnational Mergers (*Gesetz über die Mitbestimmung der Arbeitnehmer bei einer grenzüberschreitenden Verschmelzung*, MgVG). Both processes are identical in many ways and differ from the national rules of national co-determination. Representatives of the employees are supposed to establish a committee and were initially required to arrange co-determination in a respective agreement with the involved companies; however, obligatory standards of process, form and content may be slightly different. If no agreement can be reached within a six or twelve month period, the statutory co-determination process will apply subsidiarily as it is set in law, also bearing in mind the existing complexity of co-determination in the companies involved. In such cases, the standard of co-determination will be generally governed in accordance with the highest standard of co-determination in one of the companies involved. The rights of the individual works council are still set out under national law.

---

4 Sec. 1 (1) DrittelbG (*Drittelbeteiligungsgesetz* – Act on One-Third-Participation).

5 Sec. 7 (1) MitbestG.

6 Sec. 29 (2) MitbestG.

C. Establishment and Content of Employment Relationships

I. Deemed Employees

The statutory provisions do not provide for a legal definition of the term "employee". According to the rulings of the Federal Labor Court, a person working on the basis of a civil law contract who is personally dependent on an employer is regarded as an employee. Such personal dependence is deemed to exist, either in view of the integration of the employee into the employer's operations or because the person is bound by the employer's directions as to time, place and type of services performed. In the absence of a statutory definition, the status of an employee can be distinguished from the status of a self-employed person. Contrary to dependent employment, self-employment generally consists of, inter alia, lacking integration in the employer's organization, basically free time schedule, own means of production, no obligation to perform the work personally, no remuneration in the cases of vacation and sickness and the burden of the business risk. Where deemed employees may exist, the (actual) employer will face additional liabilities in respect of tax (wage withholding and VAT) and social security contributions.

II. Supply of Temporary Workers

Employers who wish to "lease out" employees (leased employees) to third parties (client) for work, generally require an authorization according to the Act Regulating the Supply of Temporary Workers (*Arbeitnehmerüberlassungsgesetz*, AÜG).[7] The Federal Employment Agency is responsible for issuing this authorization. The employer maintains contractual relations to both the employee and the client, whereas the client does not have a contract with the employee. Nonetheless, the client is entitled to give instructions and let the employee support his business according to his desires and operational needs. An employee is "leased" if he is completely integrated into the client's establishment for a certain period of time and does not continue to work for his employer alone. If the lessor does not have the permit required, an employment relationship between the client and the leased employee will be formed (by law) at the time at which the work is to commence as set forth in the lease agreement. Where an employee is leased to a client, the employer must generally grant the same essential working conditions that apply to comparable employees in the client's company (so called principle of Equal Pay). Supply of temporary workers can be often found in a large group of companies where employees are employed by an intercompany employment agency and then leased to other companies of the group. However, this is subject to restrictions.

---

7 Federal Law Gazette (*BGBl.*) I 158.

If the employer is not in possession of the aforementioned authorization for leasing out employees, the contracts between the employer and the client as well as the contract between the employer and the leased employees are invalid. In that case, an employment relationship between the client and the leased employee shall be deemed to have been concluded at the time at which the work is to commence as set forth in the contract between the client and the employer.[8]

III. Employment Contracts

No requirement exists for employment contracts to be in writing in order to be valid. The Law of Proof of Substantial Conditions Applicable to the Employment Relationship (*Nachweisgesetz*, *NachwG*) specifies, however, that an employer must provide in writing the essential provisions of an employment relationship within one month after concluding an employment agreement. This document must include the name and address of the parties, the date of commencement, a job description including the place of work, the salary including any additional payment, the working hours, the vacation claim, notice periods and reference to the applicable collective bargaining agreements and shop agreements.

Generally, all terms of the employment contract that the employer intends to use on multiple occasions are subject to the control of the General Terms and Conditions as set forth in Sec. 305 et seq. BGB considering, however, the special aspects of labor law. According to the Federal Labor Court, the employee is deemed a consumer and therefore a control of the contractual contents will be already performed if the employment contract is only used once and the employee did not have influence on the wording and contents of the employment contract. A check must be performed if the contents of the contractual stipulations might be considered to deviate from the wording of the law to the disadvantage of the employee, taking into consideration all circumstances of the individual case. If a contractual clause proves to be invalid as a result of the rules relating to the control of contents, the validity of the remaining contract will be unaffected.

The parties may agree on a probationary period for the employment agreement (which usually ranges from three to six months), pursuant to which the employment agreement may be terminated without reason on short notice, which must be at least two weeks.

In order to prevent an employer from circumventing employment protection provisions, fixed-term contracts are principally permitted only if the limitation of the employment can be justified by objective reasons. Such objective grounds may be, inter

---

8 Sec. 10 (1) sentence 1 AÜG (*Arbeitnehmerüberlassungsgesetz* – Act Regulating the Supply of Temporary Workers).

alia, a solely temporary operational need for work, the substitution of another employee (e.g. in cases of illness), probationary periods or personal reasons specific to the employee. No objective reason for the limitation is needed in the case of new hires, where the limited term of an employment contract does not exceed a maximum period of two years, or is only extended within the said two year period up to three times. However, according to the Federal Labor Court, such limitations are not permissible without objective reasons in cases where the employee had already been employed by the same employer during the last three years for a limited or unlimited period. In the case of a newly established business, the term for new hires within the first four years of business is up to four years without the requirement of an objective reason for the limitation.

IV. Wages, Salaries and Bonuses

German law does generally not prescribe a minimum wage. Minimum wages are, however, often fixed by collective bargaining agreements in different industries. Equal pay legislation exists on a federal level providing equal pay for men and women. Although not a statutory requirement, a thirteenth month salary/bonus is quite often paid at Christmas (or split between Christmas and vacation time). With regard to other bonus payments, there are different types of such payments as a reward or compensation for different reasons: supplemental payments for certain difficulties or inconveniences; profit sharing for (mostly) executive employees to participate in the company's results; commission depending on the employee's activities; performance related piecework rates; or attendance or loyalty bonuses. Additionally, in an AG, the granting of stock options has become common. Staff bonuses may be agreed upon as a voluntary benefit and can be made subject to a right of revocation on grounds to be specified in the contract, such as economic reasons or the employee's performance or conduct. The voluntary nature of the payment has to be explicitly stated, in order to anticipate company obligations in this regard.

V. Working Hours

The general legal maximum working hours are 48 hours per week (based on a six-day working week), which can be extended up to 60 hours provided, however, that within six months or 24 weeks the average will not exceed 8 hours per day. Based on a five-day working week the normal daily working time could be up to 9.6 hours. Employees must be granted a rest period of at least eleven hours after completion of the daily work shift and breaks of at least 30 minutes after six working hours. Night work must generally not exceed eight hours per working day. According to a general rule, work on Sundays or on holidays is principally prohibited, although there are many exceptions for certain businesses. However, even if one of the exceptions applies, fifteen Sundays per year must be work-free and Sunday work must be compensated for by an additional day off. All these rules pursuant to the Working Hours Act (*Arbeitszeitgesetz*, *ArbZG*)[9] do not apply to executives and managers.

Trade unions are lobbying for a 35-hour week and collective bargaining agreements often provide for a shorter weekly working time (e.g. 38.5-hour week). Overtime is strongly opposed by unions.

VI. Holidays and Vacation

All German states recognize the following public holidays: New Year's Day (1st January); Good Friday; Easter Monday; May Day (1st May); Ascension Day; Whit Monday; German Unity Day (3rd October); Christmas Day (25th December); and Boxing Day (26th December). There are also certain religious holidays in addition to these, which differ from state to state.

The minimum amount of vacation to which an employee is legally entitled is 20 working days per year based on a five-day working week or 24 days based on a six-day working week once they have completed an initial period of six months of employment. Collective bargaining agreements as well as individual employment contracts usually increase the number of vacation days (often up to 30 days or more per year) whilst state laws provide for leave for special purposes (i. e. educational leave). An employee is entitled to receive vacation pay equal to his or her current salary during vacation. Several collective bargaining agreements, as well as business practice, may also provide for an extra vacation bonus. The vacation claim generally expires at the end of a calendar year and can only be carried forward until March 31 of the following year, although collective bargaining agreements, individual employment contracts or business practice often provide for longer periods. Where the vacation could not be taken due to termination of the employment, it must be compensated.

VII. Statutory Sick Pay

An employee whose employment has existed without breaks for at least four weeks is entitled to sick pay where sickness stops the employee from performing his or her duties through no fault of the employee.

Sick pay amounts to 100 % of normal salary and is received until recovery, but not beyond a period of six weeks (for the particular illness) beyond which time the employee, if eligible, receives benefits from the state health insurance plan (sickness allowance) for the period of 78 weeks amounting to 70 % of the employee's monthly

---

9 Federal Law Gazette (BGBl.) I 1170.

gross income up to "income thresholds" of social security. A new illness gives rise to a new claim for a maximum of another six weeks if the employee was able to work in between. The employee must inform the employer about the incapacity to work and its foreseeable duration without delay and submit a medical certificate after the third calendar day of absence.

D. Dismissal

The employer's right to issue a notice of termination may be restricted by individual contracts, works agreements, collective bargaining agreements or by statute such as the Employment Protection Act (*Kündigungsschutzgesetz, KSchG*).

I. Notice Period, Probation Period

As a basic principle, either contracting party can terminate the employment by notice. The statutory period of notice for termination for an employee and for an employer during the first two years of employment with the same firm or plant is four weeks either up to the fifteenth or the end of a calendar month. If an employee has worked for two or more years in the same firm or plant, the period of notice to be observed by the employer is one month to the end of a calendar month. The longer the employment relationship lasts, the longer the period of notice required (up to a maximum of seven months, if the employment lasts for 20 years or more). For the duration of a probation period, but no longer than the first six months of employment, the employer and the employee can agree on a short notice period of two weeks. The effective date of the dismissal is not specified. If such a short notice period is agreed, each of the contracting parties can give notice up until the last day of the probation period, using the short notice period. The contracting parties are free to agree on a longer notice period for the employee, for the employer or for both of the contracting parties provided that the notice period the employee has to observe is no longer than the notice period of the employer. The statutory notice requirements apply to the extent that no specific contractual notice period exists, or said period is invalid, due to the fact that it does not meet the statutory minimum. All statutory notice periods as well as the effective dates of the dismissal may be changed in a collective bargaining agreement in the employee's favor or to the employee's disadvantage. The employee must receive the dismissal one day before the commencement of the notice period because the day the employee receives the dismissal does not count for the calculation of the notice period. If a notice period is one month to the end of a calendar month the employee must receive the dismissal on the last day of the previous month at the latest to meet the notice period.

II. Formal Requirements

Notice of termination of employment must be given in writing, and requires an original signature in order to be valid. A notice of termination sent by fax or e-mail or a handing over of a copy of the original is therefore insufficient. The dismissal must be signed by a person who is an authorized representative as registered in the commercial register. If the authorized person does not have the power to represent the employer alone but only together with another authorized person, both of them have to sign the dismissal. The dismissal could also be signed by an employee who is authorized to appoint or to dismiss staff but whose authority is not registered in the commercial register. If a person who is not registered in the commercial register signs the dismissal, the authorization must be proved by an original certificate of authority which must be handed over to the dismissed employee simultaneously with the dismissal. Otherwise the dismissed employee has a legal reason to immediately reject the dismissal without due delay. The same applies to the conclusion of settlement agreements. The original dismissal should be delivered personally or should be sent by messenger or by registered mail (if personal delivery is not possible, the delivery by messenger is preferable to registered mail). Personal delivery should not be made by a body of the employer's company because a body of company cannot be witness in a possible law suit for the receipt of the dismissal in time.

III. Termination for Good Cause

The employment relationship can be terminated for good cause without notice by either party for an important reason which makes it unacceptable for the other party to continue the employment relationship until the expiry of the ordinary notice period. The following reasons may justify inter alia a termination for good cause: commitment of a crime against the employer; breach of duty of confidentiality or of non-competition. Termination due to an important reason is only possible within the first two weeks of obtaining such knowledge. To be valid, the notice of dismissal need, in principle, not include the reason for the termination for good cause but on the explicit request of the other party the reasons must be given afterwards in writing.

IV. Employment Protection Act

If the employer wants to terminate employment without good cause he has to consider the provisions of the Employment Protection Act (*Kündigungsschutzgesetz, KSchG*). The Employment Protection Act is applicable if an employee has worked for the employer for more than six months and the employer regularly employs more than ten employees. Due to a former statutory provision, the Employment Protection Act is also applicable for employees whose employment started before 1st January 2004 if at least five other employees have been employed since this date. For hires after

31st December 2003, however, the Employment Protection Act only applies if the threshold of ten employees is exceeded. Part-time positions are only counted proportionally (up to 20 hours per week = 0.5; up to 30 hours per week = 0.75).

According to the Employment Protection Act, a termination is only legally effective if it is socially justified. Social justification within the meaning of the Employment Protection Act is limited to three principal areas of reasons for the dismissal. These reasons are reasons related to the person, the conduct of the employee or to operational changes in the employer's organization.

First, the termination of employment due to the personal circumstances of the employee may be related to the capability or qualification of the employee required for performing work that he was employed for, such as a series of short-term illnesses or a long-term illness, loss of driving license, alcoholism etc. In case of low performance, the employer has to make sure that there is no other vacant position in the company that better suits the employee's capabilities or qualifications than his current position. A termination based on personal reasons is only valid if the employee is permanently or indefinitely unable to fulfill his contractual duties and this inability disproportionately affects the employer's business interests. When comparing the legitimate business interests of the employer with the employee's interest to continue in employment, in consideration of seniority, employees' age and maintenance obligations, the employer's interests must prevail.

Second, the behavior of the employee may constitute social justification for termination, i. e. being absent from work without excuse despite repeated warnings or refusal to work. Poor performance can also be a conduct related reason if the employee is able to perform in an appropriate way but is not willing to do. Prior to issuing a notice of termination in such cases, the employer has to give a warning to the employee with regard to his or her shortcomings. Besides, an effective warning must contain the statement that any further breach of duty equal to the violation mentioned in the warning could cause labor law-related consequences, such as a dismissal, to the employee. No statutory formal requirements for warnings exist. In particular a warning does not have to be issued in writing in order to be valid. But in consideration of a possible law suit it is preferable to hand over the warning in writing in order to serve it as evidence.

Thirdly, a dismissal may be socially justified if based on operational reasons. In particular, this can be based on changes in the employer's business organization resulting in the redundancy of the relevant job due, for example, to a plant closing or reduction of the work force due to a shortage of orders. However, the employer has to carry out the so-called "social selection" and consider the social data (age, seniority, maintenance obligation, severe disability) in order to select those employees for dismissal first who are the "least disadvantaged" by the redundancy. The social selection has to be made between all employees who are comparable due to their position, qualifications and skills. If an employee claims unfair dismissal, he must sue the employer within three weeks upon receipt of the termination notice to the competent employment court. Where the employee misses this three-week limit, the dismissal is automatically regarded as socially justified and valid. If a labor court declares a dismissal as socially not justified and therefore as null and void, the employee is entitled to return to work and the employer has to pay the employee for the outstanding salaries.

V. Severance Payment

There is no statutory obligation of the employer to provide a severance payment. But often a severance payment is given to avoid or to settle a law suit because the termination of an employment relationship under the Employment Protection Act is usually complicated. As a general and rough rule, an average severance payment amounts to 50 % of the monthly gross salary for each year of service (see Sec. 1a (2) KSchG). Furthermore a claim to a severance payment could be based on a works agreement, the so called "social plan".

VI. Hearing of the Works Council

Before any notice of termination is issued the works council – if any – has to be consulted. The works council has to be informed about the reason for the dismissal and in the case of termination based on operational reasons, about the social data of the employees, which have been compared before the decision to dismiss the individual person. The relevant circumstances must be described in a way that puts the works council in a position to assess the validity of the reasons for the dismissal without needing to conduct additional research on its own. Even though the hearing of the works council does not have to be in writing, a written form is advisable due to a possible later law suit. In the event of a defect of the works council hearing attributable to the employer's sphere, the violation will render the dismissal invalid. This defect cannot be remedied at a later date. The works council can decide whether it wants to consent, to refuse or to not comment on the dismissal within one week after receiving the information. The dismissal can be given after this week or – if the works council decides faster – after its decision. Even if the works council opposes the dismissal, the employee can be dismissed.

VII. Special Protection Against Dismissal

Additional employment protection exists for works council members, disabled employees, pregnant employees and employees on parental leave or care leave, data protection officers and pollution control officers; said employees may not be terminated except for good cause. The termination of disabled or pregnant employees or employees on parental or care leave, however, requires the prior consent of the competent authorities.

E. Maternity Rights

In principle, any notice of termination issued during pregnancy and up to four months after the birth of a child is null and void to the extent that the employer was aware of the pregnancy when issuing the dismissal or was informed of the pregnancy within two weeks after issuing the termination letter. If an employee fails to inform the employer within this two week period, the employee will lose the protection against dismissal. This does not apply if the employee was unaware of the pregnancy during the two week period and informs the employer immediately after learning of it. A dismissal during a pregnancy is only valid in special cases after declaration of the consent to the dismissal by the responsible public authority. Such a special case may be a shutdown of an establishment.

During the last six weeks of pregnancy and for eight weeks after a birth, the mother must not work. If continued employment is harmful to the health of the prospective mother or unborn baby, the mother also must not work. Additionally, pregnant employees may not work overtime, nights, on Sundays, or on public holidays. During this period of maternity leave the employee is entitled to maternity pay amounting to the average salary of the last 13 weeks or the last 3 months before the month in which the pregnancy began. The employer is fully reimbursed for this maternity pay by the health insurance or the state.

F. Parental Leave

Parental Leave is available for either parent or alternatively for both parents working part-time and may be taken up to three years after a child is born. The employee must inform the employer in writing about the demand of taking Parental Leave and the time period of leave within two years after the child's birth. During the time of Parental Leave the employee is not paid by the employer but is entitled to payments from the state for a maximum of 14 months. The amount of this payment depends on the former income of the employee. A parent taking Parental Leave may not be dismissed from employment once the employee has demanded Parental Leave (at least 8 weeks before Parental Leave) and during Parental Leave. A dismissal may only be valid if the responsible public authority declared its consent to the dismissal.

G. Care Leave

Employees are entitled to be released from their duties if they care for a close family member at home. This Care Leave can last no longer than 6 months. The employee is only entitled to salary payment if the employer and the employee agreed to such a claim of payment. For the duration of Care Leave, a dismissal is only valid with the consent of the responsible public authority.

H. Requirement for Disabled Employees

Companies with more than 20 employees must have a workforce consisting of at least 5 % of individuals who are at least 50 % disabled. Employers who do not meet these hiring requirements are subject to a monthly charge per disabled employee not hired. Companies with more than five disabled employees may elect a disabled employees' representative, who has to be consulted prior to every personnel measure against disabled persons like a dismissal. Disabled workers are entitled to five additional days of leave annually and must not work over-time. Special protection against dismissal applies also for employees in an equal status, which means that the person is at least 30 % up to 49 % disabled and the equal status to a disabled person is declared by the responsible state authority. Disabled employees and employees with an equal status are entitled to special protection against dismissal and can only be dismissed with the prior consent of the responsible public authority.

I. Right to Reduce Working Time

Employees who have been employed for more than six months are entitled to a reduction in their working time and weekly allocation, provided the request does not conflict with the legitimate operational interests of the employer (e.g. no suitable substitute employee is available). However, in order to avoid an automatic change of the working time and allocation, the employer has to reject an employer's request in writing at the latest one month before the changes would become effective.

During Parental Leave, the employee may work part-time for a maximum of 30 hours per week. The employer may only deny such a request within four weeks in writing for urgent operational reasons. In contrast to the general right of reduction, the requested part-time work during parental leave does not apply automatically when the employer fails meeting the term of four weeks. In fact the employee has to sue the employer.

J. Transfer of Undertaking

Pursuant to the EU Directive on the transfer of undertakings and respective national regulation, the transfer of a business or parts of it results in the legal transfer of the transferring party's employment relationships to the acquiring party. The same applies if – after a share acquisition – the new owner decides to move (change ownership) a business from one subsidiary to another. There is the risk that the potential closedown of an operation after a share purchase may actually be deemed in law to be a transfer of undertaking.

The transfer of undertaking (change of ownership of assets) results in the legal transfer of the existing employment agreements including all mutual rights and obligations. The rules in relation to pensions depend on the national laws implementing the directive. For example, German Law (Sec. 613a BGB) provides for the legal transfer of pensions rights/expectancies of active employees, whereas pensioners' rights remain with the transferring party.

According to German Law, the completion of the next step depends on whether employees consent or object to the transfer of their employment contracts. Since a termination of employment becomes null and void if it is based on a transfer of undertaking, the employees must be informed in writing about the intended transfer, its reason the (planned) date of the transfer, the legal, economic and social consequences of the transfer for the employees and their representatives as well as any measures planned with respect to the employees. In this respect the employee is entitled to object to the transfer, within one month, after having obtained full written information about the transfer. If the employee objects to the transfer of employment, the employer may provide for ordinary notice (redundancy) based on the fact that the current position is transferred. With respect to these and other terminations, the Employment Protection Act applies to all operations with more than ten (formerly five) regular employees.

In collective labor law there is a distinction to be made depending on whether the plant is to be transferred entirely or in part. If the entire plant is to be transferred, the plant identity is maintained and the old regulations and works agreements remain valid. If the plant identity is not maintained, however, the works agreements are transformed into individual rights together with a one-year barrier to change. The same applies regarding collective bargaining agreements if the new employer is not bound by the same collective bargaining agreements like the former employer. New works agreements are, however, possible and would replace the old transformed regulations. The members of the works council lose their function when only a part of a plant is transferred but retain lasting protection against dismissal. However, for a transitional period of six months, the former works council remains competent and responsible for starting new elections in order to create a works council in the transferred part.

K. Social Security

Germany has a compulsory social security system that covers five principle areas: health and nursing care insurance, old-age benefits, unemployment benefits and workers' compensation. While the nursing care insurance was established not before 1995, the introduction of health insurance, old-age pension and workers' compensation can be traced back to the end of the 19th century. The contributions to the social security system are generally linked to the level of the employee's salary of which a certain percentage must be paid. They are principally capped, however, by an "Income Threshold" (*Beitragsbemessungsgrenze*), whereby the salary exceeding said threshold will not be accounted for in the amount to be paid. Due to the existing differences in the average salaries in the western and in the eastern part of Germany, the thresholds of the old-age and the unemployment insurance differ accordingly. Contributions to the social security system are generally shared equally between the employer and the employee. The employer withholds the employee's share of the contribution from the employee's salary and pays this, together with its own contribution, to the Federal Insurance Agency. The percentage of the respective contributions below describes the standard of 2012. The failure to withhold and pay the employee's contributions may constitute a criminal offence that will carry a fine or a custodial sentence up to five years.[10]

I. Health Insurance

The carriers of the statutory health insurance are the statutory health insurance schemes (*Krankenkassen*). Benefits from public health insurance include the payment of medical and hospital expenses and compensation for loss of salary. Contributions to the public health insurance system are only payable up to certain salary levels, which are usually increased annually. In 2012, only employees with a gross salary not exceeding EUR 50,850.00 annually or EUR 4,237.50 monthly (insurance threshold; *Versicherungspflichtgrenze*) are obligated by law to make contributions to the public health insurance system. No compulsory health insurance exists beyond these salary thresholds; therefore, persons subject to compulsory health insurance are primarily dependent employees, but may also be unemployed persons or retired persons. Employees exceeding said thresholds might therefore opt to maintain private health insurance, to continue the participation in the public health insurance system vol-

10 Sec. 266a StGB (*Strafgesetzbuch* – German Penal Code).

untarily or to have no health insurance at all (which is rare). Due to an increase of the insurance threshold in 2003, employees, who were not subject to compulsory health insurance in 2002 and who have had a private health insurance since December 2002, are entitled to keep their private health insurance, as long as their gross annual salary amounts to at least the "Income Thresholds" (*Beitragsbemessungsgrenze*) below, i. e. EUR 45,900.00; otherwise they become subject to compulsory health insurance.

As of 1st January 2009 the compulsory health fund came into force, which regulates the funding of public health insurance in Germany. Former different contribution rates of the various public health insurance companies are replaced by a uniform rate, which annually is subject to the discretion of the German Federal Government. The respective rate for 2012 is fixed at 15.5 % of gross salary, capped by the "Income Threshold" (*Beitragsbemessungsgrenze*) amounting to currently EUR 45,900.00 annually or EUR 3,825,00 monthly (see above). The rate of 15.5 % is currently divided into a share of 8,2 % borne by the employee and a share of 7,3 % borne by the employer. Additional contributions levied by the individual health insurance schemes, which may apply for different benefits, are to be borne solely by the employee. If the employee is not subject to compulsory health insurance, the employer must contribute up to EUR 279.23 per month (50 % of the official average premium) to the employee's private health insurance.

Employers who employ up to 30 employees may claim a refund for compensation paid to employees for sick or maternity leave, of 80 %, from the competent health insurance.

II. Nursing Care Insurance

The nursing care insurance is a comparably new pillar of social security legislation and was founded in 1995. Its carriers are the nursing care funds established within the statutory health insurance schemes. The benefits from nursing care insurance comprise, inter alia, allowances for privately organized ambulant nursing carried out, e.g. by relatives, benefits in kind from professional ambulant nursing services at home and several benefits in connection with a permanent stay in a nursing home. Contributions to the nursing care insurance plan amount to 1.95 % of gross salary capped again at the income threshold of EUR 45,900.00 annually or EUR 3,825.00 monthly. Employees without children must pay an additional contribution of another 0.25 %, amounting to a total contribution of 1.225 %, while the employer's contribution remains still 0.975 %. If the employee is not subject to compulsory health insurance, the employer must contribute up to EUR 37.29 per month (50 % of the official average premium) to the employee's private nursing care insurance.

III. Old-Age Benefits

Benefits from the old-age insurance include payments from the old-age pension, benefits for reduction in earning capacity and payments from the widow's and/or orphans' pension. Old-age contributions are currently levied at a rate of 19.6 % (equally shared by the employer and employee) of gross salary capped at EUR 67,200.00 annually or EUR 5,600.00 monthly (in the western part of Germany) and EUR 57,600.00 annually or EUR 4,800.00 monthly (in the eastern part of Germany). The federal carrier of the old-age pension is the German Pension Fund.

IV. Unemployment Benefits

Unemployment benefits do not only comprise payments as compensation for remuneration, they also include support and advice by employment services and recruitment agencies as well as measures and support of further education. Employers may also be granted allowances and other financial support, especially with regard to the hiring of employees (see below). Unemployment insurance contributions amount to 3.0 % (equally borne by the employer and employee) of gross salary capped as well at EUR 67,200.00 annually or EUR 5,600.00 monthly (respectively EUR 57,600.00 annually/EUR 4,800.00 monthly in the eastern part of Germany). Unemployment insurance is administered by the Federal Labor Agency in Nuremberg with state agencies in every Federal State.

V. Workers' Compensation

The intention of the workers' compensation system is both to prevent and to compensate for work accidents and work-related diseases. After the occurrence of these events the benefits may be granted in kind, e.g. medical treatments and measures for medical rehabilitation, or in money, e.g. injury benefits. The workers' compensation system is administered by associations (*Berufsgenossenschaften*) set up by all branches of trade and industry. Contributions to the workers' compensation system are made solely by the employer. The contribution amount is fixed by the various trade industry associations taking into consideration the risk of a work accident occurring in the particular branch, the record of work accidents during the previous business year, and the total annual pay of all employees affected.

As an offset for these contributions, Volume VII of the Social Insurance Code (*Sozialgesetzbuch, SGB VII*) provides for a limited liability of the employer in cases of work accidents and work-related diseases. Under this regulation,[11] the employer is

11 Sec. 104 (1) SGB VII (*Sozialgesetzbuch VII* – Volume VII oft he Social Security Code).

not obligated to provide compensation for personal injuries of his employees, if the accident was not caused intentionally.

VI. Promotion of Job Creation

Under certain circumstances an employer might apply for a promotion allowance at the competent labor agency. The labor agency grants respective promotion allowances especially for the following cases:

Hiring new, formerly unemployed employees where a new company is being formed; employment of employees in need of respective allowances (i. e. disabled persons, elderly people, less qualified employees, long-term unemployed persons); qualification allowance for younger employees; integration of unemployed persons over the age of 50.

Additionally, certain promotion programs operated by the Federal States and municipalities exist under which certain allowances for job creation can be granted.

VII. Insignificant Employment

The German government introduced legislation on "Insignificant Employment" (positions with a salary of EUR 400.00 or less) as of April 1, 2003 pursuant to which employers must pay with effect as of 1st July 2006 a 30 % lump-sum charge on income of EUR 400.00 or less, which is tax-free for the employee. The insignificance of the employment is only measured by this income threshold, whereas there is no time limitation as to permissible working hours per week or month. The 30 % lump-sum charge is divided into 15 % for the statutory pension system, 13 % for statutory health insurance (not applicable to private health insurance) and 2 % for a lump-sum tax (including church tax and solidarity tax). The employee, however, is not actually entitled to either health insurance or statutory pension benefits. With regard to statutory pension benefits, an employee may opt for membership in which case the employee must contribute the difference between the 15 % payment made by the employer and the statutory pension insurance contribution payable (currently 19.6 %) to the statutory pension system. The employee does not have this option with regard to health insurance. The employer is obliged to have the employment registered at the central office for insignificant employment of the Federal Pension Insurance for Miners-Railways-Sea (*Deutsche Rentenversicherung Knappschaft-Bahn-See*) and to pay the contributions to the worker's compensation system. In order to promote so-called "household employment", the lump-sum charge only amounts to a total of 12 % for employment in private households and is divided into 5 % each for the statutory pension insurance scheme and health insurance and 2 % for the lump-sum tax stated above. The above stated option regarding statutory pension benefits also applies. To a certain extent (max. EUR 4,000.00 p. a.) expenses for "household employment" can also be deducted from the tax liability.

A progressive regime for income between EUR 400.01 and EUR 800.00 has been introduced in order to remove the so-called low wage threshold and the sharp increase in social insurance contributions which it caused. The employee's contribution varies here from 4 % to 21 % depending on income, while the employer's share remains unchanged. The income tax is determined on an individual basis. Several "insignificant employment" jobs are generally added together. In order to facilitate the payment procedure, the contributions are all paid to a common collection point for insignificant employment at the Federal Pension Insurance for Miners-Railways-Sea.

The term "insignificant employment" only refers to social security and tax laws. Labor law does not differentiate between "significant" and "insignificant" employments exceeding or not exceeding the income threshold of EUR 400.00. That means that employments with a monthly salary below that threshold are an adequate employment with the same applicable rights and duties, e.g. with regard to continued payment of remuneration, vacation or protection against unfair dismissal.

L. Anti-Discrimination Act

The main focus of the Anti-Discrimination Act is the protection against discrimination for employed as well as self-employed personnel. The Anti-Discrimination Act provides that no discrimination must take place with regard to race and ethnic origin, gender, religion or secular beliefs, disability, age and sexual identity. With respect to discrimination in view of these criteria, it is furthermore important to distinguish between direct and indirect discrimination. Both are prohibited. Employees affected by discrimination are entitled to raise a claim against the employer. The employee has to explain how he has been discriminated against. The claim may result in compensation in the form of material and immaterial damages. It can be claimed in front of the competent labor court. To do this the employee must raise a claim within two months of becoming aware of the discrimination. The labor court then has to consider whether the employee's claim is convincing and whether, as a result, the employer is required to justify the actions of which it is accused.

Regulations in an employment contract, a works agreement or a collective bargaining agreement as well as directives of the employer which are discriminating and not justified are invalid.

Discrimination, however, will be considered to be justified in certain circumstances, i. e. for a reason based on professional requirements, for reasons based on religion or world view, or for reasons based on age and in order to balance already existing disadvantages. With respect to professional requirements, discrimination shall be justified if the criteria represent an essential and decisive professional requirement and the purpose is therefore as legitimate as the requirement is appropriate.

Discrimination due to age shall be justified if appropriate and based on legitimate purposes as expressively set out in Sec. 10 of the Anti-Discrimination Act. This would include taking into consideration the age of an employee when considering any social selection in connection with business related terminations.

Churches and religious communities continue to be entitled to select their employees by taking into consideration their religious or world view, as far as such is justified with respect to the right of self-determination of these institutions. Finally, discrimination can also be justified if it results in the balancing of already existing disadvantages, e. g. preference of elderly or disabled persons (affirmative action).

The Anti-Discrimination Act further provides for co-determination rights of so-called Anti-Discrimination Organizations, which shall represent the interests of persons discriminated against. Such Anti-Discrimination Organizations must provide for at least 75 members.

Furthermore an Anti-Discrimination Authority is established with the Federal Ministry for Family, Seniors, Women and Youth. Anyone who believes he has been discriminated against has the right to appeal the Anti-Discrimination Authority. The Authority shall provide support to these persons through information, consultation, mediation, evaluation and recommendation with regard to the abolition and prevention of the discrimination and enforcements of the individual rights.

M. Visitors to Germany

A foreign citizen who wants to visit or take up residence and employment in Germany must comply with certain immigration rules and regulations and need a residence title according to the Act on the Residence (*Aufenthaltsgesetz*) in the form of a visa, a residence permit (*Aufenthaltserlaubnis*), a settlement permit (*Niederlassungserlaubnis*) or an EC long-term residence permit.

I. Visa Requirements

Foreigners entering Germany for transit purposes or for a short stay need a visa, exempt for citizens of EU Member States. For citizens of various other countries, such as the USA, Canada, Australia, New Zealand and Japan, special regulations apply. Visa is always committed to a special purpose. Two different forms of visa exist: the Schengen visa and the national visa.

A Schengen visa grants a limited residence permit for transit purposes or for stays of up to three months within a period of six months from the date of initial entry. Obtaining a visa from one EU Member State the foreigner is allowed to travel through all of the Schengen Member States as Austria, Belgium, Czech Republic, Denmark, Estonia, Finland, France, Germany, Greece, Hungary, Iceland, Italy, Latvia, Lithuania, Luxembourg, Malta, the Netherlands, Norway, Poland, Portugal, Slovakia, Slovenia, Spain, Sweden and Switzerland.

If the foreigner wants to stay for a longer duration a national visa for the territory of Germany shall be required. The Act on the Residence does not include any provisions regarding the duration of residence with the national visa. In contrast to the Schengen visa the national visa permits only to stay in the territory of Germany and not to travel through other EU Members.

II. Permitted Activities

According to the Act on the Residence the holder of a residence title is only permitted to take up an economic activity if this is indicated in the residence title. The four types of residence titles provide different permissions of employment activities.

Foreigners who stay in Germany with a visa are not allowed to carry out gainful employments. According to the provisions of the Residence Act gainful employment includes activities for which remuneration has been agreed upon or work which requires permission to practice a profession.

Therefore activities such as attending meetings, signing contracts, installing and removing are not considered as gainful activity (and are therefore allowed) provided that the visitor is employed by a corporation located in a foreign country. Foreign employees who merely install industrial equipment or machines from foreign companies in Germany or who supervise such installations (or provide advice as consultants) are also not considered to be gainfully employed in Germany. Such activities in Germany must, however, observe the time limit of three months. As visa does not allow gainful employments it is used especially for transit purposes or for business travels.

A foreigner who is in possession of a residence permit is allowed to enter into an employment if the residence title indicates that economic activity is permitted or a statutory instrument stipulates that taking up the employment is permissible. The work permit as indicated in the residence title, as well as any restrictions, depends on the approval of the Federal Employment Agency. A settlement permit and an EC long-term residence permit entitle the holder to pursue economic activities without any restrictions. For foreigners with a special education the Act on the Residence includes a special permit. Highly qualified foreigners may be granted a settlement permit and therewith an unlimited permission to work.

III. Application Procedure

The diplomatic mission of the Federal Republic of Germany which is responsible for the area where the applicant has his ordinary residence or domicile is responsible for issuing visas. As it lasts usually between two and ten working days until a diplomatic mission decides on an application for a short stay visa it is advisable to contact the respective mission in advance about all necessary documentation and any special local requirements regarding particular visa formalities, in order to avoid time-consuming requests for additional information or documentation. An application for residence titles which entitles the holder to a longer stay or for a permission to take up gainful employment even takes several months to process. Application forms can be obtained from the competent diplomatic mission free of charge. For further information about the application procedure please see the homepage of the Federal Foreign Office (www.auswaertiges-amt.de).

IV. Requirements for Short Stay Visas (Schengen)

In issuing short stay visas, diplomatic missions in Germany are bound by the relevant provisions of the Act on the Residence, the Schengen Agreement and its implementing ordinances. The diplomatic mission must verify and ensure that the requirements of these ordinances have been met in each individual case. The identity and nationality of the applicant must be known and the purpose of the trip to Germany must be plausible and comprehensible. The applicant must be in a position to finance his living and travel costs from his own funds or income. Furthermore the applicant must be prepared to leave the Schengen area before the visa expires and documentary evidence must be provided of travel health insurance valid for the entire Schengen area. The applicant must not be a danger to law and order, the national security or for international relationships for one of the Members of the Schengen States.

V. Requirements for Extended Stays

Foreigners who require national visas or other residence titles for stays of more than three months or stays leading to the holder taking up gainful employment, must apply for such a residence title at the competent mission before arriving in Germany. This does not apply for citizens of the EU and Switzerland. Citizens of Australia, Canada, Israel, Japan, New Zealand, the Republic of Korea and the United States of America may obtain any residence permit that may be required after entering Germany.

Residence title applications must be approved by the relevant foreign authority in Germany in the place where the applicant intends to take up residence in an internal procedure. Foreign authorities are not subordinate agencies of the Federal Foreign Office but operate under the supervision of the respective interior ministries of the Federal States.

Residence title application forms for a long-term stay (longer than three months) can be obtained free of charge from the relevant mission.

The granting of a Schengen visa, the granting of a national visa and a residence permit, a settlement permit or an EC long-term residence permit shall generally presuppose that the foreigners livelihood is secure and that his identity and nationality is established. Furthermore the granting of a residence permit, a settlement permit or an EC long-term residence permit in general presupposes that the foreigner has entered Germany with the necessary visa and has already furnished the key information required for granting of the title in the visa application.

It usually takes up to seven months until a residence title can be issued because the foreign authority has to consult different other authorities before deciding about the approval. As the residence title must indicate whether the pursuit of an economic activity is permitted, the foreign authority has to consult with the Federal Employment Agency. Depending on the individual case other authorities have to be consulted to obtain their approval.

N. Working in Germany

I. Access to the German Labor Market

Foreign nationals, other than European Union (EU), European Economic Area (EEA) and Swiss nationals, may as a rule only reside in Germany for the purpose of taking up gainful employment if they have the requisite residence permit which allows gainful employment as well. They must not work without it. Australian, Canadian, Israeli, Japanese, South Korean, New Zealand and US citizens may acquire this residence permit from the competent foreigners' authority after their arrival in Germany. They may not, however, commence gainful employment until they have the permit. Nationals of all other states must apply for a work visa from their local German mission prior to entering Germany.

Access to the labor market is in principle limited to certain professional groups and requires in principle the prior approval of the employment authorities. For some job groups no approval of the employment authorities is needed, e.g. highly qualified employees. These are employees with a special technical knowledge and teaching personnel in prominent positions or scientific personnel in prominent positions or specialists and executive personnel with special professional experience who receive an annual gross salary of more than EUR 67,200 (amount in 2012). There are plans to reduce this amount to gross EUR 48.000,00. Furthermore, managerial employees with a power of attorney and members of an organ of a company do need the consent of the employment authorities for their residence title. The same applies to some employees (e.g. installer, merchandiser) who are seconded to Germany for a maximum of three months within a twelve months period.

The Employment Agency may approve the granting of a residence permit to take up employment if the employment of foreigners does not result in any adverse consequences for the labor market and no German workers, foreigners who possess the same legal status as German workers with regard to the right to take up employment, or other foreigners who are entitled to preferential access to the labor market under the law of the European Union (preferred employees) are available for the type of employment concerned and the foreigner is not employed on terms less favorable than apply to comparable German workers. For some groups of employees (e.g. foreign graduates of a German university, managerial employees and IT specialists) the employment authorities do not investigate whether a preferred employee could be employed instead.

Two different types of residence titles exist for employees who intend to hold gainful employment in Germany. The residence permit is valid for a limited duration and is granted for different purposes, inter alia for gainful employment. The settlement permit is granted without a time limit. It always includes the right for gainful employment. The settlement permit can be granted under special circumstances, e.g. for highly qualified employees (see above) and for self-employed persons who will invest at least EUR 250,000, and create five jobs, if the personal capital or a loan undertaking is available to realize the business idea. Furthermore, the settlement permit can be granted after five years of employment under a residence permit.

Most recently a so-called "blue card" is in discussion on a European level. In Germany foreigners shall obtain a blue card who receive an annual gross salary of EUR 44,800.00. For engineers and doctors an annual gross salary of EUR 34,944.00 shall apply.

II. Social Security

The German social security system generally applies to all employees in Germany on a mandatory basis. However, based on national social security provisions or on an applicable social security treaty concluded between Germany and an individual's home country, it may be possible to obtain an exemption from German social security contributions for a limited period of time.

III. Secondment

An employee seconded to Germany by his foreign employer does generally not fall within the scope of the German social security system, provided the employee remains employed by the foreign employer, the foreign employer continues to pay the employee's salary during the secondment period and the period of employment in Germany is limited in time. The period of limitation differs depending on the country and varies usually between 12 and 60 months. In order to prove that the foreign employee is exempted from social security as a result of a secondment, the employee or his or her employer must obtain an exemption certificate from the relevant authorities stating that the employee is subject to compulsory social security coverage in the employee's own country.

In the case of an EU Member State, the employee and his foreign employer may respectively apply for an exemption certificate (A-1) as proof that the domestic law remains applicable. The exemption may be granted if the employee is subject to the social security laws in his or her native country. A release from the German social security system is possible to the extent that the length of the employment does not exceed two years. In the case of an EEA Member State or a Swiss employee, the exemption certificate E 101 is applicable. Its limited duration is 12 months with the possibility of an extension up to a maximum period of another 12 months.

The same generally applies to employees who are citizens of a non-EU or EEA country which has entered into a social security treaty with Germany (such as Japan and the USA). If such an exemption does not exist, the employee in general (and depending on the social security treaty) may later claim repayment of pension contributions (only employee's part) paid into the German social security system. Such a later claim of repayment is also possible for employees from countries without a social security treaty with Germany unless they already have sufficient old age provision.

O. Income Tax

I. General

Individuals who are German residents by virtue of a permanent home or customary place of abode in Germany are subject to German income tax plus solidarity surcharge and possibly church tax on their worldwide income (unlimited tax liability) without reference to nationality. A permanent home will generally exist if an individual has accommodation in Germany at his or her disposal, this does not require ownership. A customary place of abode is given if an individual is present in Germany for a continuous period exceeding six months, whereby, once the six month period has been exceeded, residence is assumed retroactively from the first day of presence in Germany.

If an individual is not a resident of Germany, then only German source income is subject to German taxation (limited tax liability). If an individual qualifies as a tax resident of Germany and another country, a relevant tax treaty concluded between Germany and the other country of residence may apply to ascertain the country of residence for treaty purposes. The respective tax treaty may apply to restrict Germany's right to tax worldwide income under its national laws.

A non-German national who moves his/her home to Germany will usually become liable to unlimited German tax liability – subject to the provisions of an applicable tax treaty.

II. Taxable Income

There are seven categories of taxable income:

Income from agriculture and forestry; income from trading; income from professional and other independent personal services; income from employment; income from investment; rental and royalty income; other income.

Taxable income is calculated on a calendar year basis and is gross income less deductions and allowances. Various deductions and allowances are permitted, such as personal allowances, income related expense deductions, special expense deductions and extraordinary allowances.

III. Tax Rates

For a German tax resident, progressive income tax rates in a range from 14 % to 42 % apply in 2012 (plus 5.5 % solidarity surcharge and possibly church tax on the income tax liability). Church tax amounts to 8 % or 9 % of the income tax, and is capped at between 3 % and 4 % of the taxable income, depending on the Federal State of residence of the taxpayer. A so-called tax for rich individuals (*Reichensteuer*) is increasing the maximum income tax rate of 42 % to 45 % for taxable income in excess of EUR 250,000 per year (EUR 500,000 for married couples filing joint income tax returns).

The Federal Parliament introduced as part of the German "Corporate Tax Reform 2008" (*Unternehmensteuerreform 2008*) a final withholding tax on private investment income (*Abgeltungssteuer*), which came into effect in January 2009. Accordingly the various forms of private investment income in Germany are taxed at a uniform rate.

Further capital gains and proceeds from the sale of private capital assets (securities, investment shares, participations in corporations, and others, excepting real estate) are taxed at a standardized tax rate of 25 % plus a 5.5 % solidarity surcharge.

Investment income received in a business and dividends and capital gains received from a corporation in which the taxpayer holds 1% or more of the shares are not subject to the withholding tax but to the partial income system. Under this system, only 60 % of dividends distributed to a German individual shareholder by a corporation are subject to individual income tax at the shareholder level. In exchange, expenses incurred in connection with the shareholding are only 60 % deductible for individual shareholders. The same applies to taxable capital gains derived from the sale of shares in a corporation.

IV. Income from Employment

If an individual is a German resident, then all employment income – whether relating to activities carried out in Germany or abroad – is in principle subject to German income taxation. However, if Germany has concluded a tax treaty with the country in which employment activities are physically carried out, then, based on the provisions of that treaty, Germany may exempt the portion of employment income relating to activities carried out abroad from German income taxation. This exemption from German income taxation will usually only apply if certain conditions are fulfilled. A so-called split-payroll concept is often implemented to take advantage of this German tax exemption. Germany will take any tax-exempt income into account in calculating the applicable German income tax rate.

If an individual is not a German resident for tax purposes, then limited taxation will apply to tax employment income in relation to employment activities carried out or utilized in Germany. Again, a relevant tax treaty may restrict Germany's right to tax this income.

Incentives and fringe benefits received by an employee as a result of employment in Germany are generally taxable in the same way as income from employment and are subject to wage taxation at source. This applies in particular to the private use of a company car, to which special provisions apply with regard to the calculation of the benefit in kind. Further, stock options granted to an employee in relation to employment activities carried out in Germany during the German residence or possibly after German residence has expired are treated as taxable employment income. However, in most cases, the income first becomes taxable on exercise rather than on grant of the options.

V. Tax Returns

As a general rule, a German resident individual must file an annual income tax return declaring worldwide income. Married couples may file a joint return or opt for separate filing. Income tax returns must be filed by May 31st following the end of the calendar year in question, whereby an automatic filing extension to December 31st applies if the income tax return is prepared by a tax consultant.

P. Driver's License

I. General

The validity of foreign driver's licenses in Germany mainly depends on which state had issued the license and additionally on the duration of the stay in Germany.

EU citizens as well as non-EU citizens who do not have permanent residence in Germany may use their valid national driver's license or International Driving Permit in Germany for the duration of their temporary stay. It is permitted to drive all categories of vehicle indicated on the license. However, compliance with any conditions and restrictions on the driver's license is required. A translation of the domestic driver's license is principally required if it was not issued by a member state of the European Union or by a state party to the European Economic Area (EEA = Iceland, Liechtenstein, Norway), if it is not in German or if it does not comply with the provisions of the Convention on Road Traffic of 8th November 1968 (Annex 6) This prerequisite can be obtained at the competent authority of the issuing state. No translation of the license is necessary, however, if the license was issued by Andorra, Hong Kong, Monaco, New Zealand, San Marino, Senegal or Switzerland. An International Driving Permit does not have to be translated.

EU citizens as well as citizens of countries party to the European Economic Area (EEA = Iceland, Liechtenstein, Norway) who have taken up permanent residence in Germany may usually use their foreign driver's license until the end of its period of validity. An International Driving Permit is not sufficient. General restrictions may apply to different categories of a driver's license regarding, for example, the holder's age, medical requirements or the general period of validity and necessary applications for an extension. Further information will be provided by the local licensing authority. Driver's licenses issued by EU countries or countries party to the EEA will be fully recognized in Germany and need not to be transferred.

Non-EU or EEA citizens having permanent residence in Germany may use their national driver's license within Germany for a period of six months commencing from the date when normal residence in Germany was established. After six months, the domestic driver's license will no longer be recognized and every driver who has not obtained a German driver's license will be deemed to be driving without a license and penalized accordingly. The driver may apply for an extension of another six months if he or she is able to show credibly that residence in Germany will not exceed twelve months. Every foreign driver, who suspects that he or she will remain in Germany for more than six months, should therefore apply in time to get his or her foreign or international driver's license recognized and transferred.

II. Application Procedure

The holder of a foreign or international driver's license must generally first obtain an official translation and classification of the license. This usually results in costs of between EUR 30.00 and EUR 80.00. This may be done at the German Automobile Association known as the ADAC (*Allgemeiner Deutscher Automobil Club*), the German equivalent of the AAA in the USA, internationally recognized motoring organizations in the state that issued the driver's license, certified interpreters or at German diplomatic missions.

The German laws regarding recognition and transfer of foreign drivers' licenses as well as issuing of a German driver's license are complicated and depend principally on the origin of the driver's license. A number of countries (e.g. EU member states, Canada, Japan and various States of the USA) enjoy reciprocity, with the result that holders of a driver's license from said countries are not subject to written and/or practical examinations in order to transfer the license. Exact details about the conditions that have to be met and an updated list of countries, which enjoy reciprocity with regard to German driver's licenses, can be obtained from the local Driver's License Office (*Führerscheinstelle*) or from the diplomatic missions of the Federal Republic of Germany.

Even if a particular country enjoys full or partial reciprocity and exemption from written or practical examinations, a fee of approximately EUR 40.00 must still be paid in order to transcribe the driver's original license into a German driver's license.

Hans-Christian Ackermann
hans-christian.ackermann@luther-lawfirm.com

Dr. Volker Schneider
volker.schneider@luther-lawfirm.com

CHAPTER 8
PUBLIC SUBSIDIES AND STATE AID CONTROL

DR. HELMUT JANSSEN
DR. THOMAS KAPP

Many private and public companies benefit from public subsidies granted by Germany or the European Union. Different legal regimes apply: German law, EU law and WTO law. For companies usually two questions are most relevant: can they obtain a public subsidy and can they prevent competitors from obtaining subsidies?

A. Benefits Available

Some industries in Germany rely heavily on subsidies. The most striking example is agriculture. Almost half of the European Union's budget goes to the Common Agricultural Policy. Yet all industries benefit from subsidies. Some subsidies stem from the EU's budget, others from the national budget, some are co-financed, i. e. both EU and German means are used. There are specific subsidies to support one single project, but in most cases subsidies are granted on the basis of a federal subsidy scheme or one of the many regional schemes that considerably differ from each other. In 2011 approximately EUR 23.5 billion were accounted for in German state budgets – e.g., for tax holidays or financial aids.[1] Other benefits for companies are not officially accounted for, yet are not uncommon forms of state aid. An example is that a municipality transfers real estate to an investor and agrees a consideration below market value. Subsidies can take many different forms: capital injections, guarantees, preferential tax treatments, construction of an infrastructure that is of interest to only one single company etc. Nearly all subsidies, including those co-financed by the EU, are administered by German authorities. One exception are subsidies for research and technological development under a specific EU framework program that provides for moneys amounting to more than EUR 50 billion in the period of 2007 to 2013.

---

1 See 23rd Report on public subsidies of the German Federal Government published on 11 August 2011, available at the website of the German Federal Ministry of Finance www.bundesfinanzministerium.de.

B. Applicable Legal Regimes

The different legal regimes applicable to public subsidies, in essence, cover the following. German law sets forth the conditions under which a public authority may grant subsidies, provides for rules of procedure and the consequences of a misuse of public grants. EU law contains the substantive and procedural rules for granting EU funded subsidies (an area that will not be dealt with in this chapter) and establishes a system of control over national subsidies: Those subsidies which have not been approved by the European Commission are considered illegal[2] and the beneficiary has to return these (including interest) to the member state. WTO law provides for rules that aim at preventing or curing distortive effects of subsidies granted by a WTO member state[3] by regulating the actions countries can take to counter subsidies (e.g. charge an extra "countervailing duty" on subsidized imports) and providing for a dispute-settlement procedure; WTO law will not be dealt with in this chapter.

C. Typical Situations in Practice

If a company is in the position that it might benefit from public grants and incentives the obvious questions arise whether the company is entitled to obtain subsidies and up to which amount. One important feature of German subsidies law is that only in very few cases does a company have an enforceable right to be granted a subsidy. One reason for this is that usually a limited amount of public funds is set aside for a specific purpose, for example, to enable a bank to inject capital in a start-up company or to encourage a specific environment-friendly investment. While the state is obliged to treat applicants for subsidies on an equal basis, no one can claim subsidies once the means of the funds have been used. In practice the authorities have a very wide discretion.

If a company is granted a subsidy it will need to be determined under which conditions the beneficiary may keep the aid. For example, the recipient may be obliged to create a number of jobs over a period of several years. A standard condition is that the recipient did not give misleading information in his application for the aid. This becomes especially relevant when acquiring a company. The acquirer – in the course of its due diligence investigations – has to ascertain whether or not the target company will be able to keep public grants it obtained in the past. In this context it will also have to be investigated whether a national aid measure complies with EU law. Another relevant topic is challenging subsidies that are granted to a competitor. This will be dealt with further below (see Sec. J.II.).

---

2 See Art. 108 (3) TFEU (Treaty on the Functioning of the European Union).

3 See the WTO Agreement on Subsidies and Countervailing Measures.

D. National Authorities and the European Commission

Both national authorities and the European Commission are involved when state aid is to be granted. Furthermore, usually two sets of rules are to be applied: EU state aid law and national laws. Under German law the beneficiary usually only has to make sure that he uses the subsidies in the way agreed when they were granted to him. Under EU law the beneficiary has to ascertain moreover that the state aid rules are complied with by Germany. Otherwise the beneficiary faces drastic economic consequences: first of all, he has to return any payments or any other benefits received. Furthermore, contracts that violate EU state aid law are void. Companies may also be confronted with recovery claims after having acquired an undertaking which received unlawful aid. Finally, companies may consider suing for damages or recovery of aid granted to their competitors.

E. General Rule: State Aid is Prohibited

The EU competition policy aims at promoting the internal market and establishing a system of undistorted competition where every undertaking is able to operate on a level playing field. The EU state aid rules intend to avoid discrimination and subsidy races among member states. While the objectives of state aid control are straightforward and simple, the detailed rules are not. State aid regulations, block exemptions, guidelines, communications, notices, frameworks etc. cover more than a thousand pages.[4] And the body of case law, both by national courts and the European Court of Justice, grows day by day.

The fundamental rule is contained in Art. 107 (1) TFEU, the general prohibition of state aid. The concept of state aid is very broad and applies to measures which satisfy all of the following criteria:

- There must be an economic advantage that the beneficiary would not have had under normal market economy conditions: examples of potential state aid include investment grants, state guarantees, tax relief, loans at reduced rates of interest, the provision of goods and services on preferential terms and capital injections;
- The advantage has to be granted by a member state or through state resources: this comprises advantages which are granted directly by the state and advantages granted by a public or private body designated or established by the state;

4 A compilation of EU rules applicable to state aid is accessible under http://ec.europa.eu/competition/state_aid/legislation/compilation/index_en.html.

- The advantage has to favor certain undertakings or the production of certain goods which means that general measures which apply without distinction to all companies are not regarded as state aid;
- The advantage must distort competition and affect inter-state trade.

If the German state wants to award grants and incentives that fulfill these criteria, it may not do so unless approved by the European Commission. Applications for approval are called "notifications".

F. Exception: Aid Compatible with the Internal Market

Despite the general prohibition of state aid, state intervention is sometimes seen as a necessity, for example to ensure social and regional cohesion or to provide public services. Therefore, EU law recognizes a number of circumstances in which aid may be granted. One example is that "services of general economic interest" (SGEI) do not fall under the EU state aid rules. There are a lot of unresolved issues as to which activities can be qualified as SGEI. Often companies are operating on both public service and other markets. An example is a transport company that is obliged by the state to maintain transport services not only to those areas where due to the number of passengers the service generates profits, but also to those areas which are scarcely populated. In such a case the compensation granted by the state to the transport company for performing the non-profitable tasks will fall under the SGEI exception, i. e. will not need approval by the European Commission. However, several safeguards have to be observed in order to avoid over-compensation of the transport company, as any over-compensation, again, can constitute illegal state aid.[5]

There are three kinds of aid where the European Commission has no discretion and must approve the notified aid: this includes aid having a social character; aid granted in the event of natural disasters; and aid granted to certain areas of Germany affected by the former division of the country.[6] For other kinds of aid the Commission has broad discretion to assess whether to permit it or not. This includes inter alia aid for developing disadvantaged regions, aid promoting research and development and aid promoting culture and heritage conservation. The Commission also has wide discretion when assessing aid determined to "remedy a serious disturbance

5 The European Commission in 2005 issued a set of rules on these safeguard, the so-called "SGEI Package", which was updated in 2011, see http://ec.europa.eu/competition/state_aid/legislation/sgei.html.

6 Art. 107 (2) TFEU.

of a member state's economy" – all support schemes for credit institutions introduced as a reaction to the global economic and financial crisis in 2008/2009 have been accepted for that reason.[7]

The prohibition of state aid does not apply to measures which fall under a block exemption regulation. To date the general block exemption regulation[8] covers training aid, employment aid, aid for small and medium-sized enterprises, environmental aid as well as research, development and innovation aid. There is also an exemption for small amounts of aid ("de minimis" aid),[9] which means that aid not exceeding EUR 200,000.00 over a period of three years (for undertakings in the transport sector the threshold is EUR 100,000.00) is legal without an approval by the European Commission. Due to the current financial crisis the threshold for de minimis aid granted on the basis of state programs temporarily has been increased to EUR 500,000.00.[10]

G. Existing Aid vs. New Aid

Beyond these exceptions, EU law distinguishes between existing and new aid.[11] For the beneficiary this difference is crucial: Commission decisions on existing aid can only have effect in the future; thus a beneficiary does not have to return what he received in the past. Rather he has some time to adopt his position to meet the future requirements.[12] One example of an existing aid scheme which has been considered incompatible with the EU state aid rules by the European Commission was the preferential tax regime for Luxembourg Holdings. The scheme was granted under a Luxembourg law from 1929. The Commission decided that the preferential tax regime violated state aid rules and required the scheme to be repealed by the end of

7 For the temporary state aid rules established in response to the economic and financial crisis see http://ec.europa.eu/competition/state_aid/legislation/temporary.html.

8 See Council Regulation (EC) No 994/98 of 7 May 1998 on the application of Articles 92 and 93 (now 107 and 108 respectively) of the Treaty establishing the European Community to certain categories of horizontal State aid, published in Official Journal of the European Union L 142 of 14.5.1998.

9 Commission Regulation (EC) No 1998/2006 of 15 December 2006 on the application of Articles 87 and 88 of the Treaty to de minimis aid, published in Official Journal L 379 of 28.12.2006.

10 See "Communication of the Commission: Temporary Union framework for State aid measures to support access to finance in the current financial and economic crisis, published in Official Journal of the European Union C 6 of 11.1.2011.

11 See Chapter II and Chapter V of Council Regulation (EC) No 659/1999 of 22 March 199 laying down detailed rules for the application of Article 93 of the EC Treaty, published in Official Journal of the European Union L 83 of 27.3.1999.

12 See Art. 18 Regulation 659/1999.

2006, while its effects for the existing holdings had to be definitively eliminated only by the end of 2010.[13] A new aid on the other hand which is declared incompatible[14] with the internal market means that the beneficiary's past position is at stake. In practice, the focus of the control of state aid practice is on new aid.

H. Standstill and Prohibition to Implement a Measure

With regard to new aid, any measure which is not covered by an exemption regulation and which a member state puts into effect before the European Commission's approval is considered unlawful.[15] Thus, before approval an aid cannot be put into effect and both the member state and the potential beneficiary of the aid are obliged to "stand still".

To achieve approval by the Commission, EU law provides an ex ante control through a notification procedure.[16] Accordingly, any plans to grant new aid must be notified by the member state to the Commission prior to implementation.[17] In a first step of the procedure, the Commission examines whether the notified measure constitutes state aid and whether it raises doubts as to its compatibility with the internal market.[18] If the Commission does not take a decision within two months after receipt of the notification, the member state as a rule may put into effect the aid.[19] To safeguard a proper assessment the notification needs to provide all necessary information and the Commission is entitled to issue formal information requests to the notifying member states.[20]

---

13 See Commission Decision of 19 July 2006 on aid scheme C 3/2006 implemented by Luxembourg for 1929 holding companies and billionaire holding companies, published in Official Journal of the European Union L 366 of 21.12.2006.

14 See Art. 7 (5) Regulation 659/1999.

15 See Art. 108 (3) TFEU.

16 See Chapter II Regulation 659/1999.

17 Detailed provisions concerning the form, the content and the calculation of time limits in all procedures concerning state aid including the notification of new aid are set out in Commission Regulation (EC) No 794/2004 of 21th April 2004 implementing Council Regulation (EC) No 659/1999 of 22th March 199 laying down detailed rules for the application of Art. 93 of the EC Treaty, published in Official Journal of the European Union L 140 of 30th April 2004.

18 See Art. 4 (2) and (3) Regulation 659/1999.

19 See Art. 4 (6) Regulation 659/1999.

20 See Art. 2 (2) and 5 Regulation 659/1999.

Where, after the preliminary examination, the Commission finds that the notified measure might distort competition, it will initiate formal investigation proceedings.[21] The formal investigation procedure is concluded by issuing either a:

- Positive decision, stating that the notified measure does not constitute state aid or is compatible with the internal market;[22]
- A conditional decision, i. e. attaching to a positive decision certain conditions;[23] or
- A negative decision, stating that the notified measure is not compatible with the internal market.[24]

Besides this, the Commission may, until it has taken a decision, require the member state to suspend or to provisionally recover any aid.[25] Beneficiaries have to accept that they are not a party to the notification procedure. While German authorities welcome preparatory work by the beneficiaries up to the full drafting of the notification, it is still the authorities – in the end the Federal Ministry of Economics – that decides whether or not a notification to the European Commission is submitted.

I. Recovery of Unlawful State Aid

In the event that the European Commission finds that the aid is incompatible with the internal market, and if the aid has already been paid, the Commission will render a decision that the member has to recover the aid from the beneficiary.[26] In this respect, German authorities are required to recover the aid including interest in accordance with German procedural rules without delay and must safeguard immediate and effective execution of the respective recovery decision.[27] The interest shall be payable from the date on which the unlawful aid was at the disposal of the beneficiary. In 2010, the Commission ordered recovery of a total of EUR 530,000,000 in unlawful state aid, bringing the total amount of aid recovered to EUR 10,9 billion in the last 10 years.[28]

Consequently, for the beneficiary of state aid it is crucial to ascertain that the aid it received has been properly notified to and approved by the Commission since even

21 In its decision to initiate the formal procedure, the EU Commission shall besides other summarize the relevant issues of fact and law, including a preliminary assessment as to the aid character.
22 See Art. 7 (3) Regulation 659/1999.
23 See Art. 7 (4) Regulation 659/1999.
24 See Art. 7 (5) Regulation 659/1999.
25 See Art. 11 Regulation 659/1999.
26 See Art. 14 (1) and (3) Regulation 659/1999.
27 See Art. 14 (2) Regulation 659/1999.
28 See Commission's Press Release IP 11/201 of 18.02.2011, available at http://europa.eu/rapid.

the principle of German law, that legitimate expectations are protected, will usually not serve as a means to prevent recovery.

J. Judicial Review

There is abundant case law from German courts and the European Court of Justice in public subsidies and state aid law. The courts held, for example, that the prohibition on putting aid into effect without the prior approval of the Commission has direct effect, i. e. that undertakings can rely on this provision when contesting a Commission decision or an aid granted to a competitor. National judges must enforce the standstill obligation and have to safeguard the rights of individuals deriving from this principle. Consequently, there are many factual situations in which beneficiaries of state aid, their competitors or the Commission and the member states may seek judicial review. However, quite a few legal issues are open still. Court actions can be pursued at European and national courts.

I. Protection Granted by European Courts

The beneficiary can seek the annulment of any Commission decision in front of the General Court.[29] For example, the would-be recipient can attack a negative decision of the European Commission which deprives it of an expected aid. Even in the event that the Commission does not act, the beneficiary can bring an action for failure to act to the European courts.[30]

Competitors can seek the annulment of a Commission decision declaring the aid compatible with the internal market. However, it should be noted that in order to bring an action for annulment to the General Court, just being a competitor is not sufficient. Rather the competitor has to show that it is directly and individually concerned and that it has a legal interest in bringing the proceedings to court, which can be very difficult to demonstrate in practice.[31]

II. Enforcement of State Aid Rules by German Courts

The beneficiary can seek recourse to German courts if Germany conducts a recovery procedure. Competitors can sue in front of the German courts in order to prevent

---

29 See Art. 263 (2) and (4) TFEU.

30 See Art. 265 (1) and (3) TFEU.

31 In this respect, in case C-78/03 P "*Commission/ARE*" Advocate General Jacobs even stated that the case law on the standing of natural and legal persons seeking to challenge state aid decisions is plainly unsatisfactory for being complex, apparently illogical, and inconsistent.

that illegal aid is paid out to the beneficiary or to achieve that the beneficiary has to pay back the subsidy including interest. German courts can also give competitors access to those documents of the authority that show which amounts have been granted to a beneficiary.[32] Claims for damages are conceivable. Even though the European Commission keeps the exclusive power to decide on the compatibility of aid with the internal market, the enforcement of EU state aid law before national courts is strongly promoted and supported by the Commission.[33]

Dr. Helmut Janssen, LL.M. (London)
helmut.janssen@luther-lawfirm.com

Dr. Thomas Kapp, LL.M. (UCLA)
thomas.kapp@luther-lawfirm.com

32 See judgments of the Federal Supreme Court in the "Airport cases" of 10.02.2011 (BGH I ZR 213/08 and BGH I ZR 136/09).

33 See Commission notice on the enforcement of State aid law by national courts, OJ C85/1, 9.4.2009.

CHAPTER 9
UNFAIR COMPETITION LAW

DR. WULFF-AXEL SCHMIDT

German law comprises several acts against unfair competition. Although there is no "European Act Against Unfair Competition", in Europe the national laws against unfair competition are largely consistent nowadays.

The aim of competition law is to ensure the protection of free competition for the benefit of participants in commerce. In Germany, the basic rules are set out in the "Act Against Unfair Competition" (*Gesetz gegen den unlauteren Wettbewerb, UWG*). The European Law Against Unfair Competition has now been largely harmonized by the "Unfair Commercial Practices Directive" (EU Directive No. 2005/29/EC) which was implemented into German Law by the amended UWG with effect from 30th December 2008. Whilst the protection of consumers is the main objective of the reform, the UWG also explicitly seeks to protect competitors and the general public's interest in undistorted competition.

In 2004 and 2008, the UWG was thoroughly revised in order to modernize the German Law Against Unfair Competition. One of the objectives of these reforms was the deregulation of markets. The comparatively restrictive Directive, however, partly reversed this deregulation process. For instance, under the harmonized law any omission of information that could be essential in order to enable consumers to make a decision may be considered misleading – such a general duty to provide information did not previously exist under German Law.

Sec. 3 UWG now prohibits "unfair commercial practices", i. e. acts or omissions before, during or even after the conclusion of a contract. The new term replaces the term "unfair competition act" and covers all kinds of commercial acts and omissions directly related to the promotion, sale or supply of products, including their advertising and marketing. Another novelty is that breaches of General Terms and Conditions Law may entitle competitors to bring an action against the user of the respective general terms and conditions wherever those were used ("flying jurisdiction"). In order to assure legal certainty Europe-wide and a smooth functioning of the internal market, the harmonized law therefore contains a "blacklist" which defines several commercial practices considered to be automatically unfair.

Sec. 3 (1) UWG is the basic rule which provides that "unfair commercial practices" are prohibited, whilst Sects. 4 to 7 UWG provide for a non-exhaustive list of the commercial practices that would usually be considered as being unfair and, therefore, illegal. In addition, the "blacklist" defines several irrefutably illegal, misleading and aggressive commercial practices considered as being an unfair influence on consumers.

According to Sec. 8 et seq. UWG, a person or legal entity in breach of the UWG may be subject to a cease and desist claim as well as a damage claim and may also incur a penalty.

A. Unfair Influence on Customers

In principle, traders are obliged to advertise their products and services without encroaching upon the customer's independent judgment and free choice. Advertising statements regarding the quality, quantity, origin and price of products and services shall be true, accurate and not misleading. For instance, superlatives such as "the best" or "the largest" may not be used if it cannot be shown that the advertised trader, product or service is significantly better or larger in comparison to the competitors or their products or services. Signs which may be understood as indications of origin may not be used if the products are, in fact, not produced in the respective place or region. Furthermore, product information may also be misleading where an allegedly "independent" third party opinion is referred to in advertisements, for example, and where such third party is found, in fact, to not actually be acting independently from the advertising party.

As the price is one of the most important factors for a customer decision to buy, traders are easily tempted in advertising their products to go beyond what is permitted by law. As a result, there is a vast amount of case law. Price comparisons can be comparisons with one's own prices, with the manufacturer's recommended prices or else with competitor's prices. Such comparisons are generally permitted.

However, making a comparison with one's own prices, the current price is normally compared to a previous, higher price. In this regard, courts have ruled that shop-opening offers which show the offer prices next to crossed-out prices must indicate the term of validity. Comparisons with recommended retail prices must also be clearly identified as such. A particular wording is not required. Using the abbreviation "UVP" (the German abbreviation for "recommended retail price") would, for example, be permitted.

Furthermore, using artificially high prices for advertising purposes as a special form of advertising by making a comparison with one's own prices is generally prohibited pursuant to Sec. 5 (4) UWG. With this form of advertising, the trader raises his prices shortly before the advertising campaign in order to then be able to reduce them again and point out the price reduction. For example, a campaign was stopped by the courts where a store had used the slogan "20 % on all products except for animal feed" even though certain products had been cheaper during the week before the campaign than during the campaign.

"Unfair influence" on a customer may also be seen as a "psychological coercion" which encroaches upon a customer's free choice. As a consequence of an aggressive sales approach, for instance, a customer may feel obliged to purchase a product which he or she might otherwise not have been interested in. This may be the case if a customer has to enter a shop in order to receive a gift or, if a customer receives goods which he or she did not order. In order to restrict such situations which may lead to psychological coercion, regulations concerning sweepstakes, lotteries or competitions relating to the disposal of products or services are very strict. It has been impossible so far to generate profits directly through lotteries or competitions, giving that linking the sale of goods to a lottery or competition was deemed impermissible from a fair practices perspective (Sec. 4 No. 6 UWG). Indeed, lotteries and competitions can be very tempting so that when combined with a sale, they can, in individual cases, inappropriately influence a buyer's decision to make a purchase (Sec. 4 No. 1 UWG). The prohibition on linking lotteries or competitions to the sale of goods or the provision of services has been dealt with in numerous court decisions in recent years. Following corresponding decisions of the European Court of Justice, in 2010 the Federal Court of Justice has ultimately held that this prohibition violates European law.

Already prior to the decisions by the European Court of Justice, German courts had displayed a tendency towards liberalizing the prohibition of linking a lottery or competition to the sale of goods or provision of services. Whereas such a combination, in whatever form, had previously been deemed impermissible, the Federal Court of Justice held that a combination within the meaning of Sec. 4 No. 6 UWG requires that the participation in the lottery or competition be independent of the good or service offered. The Federal Court of Justice further held that if winning had a direct effect on the goods or services or the payment for such, the combination was not an unfair practice, but rather a special pricing method.

The European Court of Justice's decisions and the Federal Court of Justice's judgment that implements the requirements could materially affect the future assessment of linking a lottery or competition to the purchase of goods. Such a combination is, in the final analysis, a business act which needs to be assessed on the basis of the normal elements of unfair practices. However, linking a lottery or competition to the sale of goods or the provision of services can still be prohibited in a particular case.

As to the question whether an omission of information should be regarded as being misleading, the law provides that one shall particularly consider the relevance of the information for the business decision according to common opinion as well as the general possibility that such kind of omission influences such kind of decision.

If products or services are offered in a way that enables an average consumer to decide that he or she wants to buy these products or services without any additional act or statement of the offerer, i. e. in the case of mail orders based on catalogues or websites, the provider is in either case obliged to provide detailed information about the product or service, its identity and address, terms and conditions of the contract, a possible right of withdrawal.

The law basically prohibits advertising via telephone calls, automated calling systems, e-mails and faxes which are targeted at consumers and other market participants who have not explicitly agreed to receive such advertisements. An exception applies to direct advertising via e-mail where there is already an established customer relationship and if the customer is given the opportunity to reject this kind of advertising at any time. In case of e-mail advertising, the person or legal entity responsible for the advertising, as well as a valid address that the receiver can use to request their removal from the general mailing list, has to be displayed.

The so-called "blacklist" mentions several commercial practices considered as being an unfair influence on consumers and therefore being irrefutably illegal. For instance, a trader may state that they have signed a code of conduct when this is not true or offer products or services at a certain price without disclosing any grounds he may have for believing that he will not be able to supply these products or services at that price for an appropriate time in appropriate quantities (bait advertising). Also, a trader may not create the impression that a consumer will be prevented from leaving a certain location until a contract is concluded.

Advertising by appealing to a customer's social responsibility, so-called "social sponsoring", is a subtype of the former case group of emotional marketing. Social sponsoring appeals to an individual's social responsibility and aims at making the customer believe that by buying a particular product or particular company's products, he is doing a good deed.

Companies increasingly use social sponsoring both to improve their image and to promote a particular product. Purely image-related marketing means that a company tries to improve its public image in general, unrelated to any sales, by providing support in connection with social or environmental issues. With so-called cause-related marketing, companies advertise a product by promising to make all or part of the proceeds from the sale of such product available for a good cause.

In its earlier rulings, the Federal Court of Justice held emotional sponsoring to be an unfair practice if there was no objective relation between the offer and the emotions appealed to. In later judgments, the Federal Court of Justice took the view that the absence of an objective relation between the commitment referred to in the advertisement and the advertised product alone was not sufficient to make appealing to a person's social sense of responsibility, readiness to help others, compassion, or environmental awareness an unfair practice. With a reference to the materials prepared in connection with the amendment of the Act Against Unfair Competition in 2004, the Federal Court of Justice additionally declined any duty of the advertiser to inform prospective customers of the type and the scope or amount of the support granted to the social institution, giving as a reason that the legislative bodies had expressly decided against a general transparency requirement. As a result, it is today permissible for advertisement to not contain any explicit information about the extent of the advertiser's social commitment.

Even though recent case law is very liberal, it does not result in absolute freedom of advertising when it comes to social sponsoring: the limits imposed by the Act Against Unfair Competition still need to be observed. It is therefore still an unfair practice to perform acts of competition which are apt to interfere with a consumer's or other market actor's freedom of decision by exerting an inappropriate influence that is not related to the product concerned.

B. Unfair Restraint of Competition

The law further prohibits unfair restraints on competition. Even if such unfair restraints can only be traced back to the superior performance of a competitor, certain acts may still constitute unfair practices if that competitor intended to constrain certain other competitors or prevent competition in general. For instance, price undercutting may violate "good ethics" if this is done with an unfair intention. Competition may be restrained by an extensive distribution of free products. Plagiarism as well as taking advantage of or being detrimental to a competitor's reputation may also be considered as being unfair according to the UWG.

Comparative advertising is permitted in principle. Having been restrictive in the past, German courts nowadays adopt a more liberal approach towards comparative advertising. However, the UWG prohibits comparative advertising if it could lead to a likelihood of confusion regarding the products of competitors, for instance, or, if it contains criticism of the products or services of a competitor.

C. Violations of Other Laws as "Unfair Commercial Practices"

The general public's interest in undistorted competition may be affected by violations of other laws. Violations of laws other than those dealing directly with unfair commercial practices may therefore be considered as an infringement of "good ethics" if they result from a competitive action and have an impact on competition. For example, a breach of the law of contract may constitute unfair commercial practice, particularly in relation to distribution systems. Breaches of laws aimed at protecting important areas of public interest, for example laws related to public health, could also constitute unfair commercial practices.

Dr. Wulff-Axel Schmidt
wulff-axel.schmidt@luther-lawfirm.com

CHAPTER 10
ANTITRUST LAW

DR. HELMUT JANSSEN
DR. THOMAS KAPP

Price-fixing cartels, market sharing arrangements, territorial and customer restrictions, bid rigging, resale price maintenance, discrimination by dominant firms, creation of market dominance by way of combination with other companies – these are but a few examples of where anti-competitive practices face legal consequences in Germany. German antitrust law is highly developed. Its rules have been long-tested, and there is abundant case law. There are specialized cartel authorities, courts and members of the legal profession that deal with antitrust cases on a daily basis.

A. Main Provisions and Actors

The main provisions applicable to anticompetitive conduct in Germany are contained in the Act Against Restraints of Competition (*Gesetz gegen Wettbewerbsbeschränkungen*, *GWB*) and in Art. 101 to Art. 106 of the Treaty on the Functioning of the European Union (TFEU) and the regulations based on it (especially the Merger Regulation, see Sec. H). Both the GWB and the TFEU (or its predecessor the "Treaty of Rome") date back to 1958 and have been amended several times since. The main institutions enforcing antitrust law in Germany are the Federal Cartel Office (*Bundeskartellamt, hereinafter "FCO"*), and the European Commission. Appeals against decisions of the FCO are handled by one court with a specific jurisdiction (*Oberlandesgericht Düsseldorf*) whose decisions are subject to judicial review by a specific antitrust law body of the Federal Court of Justice (*Bundesgerichtshof*). Appeals against decisions of the European Commission can be raised with the General Court and the European Court of Justice in Luxemburg. Private actions involving antitrust law are common in Germany, especially in cases of refusal to supply. They can be brought before nearly every civil law court. Private actions for damages are a relatively new phenomenon. However, Germany has for several years become a rather popular jurisdiction to initiate legal proceedings on behalf of damaged parties in the aftermath of the discovery of cartel cases. In particular, it seems that German courts are inclined to grant damages without placing a too heavy burden of proof on the plaintiff.

B. Applicability of Antitrust Law in Germany

The GWB covers restrictions of competition that have an effect within Germany, even if such restraints have their origin abroad. The TFEU catches anti-competitive practices that restrict trade within the European Union (EU) and is applicable in parallel to the GWB. Companies that are based outside of Germany or the EU thus may need to comply with the rules in Germany, for example if foreign manufacturers agree on terms and conditions for exports to Germany.

Where trade between member states of the EU is affected, the GWB may not deviate from the TFEU. However, both acts are nearly identical so that in practice usually no distinction between them is necessary. An exception to this rule is the treatment of companies with a "strong market position" (see Sec. G), where German law can prohibit certain practices even if these do not infringe EU law. Furthermore, German and EU merger control law vary to some extent. While both the GWB and the TFEU want to protect freedom of competition, EU antitrust law also has as its objective the integration of the internal European market. Furthermore, consumer welfare seems to be a concept that is advocated more by the European Commission than the FCO. This can sometimes lead to different results in practice depending upon whether the TFEU or the GWB is applicable and which authority or court applies them.

C. Sanctions

Antitrust law infringements can lead to various sanctions. First, there are civil law sanctions. That means for example that an anti-competitive agreement can be null and void and consequently it is unenforceable in court. Another example is an anti-competitive refusal to supply where the customer can obtain a court order to supply him. A more common example recently is actions for damages. Damages are to compensate a loss and (unlike US law) may not have punitive character, hence no "treble damages" in Germany. Second, there are public law sanctions. The FCO regularly imposes fines on individuals; the maximum amount is EUR 1,000,000.00 (the European Commission as a rule cannot fine individuals). The company to which the anti-competitive conduct is attributed can also be fined. The maximum is 10 % of the turnover of the group to which the company belongs. Neither EU law nor German law treat offences against antitrust regulations as criminal acts. However, a conduct like bid-rigging constitutes a criminal offence (independent of antitrust law) and in some cases has resulted in imprisonment of managers.

D. Horizontal Restraints

Restrictions between competitors are commonly referred to as horizontal restraints. They are treated by the GWB and the TFEU in the same way. First, there is the general prohibition of such restraints. Second, there are block exemption regulations that render certain restrictions legal. And third, there is a general exemption clause. If an agreement restricts competition and falls neither under a block exemption regulation nor under the general exemptions clause, the sanctions outlined above will be triggered.

The general prohibition covers all agreements or concerted practices between competitors aiming at or causing restrictions of competition.[1] A competitor is not only a company that is currently active on a specific market; it suffices if this company could at any time enter the market (is a "potential" competitor). Similarly prohibited are decisions by associations of competing companies (trade associations) that restrict competition. Only those restrictions are caught that have an appreciable effect on competition. The typical hardcore cartels like price fixing, quota fixing, customer sharing, and big-rigging are caught by this prohibition and relentlessly prosecuted by the authorities. However, there are a lot of horizontal agreements that do not constitute hardcore cartels and are exempted from the cartel prohibition.

Agreements that fall within the scope of a block exemption regulation are, as a rule, permitted. Horizontal block exemptions cover e. g. specialization agreements[2] and research and development agreements.[3] The European Commission has issued horizontal guidelines[4] in addition to these block exemption regulations. There are specific block exemptions for agriculture, transport and insurance.

The general exemption clause permits all restrictive agreements that contribute to the improvement of production or distribution of goods or the promotion of technical or economic progress, while allowing consumers a fair share of the resulting benefit; they have to be indispensable and must not eliminate competition.[5] This

---

1 Art. 101 (1) TFEU; Sec. 1 GWB.

2 Commission Regulation (EU) No 1218/2010 of 14th December 2010 on the application of Art. 101 (3) of the Treaty on the Functioning of the European Union to certain categories of specialisation agreements (OJ L 335/43, 18.12.2010).

3 Commission Regulation (EU) No 1217/2010 of 14th December 2010 on the application of Art. 101 (3) of the Treaty on the Functioning of the European Union to certain categories of research and development agreements, (OJ L 335/36, 18.12.2010).

4 Guidelines on the applicability of Art. 101 of the Treaty on the Functioning of the European Union to horizontal cooperation agreements (OJ C 11/1, 14.1.2011).

5 Art. 101 (3) TFEU; Sec. 2 GWB.

clause is self-executing, which was different until 2004 (EU law) and 2005 (GWB). That means a formal clearance decision or any other administrative act by the FCO or the European Commission is neither necessary nor usually attainable. This general exemption clause might apply in typical cooperation situations where the parties are not heading for a hardcore restriction of competition (research and development, specialization, joint purchase, joint marketing activities, joint production, etc.). In practice, it is often cumbersome (and sometimes impossible) to claim that an agreement that is not covered by a block exemption regulation falls under the general exemption clause of Art. 101 (3) TFEU.

E. Vertical Restraints

Vertical restraints are restrictions between companies that do not operate on the same level of the production or distribution chain, but rather in terms of, e.g., manufacturer/wholesaler or wholesaler/retailer. Very often vertical restraints are beneficial for the market and customers and are consequently treated more benignly by antitrust law. There is a rather limited number of hardcore restrictions (e.g. resale price maintenance).

Technically, vertical restraints are not treated differently from horizontal agreements. That means: if a vertical agreement restricts competition (for example a clause granting territorial exclusivity to a distributor) such a restrictive clause or sometimes even the whole agreement is null and void unless it benefits from an exemption granted either by a block exemption regulation or by the general exemption clause. The most frequent restrictions in vertical relationships are exempted from the antitrust prohibition of the TFEU or the GWB by the block exemption regulation for vertical restraints.[6] One of the conditions for the applicability of this block exemption regulation is that the market share of neither company involved exceeds 30 %. Under this condition, for example, maximum resale prices, price recommendations, most favored customer clauses, and typical restrictions in distribution and in franchising contracts are admissible. The European Commission has published vertical guidelines to complement the block exemption regulation.[7] Until June 2013 there is a specific block exemption on the distribution of motor vehicles and a third one covers technology transfer agreements.

6 Commission Regulation 330/2010 of 20 April 2010 on the application of Art. 101 (3) of the Treaty on the Functioning of the European Union to categories of vertical agreements and concerted practices (OJ L 102, 23.4.2010).

7 Guidelines on Vertical Restraints (OJ C 130/1, 19.5.2010).

F. Licensing Agreements

Licensing Agreements typically raise questions that are not properly addressed by the horizontal and vertical block exemption regulations. The European Commission therefore has issued a specific block exemption regulation and guidelines for the technology transfer agreements.[8]

G. Dominant Companies

Art. 102 TFEU and Sects. 19, 20 GWB prohibit the abusive unilateral behavior of a dominant company. German and EU law apply basically the same criteria for defining the relevant market on which a dominant position may be exercised and for determining whether a company is actually dominant. In the words of the European Court of Justice dominance is

"*... a position of economic strength enjoyed by an undertaking which enables it to prevent effective competition being maintained on the relevant market by affording it the power to behave to an appreciable extent independently of its competitors, its customers and ultimately of the consumers. ... Very large market shares are highly significant evidence of the existence of a dominant position. Other relevant factors are the relationship between market shares of the undertaking concerned and of its competitors, especially those of the next largest, the technological lead of the undertaking over its competitors, the existence of a highly developed sales network and the absence of potential competition.*[9]"

According to its practice the European Commission usually considers that a market share of 50 % grants dominance. The GWB contains rebuttable assumptions of market dominance:[10] a company is considered dominant that has a market share of one third or more. Further legal assumptions are that if three companies or fewer have a market share of 50 % or more or if five companies or fewer have a market share of two thirds or more, all of these companies are considered dominant. These assumptions are rebuttable if the market situation does not allow them relevant market power. Recent reform discussions (April 2012) propose to raise the thresholds.

---

8 Commission Regulation (EC) No 772/2004 of 27 April 2004 on the application of Article 81(3) of the Treaty to categories of technology transfer agreements (OJ L 123/11, 27.4.2004) 346; and Guidelines on the application of Art. 81 of the EC Treaty to technology transfer agreements (OJ C 101/2, 27.4.2004).

9 European Court of Justice, Judgment of 13 February 1979, ECR 1979, 461, 520 – Hoffmann-La Roche & Co. AG v Commission of the European Communities.

10 Sec. 19 (3) GWB.

Unlike Art. 102 TFEU the GWB declares the abuse prohibition applicable not only to dominant companies but also to those with a strong market position. This difference means that in cross-border cases, certain behavior that is legal under Art. 102 TFEU can be prohibited by the GWB. A strong market position can exist in relation to competitors where a company has superior market power in relation to small and medium-sized competitors.[11] In relation to customers such a position exists if small and medium-sized companies depend on the supply of certain products in such a way that there are no sufficient and reasonable alternatives of supply.[12]

Companies that have a dominant position (or according to the GWB have a strong market position) may neither abuse this position nor discriminate or hinder other businesses in an unfair manner. Abuse triggers the legal consequence outlined above: substantial administrative fines and civil law consequences such as damages. There are three basic forms of abuse. The first type deals in particular with the relationship between the dominant company and its competitors. An abuse exists if the dominant company – without having any objective justification – impairs the ability of other companies to act on the market in a competitive manner. This rule applies, for example, to some rebate systems. The second type of abuse is so-called exploitation. Exploitation is deemed to exist if, for example, the dominant company requests a price or asks for business conditions different from those that would be likely if effective competition existed. The third type of abuse is discrimination: so the dominant company is prevented from requesting a less favorable price or business conditions than it requests from customers in comparable markets, unless the difference is objectively justified.

Typical cases of abuse are: imposition of unfair purchase or selling prices or unfair trading conditions; hindrance of another company in an unfair manner in business activities, especially the refusal to provide a competitor access to one's own infrastructure (so-called essential facilities); tying arrangements; the refusal to deal; and predatory pricing. Recently, the European Commission issued a communication on its enforcement priorities with respect to Art. 102 TFEU.[13] It focuses on abusive exclusionary conduct and emphasizes a more economic approach in the assessment of potentially abusive behavior. This approach is more effects-based and gives a high priority to consumer welfare. It is not yet clear, however, whether the courts will follow that line.

---

11 Sec. 20 (4) GWB.

12 Sec. 20 (2) GWB.

13 Communication from the Commission — Guidance on the Commission's enforcement priorities in applying Art. 82 of the EC Treaty to abusive exclusionary conduct by dominant undertakings (OJ 24.2.2009, C 45/7).

H. Merger Control

The acquisition of all or a substantial part of a company's assets or shares, a public takeover, or the creation of a joint venture – these are typical transactions that qualify for merger control.[14] Both the EU and the GWB merger control rules request that a merger must be submitted for approval to the European Commission or the FCO respectively before it can be implemented. Failing to do so (or disregarding a prohibition decision by the authority) renders the transaction unenforceable and the companies can be heavily fined. If certain turnover thresholds of the companies involved are exceeded, the EU merger control regulation applies exclusively (i. e. the GWB rules will not apply) and usually the European Commission will conduct the investigation. However, it is possible to request a referral of the case from the European Commission to the FCO. Should the turnover of the companies involved fall short of the EU thresholds but exceed the GWB threshold, the GWB rules will apply and the FCO will conduct the investigation. If three or more EU member states are competent to investigate the merger, a referral to the European Commission is possible.

Under the EU merger regulation[15] the acquisition of control of one company over another ("concentration") must be notified if the following turnover thresholds are exceeded:

- The combined aggregate worldwide turnover of the companies involved exceeds EUR 5 billion and the aggregate EU-wide turnover of each of at least two of the companies exceeds EUR 250,000,000 or
- The combined aggregate turnover exceeds EUR 2.5 billion on a worldwide basis, the combined aggregate turnover of all companies concerned furthermore exceeds EUR 100,000,000 in each of at least three EU member states and the aggregate turnover of each of at least two of the companies concerned exceeds EUR 25,000,000 in the aforementioned three member states and the aggregate EU-wide turnover of each of at least two of the companies concerned exceeds EUR 100 million.

Even if a concentration fulfills these criteria, the EU merger regulation will not apply if each of the companies concerned achieves more than two-thirds of its aggregate EU-wide turnover in one and the same EU member state.

14 Under German merger control the acquisition of shares representing more than 25 % of the target's capital or voting rights also qualify for merger control, in some cases even in the case of the acquisition of shares of less than 25 %.

15 Council Regulation (EC) No 139/2004 of 20 January 2004 on the control of concentrations between undertakings (OJ L 24/1, 29 January 2004).

If the concentration would significantly impede effective competition in the EU, the European Commission will prohibit it. This will occur in particular if the concentration creates or strengthens a dominant position. The procedure is split in two phases: within 25 working days after receipt of the complete notification the European Commission has to decide whether it intends to initiate a closer investigation. It must, as a rule, pass a final decision within 90 working days after the procedure has begun.

Under the GWB rules[16] a transaction has to be notified to the FCO if

- The annual worldwide turnover of all companies involved exceeds EUR 500,000,000 and
- The total turnover in Germany of one participating company exceeded EUR 25,000,000 and of another participating company EUR 5,000,000 in the business year preceding the merger.

There are exceptions for de-minimis markets and de-minimis transactions. Turnover generated from certain business transactions (for example by publishing companies or trading in goods) is calculated in a different manner than under the EU merger regulation. For both the EU and the GWB regimes, the turnover figures of all affiliated companies controlled by or controlling one of the participating companies must be added.

The FCO has to prohibit mergers that might create or strengthen a dominant market position, unless the participating companies can demonstrate that the joining of their forces would in effect promote competition and that this would outweigh the disadvantages of their dominant market position. Unlike the EU merger control law the GWB operates with various legal assumptions as to market dominance (see Sec. G).

The FCO has one month after receipt of the complete notification to decide whether it will initiate a full-fledged investigation. If it does not do so the merger is deemed approved. It has become the practice of the FCO in unproblematic cases to inform the parties before the end of the one-month deadline that it sees no reasons to prohibit the transaction. When the FCO however decides to enter a full-fledged investigation the duration of its review is extended from one to four months.

16 Sec. 35 GWB.

I. Damages

Claiming for damages on the basis of antitrust law infringements is no new phenomenon in Germany. Damages actions raised by customers against members of price cartels were, however, rare. This changed due to an amendment of the GWB in 2005. Furthermore, the European Court of Justice has held that the EU member states' law must foresee that the EU antitrust rules can be enforced by private claimants.[17] And for some years already, the European Commission has been advocating strongly the private enforcement of antitrust law. In spring 2008 it issued a so-called White Paper on damages actions for breach of the EU antitrust rules which was to be followed by a draft bill in summer 2009. After heavy criticism by member states this draft has disappeared from the agenda for the time being. A somewhat broader initiative by the European Commission ("collective redress") is slowly progressing.

German legislation facilitates private cartel enforcement. One example is the joint and several liability of all companies participating in a cartel. This means that the victim of a cartel is free to decide whether he pursues a claim against one or more participants – in any event he can claim his entire damages from any of them. Also, the claimant can base his action on a (non-appealable) decision of an antitrust authority of an EU member state, as such a decision will be treated as binding on the parties in civil litigation. In such so-called follow-on proceedings, the period of limitation is extended until six months after the final termination of the investigations of the cartel authorities. On the other hand, there are no US style class actions in Germany. However, bundling of interests is possible. Currently, there are several cases pending in which the claimants are demanding damages for losses suffered from cartel behavior. Many aspects of substantial and procedural law are not settled yet. Just recently the Federal Supreme Court[18] issued a decision according to which cartel members can call upon the passing-on defense: cartel members will not be liable if their direct customers (e.g., wholesalers) passed on the damage to the next market level (indirect customers, e.g., retailers). Also, the tensions arising from a stronger private antitrust enforcement and public enforcement are increasing. A highly relevant example is that FCO and the European Commission warrant that leniency applications and accompanying material provided by whistleblowers will be kept confidential. Whether the FCO is entitled to lock away its files from cartel victims is under heavy debate right now. Recently, the European Court of Justice has held that EU law does not prevent the national authority or judge from granting access to the

17 European Court of Justice, Judgment of 20 September 2001, ECR 2001, I-6297 – Courage Ltd v Bernard Crehan, Judgment of 13 July 2006, ECR *2004, I-1605* – Vincenzo Manfredi v Lloyd Adriatico Assicurazioni SpA.

18 Federal Court of Justice, decision of 28 June 2011 – KZR 75/10.

authorities' file.[19] While the court requires a balancing of the interests of the claimants and the functioning of the leniency program, it did not give any further indication as to such balancing. It is not yet decided how this contradiction between public and private enforcement will be resolved.[20]

Dr. Thomas Kapp, LL.M. (UCLA)
thomas.kapp@luther-lawfirm.com

Dr. Helmut Janssen, LL.M. (London)
helmut.janssen@luther-lawfirm.com

19 European Court of Justice, decision of 14 June 2011, C-360/09 – Pfleiderer vs. Bundeskartellamt.

20 For a recent decision see Amtsgericht Bonn of 18.1.2012 (51 GS 53/09).

CHAPTER 11
PROTECTION OF PLANT INNOVATIONS

THOMAS LEIDEREITER, LL.M.

Effectively protecting the results of breeding and R&D work is of utmost importance in the agricultural as well as in the horticultural industry. Effective protection requires a sophisticated strategy making use of the various available IP protection systems. Plant variety rights form an essential part of the IP strategy of breeders.

In Germany plant innovations, in particular, newly developed[1] plant varieties, may be protected by plant variety rights ("PVR"). Although similar to a patent, the PVR regime is a protection system *sui generis* and, therefore, different from the (German) patent system.[2] Various decisions of the (Enlarged) Board of Appeal ("BoA") of the European Patent Office ("EPO") have clarified the border-line between patent and PVR protection for inventions in the field of bio-technology.[3] In essence, plant varieties[4] may not be patented.[5] Also essentially biological processes, in particular any non-microbiological process for the production of plants which contains or consists of the steps of sexually crossing the whole genomes of plants and of subsequently selecting plants, are in principle excluded from patentability.[6]

In the following, we fill focus on the protection of new plant varieties under the Community plant variety rights ("CPVR") regime. Although a German national legal system of protecting plant innovations through the granting of PVR exists, it

1 "Developed" to mean "bred" or "discovered and developed" under the applicable laws.

2 Art. 27 (2) (b) TRIPS "...However, Members shall provide for the protection of plant varieties either by patents or by an effective sui generis system or by any combination thereof..."

3 Cf. the decisions in cases G2/07 and 1/08 "Broccoli and Tomato"; G1/98 "NOVARTIS II"; T-356/83 "Plant Cells", T-320/87 "LUBRIZOL" and T-49/83 "CIBA-GEIGY"

4 Art. 1 (VI) of the UPOV 1991 convention: "'variety' means a plant grouping within a single botanical taxon of the lowest known rank, which grouping, irrespective of whether the conditions for the grant of a breeder's right are fully met, can be defined by the expression of the characteristics resulting from a given genotype or combination of genotypes, distinguished from any other plant grouping by the expression of at least one of the said characteristics and considered as a unit with regard to its suitability for being propagated unchanged"

5 Enlarged Board of Appeal decision in case no. G 1/98 "NOVARTIS II"

6 Enlarged Board of Appeal EPO, decision in case no. G 0001/08 "Broccoli and Tomato"

seems advisable to seek protection for plant innovations on a European level. The applicable Council Regulation[7] (hereinafter referred to as the "Basic Regulation" or "BR") established a uniform protection system for new varieties in the entire territory of the European Union, a market of 500 million customers. Under the Basic Regulation, varieties of all botanical genera and species, including, inter alia, hybrids between genera or species, may form the object of a CPVR.

A. Scope of Protection of a CPVR

A Community plant variety right may be granted for any variety[8] that is distinct, uniform, stable and new at the date of the application[9] and which is designated by a variety denomination. The variety may be the result of the breeding activities of the breeder, i. e. it has been created by crossing and selection or other breeding methods, or it is a variety that has been discovered and developed by the breeder, e.g. in case of a mutation. CPVR protection can be obtained for a period of 30 years for tree and vine varieties or 25 years for varieties of all other species, calculated from the grant of the right.

Protection under the CPVR regime covers *variety constituents*, i. e. whole plants or parts of plants of the protected variety, if these parts are capable of producing entire plants of the variety.[10] The following acts in respect of variety constituents or harvested material of the protected variety require the authorization of the holder of the CPVR: production or reproduction (multiplication); conditioning for the purpose of propagation; offering for sale; selling or marketing; exporting from or importing to the European Union or stocking for any of the aforesaid purposes.[11] The protection also covers so-called essentially derived varieties ("EDV", e. g. mutations of a protected variety).[12] There are limitations as to the use of variety constituents of a protected variety by farmers (the so called "farmers privilege"[13]) or the breeding of new

7 COUNCIL REGULATION (EC) No 2100/94 of 27 July 1994 on Community plant variety rights (OJ L 227, 1.9.1994, p. 1).

8 For the definition see Art. 5 (3) BR which is identical to Art. 1(VI) UPOV 1991.

9 All varieties are put to the so-called "DUS test", i. e. it is verified by the office that the variety is **D**istinct (Art. 7 BR), **U**niform (Art. 8 BR) and **S**table (Art. 9). In addition, plant material of the variety must not have been made accessible by the breeder or with his consent earlier than one year (in the EU) before to the application date (earlier than four years outside the EU).

10 Art. 5 (3) BR.

11 Art. 13 BR.

12 Currently, there still is a great deal of uncertainty related to the EDV concepts. In particular, no standardized thresholds with regard to the genetic conformity of an EDV to the initial variety exist.

13 Art. 14 BR.

varieties using material of a protected variety ("breeders' exemption"[14]). Also, the concept of exhaustion applies.[15]

B. Entitlement to and Application for a CPVR

The person who bred, or discovered and developed the variety or his successor in title, shall be entitled to apply for CPVR protection.[16] After a recent amendment of the applicable regulation, an application for a CPVR may be filed by any natural or legal person, or anybody ranking as a legal person under the law applicable to that body. A former limitation with regard to foreign applicants has been lifted in 2008. However, persons who are not domiciled or do not have a seat or an establishment within the territory of the European Union may participate as party to proceedings before the competent Community Plant Variety Office[17] ("CPVO") only if they have designated a procedural representative who is domiciled or has his seat or an establishment within the territory of the European Union.[18] An application for a CPVR may be filed jointly by two or more persons,[19] in particular if two or more persons bred, or discovered and developed the variety jointly. In this case, entitlement shall be vested jointly in them or their respective successors in title.[20] The application for a CPVR may be filed at the CPVO directly or at a national office, in Germany the *Bundessortenamt* in Hannover.[21] The application must be accompanied by a detailed description of the supposedly new variety and contain a proposal for a variety denomination. Today, an online application system is provided by the CPVO for an increasing number of botanical species.

C. Examination of the Application

Upon the receipt of an application, the CPVO will conduct a formal,[22] a substantive and a technical examination of the application. In the course of the formal examination, the CPVO verifies that the formal conditions of filing an application

14 Art. 15c BR.
15 Art. 16 BR pursuant to which the holder of a CPVR cannot enforce his rights in respect of any material of the protected variety, which has been disposed of to others by him or with his consent, unless special conditions are fulfilled.
16 Art. 11 (1) BR.
17 www.cpvo.europa.eu.
18 Art. 82 BR.
19 Art. 12 BR.
20 Art. 11(2) BR.
21 www.bundessortenamt.de.
22 Art. 53 BR.

are fulfilled and that the application fee has been paid. Most importantly, the CPVO will set the formal application date, which is of particular relevance with regard to distinctness and priority, as both have to be determined with effect of the application date.

During the substantive examination it is ascertained that the object of the application is a variety and that the variety is new within the meaning of the law. In addition it is verified that the proposed *variety denomination*[23] is suitable. The variety denomination forms the intersection of the PVR and the trademark system. Comparable to international non-proprietary names for active pharmaceutical ingredients, the variety denomination cannot be individually protected by trademark rights. Accordingly, choosing the variety denomination and, possibly, using an additional commercial name that is protected as a trademark, should be considered in any IP strategy for plant innovations.

The last and more extensive and time consuming examination is the DUS test. The technical examination is performed by growing a sufficient number of plants of the candidate variety for one or more growing periods by one of the co-operating testing offices of the CPVO. Various test guidelines[24] have been drafted by the CPVO which form the basis of the DUS test. Only when the CPVO is convinced that the candidate variety fulfills the criteria of distinctness, uniformity and stability, will protection be granted.[25]

D. Costs of the Application

Different individual fees[26] will be charged by the CPVO during the process of examining the application for a CPVR. The overall fees have just recently been increased by the CPVO. Currently, an application fee of EUR 900 applies. Depending on the species, the costs for the technical examination range from EUR 1,160.00 to EUR 2,500.00 for each year of DUS testing. If a DUS report of another office can be taken over, a fee of EUR 240.00 applies. Upon the granting of a CPVR an annual fee of now EUR 300.00 is payable to uphold the title.

23 Pursuant to Art. 20 (1) letter a UPOV 1991, "The variety shall be designated by a denomination which will be its generic designation".

24 "Technical Protocols", see www.cpvo.europa.eu/main/en/home/technical-examinations/technical-protocols

25 Art. 62 BR.

26 For the current fee schedules see www.cpvo.europa.eu/main/en/home/methods-of-payment/applicable-fees

E. Objections

Any person may lodge with the CPVO a written objection to the grant of a CPVR; no personal interest or individual concern of the objector is required.[27] The objection can be based on the grounds that the DUS conditions or the novelty requirement are not complied with or that the applicant is not entitled[28] to the respective CPVR title. Also the objection may be raised against the proposed variety denomination. Objections may only be filed until the granting of a CPVR or, in case of objections against the variety denomination, within three months of the publication of the proposed denomination. However, should the denomination stand in conflict with a prior trademark right of a third party, also at a later stage the denomination may be amended.[29]

F. Appeals Against Decisions of the CPVO and Further Remedies

Against the majority of the decisions of the CPVO, an appeal may be lodged before the office's own Board of Appeal, an independent body[30] established within the CPVO. Any natural or legal person may appeal against a decision *addressed to him*. In addition, appeals may be lodged by third parties, *directly and individually concerned*[31] by the decision in question. For the procedures before the CPVO and the appeal proceedings, a set of rules is provided for in the applicable regulations.

Decisions of the Board of Appeal may be further appealed against before the General Court of the European Union ("GCEU"). It has to be noted, however, that in a landmark ruling, the GCEU has decided that it will not, in detail, judicially review the decisions of the Board of Appeal in relation to questions of botanical nature, such as the distinctness of two varieties, due to the complexity of the subject mat-

27 Art. 59 (1) BR.

28 Actually, quite frequently breeders are in disagreement as to who owns the variety in question. Although plant varieties, or the rights vested in a plant variety respectively, may be transferred (assigned) without the need for a written agreement prior to the application for a CPVR, with a view to the burden of proof it is strongly advisable to put on record any such agreement.

29 Art. 66 BR.

30 Art. 45 to 48 BR.

31 In the decision of 31 January 2008 of the General Court of Justice of the European Union ("GCEU") in case no. T-95/06 – "Nador Cott" it was held that "*In order to determine whether a person is individually concerned within the meaning of Article 68 of Regulation No 2100/94 on Community plant variety rights, that person must be affected by the decision granting protection by reason of certain attributes which are peculiar to him or by reason of circumstances in which he is differentiated from all other persons and distinguished individually just as in the case of the person addressed.*"

ter.[32] While one might very well question whether such a limitation of the judicial review by the court is in line with Art. 41(4) of the TRIPS agreement, currently applicants should nevertheless be aware of the scope of review they may achieve when appealing a Board of Appeal decision.

A decision by the GCEU may then be appealed only on grounds of law to the Court of Justice of the European Union ("CJEU"). The CJEU has already confirmed the position of the GCEU with regard to the scope of judicial review[33] and, therefore, will strictly deal with grounds of law when reviewing the decision in question.

G. Assignment and Licensing

A Community plant variety right may be the object of a transfer to one or more successors in title.[34] In this respect it should be noted that a transfer of a CPVR or a respective application requires a written agreement of the parties. Even though before the filing of the application the rights in a variety might be transferred by way of an oral agreement, it is strongly advisable to enter into a written contract at this stage to prevent lengthy discussions or even court cases about the entitlement to the variety. The CPVR[35] may also form in full or in part the subject of contractually granted exploitation rights. Exploitation rights may be exclusive or non-exclusive. It is generally recommended to enter into a formal license contract to avoid any misunderstandings as to the scope and content of the license granted. The holder of a CPVR may, in certain circumstances, invoke the rights conferred by the CPVR against a licensee who contravenes any of the conditions or limitations attached to his exploitation right.[36] In particular with a view to applicable antitrust rules, it is strongly advisable to seek legal advice when setting up the respective agreements.

H. Infringement and Remedies

With regard to the remedies in case of infringements, reference can be made to our explanations in the previous chapter Protection of Trademarks and Commercial

32 In case no. T-187/06 – SUMCOL 01, the GCEU pointed out (para. 63) "In the present case, the appraisal of the distinctive character of a plant variety in the light of the criteria laid down in Article 7(1) of Regulation No 2100/94 is of a scientific and technical complexity such as to justify a limit to the scope of judicial review."

33 C-38/09 P – SUMCOL 01.

34 Art. 23(1) BR.

35 By virtue of the law CPVR applications cannot be subject of license agreements unlike patent applications, Art. 26, 27 BR.

36 CJEU decision in case no. C-140/10 – "Greenstar-Kanzi."

Designations which apply mutatis mutandis. However, there is still no case law on the question of how to apply the provisions of the IPR Enforcement Directive[37] on CPVR, an issue of particular interest as the Basic Regulation has not been amended to incorporate the IPR Enforcement Directive and, in principle, excludes other laws to be applicable.[38] It should be expected, however, that the German courts will eventually award CPVR the same level of protection as national varieties.

I. Summary

The relatively young CPVR system is taking more and more shape not only with regard to the implementation through the CPVO but also in relation to the enforcement of rights before the national courts. Nevertheless, from a commercial point of view, it is advisable to combine Community or national PVR, which is primarily the plant material of the variety in question, with other IP rights, in particular national or Community trademark rights. A comprehensive IP strategy is surely worth investing in, in order to achieve a reasonable return on the considerable investment the development of a new plant variety requires.

Thomas Leidereiter, LL.M.
thomas.leidereiter@luther-lawfirm.com

37 Directive 2004/48/EC of the European Parliament and of the Council of 29th April 2004 on the enforcement of intellectual property rights.

38 Art. 97 (3) BR.

CHAPTER 12
INTELLECTUAL PROPERTY RIGHTS

DR. DETLEF MÄDER

The protection of trademarks and commercial designations has always been an important measure to protect the relevant names and symbols in the German market. However, as a result of the growing variety of goods and services offered and the internationalization thereof, the protection of such signs has become even more important. With regard to the level of protection, company names that are used in the market have a similar protection under the relevant laws to trademarks.

On a national level, trademark protection may be obtained with the registration of a German trademark. Such protection may be extended internationally. Moreover, a Community trademark (*Gemeinschaftsmarke*) granting protection for the whole EU and a market of 500 million consumers may be achieved by an according registration.

A. Requirements for Protection

Suitable for being registered as a trademark is a name, a company name, a term, a logo or a combination of these, which identifies a company and its goods or its services. Signs that are associated with a specific manufacturer/supplier may take the form of symbols, words, illustrations, audio signatures, color designs, packaging or the like. Additionally, a company or a product name that has acquired a secondary meaning as a trademark due to its independent value can also be eligible for trademark protection. Therefore, trademark applications may be filed with the German Patent and Trademark Office (*Deutsches Patent- und Markenamt, DPMA*[1]) for words, letters, numbers, pictures, 3-dimensional-forms and even colors or sounds.

However, protection will not be granted if trademarks consist exclusively of signs or indications which may serve to designate the kind, quality, quantity, intended purpose, value, geographical origin or the time of production of the goods or service. Moreover, protection will be refused if said signs have become customary in the current language or the established practices of trade. Furthermore, a protection will not be granted if the intended trademark is contrary to public policy or morality or if it is

1 http://www.dpma.de

likely to deceive the public with respect to the nature, quality or origin of goods or services.[2]

In contrast to other legal systems, the DPMA does not carry out any research regarding conflicting signs of third parties. As a consequence, it is strongly recommended to carry out trademark research including Community trademarks and international trademarks with protection in Germany and German company names prior to the filing of a trademark application with the DPMA. Otherwise, third parties with older rights may take legal action against the registration of a trademark or the use of such signs.[3]

Commercial designations, such as company names, enjoy similar protection under German law to registered trademarks. Although protection arises from the use of the name in the market, the filing of a trademark for commercial designations is highly recommended, especially if certain names or titles are to be used as a symbol for products or services rendered to third parties. The same applies to work titles (names or particular designations of printed works, sound works, cinematographic works, stage works etc.).

Further to the abovementioned registered trademarks and commercial designations, trademark protection may be achieved in cases where a sign has acquired secondary meaning (*Verkehrsgeltung*) or from the fact that a sign has notoriously become well-known (*notorische Bekanntheit*). However, certain levels of use and/or a very high profile need to be achieved in order to gain such protection. Thus, the court practice has set high demands for such protection, which often will be difficult to fulfill and even more difficult to prove. Therefore, the "normal" registration of a trademark is much easier to achieve.

Similar rules apply to the application and registration of a Community trademark with the Office for Harmonization in the Internal Market (*OHIM*) in Alicante, Spain.

B. Registration Proceedings

Foreigners may register trademarks on the same terms as German nationals. However, applicants having neither a domicile nor an establishment in Germany must – as customary in most other jurisdictions – appoint a qualified lawyer in Germany as its representative for filing the application.

---

2 Sec. 8 MarkenG (*Markengesetz* – German Trademark Act).
3 Sec. 9 MarkenG.

Applications have to be executed by using the official forms of the DPMA and must contain information on the applicant, the trademark and a list of goods and services for which the protection is requested. This list determines the scope of protection and cannot subsequently be extended. Therefore, it is recommended to also include such goods and/or services which might be intended to be developed in the near future. However, an obligation by law has been stipulated for the use of the registered goods and services within five years from the trademark registration. For this reason, only those goods and services should be included in the list, which are intended to and most likely will be developed within five years following the successful registration.

The DPMA and the OHIM might refuse the registration of a trademark based only on absolute or relative grounds. However, the fact that a sign has acquired secondary meaning or has notoriously become wellknown may be, both in Germany and the EU, used as a tool to overcome such obstacles for registration.

In addition, oppositions may be filed by owners of similar or identical trademarks registered earlier or filed within three months from publication of the registration, possibly delaying the process of the registration of a trademark. Contrary to German law, where oppositions may be filed after the registration and publication of such registration, a Community Trademark will only be registered after it has been published for opposition purposes. Therefore, the registration process may take much longer. Opposition proceedings – which are very formal – may delay the registration for several years.

For the protection of geographical indications of origin, applications emanating from Germany need to be filed via the DPMA – even for protection for all EU member states. Applications will first be published to give third parties the opportunity to express concerns.

C. Official Fees

The official fees of the DPMA for the registration of a national mark with protection in three classes amounts to EUR 300.00. For each further class, an additional amount of EUR 100.00 applies. Furthermore, the DPMA offers an accelerated process for the registration proceedings, which results in a shortened process of verifying the necessary qualifications of the application. Said process is highly recommended, but will incur additional costs of EUR 200.00. Hence, the official fees will amount to a sum of EUR 500.00 in the case of protection for three classes.

If a trademark protection within the EU (Community Trademark) is sought, the official fees will amount to EUR 1,050.00 for paper filings and EUR 900.00 for e-filings. As a significant cost reduction, the registration fee claimed for earlier registrations of EUR 850.00 has been omitted. The application fee also includes protection for three classes. The costs for each further class amount to EUR 150.00.

D. Opposition Proceedings

Oppositions may be filed against trademark applications by owners of similar or identical trademarks registered or filed earlier. In Germany, oppositions (regularly based on older trademarks) can be filed within three months from the publication of the trademark registration.

As to the procedure, an opposition against a German trademark application needs to be filed by using an official form from the DPMA. With this filing, no reasoning needs to be given. However, in order to give the case more chances of success and more weight, it is highly recommended to give reasons for the opposition right away instead of waiting for the later trademark holder to give his counter-reasoning to the DPMA first. After such reasoning, detailed arguments would need to be filed with the DPMA anyway.

Once an opposition has been filed, the DPMA will inform the holder of the opposed trademark application, giving him at least one month in order to respond to the opposition. Afterwards, the opponent will be informed of the holder's response, and also be granted a period of at least one month for his counter-response. It is common practice to expand these time limits. Moreover, this procedure might be repeated, depending on the arguments filed by each party. According to our experience, an opposition procedure will take at least half a year or even longer, until a decision of the first instance from the DPMA is reached. As to the costs, the official fees for each opposition amount to EUR 120.00.

Opposition proceedings against a Community Trademark are very similar, but again might take much longer than national proceedings. The notice of opposition has to be received by the OHIM in written form within the opposition period. After filing an opposition, the parties will be granted a period during which parties can negotiate a settlement, the so-called "cooling-off" period. This period is set to expire two months from the notification of admissibility, but can be extended up to a total of 24 months.

Once the cooling-off period has expired, the adversarial part of the proceedings begins. The opponent is then allowed two more months to submit all the evidence and observations he thinks necessary to make his case. After these two months, or once the submitted evidence and observations have been forwarded to him, the applicant also has two months to reply to the opposition. The applicant can either question whether the earlier marks have been used by filing a request for proof of use, or he can file observations and evidence in order to convince the responsible examiner that the opposition should fail. If the applicant files evidence and observations, the opponent is again given two months to comment on the submissions of the applicant. After these exchanges the opposition is normally ready for decision by OHIM, but also another period for comments from each party might be granted. In addition, decisions by the Opposition Division at OHIM may be questioned at the Board of Appeal and appeals to the Court of First Instance and the European Court of Justice at last instance are also possible. The current opposition fee of the OHIM amounts to EUR 350.00.

E. Assignment and Licensing

Trademarks may be sold and assigned in total or as part of the protected goods and services. However, if applicable, consequences for an international registration need to be observed. There are no specific formal requirements for licensing to be observed under German law.

However, it is generally recommended to enter certain aspects into a license contract in order to avoid disagreement, e.g. whether the license granted shall be exclusive or non-exclusive, which goods or services the license shall be granted for and if the license shall be territorially restricted. Usually the license will be part of a commercial contract, as the granting of a license will often be a condition throughout commercial negotiations.

F. Infringements and Remedies

A trademark owner may act against third parties using identical or similar signs, if such use may cause the likelihood of confusion. However, such likelihood of confusion is not necessary if a well-known sign is concerned.

Generally, in cases of infringements against trademarks, it is common to send a warning letter (*Abmahnung*) to the infringing party, claiming the trademark rights violated combined with a request to give a declaration to cease and desist the infringing behavior under a contractual penalty. Usually, a short time limit (approx. 3–4 days) will be given to respond to such warning letter.[4]

4 Sec. 14 et seq. MarkenG.

In case the infringing party does not submit to the requested declaration within said time limit, court proceedings can be initiated against the infringing party, aiming to obtain a preliminary injunction enjoining the infringing party to refrain continuing the infringing behavior. The infringing party will – after the serving of such court decision – be legally bound by the preliminary injunction. Once the request is filed, the court usually rules within a few days, assuming that no oral hearing will be appointed.

Alternatively, a petition for a preliminary injunction can be filed directly as the warning letter is not a legal requirement for such proceedings. However, as court proceedings can be expensive, it is common to send a warning letter first to avoid that the infringer accepts said injunction right away – which might lead to the fact that the applicant has to bear all of the court costs.

Overall, the proceeding should not take more than a few weeks. In addition, the right to file a preliminary injunction under German law is usually only accepted by courts if the applying party has had knowledge of the infringement for no longer than 4–6 weeks. Otherwise, a lengthy regular court proceeding has to be initiated.

A preliminary injunction will only be granted, if the infringement of the trademark right is obvious and highly visible. However, there is no guarantee that a court will not rule other than the preliminary estimate of the applicant. In such case, a prompt hearing will be summoned.

Within normal court proceedings, subsequently to claim for ceasing and desisting the infringing behavior, the owner of the trademark is entitled to claim damages. These include inter alia damages as well as the lawyers' fees according to the German lawyer's fee ordinance (*Rechtsanwaltsvergütungsgesetz*, *RVG*). The applicant can, furthermore, request information about the infringing behavior (names and addresses of producers, dealers, commercial purchasers and third parties having ordered infringing goods) in order to be able to raise his concrete damages. Some infringements of both German and Community trademarks can even be criminally punished under Sects. 143 and 143a MarkenG.

Thus, rights conferred by a Community trademark can be exhausted once goods have been correctly entered into the market of the European Community or, for German trademarks or commercial designations, the European Economic Area or the European Community. The resale of such products can possibly not be subject of a legal proceeding. Thus, it cannot generally be determined whether an infringement occurs, but rather requires a detailed inspection of the case.

G. Summary

In general, trademark protection has become very important within worldwide trade actions and the protection of business assets. Thus, internationally operating businesses should provide for obtaining protection in all countries where business is carried out.

If extensive protection is sought, a trademark should be registered in all member states of the European Union by registering a Community trademark or, for non-EU-countries, through an international trademark. However, a German trademark can be registered cheaper and much faster. Moreover, even the scope of protection may differ. Additionally, the scope of the protection of a German trademark can be extended to a protection within the EU or internationally to certain countries, gaining the advantage of the priority date of the German trademark application. Very often it seems advisable to file a national application first and – after a quicker registration – extend it internationally.

The enforcement of trademark rights can easily and with preliminary measures be achieved in Germany. Insofar, initial court decisions can be reached and served within a few days.

Dr. Detlef Mäder
detlef.maeder@luther-lawfirm.com

CHAPTER 13
COPYRIGHT LAW

DR. MICHAEL RATH

As in most European jurisdictions, copyright in Germany is intrinsically linked to the creator of the work. The German Copyright Act provides for some specifics, particularly as copyright and neighboring rights have not been comprehensively harmonized within the European Union. Therefore, it is worth taking a closer look at some of the issues relating to copyright law in Germany.

A. Requirements for Protection

Personal intellectual creations such as literary, scientific and artistic works are protected under Sec. 2 Copyright Act (*Urhebergesetz, UrhG*). The scope of copyright protection afforded to different types of works is basically identical. The degree of creativity and originality required by German law is rather low. Even instruction manuals have been found worth protecting by German courts. Artistic performances are protected as well. The performers of such works are granted so-called neighboring rights. Such rights are given even to authors of non-creative photographs or non-creative films.[1]

B. Term of Protection

The term of protection (*Schutzdauer*) of a work protected by German copyright is the lifetime of the author plus 70 years.[2] Where a work has been created by several co-authors, the term of protection will be the lifetime of the longest surviving co-author plus 70 years. Protection for neighboring rights differs from 25 years from publication for scientific editions to 50 years from publication of a sound recording. Recent EU proposals have argued for an extension of the term of protection for performers and sound recordings from 50 to 95 years.

---

1 Sec. 72 UrhG.

2 Sec. 64 UrhG.

C. Ownership

According to Sec. 7 UrhG, the author is the "owner" of his work. Such legal ownership can only be transferred by inheritance. Copyright cannot be fully assigned (the same applies for some neighboring rights). Instead, the author may grant an exclusive or non-exclusive license for the exploitation of his or her work. If the author creates a work as part of his duties to his employer, he or she still remains the owner of the copyright: there is no "work-for-hire"principle in German copyright law. An employed computer programmer, for example, will formally obtain ownership of all programs he or she has created. Sec. 69b UrhG, however, states that the employer will be entitled to exploit the software unless it is agreed otherwise between the parties. The same applies for authors involved in film productions.[3] Therefore, it is recommended that the terms of the respective employment agreement specifically state that exclusive rights of use and exploitation to works created during the employment are granted to the employer. If works are created by several co-authors (*Miturheber*), Sec. 8 (2) UrhG provides for additional requirements.

D. Exclusive Rights and Moral Rights

German copyright law grants the author certain exclusive rights (*Ausschließlichkeitsrechte*). The author may, for instance, exclusively reproduce, distribute, exhibit or broadcast the work, make it available to the public or perform it publicly. Unless copyright limitations (*Schranken*) explicitly allow third parties to use the protected works, the author has to give his explicit consent to each form of exploitation. Furthermore, moral rights (*Urheberpersönlichkeitsrechte*) protect the ideal ties between author and work. This means that if the exploiter, for example, wants to publish a work, he will need the author's prior consent as publishing would affect the author's moral right.[4] However, exploitation can be effected if certain rights can be waived, although it is important to remember that core moral rights (like the right to interfere in case of deformation, Sec. 14 UrhG), cannot be waived.

E. Limitations to Copyright

German copyright law lacks a general "Fair Use" clause, allowing free use of protected copyright or neighboring rights by third parties under certain circumstances. Instead, there are specific exemptions which regulate the free use and availability of

---

3 Sec. 89 UrhG.

4 Sec. 12 UrhG.

legal licenses in respect of a certain copyright. For instance, public libraries and other public institutions may exploit the author's work in certain ways under the terms of a legal license. Fees payable under the terms of such license are collected and distributed by certain state supervised collecting societies (*Verwertungsgesellschaften*) such as GEMA or VG Wort. Use granted "for free" is limited to specific instances such as where copies of works are used in court or administrative proceedings, where works are reproduced as part of an educational broadcast, citations, etc.

F. Licensing

Basically speaking, there are no formal requirements for licensing under German copyright law. However, the licensee can only acquire rights the licensor is entitled to grant. A license may be granted exclusively or non-exclusively, and may furthermore be contractually restricted with respect to time, content or territory. In the absence of such contractual provisions, exploitation rights are generally limited by the intention of the contracting parties (*Zweckübertragungsgrundsatz*, Sec. 31 (5) UrhG). Therefore, it is important to prepare clear and unambiguous agreements which specify which forms of use will be permitted under the terms of the license.

G. Remuneration

Authors and performers are given an equitable right to remuneration (*angemessene Vergütung*) for every use of their work.[5] Buyout-contracts, however, do not generally provide for equitable remuneration. Therefore, it is important to consider whether the amount paid for a "total buyout" can be viewed as equitable throughout the whole period of use.

The law does not fix remuneration terms, and the so-called common rules of remuneration (*gemeinsame Vergütungsregeln*)[6] which were intended to set a remuneration framework for each relevant branch, are still rather uncommon. The same applies for collective wage agreements (*Tarifverträge*). Where there is such lack of collective regulation, contracts may be individually reviewed and assessed according to "honest practices" in the relevant branch of industry.[7]

Where earnings received as a result of the exploitation of the work are obviously disproportionate to the author's remuneration (*auffälliges Missverhältnis*), the judge

5 Sec. 32, 32a, 79 UrhG.

6 Sec. 36, 36a UrhG.

7 Sec. 32 (2) UrhG.

may review the remuneration conditions. Earnings will be considered to be disproportionate to the remuneration paid if the remuneration paid is less than or equal to 50 % of what is considered to be equitable. If the exploitation of the author's or performing artist's work is mainly on German territory, the abovementioned Sects. 32 and 32a UrhG may not be excluded even in cross-border agreements.[8] This is different for contracts concerning unknown future types of exploitation and claims for equitable remuneration deriving from such type of use. A form of use will be regarded as known, if it is technically known and commercially exploitable. For new forms of use, authors and performing artists are granted certain revocation rights which need to be executed within three months after the licensee informed the author about the intended exploitation. If the parties agree on equitable remuneration for the exploitation in the new form of use, revocation rights are suspended.

H. Copyright Infringements and Remedies

According to Sec. 97, 98 UrhG, the infringer will be held directly liable for illegal exploitation of exclusive rights or violation of moral rights. This may lead to civil law claims for injunctions, damages, recall or restitution of infringing goods. Moreover, German courts have held that persons contributing to an infringement (by action or omission) may be found to be vicariously liable. Compensation for actual damages can be obtained in a number of ways. The right holder may sue the infringer for lost profits and damages, claim for damages in the amount of the required license (*Lizenzanalogie*) or claim for the infringer's profits received as a result of the exploitation. Compensation for immaterial damage, on the other hand, will only arise in the event of a severe and substantial infringement of a moral right. Despite the fact that the German copyright act lacks provisions which would enable claims to be brought in respect of specific information held, such claims have been successful in the German courts for a number of years. Sec. 101 UrhG, implemented in 2008, provides for additional rights against third parties who possess infringing copies, accepted or provided infringing services, or were involved in any of these acts. However, according to the principle of proportionality, such right will only be enforced where the infringement can be shown to be beyond reasonable doubt.

I. Copyright Enforcement

As a first reaction to a potential copyright infringement, the entitled right holder should initiate a warning letter (*Abmahnung*), demanding the infringer to sign a cease

8 Sec. 32b UrhG.

and desist statement (*Unterlassungserklärung*).[9] Attorney fees for the warning letter can be claimed if claims for infringements are justified. There is a reimbursement limit of EUR 100.00 for simple cases with minor infringements if consumers are involved.[10]

The entitled right holder may also file for a preliminary injunction (*einstweilige Verfügung*). However, an injunction should only be filed before sending a warning letter if damages are not considered to be a sufficient remedy and a preliminary injunction is needed immediately. In a main action (*Hauptsacheverfahren*), the entitled right holder can request a permanent restraint. In broadcasting or internet matters, the claimant is allowed to choose between several courts in which it could bring its claim. Some federal states have established specialized courts which deal with copyright matters. However, as jurisprudence may differ, it is advisable to thoroughly scrutinize the recent case law before requesting an injunction or filing an action.

Dr. Michael Rath
michael.rath@luther-lawfirm.com

9 Sec. 97 UrhG.
10 Sec. 97a UrhG.

CHAPTER 14
INFORMATION TECHNOLOGY

DR. MICHAEL RATH

Information Technology (IT) is of importance not only for the software industry but for all entrepreneurs using IT in their business. Therefore, all companies doing business in Germany need to be aware of the legal framework for their IT, particularly as the observance of IT Compliance and IT Governance is an integral part of general Corporate Compliance.

A. Protection of Software in Germany

The provenience for software protection can be found in the German Copyright Act (*Urhebergesetz*, *UrhG*). This law, however, contains only a few specific provisions regarding software protection.[1] Furthermore, the extent of copyright protection for software is not unlimited as it does not provide sufficient protection against the independent development of the same software solution by a third party. Also, the UrhG does not protect the utilization of the concept of the software by third parties unless the identical source code or object code is being used. This means that if a software developer produces software which has been specifically developed for the ordering party, it could be arguable whether such production means that the IT provider has a right to distribute the specific piece of software to other third parties. Supplemental protection for software can be obtained under the German Act against Unfair Competition (*Gesetz gegen den unlauteren Wettbewerb*, *UWG*) and this may in certain circumstances protect software against copying and plagiarism (cf. the chapter about competition law). In some rare cases, software may also enjoy protection under the German Patent Act (*Patentgesetz*, *PatG*). However, under German patent law a patent will only be granted for so-called "computer-implemented inventions", hence in case the software involves a technical contribution. Furthermore, at present, the rulings and court decisions in Germany and Europe are not clear regarding the extent of the technical contribution which is required for such patent protection (at least for software patents).

---

1 Sec. 2, 69a UrhG.

B. Software License Agreements

German law does not recognize a specific legal category of agreements for software agreements or license agreements. Rather, under German law, the provision of IT services and even the mere delivery of software has to be classified within the long list of existing categories of agreements set out under the German Civil Code (*Bürgerliches Gesetzbuch*, GCC). This very rudimentary classification then impacts the set of law which is applicable to certain parts of the agreement such as warranty, liability, acceptance, partial payments, statute of limitations, right to rectify defects, etc. In general, these stipulations do not really fit with the special requirements of IT-related contracts.[2] A license agreement in relation to a piece of standard software may be, for example, classified as a purchase agreement in terms of the GCC if the software is delivered "as is" without modifications for the buyer. However, if the (same) software is being provided for a certain period of time with e.g. recurring payments or combined with some sort of obligation on the part of the licensor to service and support the software, the provisions for rental agreements may apply to both this software license and the application services provided. The latter could mean that the licensor has permanent obligations to the licensee in respect of the software during the entire term of the agreement, whereas a seller of software would only have warranty obligations for a limited time period of two years (which may in any event be further reduced to one year). This would mean that if any bugs in the software were corrected by the customer rather than by the licensor, this would not, for the purposes of the law, absolve the licensor of any liability and would not be the right remedy (under the law) for the correction of any mistakes in the software.

C. Service Contracts and Service Level Agreements

As a result, the licensing of software is often accompanied by a special service contract (a support and maintenance agreement), and the provision of IT services may often be further subject to comprehensive Service Level Agreements (SLA) which define and modify the quality of the services to be provided and related remedies.[3] SLA will usually set out the penalties which will apply where there has been a failure to discharge obligations under the contract, but may also set out bonus credits which may be applicable in certain cases. However, even a SLA would also be judged according to the general rules of the GCC and must therefore be drafted with due care in order to ensure that all the provisions of the agreement are valid and enforceable and are not affected by the operation of the law.

2 See Rath et. al., Software Liability, in: Economics of Security Challenges – A Multidisciplinary assessment, ENISA Study (European Network and Information Security Agency, 2011.

3 See Rath, K&R K&R 2007, p. 362–366.

In essence this means that the drafting and interpretation of software and IT-related contracts has to be carried out in light of the special rules and principles that are not only laid down in statutory law but also by the courts. This is also the case for de facto standard license conditions which are delivered in connection with open source software and it is therefore possible that even some of the provisions contained in the General Public License (GPL) could, for example, be considered void under German law if they were put to the test.

D. Software in an Insolvency

Another important factor which should not be neglected in connection with the business continuity demands of a company is the protection of usage rights for the software in the event that the IT provider or the licensor becomes bankrupt. If the licensor becomes insolvent or an administrative receiver is appointed in respect of the licensor's assets, the receiver may terminate the license agreement that is in force.[4] Therefore, any rights to use the software could be extinguished immediately at the discretion of the receiver unless the parties have entered into some form of escrow agreement, which is entered into between the parties in relation to their respective rights to the source code of the software in the event of insolvency. However, even an escrow agreement may not always provide for sufficient protection for the core systems because such escrow agreements may also be subject to the mandatory rights of the receiver under the insolvency code. To be on the safe side, it is therefore advisable to add provisions to the software license agreement about how the source code will be treated in such an event.

E. IT Compliance and IT Governance

Companies also have to make sure that their IT is in full compliance with statutory law and further IT Governance requirements. Such IT Compliance[5] is not limited to the CEO's responsibility for copyright issues (although it is indeed advisable to conduct internal audits from time to time to verify if the number of install counts corresponds with the number of existing license agreements for the software). A license management is important because software publishers may under German copyright law – directly or through third-party associations – conduct audits where there is little or almost no evidence of non-compliance on the company's part. In this case, businesses may simply receive a notice requesting them to prove compliance with

4 Sec. 103 German Insolvency Code (*Insolvenzordnung, InsO*).
5 See Rath/Sponholz, IT-Compliance, 2009.

the licenses granted, or law enforcement officers may appear unexpectedly. Experts predict that more companies will continue to be subjected to external software audits by enforcement organizations and, where a company is found to be in breach of the relevant intellectual property rights, the business will face a demand for back-payment of license fees at punitive levels plus additional damages.

IT Compliance also includes the obligation for companies doing business in Germany to comply with applicable archiving and data retention rules.[6] This means that the CEO has to ensure that the IT systems are operated in accordance with the so-called "Generally Accepted Electronical and Optical Storage Principles" (*Grundsätze DV-gestützter Buchführungssysteme*, GOBS) and the "Principles for Digital Tax Audits" (*Grundsätze zum Datenzugriff und zur Prüfbarkeit digitaler Unterlagen*, *GDPdU*) issued by the Federal Ministry of Finance (*Bundesministerium der Finanzen*).[7] As these guidelines for archiving, data retention and tax audits are also basically applicable to business emails and attached documentation, it is obligatory for companies to make sure that all appropriate data retention policies are in full force and effect. This is also important because of e-discovery regulations in other jurisdictions (e. g. USA and UK) that may have an impact on data recovery policies even for companies in Germany (even though there is no concept of e-discovery under German procedural law).[8]

F. IT Governance and Risk Management

Although there are no explicit provisions in law (for data protection requirements see above) requiring "good information technology practices" or a specific set of measurements for IT Compliance, it is important that, in order to avoid personal liability and also to comply with due care requirements, the management is required to install a monitoring and control system that allows early detection of incidents or events that could put the existence of the company at risk.[9] Therefore, a company must also comply with certain quality and security requirements in relation to its information infrastructure. These should also cover the prevention of risks resulting from the erroneous input and processing of data. Without having a special law or regulation requiring a certain level of IT Compliance, the management of a company needs to make sure that efficient measures are in place to ensure sufficient control over its IT systems in order to enable effective IT risk management. This means that the management must ensure the existence of an internal (in case of a third party IT

6 Sec. 257 HGB (*Handelsgesetzbuch* – Commercial Code); Sects. 146, 147 AO (*Abgabenordnung* – German Tax Code).

7 These guidelines will be replaced by the so-called GOBIT in the near future.

8 Cf. Geercken/Holden/Rath/Surguy/Stretton, Cross Border E-Discovery: How to manage potential evidence in an international environment, CRi 2010, p. 65 et. seq.

9 Analogy to Sec. 91 (2) AktG, respectively Sec. 43 (1) GmbHG.

provider, external) control system or framework to support the various business processes. Mostly, those control objectives can be achieved by built-in application control functionality. This functionality is commonly found in integrated ERP environments, such as SAP. In cases where this functionality is not available, a combination of manual and automated control procedures may be needed in order to satisfy the control objective. This can be done by appointing an Information Security Officer to coordinate activities in relation to the secure handling of data.

G. IT Standards

In view of the general rules outlined above, companies are well advised to establish an IT-supported risk and service management that will prevent, or at least minimize, the potential danger of incidents occurring. In order to comply, companies may rely on industry standards such as CobIT (Control Objectives IT), service management rules like ITIL (IT Infrastructure Library), or the "IT Grundschutz Manuals" (*IT-Grundschutz-Kataloge*) issued by the Federal Agency for IT Security (*Bundesamt für Sicherheit in der Informationstechnik, BSI*). Applying these IT standards can be a key indicator of establishing IT Compliance and IT Governance. However, under statutory law there are no minimum standards or specific requirements. This means that any form of efficient IT risk management (including an IT continuity plan to ensure availability of relevant data) could be potentially compliant.

H. Third Party Provider

The implementation of policies and procedures as described before is also mandatory where IT services are not provided in-house, but by a third party IT supplier. A company therefore requires all third parties providing IT services to comply with those key elements. Arrangements which involve a third party who has access to the company's information processing facilities must be based on a formal contract containing, or referring to, all the security requirements above – this is to ensure compliance with the company's security and information handling policies and standards. When agreeing contractual relations with third parties, the company must also make sure that the standards implemented by the service provider are at least equal to those implemented within the company. Additionally, the following topics should be included in agreements with the company's IT provider (or should be installed as in-house guidelines): Information security policy; Service Level Agreements (SLA) or policies for availability, reliability, performance, levels of support, continuity planning, etc.; asset protection, including procedures to protect organizational assets, including information and software; procedures to determine whether any compromises of the assets, e.g. loss or modification of data, has occurred; restrictions on copying and disclosing information; access control regulations; establishment of an escalation process for problem resolution; regulations regarding hardware and software installation and maintenance; change management procedure; reporting and notification of security incidents.

Finally, companies should be aware that because of vast technical improvements, the life-cycles of IT systems are becoming shorter and therefore IT compliance requirements are subject to continuous change, e. g. the Cloud.[10] Still, IT Compliance and IT Governance should not be regarded as a burden. Rather, establishing service-orientated structures within the IT systems and procedures (and therefore complying with IT Governance requirements) can also tremendously contribute to the value of a company.

Dr. Michael Rath
michael.rath@luther-lawfirm.com

10 See Rath, Cloud Computing, IT-Security und der Datenschutz, DACH-Security 2010, Vienna p. 185–193.

CHAPTER 15
BANKING, FINANCE AND CAPITAL MARKETS

CLAUDIA LEYENDECKER
DR. ROLF KOBABE

The German banking sector is among the largest in the world, with big international banks such as Deutsche Bank and Commerzbank. However, the German banking system, which consists of private, public and cooperative banks, is unusual inasmuch as the market share of private banks is rather small as compared to the market share of public and cooperative banks.

The competent German regulatory authority is the Federal Financial Supervisory Authority (*Bundesanstalt für Finanzdienstleistungsaufsicht, BaFin*), which monitors banks and financial services institutions and is responsible for issuing banking licenses. The basic German banking law is the Banking Act (*Kreditwesengesetz, KWG*), which contains, inter alia, key definitions which are used throughout the legislation.

According to Sec. 1 of the German Banking Act, an enterprise is classified as a credit institution if it engages in banking business either commercially or on a scale requiring a commercially organized business undertaking. The banking business, as defined in the German Banking Act, comprises, inter alia, the deposit business, the mortgage bond (*Pfandbrief*) business, the lending business, the discount business, the broking business, the safe custody business, the guarantee business, the giro business and the underwriting business. Financial services institutions are enterprises which are not credit institutions and which provide financial services to others either commercially or on a scale requiring a commercially organized business undertaking. Financial services include but are not limited to the brokering of business involving the purchase and sale of financial instruments (investment broking), the expressing of personal recommendations to customers or its representatives referring to business with certain finance instruments, based on an examination of the personal circumstances of the investor, presented as suitable for the investor (investment consultancy), contract broking, portfolio management, proprietary trading, brokering of deposit business with enterprises domiciled outside the European Economic Area (non-EEA deposit broking), execution of payment orders (money transmission services) and dealing in foreign notes and coins (foreign currency dealing).

A. Structure of the German Banking & Finance System

German banks offer a wide variety of banking services and are usually not specialized or restricted to certain activities. Typically, German banks will offer assistance with virtually every type of banking transaction, regardless of their legal form, size, organization and business structure. Large parts of the banking sector are publicly owned or controlled, or are cooperatives.

The following banks play an important role in the development of local communities.

B. The German Central Bank

The central bank of the Federal Republic of Germany is the German Federal Bank (*Deutsche Bundesbank*) with its Central Office in Frankfurt on the Main. Established in 1957 as a corporate body under public law, the Federal Bank is part of the European System of Central Banks (ESCB) which again is composed of the European Central Bank (ECB) and the national central banks (NCBs) of all European Union (EU) Member States. The Federal Bank was the first central bank to be given full independence. It was greatly respected for its control of inflation through the second half of the 20th century. Due to its strength and former size, the Federal Bank is the most influential member of the ESCB and still plays a significant role.

After the ECB took over responsibility for currency, the Federal Bank continued to exist. Its duties were redefined by the 7th Law amending the "Bundesbank Act" (*Bundesbankgesetz*) of 30th April 2011 in Sec. 3 of the Bundesbank Act. According to the law, the Federal Bank shall participate in the performance of the ESCB's tasks with the primary objective of maintaining price stability, and, inter alia, shall arrange for the execution of domestic and international payments.

Unlike other central banks, the Federal Bank is not a lender of last resort. A key area for which it has responsibility is the monetary policy of the Euro system. Particularly, the German central bank has the principal duty, as stipulated in the Treaty establishing the European Community, of ensuring price stability in the Euro area. The German Central Bank also helps to prevent national and international financial crises. With banking supervision, which is a further key area, the GCB assists with the important operative task of securing a financially sound credit system and, hence, ensuring a stable financial system. The supervisory activities, along with other central-bank functions, enable the bank to gain a valuable insight into the banking system, particularly as a result of its involvement in the money, capital and currency markets and in the refinancing of credit institutions – this helps the bank to ensure stability in the financial markets.[1] As part of its cooperation with the BaFin, the German Central Bank is also responsible for examining approximately 2,300 credit institutions in Germany in order to assess their solvency, liquidity and risk management systems, which includes, inter alia, carrying out inspections of the banking business, e.g. in relation to matters such as compliance with the Basel II rules, giving supervisory talks and carrying out an ongoing assessment of notifications and audit reports.

C. The European Central Bank

The European Central Bank (ECB) was established in 1998 through the Treaty establishing the European Union. It is based in Frankfurt on the Main. It manages the Euro, the single currency of the EU, and ensures price stability for more than two thirds of the citizens of the EU who use the Euro as their currency. Additionally, the ECB is responsible for determining and implementing the economic and currency policy of the Eurozone. Other key tasks of the ECB are to conduct foreign exchange operations, to take care of the foreign reserves of the European system of central banks and promote smooth operation of the financial market infrastructure. Furthermore, it has the exclusive right to authorize the issuance of euro banknotes.

D. Kreditanstalt für Wiederaufbau, KfW

The German Promotional Bank (*Kreditanstalt für Wiederaufbau, KfW*) acts on behalf of the German government. The Frankfurt based KfW was formed in 1948 and is owned by the Federal Republic of Germany (80 %) and the federal states of Germany (20 %). As Germany's most important promotional bank, KfW promotes the future investments of its citizens, small and medium-sized businesses and the municipal and social infrastructure by granting investment loans, financing infrastructure and residential building projects, financing energy-saving and energy-efficient technologies and municipal infrastructure. For this purpose KfW has provided nearly one trillion euros in loans over 60 years since its founding in 1948.

At the present day KfW banking group has three business units with distinct functions, as well as several subsidiaries. KfW covers over 90 % of its borrowing needs in the capital markets. The Federal Republic of Germany is liable for all liabilities and loans of the KfW. This guarantee, which is given by the Federal Republic of Germa-

---

1 Art. 105 Sec. 5 EC Treaty.

ny, is based on Sec. 1a KfW Act and allows KfW to raise funds at advantageous conditions. Together with its exemption from corporate taxes due to its legal status as a public agency, this allows KfW to provide loans for purposes prescribed by the KfW Act at lower rates than commercial banks. KfW is not allowed to compete with commercial banks. Typically, KfW does not lend directly to enterprises or individuals, but it provides commercial banks with liquidity at low rates and long maturities, as well as with instruments to transfer risk (securitization). KfW thus acts as a second-tier bank.

KfW promotional bank (*KfW Förderbank*), the largest business unit of the group, promotes mostly energy-efficient housing and energy-saving and energy-efficient improvements in Germany. Through the subunit KfW municipal bank *(KfW Kommunalbank)* it also invests in municipal infrastructure such as public transport and sanitation. More recently, KfW promotional bank also engaged in education where it provides student and educational loans. KfW bank for small and medium sized businesses *(KfW Mittelstandsbank)*, the second largest business unit of the group, promotes German small and medium enterprises (SMEs) including individual entrepreneurs and start-ups by providing loans, equity and mezzanine financing. *DEG (Deutsche Investitions- und Entwicklungsgesellschaft*, which translates to German Investment and Development Corporation), a smaller subsidiary, and KfW development bank (*KfW Entwicklungsbank*), one of the group's smaller business units, support economic and social progress in developing and transition countries.

Through its subsidiary KfW IPEX-Bank KfW offers financing solutions for large-scale projects in Germany and for expansions, exports and imports as well as new infrastructure, climate and environmental projects abroad. It also promotes foreign investments in Germany. In 2008 KfW IPEX Bank became legally and financially independent. As a consequence it does not any more benefit from the federal loan guarantees that allow KfW banking group to refinance itself at advantageous rates. On the other side, unlike KfW banking group itself, KfW IPEX-Bank is allowed to directly compete with commercial banks.

KfW has been very active in securitization before this market collapsed during the subprime mortgage crisis. Through securitization it helped commercial banks to transfer risks from their housing and SME portfolios to the capital market. KfW also provides loans to European commercial banks to help them finance small and medium enterprises, housing and infrastructure (global loans).

E. German Banks

In Germany an extensive network of around 2,300 banking institutions with approximately 44,000 branches offer the full range of banking services. Unlike banking in the United Kingdom and the United States, where historically there was a distinction drawn between pure investment banks and commercial banks, the German banking sector stands for universal banking, i. e. most banks are both a commercial bank and an investment bank and engage in many kinds of banking activities. The finance market is supplemented by banks that specialize in particular functions (e.g. mortgage banks and home loan banks).

The German banking system is structured in three different tiers. Private Banks, which are represented by major players like Deutsche Bank or Commerzbank as listed companies or Hauck & Aufhäuser or Bankhaus Lampe as smaller and less known private companies, are the first tier. The second tier is composed of cooperative banks, first and foremost the numerous Volksbanken or Raiffeisenbanken. The third tier consists of public banks, which are a legally defined arm of the banking industry in Germany and separate into two main groups. In contrast to the private commercial banks, the main goal of co-operative banks and savings and loan banks is not profit maximization.

Although most banks conduct both corporate and private customer business, big corporations are increasingly being handled by the major banks, whereas small and medium-sized companies are handled by smaller banks that tend to operate regionally (e.g., savings and loan banks, credit cooperatives for trade, and agricultural credit cooperatives).

Over recent years, financial services have increasingly been offered by non-banking firms such as insurance corporations, department stores, mail-order firms, and car manufacturers. The financial services provided by these companies will often correspond to their original businesses so that a manufacturing company may offer loans to their customers to enable customers to purchase their products, for example.

In recent years the German banking sector also has seen mergers between many financial institutions. This has led to consolidation within the German banking sector. Although such takeovers have led to a reduction in the size of the banking branch network in Germany, the country still boasts a density of around one banking outlet per 1,766 inhabitants (including post office savings banks), which is one of the best in Europe.

F. Private Banks

Private commercial banks engage in most types of banking operations. They grant short-term loans, lines of credit, and medium and long-term loans; they also place issues and trade in securities for customers and on their own account. They may also be shareholders in companies operating in other industries or participate in a business venture. The range of services offered by banks is becoming increasingly diversified and includes new activities such as online banking and investment banking.

The German private banking sector is represented most notably by the major banks (Deutsche Bank, Commerzbank and Unicredit Bank) which maintain a vast network of branches. Historically their clients are primarily major corporations and wealthy private customers. Aside from that there are a few private banks with branch networks and a stronger regional focus, i. e. *Südwestbank* and National-Bank. Moreover, there has also been an increase in the number of direct banks with no branch network, such as ING-DiBa and Deutsche Kreditbank. Additionally, there are private real-estate loan banks which issue mortgage bonds as well as private home loan associations (*Bausparkassen*), e.g. BHW Bausparkasse AG.

Foreign banks in Germany consist of two subgroups. Some banks have established their own retail business in Germany and operate a full-coverage network of branches (e.g. Santander Consumers Bank and Targobank). Then there are the branch offices of foreign banks which care for their original customers in Germany (e.g. ABN AMRO).

Finally there are some "Privatebankiers", i. e. banks which traditionally address and care for wealthy private clients (such as Berenberg Bank). The bigger players also engage in investment banking, e.g. Sal. Oppenheim. The oldest family-owned bank is Bankhaus Metzler. The Fürst Fugger Privatbank is even older, however, just like Trinkhaus & Burkhardt, it now belongs to a group (Nürnberger Versicherung and HSBC, respectively).

G. Genossenschaftsbanken (Cooperative Banks)

German Cooperative Banks (*Genossenschaftsbanken*) mostly have the legal form of a cooperative and belong to a cooperative bank group. The German cooperative banks are based on the principles of self-help, self-responsibility and self-administration. They trace back to credit unions founded in the 19th century. While "Volksbanken" accrued mainly in municipal areas, "Raiffeisenbanken" were founded mainly in rural areas as credit cooperatives for agriculture. Besides the classic banking business, some of these banks still run commodity trade on a small scale. The term "Raiffeisen" is a reference to Friedrich Wilhelm Raiffeisen, the founder of the cooperative movement of credit unions. Furthermore there are cooperative banks with other names. They include, inter alia, Sparda banks and banks which emphazise the name of their city of origin (e.g. Kölner Bank and Münchener Bank). Finally there are other cooperative banks, such as German bank of pharmacists and medical doctors (*Deutsche Apotheker- und Ärztebank*) and some cooperative banks with a churchly background.

Cooperative banks are based on a member-structure where each member, independently from its capital share, has one vote. They typically serve smaller and medium sized businesses and individuals with lines of credit and loans as well as finance products of the cooperative bank network. On a regional level the shares of the cooperative banks are in the hands of their respective members. The shares of the two cooperative central banks (DZ Bank AG and WGZ-Bank AG) are largely in the hands of the cooperative banks. These credit institutes serve as clearinghouses and sources of refinancing. They also come up with products for the capital market and care for major corporate clients. DZ Bank is the majority shareholder of DVB Bank SE. The listed bank with its seat in Frankfurt and offices in 13 locations worldwide supports clients in the Shipping, Aviation and Land Transport sectors with financing and advisory services. The network of the cooperative banks comprises some special institutes, among this an investment fund company, a real estate fund company, a savings and loan association, several mortgage banks, a leasing company an insurance company and a number of IT service provider.

H. Sparkassen-Finanzgruppe (German Savings Banks Finance Group)

The German Savings Banks Finance Group (*Sparkassen-Finanzgruppe)* is the most important sub-sector of the German banking market. In 2010 the German Savings Banks Finance Group comprised 429 savings banks using the *Sparkasse* brand, more than half a dozen public owned state banks (*Landesbanken*) (e.g. WestLB and HSH Nordbank), ten real estate financing banks using the "LBS" brand as well as the DekaBank and a number of specialized institutes.

I. Sparkassen (Public Savings Banks)

Savings banks in Germany are called *Sparkasse*. The first savings banks in Germany were founded at the close of the 18th century in the big trading cities. Between 1850 and 1903 the idea of the municipal savings banks spread and the number of savings banks in Germany grew rapidly. Fulfilling public interests is still one of the most significant characteristics of public banks in general and the savings banks in particular. In general, savings banks are not profit oriented. Savings banks typically are universal banks and provide the whole spectrum of banking services for private and commercial medium sized customers out of a public interest.

The name *Sparkasse* is legally protected in Sec. 40 of the Banking Act. *Sparkassen* are credit institutes, typically held directly or indirectly by the public sector, e.g. the states, administrative districts or cities. On the legal base of the Banking Act, the regional savings Bank Acts and their statues, they work as commercial banks in a decentralized structure. Each savings bank is independent, locally managed and concentrates its business activities on customers in the region it is situated in.

The public savings banks and their municipal holders respectively are members of one of the twelve regional Savings Banks Associations (*Sparkassen- und Giroverbände*) as statutory bodies. They are responsible for the coordination among savings banks in a region. They also act as auditors and operate regional savings banks academies for educational and training purposes. Through their membership of the regional associations, the savings banks are also members of the German Savings Banks Association (*Deutscher Sparkassen- und Giroverband, DSGV*). DSGV was founded in 1924 as umbrella organization of all German savings banks, state banks and state home loan banks to organize decision-making processes, coordinate the strategy of the savings banks and represent its members' political and regulatory interests on national and international scale.

The total assets of the 431 savings banks amount to about 1 trillion Euros. They operate a network of over 15.600 branches and offices and employ over 250.000 people. 50 million customers maintain business activities with German savings banks. Although independent and regionally spread, the savings banks act as one unit under the brand *Sparkasse*.

II. Landesbanken (State Banks)

The *state banks* (*Landesbanken*) are mostly owned by the savings banks through the regional association and the respective federal state. Regional banks are also interlinked through cross-holdings.

State banks are led, together with the clearing houses responsible for the respective savings bank region, as a community bank traditionally. They support federal states in the procurement of the banking related business and facilitate the economy of a federal state. Beyond that, state banks may run the whole spectrum of banking business, wherefore these institutes have appeared as a general commercial bank or universal bank respectively on the market for years.

The tasks and powers of a state bank are codified in the individual country state bank laws of the federal states (*Landesbankengesetze*). The specific tasks for the savings banks include the central clearing for cashless payments and liquidity funding for the associated savings banks, e.g. by issuing mortgage or municipal bonds. They also provide many services for the associated savings banks in the region in securities and cross-country businesses. In contrast to savings banks, state banks are doing "wholesale-banking" instead of retail-banking.

With three exceptions the state banks are public-law institutions. As such they are subordinate to the federal state supervision in the respective states. Another two state banks will be transformed to private corporations in future, namely LBBW, which has to be transformed due to European order, and BayernLB, for which complete privatization until 2015 was decided by the Bavarian state parliament (*Bayrischer Landtag*).

With combined total assets of 1,620 trillion euros as of December 2010, the seven Landesbanken-Groups employ about 44.000 people.

III. DekaBank

DekaBank with its subsidiaries is the central asset manager of the German Savings Bank Finance Group. Based in Frankfurt on the Main and Berlin it provides asset management services for the savings banks and the Regional banks and their customers. The sole owners of DekaBank are the regional Savings Banks Associations and thus indirectly the savings banks.

IV. Landesbausparkassen (Regional Real Estate Financing Banks)

The German state real estate financing banks (*Landesbausparkassen*, *LBS*) are subsidiaries of the savings banks and the regional associations respectively. They focus on real estate banking. Their combined assets total 52 billion euros. The core business of the LBS is the offering of collective real estate saving products, i. e. building loan contracts (*Bausparverträge*), and providing low-interest residential mortgage loans.

V. Other Members of the Sparkassen-Finanzgruppe

In addition to several banking units, the German Savings Banks Finance Group also consists of nearly a dozen regional, public insurance groups, leasing and factoring companies, i. e. the German Leasing-Group, and numerous venture capital companies which promote small and medium sized companies.

I. Mortgage Banks and Other Financial Institutions

Mortgage banks (*Hypothekenbanken*) specialize in long-term mortgage loans and long-term loans to federal, state, and local governments. They issue bonds secured by mortgage loans and loans to public authorities.

In addition, a number of private and public banks provide highly specialized services and special forms of financing. Insurance banks and leasing companies also play an important role in the financing of industrial business.

J. Banking Regulations of the Federal Financial Supervisory Authority

Banks, financial services institutions, and insurance enterprises in Germany are monitored by the Federal Financial Supervisory Authority (*Bundesanstalt für Finanzdienstleistungsaufsicht, BaFin*), which reports to the German Federal Ministry of Finance (*Bundesministerium der Finanzen, BMF*). Following the adoption of the Act on Integrated Financial Services Supervision, the former offices for banking supervision, insurance supervision, and securities supervision were combined to form the BaFin in 2002.

The fundamental supervisory legislation with regard to banks is the Banking Act, which not only covers banks, but also financial service providers, i. e. investment firms which cannot be classified as a credit institution. A company covered by the Banking Act must obtain a license from the BaFin, is subject to supervision by the BaFin and must have a capital endowment which corresponds to the risks involved in the company's business.

The BaFin's main task is to ensure the functioning, stability and integrity of the German financial system. It has many specific duties: it regulates banks by enforcing standards of professional conduct and monitors banks to ensure that they comply with the capital adequacy requirements and to ensure that they maintain sufficient liquid funds. It also ensures that the banks comply with statutory risk limits and demands bad debt provisions that are in line with the banks risk exposure. Thus, banks, financial services institutions and insurance undertakings are reminded that they need to ensure that they control their business dealings in such a way that they are always able to meet their payment obligations.

The BaFin directorate for Insurance Supervision grants the regulatory authorization required by enterprises in order to carry out insurance. Together with the BaFin, the German central bank participates in the ongoing supervision of the banking system. Its participation is governed by Sec. 7 of the Banking Act. Amongst other things, the German central bank analyses the reports and returns that institutions have to submit on a regular basis and assesses whether their capital and risk management procedures are adequate. According to the 2010 annual report, BaFin currently supervises 1,923 banks and securities trading companies, 717 financial services institutions, 603 insurance undertakings and 30 pension funds.

K. German Stock Exchanges

The most important stock exchange in Germany is the Frankfurt Stock Exchange (Frankfurter Wertpapierbörse, FWB). The institution operating FWB is Deutsche Börse AG. In addition, there are stock ex-changes in Berlin, Düsseldorf, Hamburg, Hanover, Munich, and Stuttgart. The German Exchange Supervisory Authority, an institution of the German federal states (*Bundesländer*), monitors the setting up, closing down, and operations of stock exchanges, and ensures that trading is properly conducted.

The Frankfurt Stock Exchange offers a wide range of services, providing access to both the equity and derivatives markets for companies as well as investors, in particular access to the electronic trading platform Xetra – one of the leading electronic trading platforms in the world. After the London Stock Exchange, FWB is the most important market for securities and derivatives in Europe.

At the beginning of 2003, FWB introduced a new segment of the equity market. The goal was the division of the market into two separate segments with different standards of transparency as well as a new concept of sector indices. The legal basis for the new segment is the 4th Financial Market Promotion Act (*4. Finanzmarkt-Förderungsgesetz*), which resulted in a comprehensive reform of the law governing stock exchange transactions. The stock exchange admission segments distinguish between the General Standard with statutory minimum transparency requirements and the Prime Standard with high international transparency criteria. Admission to the Prime Standard requires quarterly reporting, the application of international accounting standards (IAS/IFRS, U.S. GAAP), publication of a financial calendar, staging of at least one analyst conference per year, and ad hoc disclosures also in English.

The shares in the Prime Standard are quoted in the Xetra trading system. Only Prime Standard issuers qualify for all FWB indices. The largest companies by market capitalization and sales are included in the DAX (the German Share Index). Smaller and midsized companies are included in MDAX and SDAX, if they operate in the classic industry branches, and in TecDAX if they operate in the technology sector.

The admission of a security to the Frankfurt Stock Exchange is determined by the listing board for the official market or the listing committee for the regulated market. The admission criteria vary according to the market segment. All issuers must prepare an offering prospectus containing the information needed to evaluate the securities. Admission to the General Standard requires no further involvement from the issuer. However, if admission is sought to the Prime Standard, an application must be made by the issuer, with admission being contingent on the company's compliance with the transparency criteria.

I. Capital Market Access for Medium-Sized Companies in Germany

The German capital market as a long-term source of debt finance still plays a subordinate role in German corporate finance. Its share of corporate finance lies significantly below the level of leading Western industrial nations. The comparatively uncomplicated house bank credit financing led to the capital markets not being able to develop into an alternative source of financing to the same extent as it did in Anglo-Saxon countries. However, this significantly changed with the implementation of Basel II. Banks stopped lending as lightly at previous attractive conditions. This trend increased even more with the onset of the financial crisis and Basel III will increase this development even more. Companies must either pay higher interest or bring in more collateral. In addition, numerous small and medium-sized companies are seeing themselves confronted in the short-term with replacing the standard mezzanine capital issued and securitized in 2007.

To offer these companies a financing alternative and access to the capital market, the Stuttgart stock exchange presented the "bondm" based in the "regulated" inofficial market segment for medium-sized companies bonds in May 2010. The companies in this segment are committed to guaranteeing minimum standards of transparency and publicity for investors on a continuing basis. These standards are stricter than the usual rules and regulations governing the open market. In addition to the securities issuing prospectus, audited annual financial statements, six months' reports and the financial calendar, these companies also have to publish quasi ad hoc announcements.

Since then bondm has become a success story. Ever more small and medium sized enterprises are discovering the bond market as an additional source of finance and as a financing alternative to traditional bank credits. Private investors are also strongly interested for the high-yielding securities of SME. Due to the great interest of the corporations and the private investors, further stock exchanges founded special segments for such bonds. By now five stock exchanges have established special segments which aim at middle-class issuers and private investors. To date, the stock exchanges in Stuttgart (bondm), Düsseldorf (*Mittelstandsmarkt*), Frankfurt (Entry Standard), Hamburg-Hannover (*Mittelstandsbörse*) and the Munich (m:access bonds) have placed more than two billion euros of debt. Some companies like the airline Air Berlin or the providers of alternative energy, solar power and wind SAG kingdom, have tapped into the market with a second bond. On 1st September 2011, the Stuttgart stock exchange even launched an index for the bondm trading segment which tracks the performance of the corporate bonds listed and traded in bondm segment for medium sized enterprises.

L. Capital Markets

No legal definition of the term "capital market" exists in European or in German law. It is generally accepted that a capital market is not necessarily a physical market place with a trading floor. Instead, the term "capital market" refers to the notional place where funds from investors (retail investors, professional investors, etc.) and the borrowing requirements of companies seeking external financing meet with the help of financial intermediaries. Such capital markets include stock exchanges, other organized markets and OTC markets.

The term "capital market" should be distinguished from money market and can be classified into primary and secondary, domestic, foreign and international markets as well as regulated and unregulated market, all of which have slightly different meanings, as illustrated below.

I. Money Markets vs. Capital Markets

Money and capital markets can usually be distinguished by reference to the maturity of the instruments issued. "Money market" instruments rarely exceed a maturity of two years, whilst "capital market" instruments usually have a maturity of between two and 30 years.

II. Domestic Markets vs. Foreign Markets and International Markets

Whereas money markets and capital markets are distinguished by reference to the maturity of the instruments traded, domestic, foreign and international markets are distinguished by reference to the place where the funds to be invested and the borrowing requirements meet. Where securities are offered only in an issuer's home market, this is known as a "domestic market" or a domestic offering. Securities offered in a "foreign market" are those offered in a country other than an issuer's domestic market. An "international market" or a "Euromarket" is a market where securities are offered by foreign borrowers to foreign investors in various countries in a currency that is not the currency of the respective financial center.

III. Primary Markets vs. Secondary Markets

Referring to the parties involved in transactions, the capital market can be divided into "issue markets" or "primary markets", where issuers and investors meet, and "circulation markets" or "secondary markets", where offering and buying investors meet. Capital market titles are initially placed on the primary market where initial purchasers and initial suppliers meet. While the focus in the primary market is on information about the new capital market title and the issuer, it is on the execution of the securities trading in the secondary market. As secondary market transactions involve the sale of securities to further investors after their initial placement by initial investors, this requires a liquid market, as well as transferable and marketable securities.

IV. "Regulated" vs. "Unregulated" Capital Markets

Finally, it is possible to distinguish between "regulated" or so-called "white" capital markets, which are subject to direct state supervision, and "unregulated" or so-called "grey" capital markets, for which no direct state supervision exists. Basically, unregulated markets are markets for products characterized by higher risks. As a typical secondary market does not normally exist for the products traded on the unregulated market, the marketability found by investors on the regulated market does not exist on the unregulated market.

As early as the 1970s, the German limited partnership (*Kommanditgesellschaft*, KG) model was established to raise private equity for the financing of projects. To raise the necessary funds initiators set up the legal entity and place the equity among individuals as private investors. The main objective of the German limited partnership model is the project financing by investors participating in single purpose companies which are organized in the legal form of a limited partnership. For the understanding of the structure it is important that no special corporate legislation is necessary to set up the model. The legal entity form of the KG was in general established at the beginning of the last century and is a common legal entity form for German medium-sized companies. The general concept of a KG is understood and accepted by private and institutional investors, financing banks, business partners and other stakeholders. Since the 1970s the German KG model has become a successful funding instrument of project finance for various asset classes (real estate, ships, renewable energy, private equity, life insurance policies, etc.) and significantly increased in terms of the volume and value of transactions. In 2010 the fundraising in the KG model market amounted to EUR 5.8 billion.

In recent years the legal environment for the German KG model has changed dramatically with respect to the financial supervision of the funds prospectuses used for the equity placement. Since 1st July 2005 the public offering of shares for which no securities are issued (e.g. shares in trust funds and in other closed funds) is subject to the obligation to publish an issue prospectus which is checked by BaFin on completeness.

M. Legal Sources of German Capital Market Law

Capital market law comprises all norms and principles which are relevant for the capital market and govern the issue and trading of fungible assets and regulate both the protection of individual investors and the protection of the functions of capital markets and business purposes. Capital market law is a conglomerate of statutory provisions from different acts and legal areas such as corporate law, securities law and stock exchange law, investment law, civil law and commercial law, among others.

I. Objectives of Capital Market Law

The primary objective of capital market law is to enable the existence of an efficient market for securities. It serves to maintain the international competitiveness of national economies and to secure private old-age provision as well as the financing requirements of the public sector. The protection of the single functions of the capital market, which include allocation, operational efficiency and institutional efficiency, therefore requires a set of rules and conditions, albeit basic.

II. Important German Capital Market Acts

The most important legal sources of German capital market law are:

- Banking Act (*Kreditwesengesetz, KWG*);
- Exchange Act (*Börsengesetz, BörsG*);
- Securities Trading Act (*Wertpapierhandelsgesetz, WpHG*);
- Securities Acquisition and Takeover Act (*Wertpapiererwerbs- und Übernahmegesetz, WpÜG*);
- Securities Prospectus Act (*Wertpapierprospektgesetz, WpPG*);
- Safe Custody Act (*Depotgesetz, DepotG*);
- Mortage Bond Act (*Pfandbriefgesetz, PfandBG*)
- Investment Act (*Investmentgesetz, InvG*);
- Financial Supervision Act (*Finanzdienstleistungsaufsichtsgesetz, FinDAG*);
- Investor Model Proceedings Act (*Kapitalanleger-Musterverfahrensgesetz, KapMuG*);
- Payment Services Regulation Act (*Zahlungsdiensteaufsichtsgesetz, ZAG*).

Other laws contain the odd provision which is of relevance for capital market law or which is directly and technically related to capital market law. For example, the German Civil Code (*Bürgerliches Gesetzbuch, BGB*) contains, inter alia, rules on contracts of agency (Sec. 675 et. seq. BGB) and rules on payment services (Sec. 675c et. seq. BGB). The Money Laundering Act (*Geldwäschegesetz, GwG*) stipulates a duty for banks and financial service providers to establish the identity of any person depositing or withdrawing amounts of money or securities with a value of more than 15,000 euros and if a suspicion of money laundering – as defined in Sec. 261 German Criminal Code (*Strafgesetzbuch, StGB*) – exists, to notify the facts of the case to the law enforcement authorities. An example of a capital-market-oriented penal provision is Sec. 264a German Criminal Code (investment fraud). The Payment Services Regulation Act (*Zahlungsdiensteaufsichtsgesetz*, ZAG) which applies to "payment institutions", i. e. entities that provide "payment services" on a professional basis without being either a credit institution or an electronic money institution.

III. Regulations and Notices Issued by the BaFin; Bylaws and Other Sets of Rules

The BaFin and the German Federal Bank have the authority to enact non-legislative rules, an option that they have made use of in the past. A legal particularity is that the regulations issued by the BaFin, which are of particular relevance in practice, are only administrative rules which interpret statutory provisions and therefore are only binding for the BaFin internally, and do not have any external effect from a legal point of view. Examples of such regulations are the Good Conduct Regulation (*Wohlverhaltensrichtlinie*) and the Compliance Regulation (*Compliance-Richtlinie*), which specify the conduct-related duties of investment service providers and their organizational duties. The so called Issuers' Guideline (*Emittentenleitfaden*), issued by the BaFin on 28th April 2009, which specifies, inter alia, the insider provisions of the Securities Trading Act, is also quite important. The regulatory authorities additionally use general decrees, administrative measures and informal measures. BaFin calls its official statements "circular letters" (*Rundschreiben*), "announcements" (*Bekanntmachungen*), "information leaflets" (*Informationsblätter*) or "letters to the management" (*Schreiben an die Vorstände*).

The general terms and conditions used by credit institutions are of importance in legal transactions. They include the general terms and conditions of the banks, the special conditions for securities transactions and the special conditions for time bargains.

Stock exchange dealings are based on a large variety of rules; at the Frankfurt Stock Exchange the most important of these rules are the Terms and Conditions of the Frankfurt Stock Exchange and the Open Market Guidelines. Similar arrangements can be found on the derivatives exchange Eurex and when executed transactions are handled via Clearstream Banking AG.

IV. Recent Developments of the European and German Financial Supervisory legislation

Since 1974, when the Basel Committee on Banking Supervision was founded, the banking sector in the EU, and amongst G10 nations, has been working along increasingly similar lines. EU and G10 nations worked together on this committee to develop an international supervisory code and network to improve the quality of banking supervision, and the committee's consultative paper on the New Basel Capital Accord (Basel II) of 2004, last updated in July 2006, had wide reaching effects in the international banking sector.

The purpose of Basel II was to create an international standard that banking regulators can use when drafting regulations which set out how much capital needs to be put aside to guard against the types of financial and operational risks that banks face. Basel II was designed to help protect the international financial system from the types of problems that might arise in case a major bank or a series of banks collapses. In practice, Basel II attempted to accomplish this by setting up rigorous risk and capital management requirements designed to ensure that a bank holds capital reserves which are appropriate for the levels of risk to which the bank exposes itself through its lending and investment practices.

The European Union has implemented Basel II via the EU Capital Requirements Directive, which consists of Directive 2006/48/EC (Banking Directive) and Directive 2006/49/EC (Capital Adequacy Directive), published on June 30, 2006. Germany implemented the relevant parts of the Capital Requirements Directive on 1st January 2007. Major laws, regulations and rules in this context in Germany are: Banking Act (*Kreditwesengesetz, KWG*); Solvency Regulation (*Solvabilitätsverordnung, SolvV*); Regulation governing Large Exposures and Loans (*Großkredit- und Millionenkreditverordnung, GroMiKV*); Minimum Requirements for Risk Management (*Mindestanforderungen an das Risikomanagement, MaRisk*).

On 1st January 2004, the Investment Modernization Act (*Investmentmodernisierungsgesetz, InvModG*) which transposed directives 2001/107/EC and 2001/108/EC of 21st January 2002 (UCITS III) into German law, came into force. This Act had several consequences: firstly, it broadly overhauls and consolidates the investment-related fiscal regulations which were previously contained in the German Capital Investment Companies Act (*Gesetz über Kapitalanlagegesellschaften*, KAGG) and the German Foreign Investment Funds Act (*Auslandsinvestmentgesetz, AuslInvestmG*). Furthermore, it integrated hedge funds into the range of regulated investment funds capable of being marketed in Germany. These provisions were incorporated into an Investment Act (*Investmentgesetz, InvG*) and a corresponding Investment Tax Act (*Investmentsteuergesetz, InvStG*). One key feature of the legislation was that, for the first time, it was possible to establish domestic hedge funds as investment funds managed by an investment management company (*Sondervermögen einer Kapitalanlagegesellschaft*) or as investment companies (*Kapitalanlagegesellschaft*). Therefore, hedge funds are obliged to meet the same requirements as investment funds, e.g. in respect of sales prospectuses, contractual terms and conditions (articles of association), and accounting.

With the German Act on the Reorganization of Mortgage Bond Legislation (*Gesetz zur Neuordnung des Pfandbriefrechts*), which entered into force on 19th July 2005, the German legislature further improved the regulatory framework for this product of the financial center of Germany in a uniform manner for all credit institutions and to further increase the already high acceptance of the German mortgage bond. Its centerpiece was the new German Mortgage Bond Act. The reformation significantly contributed to strengthening Germany as a financial center. With this legal basis the special bank principle and the business circle limitation of the institutes have been dropped. The morgtage bond issuing business is still subject to a special supervision by the BaFin, though.

A law concerning REITs was enacted on 1st June 2007 and was retroactive to 1st January 2007. With the "G-REIT Act" the German legislature introduced the German Real Estate Investment Trust – or, G-REIT, which for the most part follows various international paradigms. Yet, the bill testifies to a number of specific variations "Made in Germany" with regard to corporate, capital market and tax related G-REIT parameters. The taxation-related linchpin of the REIT legislation is the idea of tax exempting the REIT, binding it to distribute most of its profits to its shareholders, and collecting taxes on shareholder level, a concept conceived as supporting above all tax transparency which was highly controversially disputed during the legislature procedure.

On 20th January 2007, the Transparency Directive Implementation Act (*Transparenzrichtlinieumwandlungsgesetz, TUG*) came into effect implementing the European Transparency Directive. It entailed some significant changes to the disclosure requirements of German listed corporations, such as a newly introduced confirmation of the balance sheet (*Bilanzeid*). In addition, material alterations to the share ownership notification rules in the German Securities Trading Act (*Wertpapierhandelsgesetz, WpHG*) have been made.

On 1st November 2007, the Financial Market Implementation Act (*Finanzmarktrichtlinie-Umsetzungsgesetz, FRUG*) came into effect. Together with two accompanying directives the FRUG implemented the Markets in Financial Instruments Directive (MiFID) into German law, which was itself supplemented by a MiFID Implementing Directive and a Commission Regulation. Altogether this legislation was part of the Financial Services Action Plan of the European Commission aiming at the formation of a single market for financial services. The new legislation lead most notably to material changes in the German Securities Trading Act. On the one side numerous new regulations have been added, on the other side previously existing regulations have become much more detailed. In addition to the MiFID-related concerns including pre- and post-trade transparency and best execution, the regulations' influence on day-to-day consulting and product marketing is becoming increasingly apparent. Thus the WpHG has finally become "the constitution" of German capital market law.

In June 2008 the Bundestag passed the Risk Limitation Act (*Risikobegrenzungsgesetz, RBG*). The main goal of this act is to prevent undesirable activities by financial investors. This is supposed to make the shareholder structure more transparent and to oblige larger investors to disclose their strategic objectives. Together with the Risk Limitation Act, simultaneously the German legislature adopted the Act on the modernization of the framework conditions for equity investments (*Gesetz zur Modernisierung der Rahmenbedingungen für Kapitalbeteiligungen, MoRaKG*) with the aim to raise more equity capital for young and medium sized companies by giving tax incentives for risk capital investments. An essential part of the act is the Venture Capital Act (*Wagniskapitalbeteiligungsgesetz, WKBG*) which "introduces" the Venture Capital Investment Company (*Wagniskapitalbeteiligungsgesellschaft,VCIC*). A VCIC is classified according to tax law as investment managing and is not subject to the trade tax. The law was subject to a standstill clause pending Commission approval. On 30 September 2009 the Commission took a negative decision under State aid rules on the business tax break (*Gewerbesteuerbefreiung*) and on the right of target enterprises acquired by VCICs to carry forward losses. At the same time, the Commission authorized income tax benefits for private investors subject to certain conditions.

In response to the financial markets crisis, the Basel Committee on Banking Supervision formulated various new banking regulatory rules, which the European Union compiled in the EU Capital Requirements Directive II (CRD II) in 2009. Germany implemented CRD II, the Risk Management Directive, the Directives 2009/44/EC and 2009/83/EG and, partially even before it's enacting, the Capital Requirements Directive III (CRD III) by 31 December 2010 through an omnibus act which revised, inter alia, the Banking Act, the Mortgage Bond Act, the Securities Acquisition and Takeover Act and the Commercial Code. The new rules primarily relate to regulatory capital and introduced changes to the Banking Act with regard to:

- Standardized principles for the acceptance of hybrid capital as core capital;
- The regulations on securitizations and resecuritizations and stricter rules on disclosure requirements; the German legislator doubles the 5 % retention rule stipulated by the EU Directive, i. e. the German law includes a 10 % retention rule for securitizations originated by German institutions, to be introduced in 2013;
- The revision of large credit regulations and risk mitigation;
- The consolidation of cooperation between regulatory authorities within the European Union; and
- Remuneration policies.

A greater part of CRD III will be transformed by the end of 2011 through a regulation revising the Solvency Regulation as well as a circular letter.

The Basel Committee has agreed and published new capital and liquidity rules for banks on 16th December 2010 (the so-called Basel III regulatory frameworks for capital and liquidity). On 13th January 2011 it published a press release on the loss absorbency of capital at the point of non-viability. The third of the Basel Accords was developed in a response to the deficiencies in financial regulation revealed by the global financial crisis. It strengthens bank capital requirements and introduces new regulatory requirements on bank liquidity and bank leverage. The Basel III frameworks, which contain partly fundamental changes and a variety of measures, shall be incorporated into national law by the end of 2012 so that the rules can become effective on 1st January 2013. In the EU the frameworks will be implemented in the context of the Capital Requirements Directive IV (CRD IV) whose regulations then are transferred into German law. There will be transition periods which provide a gradual introduction of the new regulations not later than 1st January 2019.

Claudia Leyendecker, M.C.J. (New York)
claudia.leyendecker@luther-lawfirm.com

Dr. Rolf Kobabe
rolf.kobabe@luther-lawfirm.com

CHAPTER 16
DISTRIBUTION LAW

VOLKER STEIMLE

Control and influence on the one hand as well as distribution costs and the economic risks on the other are basic criteria for finding the ideal distribution channel. The most important types of distribution intermediaries in Germany are commercial agents, distributors and the use of franchisees. Since there is no written law on distributorship and franchising – as in almost all other European countries – the German Commercial Code as well as the Act of Insurance Contracts are the most important legal sources to be considered to establish an effective distribution business in Germany.

A. Introduction

German law offers a variety of possibilities and legal vehicles to a foreign manufacturer or service provider who wishes to distribute its products in Germany. The manufacturer may establish its own distribution company, which gives it the maximum influence on the behavior of "its" distributor, e.g. pricing, selection criteria, service levels, sales personnel etc. in the foreign market. On the other hand, this entails not only considerable expense, but also requires extensive organization and control. Another option is the sale of goods through independent traders where there is a mere buyer/seller relationship (importers, wholesalers, retailers). In this case, the manufacturer has no fixed costs so there should be no risks or problems with the profitability of the distribution, but this means the loss of almost any influence on the handling of the distribution and the positioning of the brand. This lack of an effective coordination may damage the value of a brand and impair the manufacturer's business. The manufacturer must therefore balance control and influence on the distribution of its products, against participation in distribution costs and economic risks, when deciding which distribution channel ideally fits its purposes.

In order to avoid these extremes, small to medium sized manufacturing companies in particular tend to engage independent sales intermediaries who are still subject to a certain degree of control. These relationships may be established as exclusive relationships. Eventually, the distribution structure that meets the best objectives of a foreign company that wants to successfully enter the German market should not lose sight of tax issues.

The most important types of distribution intermediaries in Germany are commercial agents (*Handelsvertreter*) and distributors (*Händler*). The use of franchisees and commission agents is also quite common. In general, foreign suppliers are not subject to specific regulations with regard to their distribution channel. However, if they choose to not rely on a direct distribution but on the aforementioned independent sales intermediaries, a variety of mandatory rules have to be considered. German law provides regulations for commercial agents and commissionaires in Sects. 84–92c respectively Sects. 383–403 of the German Commercial Code (*Handelsgesetzbuch*, *HGB*). In addition to this, the law on commercial agents has been addressed and harmonized in the European Member States based on a Directive of 1986,[1] and there are special regulations for commercial agents who act as insurance agents in Sects. 59–68 of the Act on Insurance Contracts (*Versicherungsvertragsgesetz*, *VVG*). In spite of the practical importance, Germany and almost all other European countries still lack codification of distributor and franchising law.

The main difference between commercial agents and distributors is that commercial agents are only intermediates in transactions between the manufacturer and its customers concluded in the manufacturer's name and for its account, whereas a distributor purchases the contracting partner's products in a long-term business relationship and resells them in its own name and for its own account. As a result of this, the commercial agent's remuneration consists of either a commission or a fixed amount (or a combination thereof), whilst the distributor's remuneration usually comprises the profit it achieves as a result of the difference between the original purchase price and the final sale price, i. e. the original purchase price will often reflect discounts and rebates on the list price of a product which are granted to an agent by the manufacturer. Moreover, in contrast to a relationship with a distributor, the fiduciary duties[2] owed by a commercial agent to its principal are more extensive. As a result the principal has more influence over the behavior of the commercial agent in the market and the commercial agent is supposed to be more dependent on its principal for certain protection.

The franchisee is distinguished from a commercial agent by selling goods or offering services in its own name and on its own account like a distributor. In contrast to a distributor, however, the franchisee is far more integrated into the organizational and advertising system provided by the franchisor since it is entitled – and also obliged – to use the brand, selling and production techniques developed by the franchisor. This means that this relationship is typically subject to a detailed contractual arrangement.

A commission agent sells goods in his own name, but for the account of the principal, Sects. 383 et seq. HGB. Commissionaire agreements are not very widespread but

---

1 EWG/653/1986.

2 Martinek/Semler/Habermeier/Flohr 3rd ed., 2010, § 4 Tn. 9.

are used where the intermediary has a strong position in a narrow market, e. g. in the financing sector, stock exchanges etc. They sometimes are used in order to optimize the tax structuring on intragroup supply chain management arrangements.

As a very rough guideline, one could say that a commercial agent provides for the highest degree of control by the principal, followed by the commissionaire and then the franchisee. The least degree of control is provided by a distributor arrangement, although this depends upon whether exclusive or non-exclusive distribution is being considered. The degree of control is mirrored by the business risks assumed (e.g. in relation to the keeping and financing of inventories, after-sales obligations, obtaining of permits for the relevant products etc.) and – consequently – the profit margins typically to be granted to the intermediaries for the different distribution channels.

B. Commercial Agency

I. Conclusion of the Contract

As a general rule, agency agreements do not need to be in writing and can therefore be concluded orally or even tacitly. However, the HGB provides two exceptions. First, a del credere agreement, under which the commercial agent guarantees the fulfillment of the customer's obligations resulting from a transaction, must be concluded in writing (Sec. 86b HGB). Second, a post-contractual non-competition undertaking is only binding when in written form, cf. Sec. 90a HGB. Notwithstanding these requirements, a commercial agent may also claim that a written document containing the oral agreements and signed by the principal has to be established anyway, Sec. 85 HGB.

II. Contractual Obligations of the Commercial Agent

The main obligation of the commercial agent is to seek to arrange the conclusion of transactions for the principal on an ongoing basis. Not only is it the responsibility of the commercial agent to maintain and increase the business with existing customers, but also to acquire new customers for the products of the principal and to regularly give reports thereon.

The extent and limits of a commercial agent's activities largely depend on the contractual agreement.

In the absence of an explicit contractual agreement that provides otherwise, German courts tend to accept that an implied undertaking is given by the commercial agent not to represent competing manufacturers during the term of the agency agreement.[3] However, this is not a post-contractual non-compete restriction which would require not only explicit written agreement but would also be restricted to a maximum duration of two years starting on the date on which the contract was terminated. To be valid, such a post-contractual non-compete restriction also needs to vest the commercial agent with a claim for a reasonable compensation during the period in which competition is restricted.

As a general principle, the commercial agent is obliged to obey the instructions of its principal. This applies to all respects of the distribution and allows the principal to e.g. fix the resale prices or any other terms to be agreed with the customers. Restrictions on this principle arise, as a general rule of thumb, if the parties have chosen the contractual vehicle of agency to circumvent the rules of cartel law.[4] Further care has to be taken that the commercial agent's independence is not impermissibly impaired. Otherwise the commercial agent may be regarded as an employee of the principal or a comparable person and, as a result, the regulations of labor law will apply.[5]

As an option, del credere agreements and commitments to collect customer receivables can be agreed. In particular, the conclusion of collection agreements often makes sense in cross-border agency agreements. The commercial agent residing within the relevant market is generally better positioned in this regard than the principal residing abroad who is not necessarily familiar with local law and customs like payment habits. Besides these, some further duties which are not mandated by the HGB, can often be agreed.

III. Contractual Obligations of the Principal

The German Commercial Code sets out a number of obligations with which the principal is required to comply where a relationship has been established with a commercial agent. The main obligation is to remunerate the commercial agent for the successful arrangement or conclusion of transactions, Sec. 87 (1) HGB. Remuneration may consist of either a commission, being a success fee, a fixed remuneration or a combination thereof (a so-called guaranteed commission). Unless explicitly agreed otherwise, the commission is only to be paid if a contract with a customer is eventually concluded and if the customer under the relevant contract pays the purchase price, Sects. 87a (1) and 2 HGB. If the commercial agent is granted a guaranteed contractual territory (*Bezirksvertretung*), the commission is due irrespective of whether the contract with the customer was actually concluded or arranged by the

3 BGH NJW 1969, 1662, 1664.
4 BGH NJW 1986, 2954, 2955 ("Telefunken").
5 BGH NZA 1999, 53, 55 ("Eismann").

agent or not. It is in the principal's interest to avoid this by way of the relevant provisions in an agency contract. Where there is a fixed commission, the commercial agent is promised a minimum commission irrespective of its business results. Since the principal here incurs costs, irrespective of whether the commercial agent is successful or not, it is more common to agree upon a commission which depends on concrete business results. A guaranteed or fixed commission however may be suitable for a period during which business relations are being built up in new sales territories, for example.

Special problems can arise regarding commissions which are based on sales that have been arranged during the effective period of the agency agreement but which are only due at the end of said agreement (so-called overhang commissions[6]) or when the transaction concluded or arranged by the agent consists of a long-term framework agreement with the customer which survives the duration of the agency agreement.[7]

In addition to the obligation to remunerate the commercial agent for its activities, the principal is committed to provide all necessary information to its commercial agent.[8] The importance of fiduciary duties also should not be underestimated. The principal has to support the fulfillment of the commercial agent's obligations and has to refrain from doing anything that might conflict with the commercial agent's interests, to a reasonable extent.

Tax problems regarding the commission to be paid should always be considered in detail when an affiliated company of the principal performs the distribution. In that case, the "arm's length" doctrine requires special tailoring for the relevant conditions.

IV. Ending the Contractual Relationship

A contractual relationship which is entered into for a specific period ends upon expiry of the period. An agreement of indefinite duration will usually be terminated following expiry of a statutory notice – this will be based on the length of time which the agreement has been in force. The period ranges from one month in the first year of the contract to a maximum of six months from the fifth year onwards, Sec. 89 HGB. It may be extended by contractual agreement, but not shortened. If the notice period is extended, the agreement cannot provide that the notice period for the commercial agent shall be longer than that for the principal. It is also possible to enter into a cancellation agreement, to which no notice period applies.

6 Sec. 87 (3) HGB.
7 See Baumbach/Hopt 34th ed. 2010, § 87 HGB, Tn. 41.
8 BGH Decision of 4.5.2011, VIII ZR 11/10.

The contractual relationship may also be terminated for good cause at any time without observing a notice period. In this case, it is crucial that the terminating party cannot reasonably be expected to continue the contractual relationship until the end of the aforementioned period. Typical examples of a situation where the relationship may be terminated for good cause would include the commercial agent representing a competing company or the principal repeatedly breaching its obligation to pay commission. If the contractual relationship is terminated validly for good cause by the principal, because of a breach of contract which is the responsibility of the agent, the commercial agent will usually lose any claim it might have to compensation.

V. Compensation Claims

The commercial agent is entitled to compensation following termination of the contractual relationship in respect of recurrent new customers acquired by it during the term of the contract, Sec. 89b HGB. This also applies to those recurrent customers with whom the agent has significantly developed an existing customer relationship. The purpose of this provision is to remunerate the commercial agent for the customer base which it has acquired for the benefit of the principal and to the extent that it is of lasting value to the latter.[9] The claim for compensation cannot be waived by the agent or otherwise be contractually derogated, and is only excluded in limited circumstances in particular if the commercial agent terminated the agreement itself, other than for good cause, or if the principal terminated it for good cause within the responsibility of the agent, Sec. 89b (3) HGB.

In such cases, the commercial agent is entitled to receive a compensation equivalent to the benefit acquired by the principal from the acquisition of customers by the commercial agent. In most cases this will amount to the commissions the commercial agent would have earned from future transactions with the recurrent customers that were acquired, intensified or reactivated by it.[10] The calculation of the compensation is often very difficult. Furthermore, it is important to consider if there are any special circumstances which may reduce the claim in good faith – here, in particular, the "bandwagon effect of the brand" is relevant.[11] The claim is, however, limited and may not exceed the average annual commission based on the last five years of the commercial agent's activities. In practice, this cap usually determines the amount of the compensation claim to be paid.

9 BGH NJW 1957, 1029, 1030 et seq.

10 This way to calculate the compensation to the commercial agent is in compliance with the legal situation applicable until 2009, which will in practice apply in the vast majority of cases still today.

11 Depending on the strength of the relevant brand this typically results in deductions of up to 25 %.

VI. Choice of Governing Law

If the commercial agent and the principal reside in different countries, it is advisable for both parties to agree on the law governing the agreement and the choice of forum in advance. Otherwise it is usually the national law of the commercial agent's seat or headquarters which will apply. Where this is done in a standard form contract, some caution needs to be applied. The German Courts of Appeals in Celle, Bremen and Dresden – confirmed by a ruling of the German Federal High Court[12] – have held in the case of franchisees of the network of "Subway" restaurants that a contractual clause between the Dutch principal (i. e. the Dutch affiliate of the US Franchisor "Subway") and German franchisees providing for arbitration to be held in New York is invalid.

Certain limits are, however, imposed on the choice of the applicable law. As with most other national laws, German law provides a number of regulations which apply to contracts irrespective of the law chosen. This principle has been emphasized by a ruling of the European Court of Justice[13] and restricts the effects of a choice of non-EU-laws. In particular, rules relating to the protection of the agent concerning, for example, the commercial agent's claim to remuneration or the claim for compensation along with the minimum notice periods for termination: all have to be considered since these have now been harmonized throughout the EU.

A different approach is possible if the commercial agent performs its activities solely outside the territory of the European Union or the European Economic Area. In this case, Sec. 92c HGB allows derogation from mandatory regulations, e.g. the compensation claims, shorter notice periods etc.

C. Distributors

I. Distribution Agreement

The distribution contract is defined as a framework agreement under which the distributor is obliged to sell the manufacturer's goods in its own name and for its own account, thereby integrated into the sales organization of the manufacturer. Again, such an agreement can be concluded informally, i. e. orally or tacitly. Compared to a commercial agent, the distributor is usually less restrained by instructions of the

---

12 cf. Schulz, Niedermaier *Unwirksame Schiedsklausel in Franchiseverträgen durch Wahl des Tagungsortes im Ausland?*, SchiedsVZ 2009, 196.

13 Ruling of November 9, 2000 (C-381/98).

principal but, on the other hand, he generally takes over more obligations i. e. maintaining a warehouse, a stock of spare parts or providing after-sales services.

Alongside rights to remuneration, which are typically granted by way of a dealer's margin/dealer's discount, the contractual obligations of the principal are comparable to those of the principal and a commercial agent where the distributor is equivalently integrated into the sales organization of the principal.

A territorial protection or exclusivity clause is often included in distribution agreements, providing that only the distributor may sell the manufacturer's products in the contractual territory. Since such clauses prevent a manufacturer from appointing other distributors in a certain territory or from concluding transactions directly and therefore may impair competition, they often require exemption, regularly under European competition law. Even if the parties agree on an exclusivity clause, it is not unusual for a manufacturer to reserve the right to supply certain major customers with whom business relations already existed before concluding the distribution agreement.

Distribution systems between non-competing companies are widely covered by the EU Block Exemption Regulation for Vertical Restraints[14] (*Vertikal-Gruppenfreistellungsverordnung*), which applies to products and services in all industries except for motor vehicle distribution and technology transfer, which are governed by their own special Block Exemption Regulations.[15] If the share of the supplier (for exclusive purchase agreements: of the buyer) in the relevant market does not exceed 30 %, most of the vertical restraints of competition are exempted by law from the general prohibition of restraints of trade. Some particularly restrictive clauses, however, are "blacklisted" and do not benefit from said exemption (e.g. minimum or fixed resale price maintenance, granting of excessive territorial protection and certain other restraints of inter-brand or intra-brand competition). Non-competition clauses, which also include exclusive purchasing agreements, may not exceed five years' duration. Agreements that are not covered by the Block Exemption (e.g. because the market share threshold is exceeded) but are also not "blacklisted" may still benefit from exemption, which needs, however, to be established for each individual case.[16]

German competition law, which applies as well to cases that are purely domestic, has been harmonized with the European scheme. As a result, German competition law is now less restrictive than in the past and the parties have more freedom in forming

14 EU/330/2010.

15 EU/461/2010 on the distribution of motor vehicles and EC/772/2004 on technology transfer – presently under review.

16 Art. 101 (3) AEUV.

their distribution contracts, e.g. on recommended retail prices or most preferred customer clauses.

II. Ending the Contractual Relationship

A distribution agreement concluded for a specific period ends upon expiry of the specified period. An agreement not limited by time can be ended by termination for good cause at any time, without observing a notice period. As a result of the lack of codification of the law of distributorship, problems often arise regarding the question of which notice period applies when there is no good cause for the termination. German courts show a tendency to decide that the period of notice for a distributor contract needs to be longer than the one for an agency contract, because the distributor is often forced to undertake relatively high investments which would be devalued by the possibility of a short notice period. Therefore, a minimum notice period for termination of one year is considered reasonable in most cases (exclusive distributorship).[17] Longer periods may be required depending on the industry and the duration of the contractual relationship. Two years may be required, for example, for the distribution of motor vehicles based on the EU Block Exemption Regulation EU/1400/2002, which has, however, been replaced by a new Block Exemption Regulation (EU/461/2010) which no longer provides for such a requirement.

III. Claim for Compensation and Repurchase of Delivered Products

When ending a distribution agreement the key issue is whether, as with commercial agents, a distributor can claim compensation in respect of the recurrent customers it acquired during the term of the agreement. German courts have generally held this to be the case if the status of the distributor is equivalent to the relationship between a commercial agent and its principal.[18] Thereby, no claim for compensation exists if the contractual relationship does not exceed a mere buyer/seller relationship. In practice, the decisive question here is whether the distributor is contractually obliged to disclose his customer base to the principal.

The principles for the calculation of the compensation are in most parts comparable with those applicable to a commercial agency agreement. However, there is a difference concerning the basis of calculation. The claim for compensation of a commercial agent is based on its commission. The dealer's margin, by contrast, also contains remuneration for activities which are usually not taken over by a commercial agent,

17 cf. Court of Appeals Stuttgart, NJW-RR 1990, 491, 491 et. seq.
18 Starting with BGH NJW 1959, 144, 145 et seq.

e.g. after-sales, financing of inventories etc. This part of the dealer's margin does not have to be compensated for, i. e. the dealer's margin has to be reduced to the level of an agent's commission for the purpose of calculating the compensation claim.[19]

For the calculation of the compensation the problem of the "bandwagon effect of the brand" is even more acute than in an agency agreement. The success of a product in the market does not solely depend on the dealer's selling skills and efforts but also on the customer's general experience with products of the relevant brand and on centrally controlled advertising campaigns of the principal. This may result in a mitigation of the compensation claims. In any case, if the distributor was committed to keep a minimum of products in stock during the term of the contract, the principal is obliged to repurchase the remaining goods in stock after the end of the contract.[20]

IV. Choice of Law

Similar questions apply here as already pointed out with regard to the commercial agent. There are, however, further uncertainties since the law of distributorship is not codified in Germany. This may allow an argument that the afore-said ruling of the European Court of Justice on the compensation claim of the commercial agent being mandatory, despite a choice of law, is not applicable here. This should even more be the case, since there are quite a number of European countries that do not provide for such a claim for dealers.[21]

D. Franchise Agreements

Franchising is a contractual method for marketing and distributing the goods and services of a company through a dedicated or restricted network of distributors. Ideally, it is a contractual relationship between a principal with a proven business system and an ambitious "independent" distributor willing to follow its system. It is most successful where homogenous goods or services can be offered in large quantities under a joint brand that penetrates the consumer consciousness. The franchisee constitutes an independent entity even if it appears to be part of the franchisor and the same legal principles are applicable as with commission agents and distributors. Because of this, it is the prevailing opinion that under German law a franchisee may claim compensation similar to that of a commercial agent or a distributor after the

---

19 BGH, see above.
20 BGH BB 1994, 885, 890 et seq. ("Daihatsu").
21 E.g. France, Italy, Netherlands.

end of the contractual relationship – German courts, however, have not finally decided on this matter.

The afore-mentioned Block Exemption Regulation for vertical relationships EU/330/2010 also governs franchise agreements in terms of anti-trust law. There remain, however, a number of issues of concern under this new regulation including exclusivity and non-competition clauses.[22]

Volker Steimle
volker.steimle@luther-lawfirm.com

22 See for more guidance Guidelines on Vertical Restraints (2010/C 130/01), para. 189–191 on Franchising.

CHAPTER 17
LITIGATION, ARBITRATION AND MEDIATION

DR. RICHARD HAPP

There are different ways available for resolving disputes, including by litigation in front of the competent public courts, by decision of a panel of arbitrators either constituted ad hoc or under the rules of institutional arbitration, or by mediated agreement of the parties.

A. Litigation

I. The Court System

Courts in Germany are divided into ordinary courts (*ordentliche Gerichte*) and specialized courts (*Fachgerichte*). Ordinary courts exercise jurisdiction over all matters not allocated to any of the specialized courts (administrative, tax, labor or social courts), i. e. civil and criminal law. Situated above those regular branches is the Federal Constitutional Court[1] (*Bundesverfassungsgericht, BVerfG*). The court has the power to review laws and cases submitted to it by other courts, local or federal parliaments and even individuals. Besides, since Germany is a Member State of the European Union and the Council of Europe, it is – under specific circumstances – possible for foreign investors to submit cases to the Court of Justice of the European Union and the European Court of Human Rights.

II. Structure of the Civil Section of the Ordinary Courts

The branch of the court system which might be of most importance for a foreign company is the civil section of the ordinary courts. The composition of the ordinary courts is governed by the Courts Constitution Act (*Gerichtsverfassungsgesetz*, GVG).[2] Within the ordinary courts, there are a number of different hierarchy levels, which

---

1 http://www.bverfg.de/en/index.html.

2 *Gerichtsverfassungsgesetz* (GVG) (Courts Constitution Act) 1877 (F.R.G.). An English translation is available at http://www.gesetze-im-internet.de/englisch_gvg/index.html.

range from low to high: Local Courts (*Amtsgerichte*, AG); Regional Courts (*Landgerichte*, LG); Higher Regional Courts (*Oberlandesgerichte*, OLG); and the Federal Court of Justice[3] (*Bundesgerichtshof, BGH*). Although the courts are divided into state courts at the lower levels and federal courts at the higher levels, all courts apply the same law. Unlike in the United States, for example, there are no parallel tiers of state and federal courts.

In Local Courts, civil cases are tried by a single judge.[4] In Regional Courts, simple cases are tried by a single judge and complex cases by a bench of three judges.[5] Also, there is a specialized commercial division (*Kammer für Handelssachen*) at most regional courts which consists of a professional judge plus two appointed expert laymen from the commercial sector. A claimant can choose to file his claim with the commercial division if the dispute is of a commercial nature. The Higher Regional Courts and the Federal Court of Justice generally comprise a panel of either three or five judges respectively. In order to ensure that any case is tried in front of a competent judge, panels specialized in specific areas of law (e.g. anti-trust law, corporate law) have been established by many courts.

III. Subject Matter and Territorial Jurisdiction of the Courts

At entry level, local and regional courts may have subject matter jurisdiction;[6] only in limited cases also the higher regional court has jurisdiction at first instance.[7] In general, the jurisdiction of the local/regional courts is dependent on the amount in dispute: Local courts have jurisdiction over claims worth up to 5,000.00 EUR whereas claims with a value exceeding this amount are tried at regional courts. Exceptions to this rule are made, for example, in disputes on family law or the leasing of apartments.[8]

Territorial jurisdiction of German courts can be established by several means. First, it is possible for the parties of a dispute to choose a specific German court, either in advance by inserting a *choice of forum* clause into a contract or after the dispute arose by agreeing on the jurisdiction. If the parties have not reached an agreement, the territorial jurisdiction is determined (as in all EU Member States) by the Brus-

---

3 Further information can be found at http://www.bundesgerichtshof.de/EN/Home/home_node.html.

4 Gerichtsverfassungsgesetz (GVG) Sec. 22 (F.R.G.).

5 Sec. 75 GVG; *Zivilprozessordnung (ZPO)* (Civil Procedure Act) Sec. 348 (F.R.G.).

6 Sects. 23, 71 GVG.

7 Sects. 118 GVG. A pertinent example is matters relating to arbitration proceedings. This is explained in more detail below.

8 Sects. 23 (I no. 2) GVG.

sels-I Regulation[9] adopted by the EU, as well as the German Civil Procedure Code (*Zivilprozessordnung*, ZPO).[10] Unless there are specific rules, the courts at the place of domicile of the defendant have jurisdiction. Nevertheless, there are many special rules on jurisdiction: in the case of contracts, the place of performance is decisive, while in case of a tort the courts at the place where the harm occurred have jurisdiction.

IV. Appeal and Revision

First instance judgments can be appealed (*Berufung*) on issues of fact and law if the amount in dispute on appeal exceeds 600 EUR or if the appeal has been explicitly allowed in the judgment of first instance.[11] In general, appeals are brought before the next highest court in the hierarchy.[12] Judgments of the appellate courts can be brought for a second review at the Federal Court of Justice.[13] This legal remedy (*Revision*) has to be based on alleged errors of law and is only permissible if it has been granted in the contested judgment, although a complaint can be filed against a refusal of this grant with the Federal Court of Justice.[14]

V. Basic Principles of German Civil Procedure and Differences to Common-Law Civil Procedure

The German Constitution, the Basic Law[15] (*Grundgesetz*, GG), guarantees all natural and legal persons the right of due process. Due process includes, inter alia, the right to be present at the trial, to be heard in court, and to have a fair and public trial presided over by unprejudiced and neutral judges.

Contentious civil court proceedings in Germany are governed by the Civil Procedure Code. Court proceedings start by the plaintiff filing a lawsuit with the court of first instance, which will be served on the defendant by the court. Once the case is pending, the court will decide on the further procedure. Either, it can immediately conduct an oral hearing (*Früher erster Termin*);[16] or it can require the parties to file several rounds of written briefs before an oral hearing will be conducted (*Schriftliches*

---

9 Council Regulation (EC) No 44/2001 of 22 December 2000 on jurisdiction and the recognition and enforcement of judgments in civil and commercial matters, OJ L 12, 16.1.2001, p. 1.

10 Sects. 12–40 ZPO.

11 Sec. 511 (2) ZPO.

12 Sects. 72, 119 GVG; special rules apply in the case of family matters.

13 Sec. 542 ZPO.

14 Sec. 544 ZPO.

15 *Grundgesetz für die Bundesrepublik Deutschland.* English translation available under http://www.gesetze-im-internet.de/englisch_gg/index.html.

16 Sec. 275 ZPO.

Vorverfahren).[17] At the beginning of an oral hearing, the judge is required to discuss with the parties the prospects of an amicable settlement; besides, German courts are expected to encourage an amicable settlement of the dispute at every stage of the proceedings.[18] This is a cornerstone of German Civil Procedure, but might be very unusual for foreign parties.

There are some further peculiarities of German civil procedure compared, e.g., with Anglo-American civil procedure: The judge plays a central role; there is no right that the case be heard in front of a jury. Although civil proceedings are of an adversarial nature, the judge is not allowed to lean back and let the parties do the work. To the contrary: the judge has to give the parties directions in case they missed relevant legal or factual issues.[19] The judge is also required by law to further an amicable settlement in all stages of the procedure. In case of witness or expert examination, the judge himself will conduct the examination. The parties can only ask questions afterwards. As witnesses are directly examined by the judge in the first place, it generally is not possible to replace direct examination with written witness statements or interrogatories; nor is it possible to cross-examine a witness.

Furthermore, the parties only have to establish facts but not the law. This is described by the Latin legal maxims "*iura novit curia*" (The court knows the law) and "*da mihi facta, dabo tibi ius*" (Give me the facts, I will tell you the law). Nevertheless, the parties' briefs in general will contain extensive discussions on what the valid law is. When the judge has to apply foreign law, these maxims do not apply and the parties have to establish the rules of the foreign law applicable.[20]

Contrary to Anglo-American legal procedure, no pre-trial discovery exists in which the parties can require the other party to disclose all potentially relevant information.[21] Rather, the parties only have to produce evidence during trial in case a certain fact, which is actually relevant for the outcome of the case, is disputed by the parties; the decision, whether evidence for establishing a certain fact is considered necessary, is solely for the judge. Thus, the production of evidence (and the connected costs) is reduced to a minimum. On the one hand, hearings in German civil law proceedings will – even if the examination of several witnesses will be conducted – usually not take longer than 4 to 5 hours, as the examination is limited to the relevant facts. On the other hand, due to the absence of a pre-trial discovery, it can be

17 Sec. 276 ZPO.

18 Sec. 278 (1) ZPO.

19 Sec. 139 ZPO.

20 Sec. 293 ZPO.

21 Discovery orders by, e.g., US courts, are very difficult to enforce in Germany, see Geercken/Holden/Rath/Surguy/Stretton, Cross Border E-Discovery: How to manage potential evidence in an international environment, CRi 2010, p. 65 et. seq.

difficult for a party to get access to information about relevant facts which are "under control" of the other party.

VI. Summary Proceedings for Order to Pay Debts

Taking into account that many disputes over a right to receive payment are quite uncomplicated from a legal point of view, there is a need for an efficient, fast, and convenient procedure to recover overdue outstanding debts. German law does provide such an instrument by allowing creditors to file a motion requesting that the court issue an order to pay against the debtor (*Mahnverfahren*).[22] The motion is granted without reviewing the merits of the claim. The plaintiff just has to allege that a certain amount of money is due for payment. If the debtor identified in the court order does not contest the claim within two weeks upon service of the order, the creditor can apply for an enforceable order that has the same standing as a judgment (*Vollstreckungsbescheid*). If the debtor objects, the creditor has to decide whether or not to pursue his interests in a regular civil trial.

VII. Provisional Measures

To secure the legal and factual position of a party before or during a lawsuit, German procedural law offers the option of obtaining an interlocutory injunction (*Einstweilige Verfügung*)[23] or an attachment order/judgment (*Arrest*) against the other party.[24] As a general rule, the attachment order/judgment aims at securing a future enforcement of a judgment for monetary claims; interlocutory injunctions concern all other claims. An interim payment order/judgment is only likely to be granted under very exceptional circumstances as in the case of maintenance claims.

As a general rule, interlocutory injunctions may not pre-empt a final decision by the courts. Thus, for instance in order to secure a claim for restitution, the court will order the respondent to turn over the disputed item to a bailiff (*Gerichtsvollzieher*), but not to the applicant. It is worth noting that the court has a large discretion in deciding what measure is considered appropriate to secure the applicant's claim;[25] the applicant's submission is rather a proposal what the court could order. To secure claims for money, an order or judgment of attachment against the assets of the defendant can be obtained. If later on the provisional measure is held by a court to have been unjustified, compensation for damages must be paid to the defendant.[26]

22 Sec. 688–703d ZPO.
23 Sec. 935, 940 ZPO.
24 Sec. 916 ZPO.
25 Sec. 938 ZPO.
26 Sec. 945 ZPO.

Depending on the subject matter and its complexity, a court can issue an interlocutory injunction or an attachment order immediately; it is not unusual to submit a request in the morning and obtain the injunction after lunch. If the court considers an oral hearing necessary before it will grant the injunction, it might take one or two weeks. In case there is an oral hearing, the court will render a judgement (*Urteil*); otherwise, the attachment/the interlocutory injunction will issued as "order" (*Beschluss*).

The respondent can appeal a judgment or file an objection against an order.[27] The court can also order the applicant to file a full lawsuit on the merits within a certain time or else the judgment/order will be vacated.[28]

VIII. Independent Proceedings for Taking of Evidence

Irrespective of whether a claim is already pending, German procedural law gives parties the option to take evidence in independent proceedings (*Selbstständiges Beweisverfahren*).[29] As a prerequisite, there must be cause for concern that evidence will be lost or will deteriorate before the court officially decides to take evidence. If no lawsuit is pending, such proceedings are also permissible if the party initiating the proceedings has an interest to have determined:

- The condition of a person or an object, or
- The causes for damage or an injury, or
- The necessary efforts to remedy a damage.[30]

Thus, such proceedings are common in cases concerning construction disputes or damage claims for personal injury, or where goods damaged are perishable. The evidence taken in such proceedings can later be introduced into the lawsuit as regular evidence.[31] If the applicant succeeds in a later lawsuit, it can claim reimbursement of the costs connected with the independent evidence proceedings; if it does not file a lawsuit because, for instance, the evidence shows that it will not succeed, the court can order the applicant to reimburse the respondent's costs resulting from these proceedings.[32]

---

27 Sec. 924 ZPO.
28 Sec. 926 ZPO.
29 Sec. 485–494a ZPO.
30 Sec 485 ZPO.
31 Sec. 493 ZPO.
32 Sec. 494a ZPO.

IX. Duration of Proceedings

It is difficult to give an estimate on the general duration of civil trials in Germany, as the duration of a trial very much depends on the court with which the case is filed and its caseload. For an average simple claim filed with a regional court, the first instance might be concluded – and a judgment rendered – within six to eight months from the date of the filing. However, this very much depends on the docket of the individual court, and appeal proceedings can vary between one to three years.

X. Costs of Proceedings

The costs of a lawsuit will comprise court fees and extrajudicial costs such as the attorneys' fees, which will both ultimately have to be paid by the party losing the case. Court fees are calculated pursuant to the Court Fees Act (*Gerichtskostengesetz*, GKG) and depend on the value of the claim/the amount in dispute, which corresponds to a statutory defined base fee (e.g. in the case of a disputed amount of EUR 10,000.00/ 100,000.00/1,000,000.00 the court fees are EUR 588.00 EUR 2,568.00/13,368.00). Before the court will serve a lawsuit, the claimant has to advance the court fees.[33] However, the claimant will generally be reimbursed by the defendant if/to the extent the lawsuit is successful.[34]

Similarly, the claimant can demand the reimbursement of its attorney's fees on the basis of the statutory attorney fees if and insofar he wins. The attorneys' fees are regulated by the Attorney Fees Act (*Rechtsanwaltsvergütungsgesetz*, *RVG*). These fees are calculated pursuant to the value in dispute and finally depend on the status of the proceedings: raising the lawsuit, arguing the case during the oral hearing and settling the case each entail separate fees. Although it is possible to agree on higher fees or hourly rates, German law widely prohibits contingency fees, which may only be agreed upon in special circumstances and if the client would otherwise be precluded from litigating. It is not possible for the attorney/client to agree on fees lower than those prescribed by statute.

The statutory fees for the attorney in case of a disputed amount of EUR 10,000.00/ 100,000.00/1,000,000.00 value at EUR 1,469.65/4,051.95/13,399.40 in case there is an oral hearing; in case there is no oral hearing, the fees are EUR 775.64/2,118.44/ 6,979.11.[35] As has been mentioned before, these costs will be reimbursed in case the lawsuit succeeds. In case it does not, the claimant will have to bear its own attorney's

33 Sec. 12 GKG.

34 Sects. 91, 92 ZPO.

35 No liability is accepted for potential errors in these calculations or subsequent changes in the law, any potential party is advised to consult with its lawyer in advance to get a binding opinion.

fee plus the defendant's fees, having the same amount. In case of only partial success, the costs will be shared between the parties in a proportion determined by the court.[36]

XI. Enforcement

Final judgments can be enforced without any precondition, while judgments that still can be appealed generally are only enforceable after a security has been deposited.[37] There are several possibilities to enforce a monetary judgment. First, a bailiff can be requested to seize movable property of the debtor and to initiate a forced auction.[38] Second, the court can be requested either to order the forced sale or the forced administration of the debtor's real estate.[39] Or third, the court can be requested to attach rights or receivables of the debtor against third parties;[40] however, the attachment of receivables requires that the claimant-creditor specifies (name of the third party creditor, ground of the receivable) the receivables to be attached. This can pose a high burden on the claimant-creditor because generally he can only guess whether the debtor-defendant has claims against third parties.

XII. Foreign Judgments and Court Proceedings

Germany is member of the European Union. Thus, the European Regulations and Directives concerning civil procedure apply. Probably the most important legislation in this regard is the so-called Brussels I-Regulation on jurisdiction and the recognition and enforcement of judgments in civil and commercial matters. The Regulation prescribes the jurisdiction of the Member States' courts for citizens residing in the EU. Furthermore, it provides that judgments given in a Member State shall be recognized in the other Member States without any special procedure like an *exequatur* being required.[41] Also, all other Member States' courts have to stay proceedings until the court seized first has established whether it has jurisdiction.[42]

Besides, Germany is a Contracting party to only few bilateral and multilateral treaties on the jurisdiction and the mutual recognition and enforcement of judgments.

---

36 Sects. 92 ZPO.

37 Sects. 704, 708–710 ZPO.

38 Sects. 803, 814 ZPO.

39 Sects. 866 ZPO; *Gesetz über die Zwangsversteigerung und die Zwangsverwaltung* [ZVG] (Act on Forced Sales and Forced Administration).

40 Sects. 829, 857 ZPO.

41 Art. 33 (1) Council Regulation (EC) No 44/2001 of 22th December 2000 on jurisdiction and the recognition and enforcement of judgments in civil and commercial matters, OJ L 12, 16.1.2001, p. 1.

42 Art. 27 Council Regulation (EC) No 44/2001.

Judgments of other States will be enforced if reciprocity is guaranteed and if the court had jurisdiction according to the German principles of civil procedure.[43]

B. Arbitration

I. Overview

Arbitration, in particular in commercial matters, has a long tradition in Germany. The first codification of arbitration law on a federal level was in 1879. Since 1879 it is integrated in the tenth book of the German Code of Civil Procedure.[44] Since a reform of the ZPO in 1998, the German law on arbitration is based on the UNCITRAL Model Law on International Commercial Arbitration of 1985. This modernization was considered necessary in order to harmonize German arbitration law with international standards. To make the law easily accessible for foreign users, the drafters decided to stick as closely as possible to the wording of the UNCITRAL Model Law. Consequently, the provisions of the German arbitration law contained in the ZPO are to a large extent a verbatim adoption of the UNCITRAL Model Law. Germany is a contracting State of the 1958 New York Convention,[45] as well as of the 1961 Geneva Convention.[46]

It is one of the special characteristics of German arbitration practice that not only the parties but also the arbitral tribunal may – and frequently will – suggest settlement negotiations, subject to the agreement to the parties. Different from the situation under common law, the unsolicited suggestion of settlement proceedings is not considered to make the arbitral tribunal biased. As has been explained above, German courts are expected to encourage an amicable settlement of the dispute at every stage of the proceedings, and this is usually also expected by parties of arbitral tribunals. Experienced arbitrators, however, are aware of this difference when dealing with foreign parties.

II. German Arbitration Law – Scope of Application

German arbitration law applies to all civil matters as far as the place of arbitration is located in Germany;[47] it applies to both international and domestic arbitration.

43 Sects. 328 ZPO.

44 An English Translation can be found at www.dis-arb.de/en/51/materials/german-arbitration-law-98-id3.

45 Convention on the Recognition and Enforcement of Foreign Arbitral Awards of 10th June 1958 ("New York Convention").

46 European Convention on International Commercial Arbitration, 21th April 1961.

47 Sects. 1025 (1), 1030 ZPO.

A restriction to commercial disputes has not been included in German arbitration law. According to Sec. 1030 (1) ZPO, "*Any claim involving an economic interest (vermögensrechtlicher Anspruch) can be the subject of an arbitration agreement.*" However, disputes that would be submitted to the jurisdiction of financial or social courts are thereby excluded from arbitration.

Besides, certain provisions of the ZPO on arbitration also apply if the place of arbitration is situated outside Germany or has not yet been determined.[48] This concerns, first, the provisions on the relationship between the arbitration agreement and the jurisdiction of the State courts. Second, it concerns the supporting functions performed by State courts concerning the gathering of evidence.

In addition, if the place of arbitration has not yet been determined and the respondent or the claimant has his place of business or habitual residence in Germany, the German courts are competent to perform court functions concerning the composition of the arbitral tribunal (e.g. appointing "missing" arbitrators); concerning appointing or challenging arbitrators; or concerning terminating of the mandate of the arbitrator if he is unable to perform his functions.[49]

III. Form and Effect of the Arbitration Agreement

According to Sec. 1029 (2) ZPO an arbitration agreement may be concluded as a separate agreement (*Schiedsvereinbarung*) or be concluded as a clause in a contract (*Schiedsklausel*). Irrespective of its form, pursuant to Sec. 1040 (2) sentence 2 ZPO, an arbitration agreement is legally distinct and autonomous from the main contract. Thus, if a contract in which the arbitration agreement is incorporated is void, this generally has no impact on the validity of the arbitration agreement itself.

As a rule, arbitration agreements must be either in writing or in some other form or communication evidencing an agreement between the parties, via fax or any other medium of data transmission.[50] It need not be signed by both parties. An arbitration agreement can also be made in a document signed by the parties which refers to an arbitration clause contained in another document.[51] That is the case if an arbitration agreement or an exchange of correspondence refers to the standard terms and conditions of business of one of the parties which include an arbitration clause and thereby incorporates the arbitration clause into the agreement. According to Sec. 1031 (4) ZPO, an arbitration agreement is also concluded by the issuance of a bill of lading which contains an express reference to an arbitration clause in a charter party.

---

48 Sects. 1025 (2) ZPO.

49 Sects. 1034 et seq. ZPO.

50 Sects. 1034, 1031 (1) ZPO.

51 Sec. 1031 (3) ZPO.

The effect of a valid arbitration agreement is that it excludes the jurisdiction of the state courts for the decision and confers jurisdiction on the arbitral tribunal. Hence, a state court must refuse to exercise jurisdiction and declare the court action as inadmissible if an arbitration agreement is invoked by the defendant (*Schiedseinrede*).[52] Independent from time limits set by the court for a submission of the statement of defense, the objection may be raised until the beginning of the oral hearing on the merits. The objection is even open to a defendant who has already submitted written pleadings on the merits without challenging the jurisdiction of the court.

IV. Competence of the Arbitral Tribunal

Under German arbitration law, the arbitral tribunal may rule on its own jurisdiction and, in this context, on the existence or validity of the arbitration agreement. However, it is important to know that the arbitral tribunal's decision is still subject to control by the state courts. Sec. 1040 (3) ZPO should be regarded as a mandatory provision that the parties cannot derogate. It provides:

> *"If the arbitral tribunal considers that it has jurisdiction, it rules on a plea referred to in subsection 2 of this section in general by means of a preliminary ruling. In this case, any party may request, within one month after having received written notice of that ruling, the court to decide the matter. While such a request is pending, the arbitral tribunal may continue the arbitral proceedings and make an award."*

This means in particular that it is not possible for the parties to confer on the arbitral tribunal the final (and binding for the state court) *Kompetenz-Kompetenz* in respect to the decisions on the validity of the arbitration agreement. The arbitral tribunal should in general rule on the objection to its competence by means of a preliminary ruling (*Zwischenentscheid*) which will then be subject to court control.[53] However, the arbitral tribunal may also choose to decide on the jurisdiction issue in its final award on the merits, which will then be subject to court control when it is challenged or enforced.

V. Role of the Courts

In general, an arbitration agreement excludes the jurisdiction of the state courts. In arbitral proceedings, state courts are only authorized to act in certain, expressly mentioned functions. The function of state courts is largely reduced to supporting or controlling the arbitral tribunal.

---

52 Sec. 1032 (1) ZPO.
53 Sec. 1040 (3) ZPO.

First, the respondent can challenge in the state courts that there is a valid arbitration agreement concluded between the parties which concerns the dispute at hand.[54] Second, in case the parties cannot agree on the composition of the tribunal or the nomination of a sole arbitrator or the umpire, they can request the state courts to do so.[55] Third, in case a party has doubts as to the impartiality of one of the arbitrators, it can challenge the arbitrator in the state court under certain circumstances.[56] Fourth, a party can request preliminary measures of protection in the state courts[57] even after the tribunal has been constituted. Fifth, since the arbitral tribunal has no power to summon witnesses to testify, the arbitral tribunal can ask the state courts for assistance.[58] Finally, the state courts will decide about the challenge and the enforcement of the arbitral award as explained afterwards.[59]

The competence for these actions is vested in the Higher Regional Courts. Most Higher Regional Courts, at least in major arbitration centers such as Hamburg, Frankfurt or Cologne, have specialized arbitration divisions. This ensures that proceedings are conducted in front of judges with the necessary competence.

VI. Challenging of Awards

Recourse to a court against an award may be made only by a motion to set aside the award for one of the grounds stipulated in Sec. 1059 (2) ZPO. Besides, the parties may designate in their arbitration agreement that each party has the right, within a certain time after receipt of the award, to commence state court proceedings for a review of the award. While German state courts had not accepted such agreements as valid arbitration agreements in the past, the Federal Court of Justice overruled these decisions and held that the parties may arrange the arbitration agreement and the binding effect of the arbitral award subject to the fact that neither party initiates court proceedings within a specific period of time.[60] But such conditioned arbitration agreements are rather the exception and they should only be drawn up by experienced lawyers.

VII. Enforcement of Awards

The German arbitration law formally distinguishes, for purposes of recognition and enforcement of awards, between domestic and foreign arbitral awards. With regard to

---

54 Sec. 1032 (2) ZPO.
55 Sects. 1034, 1035 ZPO.
56 Sec. 1037 ZPO.
57 Sec. 1033 ZPO.
58 Sec. 1050 ZPO.
59 Sects. 1059–1061 ZPO.
60 BGH, 1.3.2007 – III ZB 7/06, NJW-RR 2007, 1511.

domestic awards, the court shall deny a declaration of enforceability and set aside the award if one of the grounds listed in Sec. 1059 (2) ZPO is given.[61] In contrast, the recognition and enforcement of foreign arbitral awards shall be granted in accordance with the New York Convention.[62] Foreign awards shall be recognized as binding and may be enforced by filing to the Higher Regional Court, unless there are grounds for setting aside. The German Code of Civil Procedure does not provide a system for setting aside foreign awards. However, the Higher Regional Court has the power to refuse the recognition and enforcement of the foreign award.

German courts have taken a very arbitration-friendly approach in interpreting and handling the New York Convention. Hence, the courts have granted recognition and enforcement of foreign awards whenever possible and a refusal to recognize or enforce an award has been the very exception. As a consequence, the Federal Court of Justice has ruled that in the light of Art. VII New York Convention, establishing the principle of the most favorable treatment, the arbitration agreement does not need to meet the form requirements of Art. II New York Convention. Hereafter, the arbitration agreement has to fulfill the form requirements of Sec. 1031 ZPO which are more permissive than the form requirements of Art. II New York Convention.[63]

VIII. Institutional Arbitration

Germany has two major arbitral institutions offering full services. The German Institution for Arbitration (*Deutsche Institution für Schiedsgerichtsbarkeit*, DIS)[64] is a registered association. It is the main arbitral institution in Germany with approximately 1000 members from Germany and abroad, with the aim of promoting national and international arbitration. The DIS offers an administered arbitral procedure under the DIS Rules, currently from 1998. The German Maritime Arbitration Association (GMAA) is active in the field of international maritime and transport law.[65] It does not offer an administered procedure, but provides specialized rules of arbitration and a list of expert arbitrators.

C. Mediation

Whereas a judgment or an arbitral award is a legal solution imposed by a judge or arbitrator, mediation tries to assist the parties in finding their own consensual solu-

61 Sec. 1060 ZPO.

62 Sec. 1061 ZPO.

63 Federal Court of Justice, Decision of 21th September 2005, SchiedsVZ 2005, 306–308.

64 http://www.dis-arb.de.

65 http://www.gmaa.de.

tion to a conflict. Mediation can offer certain advantages in contrast to a lawsuit, especially where long-standing business relationships are affected. As mediation is not a legal proceeding in the strict sense, the parties are free to enter or leave the mediation process at any time. To date, mediation has not gained significant status as a means to settle business disputes. However, to give mediation a stable legal framework, a draft mediation act is – at the time of writing – under discussion in the German parliament; the draft legislation is based on a European Directive.[66] The draft, if enacted as currently under discussion, would regulate issues such as independence of the mediator, confidentiality of the proceedings, enforceability of any settlement reached in the mediation and the relationship between court proceedings and mediation.

Dr. Richard Happ
richard.happ@luther-lawfirm.com

66 Directive 2008/52/EC of the European Parliament and of the Council of 21th May 2008 on certain aspects of mediation in civil and commercial matters, OJ L 136, 24th May 2008, p. 3. On 15th December 2011, the German Bundestag passed the law. On 10th February 2012 the German Bundesrat decided to call on the mediation committee (*Vermittlungsausschuss*). As of 25th April 2012 the law has not yet been passed.

CHAPTER 18
REAL ESTATE – REAL ESTATE LAW

RÜDIGER BONNMANN

The public building law in Germany restricts the builder's general freedom of action for public benefits and forms the statutory framework for the freedom to build on property which results from Art. 2 and Art. 14 of the German Constitution (Grundgesetz).

A. General

In general, a building permit is required for the construction, alteration, demolition or change of use of a building. The admissibility and thus the approval of a building project are in the first instance governed by planning law and building regulation law. As a result of the typical federal system in Germany, planning law is federal law and building regulation law is federal state law. Planning law is codified in the Federal Regional Planning Act (*Raumordnungsgesetz*, *ROG*) and the Federal Building Code (*Baugesetzbuch*, *BauGB*) and regulates the use of land in one entire area (i. e. it sets out roads and building plots etc.). Planning law therefore determines whether a building project fits into its surroundings. The permit itself is governed by the provisions of building regulation law. Building regulation law is codified in the state building regulations of each German federal state (*Bundesland*) and sets out requirements for both design and construction.

B. Building Permit

For the construction, alteration, demolition or change of use of a building, a building permit is required, unless it is a matter of residential buildings or buildings and structures that exceptionally do not require a permit. To reduce the regulatory burden, an amendment to several building regulations has waived the requirement of a prior building permit before construction can start in certain areas of (well defined) local zoning plans and more simple apartment buildings of restricted volume.[1] In these cases – after having checked all requirements of the applicable building regulations,

1 See state building regulations, e.g. in North Rhine Westphalia ruled in Sec. 63 et seq. BauO NRW (*Bauordnung NRW* – Statutory Building Code).

and after having notified the building authority accordingly, submitting all necessary technical plans etc. – the construction activity may be started. In such instances, the building authority may request that the normal building permit procedure be initiated within one month after notification, although only in cases of non-observance of legal requirements or if the project is particularly complex. In all other cases, the building authority must restrict its interference to any later deviations or conflicts with building regulations.

Provisions in the building regulations stipulate the time when it is necessary to obtain a building permit and what conditions need to be met in order for the permit to be granted. A further building permit is not necessary if a building permit has already been granted under other provisions, although some projects will always require formal planning permission, such as waste dumps or nuclear plants.

I. Claim for Building Permit

The state building regulations of each German federal state ascertain whether the building owner has an entitlement to a building permit. To harmonize the federal states' legislation, a Model Construction Regulation (*Musterbauordnung*) exists on a federal level, serving as a guideline for the federal states' legislation.

According to Sec. 72 of this Model Construction Regulation,[2] the building permit has to be granted by the Building Supervisory Authority (*Bauaufsichtsbehörde*) if the building project does not violate any public law. In this case, public law means in the first instance the state building regulations of the federal state and the planning law. Besides planning law and state building regulations, some further regulations have to be observed.

II. Building Regulations

The Building Supervisory Authority examines any violations of the state building regulations: The primary objective of a State's building regulation law being the prevention of hazards, the regulations place special emphasis on the safety of buildings to ensure that the inhabitants of or visitors to such buildings do not suffer injury from constructional defects. The building regulations also define requirements for social standards and environmental protection. Building regulation law also pursues architectural objectives, for instance placing a prohibition on buildings that detract from their surroundings or are an eyesore.

---

2 E.g. in North Rhine Westphalia ruled in Sec. 75 BauO NRW.

The following are the most important demands of the Building Regulations:

- The provision of e.g. roads and services to allow plots to be developed;
- The separation area (typically between a building and site boundary or adjoining building);[3]
- The obligatory provision of a specified number of parking spaces;[4]
- Fire prevention and protection;[5]
- Energy efficiency.[6]

III. Planning Law

Besides, the Building Supervisory Authority examines any violations of the federal planning law before granting a building permit. In the first instance, the Federal Building Code (*BauGB*) is examined as part of the planning law. The admissibility of building projects under the Federal Building Code is regulated by Sec. 29 et sequ. Different provisions apply depending on whether or not a local zoning plan exists for the property to be developed. *Local zoning plans* are generated by each community for the area under its jurisdiction, containing requirements for the development of a special area. They include requirements about the type of building areas and/or the land use intensity. The whole procedure to generate the local zoning plan is regulated in Sects. 1 to 29 of the Federal Building Code. Zoning is generally carried out in two steps: First a land-use plan and a preparatory and rough local development plan are drawn up. These are then used to draft the detailed local development plan which sets out the legally binding detailed planning for the zoning area. Sec. 3 stipulates that the public is to be involved in the generating process: the public has to be informed at the earliest possible stage about the general aims and purposes of planning, as well as about significantly different solutions being considered for the redesign or development of an area. The public is to be given suitable opportunity for comment and discussion. This procedure safeguards public influence.

In these local zoning plans, the community has the possibility to define a building area based on the German Ordinance on land usage (*Baunutzungsverordnung*, BauNVO). This German Ordinance on land usage completes the Federal Building Code and was enacted on the basis of Sec. 9a of the Federal Building Code. The German Ordinance on land usage contains requirements about the type of building areas (Art. 1 to 15) and the land use intensity (Sects. 16 to 23). Ten different types of building areas are defined in Art. 2 to 15, namely areas of small housing estates, pure

3 E.g. Sec. 6 BauO NRW.

4 Sec. 51 BauO NRW.

5 Sec. 17 BauO NRW.

6 Special provisions in the *Erneuerbare-Energien-Wärme-Gesetz (EEWärmeG) and the Energieeinsparverordnung (EnEV 2009).*

residential areas, general residential areas, special residential areas, village areas, mixed areas, core areas, trade areas, industrial areas and special zones. To simplify the zoning plans, the community now has the right to set out one of the above-mentioned building areas in the local zoning plan. Due to this setting, Sects. 2 to 14 of the German Ordinance on land usage are automatically part of the local zoning plan.

If a detailed local zoning plan exists in the community, only those building projects which do not conflict with the detailed local development plan and which ensure that public services are not adversely affected, will be approved by the Building Supervisory Authority (Sects. 30 and 31 Federal Building Code). This includes ensuring that the property is satisfactorily connected to the public roads, electricity and the fresh/wastewater networks.

If no detailed local development plan is available, the admissibility of the building project depends on whether the building is to be constructed inside or outside a developed area:

In undeveloped outlying areas only special projects, for example agricultural or forestry projects or projects destined to supply the public with electricity and water etc., are allowed, according to Sec. 35 of the Federal Building Code.

According to Sec. 34 of the Federal Building Code, inside a developed area most building projects are allowed as long as they fit into the surroundings as defined by other buildings. If no local zoning plan exists and the building project is to be constructed inside a developed area, the admissibility of the project depends on whether its surroundings are comparable to one of the surroundings defined in the German Ordinance on land usage[7] or whether the surroundings of the specific building project are not comparable with one of the defined building areas.[8] Anyway, despite these ten strictly defined areas, the Building Supervisory Authority is always entitled to determine by equitable discretion whether the building project fits into the surroundings.

IV. Further Regulations

Besides, further regulations have to be complied with before granting the building permit. Typical regulations to be considered are, for example, Sec. 9 Major Road Law (*Fernstraßengesetz*), which regulates a ban on construction next to federal motorways, Sec. 22 et. seq. Federal Emission Control Act (*Bundesimmissionsschutzgesetz*) or Sec. 33 (2) Highway Code (*Straßenverkehrsordnung*).

---

7 In this case Art. 34 Sec. 2 Federal Building Code and the German ordinance on land usage (BauNVO) are applicable.

8 In this case only Art. 34 Sec. 1 Federal Building Code is applicable and a resort on the German Ordinance on land usage is not possible.

V. Content, Effect and Period of Validity of the Building Permit

The building permit declares content, effect and coverage of the building project. It declares bindingly that the building project does not violate any public law at the time of granting. Other statutory obligations to require a permit remain unaffected. This means that subsequent approvals such as personal approvals have to be obtained notwithstanding.[9] The building permit verifies that no public law is violated and that a property is built in compliance with the building permit; the permit has a binding effect as long as the given permit is not withdrawn. At the time of the announcement of the building permit, the construction of the building project can start. In general, the building owner is not obligated to construct the building project just because a building permit has been granted.[10] If the building owner does not start erecting the building within three years after obtaining the permit, the building permit expires, i. e. the period of validity is three years. Upon application, the permit can be extended by a period of one year.

C. Latest Amendments

Due to the current events in Fukushima in March 2011, the German Authorities quickly enacted a new "Act concerning the support of climate change in the communities" (*Gesetz zur Förderung des Klimaschutzes in den Städten und Gemeinden*), which came into effect on 30th July 2011. This Act amends certain provisions of the existing Federal Building Code. The primary objective of this new Act is to improve climate protection by supporting and advancing the construction of power plants producing renewable energy. It is now expressly stated that climate protection is an objective which has to be considered in the Planning Law. Especially the statutory basis for the repowering of wind turbines and for the construction of photovoltaic plants have been changed and simplified.[11]

D. Outlook

In addition to the abovementioned amendments to the Federal Building Code by the "Act concerning the support of climate change in cities and communities", further fundamental reforms of the existing Planning Law are envisaged:

---

9 In North Rhine Westphalia: Sec. 75 (3) BauO NRW.

10 Exception: Art. 176 Federal Building Code.

11 http://www.bgbl.de/Xaver/start.xav?startbk=Bundesanzeiger_BGBl.

In particular, the German Ordinance on land usage (BauNVO) will be changed: for example, since German courts have ruled that children's noise has to be accepted by citizens, the building of day care centers for children in residential areas will be generally authorized in the Planning Law.

Rüdiger Bonnmann
ruediger.bonnmann@luther-lawfirm.com

CHAPTER 19
REAL ESTATE – PROPERTY LAW

DR. MICHAEL FRITZSCHE

Investors seeking to invest their money into real estate in Germany are confronted with a wide array of legal forms, rules and approval requirements from different areas of public law, and particularly a wide range of provisions relating to planning permission, building regulations and environmental laws.

A. Legal Forms of Ownership in Germany

Full ownership is the most common way that real estate is owned in Germany. It generally covers the totality of the legal rights, entitlements and obligations attached to property, but is subject to general restrictions imposed by law or rights of third parties (e.g. neighbors).

There are three types of full ownership in Germany:

- Sole ownership (*Alleineigentum*):[1] the owner is one individual person or one legal entity.
- Part ownership, in particular condominium for residential purposes (*Teileigentum, Wohungseigentum*):[2] the property of a building may divided into several units of the total ownership according to its usable area, e.g. apartments/flats, offices, shops, commercial areas, each unit belonging to different part owners (individual or company). The same person may also own several units. Usually, the division is such that "exclusive parts" (*Sondereigentum*) are dedicated to the sole ownership of a respective part-owner, while the remaining "common parts" (*Gemeinschaftseigentum*) of the property are jointly owned by all related part owners (e.g. according to their shares of ownership), open for common use according to set-out rules. Each part owner has a comparable position like a sole owner in a wholly owned property and is entitled to the full use of its part ownership, e.g. may sell it, charge it and let it to tenants. But it is bound to the joint administration (possibly by a nominated manager) and certain co-determination rights of the other part owners (also including, if not waived, their consent in case of transfer).

1 See Sec. 903 et seq. BGB.
2 *Wohnungseigentumsgesetz* (WEG) [Law on Condominiums and Part-Ownership] 1951.

- Co-ownership (*Miteigentum nach Bruchteilen*):[3] several persons or companies share the ownership of a property, but each co-owner has an individual interest in it. Each co-owner may convey or encumber its interest without the consent of the other co-owner(s).
- Joint ownership (*Gesamthandseigentum*):[4] the ownership is held by two or more persons or companies forming a specific partnership in this respect (*Gesellschaft bürgerlichen Rechts, GbR*) or, in the case of hereditary succession, a community of heirs (*Erbengemeinschaft*). The individual joint owner cannot claim any share of the property as its personal share. It may not sell or encumber its share of real property but only its interest in the joint ownership.

While the above forms of full ownership always and necessarily include the ground and the building erected thereupon, i. e. tie the buildings and installations to the property of the land when firmly connected to it, German law also provides for a specific form of ownership just relating to the building as opposed to the separate property of the land owner.[5] Such a restricted form of ownership is called *Erbbaurecht* and may be translated as heritable building right or hereditary building right (HBR). Thus, the alienable HBR – also referred to as "leasehold" (in UK terminology) – allows the beneficiary to construct and own a building on foreign land for a certain period of time, e.g. 20, 50, 99 years or for the lifetime of the building. To compensate for the restriction of the landowner's rights, the HBR holder is usually obligated to pay a ground rent (*Erbbauzins*), which is payable on a regular (mostly monthly or annual) basis. Upon termination, all buildings erected become the property of the land owner of the real estate who may have to compensate the holder of the HBR with the time value (unless agreed otherwise).

B. Encumbrances and Charges of Real Estate Property Rights (Rights in Rem)

The above rights of ownership may be encumbered or charged in different ways, e.g.

- The right to use in favor of third parties (servitudes, *Grunddienstbarkeiten, Reallasten*);[6]
- The obligation to comply with certain restrictions on the own property – or to tolerate a specific use of a neighboring property (public easements, *Baulasten*);

3 Sec. 741 et seq. BGB
4 Sec. 705 et seq. for GbR and Sec. 2032 seq. for community of heirs.
5 See "*Erbbaurechtsgesetz*" (ErbbauRG) [Law on Hereditary Building Rights] 1919.
6 Sects. 1018, 1105 et seq. BGB

such public easements mainly refer to restrictions of use in relation to the building rights like distances between neighboring buildings or the right to use a playground or parking lot on a neighboring property;

- Security for payments of the land owner (or a third party) in favor of the creditor, like mortgages (*Hypotheken*)[7] which are directly linked to a specific liability, land charges (*Grundschulden*)[8] which may secure any current liability, i. e. is exchangeable, or annuity charges (*Rentenschulden*)[9] which secure regular, repeated payments (installments);
- Or, as opposed to an encumbrance, creating the entitlement to use neighboring properties or to request the tolerance for specific uses of/on the own property (reversed servitudes or easements).

All such rights ad rem are alienable and may be transferred to third persons, they may be granted for a specific period of time or without such limitation, e.g. until the beneficiary consents to the deletion of such right (which it may be obliged to according to contract).

While servitudes and easements may be granted to the respective owner of a neighboring property (ad rem), similar rights may also be granted to specific persons (ad personam), e.g. in favor of an individual (*beschränkt persönliche Dienstbarkeit*),[10] and/or may consist of a specific entitlement to use.

The most important right is an usufruct (*Nießbrauch*),[11] which is meant to give to the beneficiary – similar to ownership in the above terms – the right to reap the fruits of a property or to use the property in a specific way – in contrast to other servitudes or easements – not only for a certain use but for the use of the plot of land in its entirety, i. e. including the accessories. At the same time, the holder of a usufruct normally is obligated to bear all costs relating to the real estate such as public charges, insurance costs and usually the costs for repairs. Usufruct is an inalienable and non-inheritable right in rem and may be granted for the life of the holder or a limited period of time. For the land owner, it provides the possibility to profit from the land on a long term basis without giving up the ownership, whereas for the other party it grants a position similar to ownership and thus confers more stability than a mere contractual obligation like a lease agreement.

7 Sec. 1113 et seq. BGB.
8 Sec. 1191 et seq. BGB.
9 Sec. 1199 et seq. BGB.
10 Sec. 1090 et seq. BGB.
11 Sec. 1030 et seq. BGB.

C. Land Survey Register (Cadaster Map) and Land Register (Properties), Notarization

In Germany, the entire territory is surveyed in cadastral plots and recorded in two registers for different reasons and held by different authorities.

With the exception of certain plots which serve a public purpose, all plots of land are recorded in the land survey register which is kept by the competent cadastral offices (*Katasterämter/Vermessungsämter*) of the townships (*kreisfreie Städte*) and counties (*Landkreise*) and consists of the cadastral map (*Liegenschaftskarte/Flurkarte*) including cadastral figures (*Liegenschaftskarte/Flurkarte*) and the cadastral register (*Liegenschaftsbuch*). The land is divided into districts (*Gemarkung*), cadastral units (*Flure*) and plots (*Flurstücke*). Details such as position and size of land are entered into the cadastral registry. Thus, each and every plot of land within Germany is identified and may be referred to without ambiguity. There is a legal presumption that all facts registered in the land survey register are accurate.

In addition to the land survey register, the purpose of the land register, which is kept by the land registry at the local courts (*Amtsgerichte*), is to record the legal interest in the land. Every land register "sheet" (*Grundbuchblatt*) consists of an inventory and three divisions (*Abteilungen*) and discloses each individual real estate property (possibly consisting of one or several plots, but never consisting of plots with different ownership) and provides, in the inventory, information on the composing plots (i. e. their denomination and address, character of use, e.g. building, industrial, agricultural land, free area). In division I, it (bindingly) indicates the legal entitlement to the property by stating all its former owners and the current owner (since the establishment of the file). Existing encumbrances, rights ad rem and restrictions like preemption rights or servitudes are displayed in division II, and mortgages, land charges or annuity charges are detailed in division III of the land register. In most parts of Germany, in addition to the land register, the local authorities hold a separate register of public easements (*Baulasten*, as detailed above). Accordingly, to learn all about the current legal situation of the property, this register must also be checked (e.g. in Bavaria and Brandenburg, there are no such separate registers, but respective easements are entered into division II of the land register).

All property transactions, charges and encumbrances relating to real estate, which furthermore have to be notarized as a prerequisite of application to the register, have to be filed to and entered into the land register. Such transactions do not become effective without registration. Condominium, part-ownership and the HBR are entered into separate sheets of the land register. In addition, the creation of the HBR is registered in the land register of the underlying real estate property as an encumbrance (in division II of such land register). A separate land register sheet allows the condominium/part-ownership and the HBR to be treated similarly to full ownership and thus enables the owner to register securities (for financing), encumbrances and other restrictions.

In contrast to other countries, in Germany there governs a legal presumption of the accuracy of all entries in the land register and of the non-existence of rights not registered therein. Such a presumption, however, in case of errors or wrong entries, may be disproved by respective evidence (e.g. notarial deeds). Thus, a person who by legal transaction acquires in good faith from the registered owner a title is protected by law, even if the land register did not reflect the correct legal situation, i. e. the "book owner" was not the true owner. This ensures the greatest possible transparency and reliability. The potential purchaser of the real estate property therefore needs no expensive insurance against title defects, as for example is usual in the USA, to protect against deficiencies in the land register records. A possible difference between the registered owner and the true owner may, in particular, result from legal transactions or disposals which do not need to be or have not yet been registered in the land register (e.g. if property is passed on to heirs or legal successors).

In certain instances (and regions), the registration of a legal title may take several months, depending on the work load at the register, or on requirements not fulfilled (e.g. payment of real estate transfer tax before the new owner is registered). Due to such significant periods of time between notarization (of the respective declaration or agreement) and the registration, the beneficiary of such registration (e.g. the new land owner, creditor of securities) needs to secure its rights by registering a so-called priority notice (conveyance in case of transfer of property, *Auflassungsvormerkung*) in the above division II of the respective land register sheet. This instrument protects against any jeopardy by later transaction or encumbrance of the said property, i. e. such later transaction/encumbrances would not become valid in respect of the conveyed beneficiary. Such priority notice may be registered relatively quickly (within a couple of days, at latest within a few weeks), and thus secures the entitlement of the beneficiary to obtain registration of its full right concerned (e.g. ownership, security).

Dr. Michael Fritzsche
michael.fritzsche@luther-lawfirm.com

CHAPTER 20
REAL ESTATE – COMMERCIAL AND RESIDENTIAL LEASE AGREEMENTS

INGO ERBERICH

Before investing in real estate, some background knowledge about lease agreements and the legal framework which applies to them is essential to enable a potential purchaser to investigate and assess the value of a property. Lease agreements in Germany are governed by the German Civil Code, in particular Sects. 535–597 BGB. In general, the German Civil Code distinguishes between residential and commercial lease agreements and in Germany the law relating to landlord and tenant is often considered to be "tenant friendly".

Residential leases are fairly strictly regulated by statute[1] and any deviation from the legislation is only allowed in specific circumstances. The law in relation to commercial leases allows the parties greater freedom of contract, but is equally regulated[2] and many of the same statutory rules relating to residential leases will also apply.

A. Rental Term

In general, residential leases are unlimited in time. A landlord may only terminate or restrict the lease term for a limited number of permitted reasons, e.g. if he wants to use the property for himself or his family.[3] The landlord may also terminate a residential lease of a dwelling in a building inhabited by the landlord himself and having no more than two dwellings, without the need for a justified interest. Residential leases are generally terminable by the tenant by giving not less than 3 months' notice to the landlord.[4] The length of notice which a landlord is required to give to their tenant increases the longer the tenant has been a tenant at the property.[5]

---

1 Sects. 549–577a BGB.
2 Sects. 578–580a BGB.
3 Sects. 575 BGB.
4 Sects. 573c (1) BGB.
5 Sects. 573c (1) BGB.

Commercial leases, which are expressed to be unlimited in time, are terminable by either party giving the other not less than six months' notice, unless otherwise agreed in the lease agreement. In commercial lease agreements it is common for the lease term to be fixed for a certain period of time and such arrangements may also include an option by which the term of the lease can be extended in the future. However, even a commercial lease with a fixed rental term can be terminated by either party giving the required statutory notice if the specific written form requirements relating to the content of the lease are not fulfilled. Therefore, specific care needs to be taken to ensure that all commercial lease agreements meet such requirements.

B. Increase of Rent

With residential leases the rent payable by the tenant may be increased at the request of the landlord as long as certain conditions are met.[6] In particular, the rent may not be increased more than once in any one year, may not be raised by more than 20 % over a 3 year period and may not exceed the level of comparative rent customary in such an area.[7] Alternatively, a stepped rent[8] or an indexed[9] rent may be predetermined by the parties. In commercial lease agreements the parties will usually agree that, subject to certain requirements, the rent will be increased on an indexed basis. A stepped rent may also be agreed.

C. Rent Reductions

In a situation where the tenant's use of the property is adversely affected, the tenant is entitled to pay a reduced rent to the landlord.[10] However, the deficiency which impacts the tenant's use of the property must be material,[11] cannot be based on the tenant's fault,[12] and the tenant may not have known it at the time of concluding the lease agreement.[13] In such circumstances the landlord's legal right to claim for payment of the agreed rent is automatically reduced by the operation of the law[14] and in residential leases, the tenant's right to pay a reduced rent cannot be excluded or re-

6 Sects. 557 et seq. BGB.
7 Sec. 558 BGB.
8 Sec. 557a BGB.
9 Sec. 557b BGB.
10 Sec. 536 BGB.
11 Sec. 536 (1) BGB.
12 Sec. 326 (2) BGB.
13 Sec. 536b BGB.
14 Prevailing opinion and case law, see BGH, NJW-RR 1991, 779.

stricted by contract.[15] In commercial leases it is possible for the landlord and tenant to agree to exclude such statutory protections.

D. Operating Costs

The general principle is that the rent payable by a tenant shall be inclusive of any operating costs relating to the property. The landlord is only entitled to charge operating costs to the tenant if it is explicitly agreed upon in the respective lease agreement.[16] However, such agreements are quite common. Often tenants are required to pay a monthly advance payment in respect of operating costs[17] and, in this case, a yearly reconciliation of the sums paid by the tenant against the actual costs must be made within 12 months of the end of the respective year.[18] In some cases a lump sum is agreed upon.[19] The Operating Costs Regulation (*Betriebskostenverordnung, BetrKV*) lists the most important operating costs for buildings and can be used by the parties when agreeing on which operating costs shall be recoverable from the tenant. This list of operating costs is often extended, particularly in commercial lease agreements. The most important operating costs are real property taxes, insurances, electricity, heating, water/drainage, waste disposal, street cleaning, chimney cleaning, caretaker, security, operation and maintenance of air condition and ventilation, operation and maintenance of lift/elevator, operation, maintenance and partly even repair (see below) of other technical installations.

E. Maintenance and Repairs

The general principle is that the landlord must carry out and bear the costs of all maintenance, repairs and renovation works relating to the property,[20] unless it is validly agreed that such costs will be borne by the tenant. However, the passing on of such costs to the tenant may often be deemed to be void,[21] if the obligations are incorporated in general terms and conditions.[22] In this case it is important that the statutory provisions in Sec. 305 et seq. BGB (*Bürgerliches Gesetzbuch* – German Civil Code) are observed to ensure that it is possible to require the tenant to pay such costs.

15 Sec. 536 (4) BGB.
16 Sec. 556 BGB for residential leases.
17 Sec. 556 (2) BGB.
18 Sec. 556 (3) BGB.
19 Which is also provided in Sec. 556 (2) BGB.
20 Sec. 535 (1) BGB.
21 Sec. 307 et seq. BGB.
22 Sec. 305 (1) BGB.

It is also generally accepted that maintenance and repairs relating to the internal part of the leased premises will normally be carried out by the landlord but charged to the tenant as ancillary (or operating) costs in addition to the rent. Alternatively, the tenant may agree to take care of the interior of the leased premises himself directly when this becomes necessary, especially by performing decorative repairs (*Schönheitsreparaturen*) i. e. painting the walls or waxing the floors. In a number of recent cases, many clauses which refer to the performance of decorative repairs have been found to be void, and particular care should therefore be taken in formulating such provisions.

The costs relating to major construction works i. e. work on structural parts, load-bearing walls, facades, roofs (*Dach und Fach*) etc. may only be allocated to the tenant where such an arrangement has been included in an individually negotiated lease agreement.

F. Competition Protection and Obligation to Conduct Business

The landlord is required by law to protect the tenant from any disruptive competition even though the lease agreement may not provide for a specific clause to this effect. Special competition clauses may be agreed among the parties. However, in general terms and conditions the combination of an exclusion of competition protection and an obligation to conduct business may be deemed to be invalid, particularly if the tenant is also restricted to carrying out business in relation to a certain assortment of goods only.

G. Securing Tenant Usage Rights

Most commonly in commercial lease agreements, the tenant often has an additional interest in relation to his right of use of the premises. Limited personal rights (*beschränkte persönliche Dienstbarkeiten*)[23] granted in favor of the respective tenant can be registered with the land register and may give the tenant additional entitlement irrespective of the terms set out in the lease agreement. Such rights might prohibit a purchaser from acquiring the property by way of a forced auction sale in the event of the insolvency of the landlord (*Zwangsversteigerung*), for example, or from terminating the lease agreement in certain specific situations provided in the legislation. Care should be taken as such rights may be considered to reduce the value of

23 Sec. 1090 et seq. BGB.

the property, and may therefore affect the ability of a potential landlord to secure future financing.

H. Tenancy Law Amendment Act – Draft of 11th May 2011

The German Federal Department of Justice drafted a Tenancy Law Amendment Act in May 2011[24] and in October 2011,[25] in which the legal rights of the landlord are intended to be sustained. For example the landlord shall be legally entitled to terminate the residential lease without notice if the tenant does not pay the security deposit. The catalogue of actions of modernization, which the tenant is obliged to tolerate, is to be extended as well. Nevertheless the Tenancy Law Amendment Act needs to pass the legislative procedure before becoming binding German Law.

Ingo Erberich
ingo.erberich@luther-lawfirm.com

24 Ref-E, NZM 2011, 424; http://www.mietgerichtstag.de/materialien_zum_mietraendg.php.
25 Ref-E, IBRMAT Nr. 677; http://www.mietgerichtstag.de/materialien_zum_mietraendg.php

CHAPTER 21
REAL ESTATE – ARCHITECTURAL AND CONSTRUCTION LAW

JUTTA WITTLER

The German Civil Code (BGB) does not provide adequate statutory requirements in respect to construction law. Therefore, the German construction praxis is used to work with the VOB/B (Award and Construction Contract Rules, Part B: General Contractual Conditions for the Execution of Building Works), and contracts which are developed on that basis. For Architects and Engineers the HOAI (Scale of Architects' and Engineers' Fees) is applicable. The HOAI is not a contract, rather a sort of price regulation. It lays down certain pricing rules for agreed contractual terms.

A. Architects and Engineers

Under German building law, it is mandatory to use the services of an architect to realize a building project. In collaboration with the builder and with other specialists (e. g. structural/construction engineers, consulting engineers for technical systems, etc.), the architect develops the idea for the building project and its realization.

I. Scope of Services and Fees

The scope of services depends on the architect's contract according to Sec. 631 et seq. German Civil Code (BGB) and, in terms of fees, the Scale of Architects' and Engineers' Fees of September 1976, last amended in 2009 (*Honorarordnung für Architekten und Ingenieure, HOAI*). The HOAI divides an architect's performance into descriptions and stages of performance. The HOAI is not a contract, rather a sort of price regulation. Hence, it does not govern the terms of the architect's contract, but lays down certain pricing rules for agreed contractual terms. That is why the parties are not required to regulate all various stages for performance in a contract. However, to avoid ambiguities, it is advisable to define each stipulated element of performance in accordance with the project requirements. The HOAI is not applicable if a foreign architect is involved in a German construction project or a German architect is involved in a foreign construction project.[1]

There are some additional rules that apply to fee agreements. Fees can only be effectively fixed by the act of party when the contract is awarded. The minimum rates laid down in the HOAI may only be undercut in exceptional cases. If contractual fee arrangements are invalid because the requirements are not met, the minimum rates laid down in the HOAI will apply.

II. Organization Phases

The organization of the planning stage follows indirectly from the HOAI, according to which it is divided up into nine basic services (phases):

Basic calculations (clarification of requirements, consultation on scope of entire project – *Grundlagenermittlung*); initial planning (analysis of basic situation, harmonization of objectives, etc. – *Vorplanung*); draft planning (detailed work on the planning concept, step-by-step working out of the solution in draftsman's terms, etc. – *Entwurfsplanung*); planning approval (preparation of documents for submission as required by public law for obtaining approval, etc. – *Genehmigungsplanung*); works plan (working out in detail the results of phases 3 and 4, etc. – *Ausführungsplanung*); preparation of placement of order (calculation and collation of quantities as the basis for drawing up a description of work, making use of the contributions of others involved in the planning, etc. – *Vorbereitung der Vergabe*); collaborating on the placement of order (collation of documents on conditions for all types of work, obtaining quotations, etc. – *Mitwirkung bei der Vergabe*); project supervision (supervising the implementation of the project for compliance with building approval or consent, etc. – *Objektüberwachung*); project supervision and documentation (physical inspection of project to identify defects, etc. – *Objektbetreuung und Dokumentation*).

III. Timing

The contract usually does not stipulate a deadline to be observed by the architect or engineer. This is considered to be one of the main obligations of the builder. If, for example, the architect fails to provide the works plan within a reasonable period of time and this leads to the postponement of the contractual deadline, the principal may successfully sue for damages if it can prove that the delay was caused by the architect's actions.

---

1 Section 1 HOAI 2009; OLG Brandenburg – 4U 112/8 (IBR 2012-Werkstatt-Beitrag) depending on applicable law.

IV. Liabilities and Insurance

The builder assumes liability in relation to third parties; he is responsible to the authorities and other third parties involved. In relations inter se, the liabilities are divided up among those involved with the planning, who in turn are responsible to the builder under their contracts for work and services. A joint obligation exists between a planning architect and a contractor, if a constructional defect can be traced back to a planning error of the architect and an execution error of the contractor. The architect, however, bears chief responsibility for the planning and project supervision. A planning architect is an auxiliary person of the builder in relation to the contractor. In the event that a constructional defect can be traced back to a planning error exclusively and not identifiable for the contractor there is no room for a joint obligation.[2]

The German Civil Code provides that the architect/engineer shall accept liability for hidden or apparent defects within a 5 year period (Sec. 634a (1) No. 2 German Civil Code). This warranty period commences on the day of acceptance of the services of the architect, usually after the project supervision and documentation stage. In the event of liability for willful default, the liability is subject to a 10 year limitation period.

Mistakes made at the planning or project supervision stage are in most cases covered by the architect's liability insurance. As a rule, every architect has such a policy, as he is not otherwise authorized to submit building particulars and plans.

V. Termination

The contract usually includes special clauses which entitle both parties to terminate the contract. In the absence of a contractual provision, both parties are entitled to terminate the contract with good cause if the other party is in breach of contractual obligations and/or endangers the success of the project.

The architectural or engineering contract may be terminated at any time by the principal without cause. In this case, the principal has to pay damages to the architect. Contracts drafted by the architect normally provide for a lump sum of 60 % of the fees relating to the uncompleted services to be paid to the architect. As the Federal Appeal Court decided at the beginning of 1996 that these contractual clauses are not valid, the architect is now forced to explain and to prove the actual damage caused by the termination of the contract.

---

2 Werner/Pastor, Der Bauprozess, 13th edition, 2011, p. 1337.

According to Sec. 649 German Civil Code the customer may terminate the contract at any time up to completion of the work. If the customer terminates the contract, then the contractor is entitled to demand the agreed remuneration; however, he must allow set-off the expenses he saves as a result of cancelling the contract or acquires or willfully fails to acquire from other use of his labor. There is a presumption that the contractor is accordingly entitled to five percent of the remuneration accounted for by the part of the work not yet provided.

VI. Intellectual Property Rights

As outlined before in the chapter about Copyrights, the UrhG protects artistic works, works of architecture and applied art and the plans for such works, and illustrations of a scientific or technical nature, such as drawings, plans, maps, sketches, tables and three-dimensional representations. The sole criterion for this is not the pursuit of artistic ends, but whether a personal intellectual creation has been produced. Thus, the planning and construction of buildings are, as a rule, protected by copyright.

Whether in any particular case the architect has granted any rights to use his copyrighted material (especially with regard to alterations, extensions, renovation of the building) depends on the contractual purpose in the absence of any express agreements to that effect. In general, however, it is safe to say that, if the architect has been entrusted with all the architectural work until completion of construction, he is not entitled to retain any such rights. Instead, the architect may subsequently exercise his right to imitate his own work.

With signing of the contract the architect does not alienate his copyright regarding the building plans or the building construction to the builder, due to the fact that the copyright is not alienable (Sec. 29 UrhG).[3] Only the exploitation right of the copyright can be aliened (Sec. 31 UrhG).

B. Building Contracts in General

Building contracts in Germany are generally governed by Sec. 631 to 651 German Civil Code (BGB). However, these provisions only deal with "contracts for work" in general and cover a wide range of contractual agreements, not necessarily only classical building contracts. Therefore, very often the VOB/B (Award and Construction Contract Rules, Part B: General Contractual Conditions for the Execution of Building Works – *Vergabe- und Vertragsordnung für Bauleistungen, Teil B: Allgemeine Ver-*

3 Werner/Pastor, Der Bauprozess, p. 1311.

tragsbedingungen für die Ausführung von Bauleistungen) is incorporated into a building contract. The VOB/B contains provisions regarding the legal relationship between the principal and the contractor and is "tailor-made" for building contracts. Since the provisions of the VOB/B constitute general terms and conditions, the content of every single provision can be subject to the restrictions laid down in Sec. 305 to 310 BGB and these provisions could therefore be invalid. However, this is not the case if the VOB/B is agreed "as a whole", i. e. without any changes.[4]

There are different types of contractors, e. g. the general contractor (*Generalunternehmer*) who performs all kinds of building work for a construction, but usually transfers substantial parts of his work to sub-contractors (*Subunternehmer*). If the general contractor takes over the overall planning it is referred to as total contractor (*Totalunternehmer*). A general contractor who does not carry out any of the building work himself is called *Generalübernehmer*.

I. Scope of the Building Work

The scope of the building work covered is defined in the building specification normally contained in an attachment to the contract. Additional services which are closely connected to the building work are included within the contractual scope of the building work even if it is not explicitly stated (see for example Sec. 4.1 VOB/C).

Change requests regarding the scope of the building work owed are quite common. Therefore, supplement agreements (*Nachträge*) are usual and of significant importance. At the time additional work and therefore a possible supplement is under consideration, the principal will not normally be able to choose another contractor because of the advanced construction process. This often results in high priced supplements. Careful planning of the whole project in advance can help to avoid such expensive supplements at this stage.

II. Remuneration

There are various types of remuneration provisions, for example:

Unit-price contract (*Einheitspreisvertrag*): the remuneration for work is the product of the measured quantity and the fixed unit price. However, according to the VOB/B, the single unit price can be dependent on the total quantity. The unit-price contract is the normal remuneration type according to the German construction contract procedures Part B (VOB/B).[5] According to Sec. 2 (2) VOB/B the sum payable shall

---

4 BGH – VII ZR 226/05.

5 Section 2 (2) VOB/B.

be calculated on the basis of the unit prices specified in the contract and of the work actually executed if no other method of calculation (e.g. lump sum payment, hourly wage rates, cost reimbursement) has been agreed. If the quantity of a work or part for which a unit price has been agreed differs on completion from that provided for in the contract by no more than 10 %, then the unit price agreed shall apply (Sec. 2 (3) no. 1 VOB/B).

Lump-sum contract (*Pauschalvertrag*): a total price is agreed on in advance for the entire scope of work to be exercised. As a consequence the remuneration to be paid is in general independent of the actual work exercised. There are different types of lump-sum contracts. The global lump-sum contract is based on global elements in the form of a functional service description.[6] The works and services are not specified in detail. The detailed lump-sum contract is based on a detailed service description. This detailed service description determines the basis of the contract in terms of type and amount of the works and services to be performed. Additional works and services demanded afterwards are not covered by the detailed lump-sum.[7]

Hourly-rate contract (*Stundenlohnvertrag*): the remuneration is based on the amount of time spent by the contractor. This type of contract is very rare and normally only used for smaller projects or when agreeing on additional work occurring during the construction process. The hourly-rate contract is the exception while the unit-price contract is the rule. According to Sec. 2 (10) VOB/B work shall only be remunerated on an hourly wage rate basis if this has been expressly agreed before the work commences.

According to Sec. 641 BGB the remuneration must be paid upon acceptance of the work. If the work is to be accepted in parts and the remuneration for the individual parts is specified, then the remuneration is to be paid for each part when it is accepted. The customer is obliged to accept the work produced in conformity with the contract, except to the extent that, in view of the quality of the work, acceptance is excluded, Sec. 640 BGB. A final invoice (*Schlussrechnung*) is no condition precedent for the payment of the remuneration. According to Sec. 632a BGB, part-payments on account (*Abschlagszahlungen*) can be claimed by the contractor. The contractor may demand a part payment from the customer for work carried out in accordance with the contract in the amount in which the customer has received an increased value by virtue of the work. The part payment may not be refused because of minor defects. On the contrary, if the parties agreed on the VOB/B, the final payment (*Schlusszahlung*) is due after the acceptance of the work, the submission of a verifiable final invoice and the check of the final invoice by the principal (at the latest two months after receipt of the invoice). Part-payments on account can be claimed by the contractor in advance.

6 Werner/Pastor, Der Bauprozess, p. 744.
7 Werner/Pastor, Der Bauprozess, p. 745.

III. Passing of Risk

Until final acceptance of the building work, the contractor bears the risk of accidental loss or destruction and deterioration of the building work. Once the building work has been finally accepted, the risk passes to the customer. If the customer is in default of acceptance, then the risk passes to him as well. The contractor is not liable for any accidental destruction or accidental deterioration of the materials supplied by the customer.

Acceptance in terms of Sec. 640 BGB means that the principal accepts the building work as performed in accordance with the contractual provisions and without substantial defects. Very often a so-called formal acceptance (*förmliche Abnahme*) is required.

IV. Liability for Defects

In case of defects the principal/customer may have the following rights and remedies (partly dependent on certain further preconditions):

Demand supplementary performance; remedy the defect himself and demand reimbursement for required expenses; terminate the contract or reduce the remuneration; claim compensation or reimbursement of wasted expenditure.

If a defect is caused by several persons (e.g. contractor and architect), they can be held jointly liable.

V. Delay

If the contractor fails to carry out the building work owed within the agreed time limit, the principal can – in general after setting an additional period of time for performance – withdraw from the contract. Under certain preconditions the principal also has a claim for compensation. Very often a contractual penalty is agreed on in the building contract.[8]

Jutta Wittler
jutta.wittler@luther-lawfirm.com

---

8 BGH – VII ZR 210/01

CHAPTER 22
REAL ESTATE – GREEN BUILDING

DR. ULRIKE FREIGANG

Where a building is developed or refurbished legal aspects concerning energy and energy consumption have to be considered. The German Renewable Energies Act and the Energy Saving Regulation are implementing the EU guidelines to reduce the energy needs and support the use of renewable energies. Those regulations have an impact on many scopes of the real estate industry like Rental Relationships, Construction and Transactions.

A. Legal Foundation

Buildings account for 40 % of total energy consumption in the European Union. Therefore, reduction of energy consumption and the use of energy from renewable sources in the building sector constitute important measures needed to reduce the Union's energy dependency and greenhouse gas emissions.[1] In Germany, there are inter alia two respective laws relevant for the building sector, namely the Renewable Energies Act (*Erneuerbare-Energien-Wärmegesetz, EEWärmeG*) and the Energy Saving Regulation (*Energieeinsparverordnung, EnEV*), which have a direct impact on various legal aspects connected with real property.

I. Renewable Energies Act

Renewable Energies Act, EEWärmeG, took effect in January 2009.[2] When developing or executing major refurbishment measures/extensions, the respective owner has to ensure that a certain percentage of the needed heat energy is obtained from renewable energy sources. The individual percentage rate depends on the nature of the source (e. g. 15 % solar or 50 % biomass etc.). Alternatively, the owner may undertake other compensating and climate friendly measures, such as the use of a highly

---

1 Statement of the European Parliament and the Council of the European Union in Directive 2010/31/EU of 19th May 2010 on the energy performance of buildings.

2 EEWärmeG, BGBl. I S. 1658; last amended on 28th July 2011 by Act to the Reorganization of the Legal Framework to the Promotion of the Generation of Electricity from Renewable Energies (*Gesetz zur Neuregelung des Rechtsrahmens für die Förderung der Stromerzeugung aus erneuerbaren Energien*).

efficient combined heat and power plant (CHP) which would cover up to 50 % of the needed heat energy.

II. Energy Saving Regulation

Current Energy Saving Regulation, EnEV 2009, came into force in October 2009.[3] In summary, it aims to reduce energy needs by an average of 30 % overall and further support the use of renewable energies. Energy efficiency shall be increased by an average of 15 % compared to today's levels.

To this effect, EnEV provides for certain construction regulations which ensure the reduction of energy needs of a building. It further sets out several obligations to refit old buildings, for example: (i) certain heating and warm water pipelines need to be appropriately insulated; (ii) from January 2020, off-peak-storage-heating installed prior to 1990 must not be operated any more; (iii) either the roof or top floor ceilings of heated rooms are to be appropriately insulated; from January 2012 this also applies to any accessible top floor ceilings of heated rooms.

EnEV also imposed the necessity of an Energy Performance Certificate (*Energieausweis*) for residential and commercial buildings. The Energy Performance Certificate evaluates the energy efficiency of a building either setting out the actual energy needs within the last three years (Consumption Certificate; *Verbrauchsausweis*) or the extent of the energy typically needed (Necessity Certificate; *Bedarfsausweis*). It must be provided where: (i) a building is newly developed or comprehensively refurbished, to the appropriate authorities on demand; (ii) a building is sold or leased, to the prospective purchaser or tenant. If services are offered to the public in a building with more than 1,000 m^2 floor space, the Energy Certificate needs to be displayed in a visible position.

Where there is a violation of certain EnEV requirements an administrative offence may be committed, which may be penalized with a fine of up to EUR 15,000.00, concerning certain construction regulations with a fine of up to EUR 50,000.00.

With Directive 2010/31/EU of 19th May 2010 on the energy performance of buildings[4] a further tightening of the required energy efficiency standards of buildings must be transformed into German national law until 9th July 2012 at the latest. The Directive tightens construction requirements concerning development and refurbishment. By 31st December 2020, all new buildings shall be nearly zero-energy

3 EnEV 2009, BGBl. I S. 1519, was updating EnEV 2007, which transformed EU Directive 2002/91/EC of 16th December 2002 into German national law.

4 OJ L 153, 18/6/2010, p. 13.

buildings, and after 31st December 2018, new buildings occupied and owned by public authorities shall be nearly zero-energy buildings. The Directive further specifies the Energy Performance Certificate in greater detail in order to make it possible for owners or tenants to compare and assess the building's energy performance. The directive will be transformed into German national law by EnEV 2012.

III. Impact on Construction Law and Works Contract

Both EEWärmeG and EnEV set out public law construction regulations which are to be observed when applying for a building permit. Hence, with regard to developments currently at the planning stage, though not in force so far, the more severe requirements of EnEV 2012 need to be taken into account if the building application is expected to be filed with the authorities after the prospected enactment date 9th July 2012 (at the latest).

With regard to the works contract, the contractor should be aware that the building, the refurbishment or extension works respectively, must comply with the laws in force at the date of final take over, including EEWärmeG and EnEV. Otherwise, the contractual works may be deemed to be defective. The employer might claim bad workmanship. The contractor, therefore, is advised to consider the tighter requirements of EnEV 2012 when negotiating the works contract. Further, as to snagging works requesting major renovation, it must be considered that the tightened requirements of EnEV 2009 (EnEV 2012 respectively) apply, which may result in an immense cost increase.

IV. Impact on Real Estate Transactions

Where the building for sale does not comply with applicable provisions under EEWärmeG and EnEV, this may constitute a defect of the building. Subject to the provisions of the transaction agreement, this defect may result in a warranty claim against the vendor. The Energy Performance Certificate however is a rather formal requirement, which is just meant to inform the purchaser (or tenant). Thus, unless otherwise agreed in the transaction agreement, if the Certificate is not provided or contains false information the purchaser is generally not entitled to claim for damages against the vendor. EU Directive 2010/31/EU provides the possibility for the Member States to regulate tighter effects of the Certificate.[5] Under EnEV 2012, a change of the mere informative character of the Certificate[6] is however not intended so far.

---

5 Directive 2010/31/EU, Art. 12 (7): "The possible effects of energy performance certificates in terms of legal proceedings, if any, shall be decided in accordance with national rules".

6 Sec. 5a EnEG (*Energieeinsparungsgesetz* – Energy Saving Act), which applies in addition to EnEV, bindingly provides: "Energy Performance Certificates only serve for information".

V. Impact on Lease Agreements

In case of leases (or sub-leases) the landlord (or the main tenant) is obliged to provide the Energy Performance Certificate to the potential (sub-) tenant for information without undue delay, on reasonable demand at the latest. However, due to the fact that it is simply a notification, unless otherwise provided for in the lease agreement, the (sub-) tenant may not claim for a defect of the lease object where the landlord does not provide the Certificate or the lease object does not comply with the energy data set out therein.

The costs connected with the issuance of the Energy Performance Certificate may generally not be allocated to the tenant. The landlord may, however, possibly claim a rent increase if it is required to modernize the lease object, in order to implement the measures recommended in the Energy Certification to improve the energy efficiency of the building.

VI. Impact on Protection of Historic Monuments

The requirements of EnEV may be departed from in the case of historically important buildings and other constructions which are considered to be worthy of preservation, if the execution of the requested measures causes damages to the monument's structure or could result in unreasonably high expenses. It is to be assessed by the building owner or the other responsible persons named by EnEV whether this exemption applies. Failure to accurately identify whether this exemption is applicable is at the risk of the relevant person. If incorrect, up to EUR 50,000.00 may be fined.

VII. German Seal of Quality for Sustained Development

The German Seal of Quality for Sustained Development (*Deutsches Gütesiegel für Nachhaltiges Bauen*, hereinafter: DGNB Seal)[7] stands for the first comprehensive German certification system which assesses the sustainability of a development. It may be awarded to newly-developed, re-developed and refurbished buildings. In order to achieve one of the ratings (bronze, silver or gold), the respective building has to fulfill a wide range of quality requirements (63 criteria), covering all main aspects of a building's sustainability (environmental, economic, social cultural and functional, technical, process and location/site quality).

---

7 Developed by the German Federal Ministry of Transport, Construction and Urban Development (*Bundesministerium für Verkehr, Bau und Stadtentwicklung, BMVBS*) in collaboration with German Sustainable Building Council (Deutsche Gesellschaft für Nachhaltiges Bauen e.V., DGNB).

Due to the wide range of the quality categories, DGNB Seal particularly certifies (beyond a construction in compliance with environmental protection requirements) low life-cycle costs and high comfort for its users (e. g. a healthy working environment), which should increase the real estate's market value and marketability.

From the planning stage through to the final taking over of the building, the fulfillment of the requirements must be checked by an expert, who monitors the necessary measures in a specification book (*Pflichtenheft*). On the basis of this book, a preliminary seal may be granted which certifies the future award of DGNB Seal. This preliminary seal may be used as a quality certificate when selling, leasing or otherwise utilizing the real estate.

With regard to the works contract, in collaboration with the above expert, the necessary measures to obtain a certain degree of DGNB Seal should be defined and covered by the scope of services owed by the employee.

When letting the real property, if leasehold improvements by the tenant are agreed upon in the lease agreement, it should be considered that a once granted seal may be withdrawn so that the tenant should not be entitled to renovation that contravenes the requirements of the DGNB Seal.

DGNB Seal is intended to achieve international acceptance as "Made in Germany". It shall be applied internationally to very different types of constructions. It will, however, compete with a number of existing and internationally accepted certification systems, such as the British BREEAM, American LEED, French HQE, Japanese CASBEE and Australian Green Star.

Dr. Ulrike Freigang
ulrike.freigang@luther-lawfirm.com

CHAPTER 23
EMISSION TRADING

DR. STEFAN ALTENSCHMIDT, LL.M.

Since 2005, large emitters of CO_2 in Germany and the rest of the EU are obliged to take part in the EU's Emissions Trading Scheme (ETS). The ETS is based on the "cap and trade"-principle: The EU and its Members States have defined a limited budget of greenhouse gas emissions and have split up that budget in tradable allowances, each of which represents the entitlement to emit one tonne of CO_2 (or the equivalent amount of other greenhouse gases). Emitters are required to surrender one allowance per tonne of CO_2 emitted by them. The scheme is an instrument of market-based environment policy[1] *and aims to achieve emissions reductions for the least possible costs. Emissions trading schemes were for the first time introduced into international law in 1997 by the Kyoto Protocol which set, based on the 1992 UN Framework Convention on Climate Change, binding emissions reduction targets for Germany, the EU and other industrial states.*

The ETS in Germany is governed by the EU's Emissions Trading Directive[2] which has been implemented by the Emissions Trading Act,[3] two Allocations Acts[4] and various regulations.[5] At present, more than 1,600 German installations and their CO_2 emissions are subject to emissions trading. Power stations are affected as well as the glass, cement and lime industry, the production of paper and pulp, the steel industry and some other energy intensive activities. Since 2012, aviation is included, covering nearly every flight that starts or ends in the EU and provoking sharp protests from the US and China. Another extension of the ETS takes places on 1st January 2013 when, beside others, the chemical and the aluminum industry join and some more greenhouse gases – like N_2O – become part of the scheme.

An installation that is covered by the ETS is subject to a number of obligations: It requires an emissions permit that grants the right to emit greenhouse gases (emissions permit), is obliged to monitor and report its emissions on a yearly basis (monitoring

1 Market based policy instruments were developed in the 1950 s and 1960 s by several economist, e.g. by *Dales* (Pollution, Property and Prices, 1968).

2 Directive 2003/87/EC, as amended by Directive 2004/101/EC, Directive 2008/101/EC and Directive 2009/29/EC.

3 German Greenhouse Gas Emission Trading Act (*Treibhausgas-Emissionshandelsgesetz* – TEHG).

4 German Allocation Act 2007 (Zuteilungsgesetz 2007 – ZuG 2007), German Allocation Act 2012 (*Zuteilungsgesetz 2012 – ZuG 2012*).

5 E.g. German Allocation Regulation 2012 (Zuteilungsverordnung 2012 – ZuV 2012).

& reporting) and has to surrender allowances in a number that is equivalent to the amount of its CO_2 emissions to the German Emissions Trading Authority (surrendering of allowances). The duty to surrender allowances is of specific importance: missing the relevant deadline (30th April) will trigger a penalty of EUR 100.00 per allowance that has not been surrendered in due time. Payment of the penalty does not release the operator from its obligation to surrender the required allowances. Companies not complying with the deadline will be published by the authority ("naming & shaming") which puts even more pressure on businesses to meet the strict obligations or to prove a case of force majeure.

There are various ways to obtain allowances. As the ETS is a cap and trade instrument, buying allowances from other operators and at market places like the European Energy Exchange or taking part in auctions organized by the Member States is the easiest opportunity but is subject to market conditions. During the current trading period 2008–2012, the allowance price has fluctuated between EUR 6.00 and EUR 15.00 per ton of CO_2 while some banks see a potential price of up to EUR 24.00 during the next trading period (2013–2020). Operators are also, subject to specific limits and deadlines, entitled to make use of carbon credits stemming from the Kyoto Protocol's flexible instruments Clean Development Mechanism (CDM) and Joint Implementation (JI).

As emissions trading constitutes a substantial burden for operators and their competiveness in international trade, the EU Commission accepted in its 2000 Green Paper on Emissions Trading[6] that – at least for a substantial transition period – a large amount of the allowances have to be allocated free of charge. The ETS Directive required Member States in the first trading period (2005–2007) to issue a minimum of 95 percent cost free, lowering that minimum to 90 percent in the second trading period (2008–2012). So far, the allocation has been done on the basis of National Allocation Plans (NAPs), most of them applying the Grandfathering principle and even catering for a special reserve for newcomers. The German NAPs and their enforcement by the German Emissions Trading Authority have triggered numerous legal challenges and court cases that have been involving even the Federal Constitutional Court which is the highest German legal instance.

From 2013, the cost-free allocation will be based on EU-wide and harmonized allocation rules set by the EU Commission.[7] These rules are based on benchmarks, limiting any free allocation to the standards of best available techniques and taking into account further possibilities to increase energy efficiency and to reduce emissions. The EU has, with some minor exceptions, excluded the generation of electricity from any free allocation, arguing that the power sector is able to pass on extra carbon

6 Green Paper, COM(2000) 87, March 2000.

7 Commission Decision of 27th April 2011, Official Journal L 130, 17.5.2011.

costs to its customers. The free allocation to other sectors is, in general, limited to 80 percent in 2013, decreasing on a linear basis to 30 percent in 2020 and to nil percent in 2027. However, sectors that are subject to international competition with countries outside the EU will benefit from a full 100 per cent cost-free allocation in order to prevent carbon leakage.[8] There will be a limited reserve for new entrants and allocation from this reserve will be done on a first come-first serve basis.

The allocation of allowances in Germany requires the filling of a formal application with the German Emissions Trading Authority. These applications are subject to strict deadlines and formal requirements, e.g. the using of specific electronic templates, and have to be verified by independent experts.[9]

With substantial sanctions in place, carbon compliance is of major importance for every business that is subject to the ETS. Businesses have to establish which parts of their activities are affected, have to meet monitoring and reporting duties and have to comply with deadlines for the surrendering of allowances and the filing of applications for a cost-free allocation. Special care is required in a Due Diligence process as it is sometimes not obvious whether an installation is subject to the ETS or not – the trading scheme affects large integrated steel works as well as medium sized boiler houses in food processing factories. Under German law, any obligation stemming from the ETS is automatically transferred to a new operator which should be reflected in M&A transactions by way of special guaranties and warranties.

Dr. Stefan Altenschmidt, LL.M.
stefan.altenschmidt@luther-lawfirm.com

---

8 Commission Decision of 24th December 2009, Official Journal L 1, 15.1.2010.

9 The German Emissions Trading Authority's webpage provides useful background information (http://www.dehst.de).

CHAPTER 24
PRODUCT LIABILITY

VOLKER STEIMLE

German law provides different legal concepts under which the manufacturer, the seller, the importer, the supplier of components or other persons involved in the supply chain may be liable for their products. These are in particular Sec. 433, 631 et seq. German Civil Code, the law of torts (Sec. 823 et seq. BGB) and the Product Liability Act.

A. Statutory Warranty for Defects of Quality

I. Overview

The delivery of a product which is free from defects is part of the seller's obligation of due performance, Sec. 433 BGB. The seller is liable for those defects, be it technical defects or defects in law, which the relevant product has at the moment the risk passes from the seller to the buyer. In such case, German sales law provides for a system of claims that are contingent upon each other, Sec. 437 BGB.

First of all, the buyer may claim, at his option, rectification of the defect or the supply of another product free of defects. In consequence thereof, the buyer has to give the seller a second opportunity for due performance before he may resort to any other legal remedies he may have. The buyer is not allowed to directly rectify the defects at the seller's cost. It is highly disputed which ancillary costs related to the rectification of a defect have to be borne by the seller, in particular if the defective products have been processed or fitted into another product by the buyer. For B2B-contracts the situation is presently seen as follows by the courts:

If the initial undertaking of the seller was (only) the delivery of the product, i. e. without any undertaking of processing or installing the goods, the seller is not obliged to bear the costs of dismantling the defective goods as part of the rectification.[1] The same applies to the costs of installing the rectified goods again.[2] An obligation to bear the costs of both, dismantling of the defective goods and new installa-

1 BGH NJW 2009, 1660, 1661.
2 BGH NJW 2008, 2837, 2838.

tion of the rectified goods, can only result from a claim for damages, as far as B2B-contracts are concerned (cf. below). Only if the seller does not satisfy the buyer's afore-mentioned claims within a reasonable time-limit set by the buyer, further rights or claims will arise. At this stage the buyer can either withdraw from the contract (*Rücktritt*) or reduce the purchase price (*Minderung*); also claims for damages (*Schadensersatz*) or compensation in respect of expenses incurred (*Ersatz vergeblicher Aufwendungen*) are possible. As described in more detail below, these claims require not only a defect of the delivered product but also responsibility for said defect to be assumed by the seller or for the seller's inability to remedy the deficiencies.

The sold goods are defective in the sense of German sales law if they do not correspond to the conditions (specifications) agreed upon between the parties in the contract. So the starting point in this regard is not an objective view as to whether the goods are fit for a certain purpose or are acceptable according to technical standards, "usual standards" etc., but the (individual) agreement between the parties (so-called *Beschaffenheitsvereinbarung*). For example, irrespective of technical performance, a blue car will be considered to be defective if the parties have agreed upon the delivery of a red one. This explains the special emphasis that should be laid on the proper establishment of a detailed description of the sold/purchased goods and their requisite features, preferably by way of a detailed specification sheet (*Lasten-/Pflichtenheft*). Only as far as the parties have not agreed upon the specific details of the goods, the following criteria will be considered (in the following order):

Suitability for the contractually presumed purpose; suitability for the usual purpose; possession of the quality that is standard for products of the same kind and that the buyer may expect (which is also the fact, if the product diverges from public statements of the seller, the manufacturer or his agents, particularly in sales promotions or in designations about special characteristics of the product, unless the seller did not know and did not need to know these statements).

In addition, a defect exists if assembly is not carried out properly by the seller or if assembly instructions are insufficient.

II. Claims for Damages and extent of Seller's Responsibility

If the seller refuses to rectify defects, is unable to do so within an appropriate period of time or if consequential damages have been caused by a defect which cannot be remedied by the rectification, the buyer may be entitled to damages against the seller, Sec. 437 (1) BGB. The crucial point with such claims for damages is, however, that these require that the violation of the seller's obligations is within the responsibility of the latter, in particular that the defect has been caused within the responsibility of the seller, i. e. intentionally or negligently.[3] While this will typically be the case where the seller is at the same time the manufacturer, this is hardly ever the case where the seller is only the distributor or importer of the relevant products.

The seller is not only liable for its own willful action and negligence, but also for the faults of his vicarious agents.[4] German courts do, however, not consider the manufacturer to be a vicarious agent of the seller, if the seller is only a distributor or importer who is simply dealing with the relevant products and has no own undertaking to manufacture them. If, however, the seller has given guarantees for certain features of the products, the seller is liable regardless of fault. This is one main reason why a guarantee for certain features of the sold goods – which guarantee is not to be mistaken with the normal contractual warranties – substantially improves the legal position of the buyer. The interpretation of a certain undertaking of the seller as a guarantee requires that the seller agreed on a (voluntary) supplementary liability and responsibility for the relevant feature. Other consequences of the agreement of a guarantee are, inter alia, that it becomes even more difficult for the seller to arrange for a limitation of liability (e.g. by limiting the duration of warranty periods or excluding consequential damages etc.).

In the absence of any contractual stipulations that provide otherwise, the amount of compensation is not restricted in any way, e.g. to the defective product itself, and also includes damages to other goods or rights of the buyer. So the buyer's claim may, for example, include the costs of the purchase of a substitute product, loss of profits or damages the buyer himself has to pay to third parties. Also immaterial damage, e.g. compensation for pain suffered (*Schmerzensgeld*) can be claimed.[5] If the seller delays in remedying any of the deficiencies, the buyer can also claim damages for the loss he suffers as a result of the delay (*Verzugsschaden*).[6] Instead of claiming damages, the buyer can demand compensation for expenses he has incurred relying fairly upon the receipt of the benefit, Sec. 284 BGB.

III. Exclusion of Claims

The buyer's claims for defects are excluded where it can be shown that he knew or should have known without gross negligence of the defects at the time the contract was concluded.[7]

---

3 Sec. 276 BGB.
4 Sec. 278 BGB.
5 Sec. 253 BGB.
6 Sec. 286 BGB.
7 Sec. 442 BGB.

IV. Obligations of Buyer

Where there is a transaction between merchants, i. e. a B2B-contract (*Handelskauf*), all warranty claims cease to exist if the buyer does not comply with his duty to examine the products without undue delay after delivery and, in case of defects, give notice of them without undue delay.[8] The admissible periods to perform such inspections under German law vary, depending on the nature of the relevant product. They tend in any case to be shorter than those applying e.g. under the United Nations Law on the International Sale of Goods (CISG).

This obligation to inspect all incoming products without undue delay after delivery (even if by random examination) often results in the loss of substantial claims, since the requirements imposed by German courts for inspections in compliance with Sec. 377 HGB are often difficult to meet within the reality of modern supplier systems. To avoid such loss it is therefore crucial to install proper quality assurance agreements, delegating the responsibility for such inspections from the buyer to the seller.

V. Warranty Period

The statutory warranty period for movable products is two years starting with delivery. A five year warranty period applies when the delivered (and defective) goods have been used for a building and caused a defect to said building.

VI. Possibility of Deviating Contractual Regulations

The seller's warranties for defects can be excluded (by way of individual agreement) or limited, unless the seller has given a guarantee for certain features of the sold products.[9] Substantial restrictions apply, however, to limitations of warranty in general terms and conditions (*Allgemeine Geschäftsbedingungen*, AGB). For example, it is not possible to exclude or even limit the liability for gross negligence or for damage to life or health of human beings in whatsoever way.[10] German courts have established a vast body of jurisprudence on clauses that are not upheld in court. As a result there is to say that meaningful limitations of liability can only be achieved by way of an individual agreement under German law.

---

8 Sec. 377 of the German Commercial Code (*Handelsgesetzbuch*, HGB).

9 Sec. 444 BGB.

10 This applies not only to consumer contracts but also to B2B-contracts.

The statutory warranty period can be shortened as well as extended by way of agreement[11] although as part of the general terms and conditions it can only be shortened to one year – this is the minimum warranty period for the sale of new goods (other than building materials).

VII. Special Provisions for Consumer Goods

Special provisions apply to a "consumer goods purchase", i. e. the purchase of a product by a consumer from a merchant for private use, e.g.: deviations from the statutory warranty provisions to the disadvantage of the buyer cannot be validly agreed in advance, Sec. 475 (1) BGB. If a defect appears within six months from the passing of the risk, it is assumed that the product was already defective at the moment the risk was passed.[12] This implies a shifting of the burden of proof to the disadvantage of the seller. Even by way of an individual agreement the warranty period cannot be limited to less than two years for new goods, respectively one year for used goods, Sec. 475 (2) BGB. The seller may take recourse against the manufacturer for all costs incurred with respect to the fulfillment of the seller's obligations vis-à-vis the consumer under the same legal regime as it is available to the consumer. This may take up to five years from delivery of the defective product or two months from fulfilling the consumer's claims, whichever is earlier.

VIII. Law on Works Contracts

Where the seller has manufactured the products specifically for the buyer the agreement between the parties is not a sales but a works contract, in respect of which German law sets out special provisions. An exception to this occurs where the entrepreneur is obliged to manufacture and deliver movable goods – in this case the law on sales agreements is still applicable, Sec. 651 BGB. Most of the supply agreements in a B2B-relationship are therefore governed by sales law. In addition, many of the differences between the law on sales and the law on works contracts were removed in the meantime so that the liability of the supplier in a works contract is now very similar to that of a sales contract.

B. Liability Under Law of Torts

Where a manufacturer brings a defective product onto the market he may not only be contractually liable but may also be liable under the statutory law of torts

11 Sec. 202 BGB.
12 Sec. 476 BGB.

(*deliktische Haftung*). The statutory liability under the law of torts for unsafe products, which may apply in addition to contractual obligations between the parties involved, is governed particularly in Sec. 823 (1) BGB (*Produzentenhaftung*).

I. Overview

The product liability under Sec. 823 (1) BGB requires that the defective product has caused an infringement of so-called "absolute rights", e.g. life, health, property etc. – a mere financial loss without the infringement of said rights is not sufficient. Product liability is based on the general obligation to avoid hazards to the public (*allgemeine Verkehrssicherungspflicht*). For manufacturers this means that they have to take all measures that are necessary to prevent their products from harming the life and health or property of their customers or third parties. Here, the principle of commensurability applies: the bigger the possible danger is the greater the manufacturer's duties to maintain safety.

II. Manufacturer's Obligations to Maintain Safety

German jurisprudence has structured these obligations as follows:

Development and testing, as well as sourcing and manufacturing of the products have to comply with state of the art of science and technology. The same applies to the instruction of the user of the products. The manufacturer has to organize its business in a way that the afore-said sources of faults are eliminated to the extent possible. If so, he is not liable when a defect arises from a unique fault, e.g. an employee's malpractice or malfunction of a machine (so-called *Ausreißer*).The manufacturer has to issue proper warnings about possible risks aligned with the product and its use. After bringing the product onto the market, the manufacturer has to observe whether the product shows risks the manufacturer was not aware of before. This also comprises risks which result from typical accessories to the product, even where they have been manufactured by a third party. If the manufacturer becomes aware of such risks, he is obliged to issue warnings or even start a recall-campaign to prevent the products from endangering the life and health of the users or innocent bystanders.

The key question in most court cases, as it will be in all other jurisdictions, is whether the product that caused damage to its user or to third parties needs to be considered unsafe for the purposes of Sec. 823 BGB. In assessing the question what level of safety the user may rightfully expect from the product, courts will have due regard to the nature of the products, the way of use (use by consumers or by trained personnel?), the presentation of the product and its features by the manufacturer in advertisements, in owner's manuals, on the packaging etc., any warning instructions – particularly if placed on the product – and to a certain extent also the price of the product. Where applicable technical standards are not met, e.g. German "DIN-Norm", courts will treat this as a substantial indication of the product being unsafe. As a result, this works as shifting the burden of proof to the manufacturer who will then have to demonstrate that his products are safe in the afore-said sense despite the fact that the relevant DIN-Norm etc. is not complied with.

III. Persons Liable

Liability under the law of torts may not only apply to the manufacturer (or assembler) but e.g. also to the distributor of products (in respect of specific distributor's duties as the duty of inspection, instruction or advice). This needs to be kept in mind as an entrepreneur who brings a product onto the market under his own brand that has been manufactured by a third party for him may also be liable hereunder (so-called "quasi manufacturer"). If there is more than one manufacturer in the afore-mentioned sense who has contributed to the damage, they all are liable as joint and several debtors (*Gesamtschuldner*).

IV. Extent of Manufacturer's Liability

The manufacturer has to compensate the injured party for all direct and indirect financial losses resulting from the infringement of the "absolute right". This may also comprise loss of profits and compensation for pain and suffering (*Schmerzensgeld*). In principle, the damage to the defective product itself is not covered here. The latter is only part of the contractual warranty for defects. This restricts the practical use of this legal concept for the purpose of taking recourse in the supply chain. This situation is, however, treated differently if the defectiveness of the product is restricted to a single part of it which affects other faultless parts of the entire product (so-called "*weiterfressender Mangel*").

V. Statute of Limitation

What makes this legal concept particularly important is the fact that the statute of limitation is substantially longer than the one under contractual liability. In principle, claims for compensation based on Sec. 823 BGB become time-barred within three years from the end of the year in which the claim came into existence and the claimant became aware of the damage and the person responsible for it.[13]

13 Sects. 195, 199 (1) BGB.

The second subsection of Sec. 823 BGB covers a further area of product liability. Here, the liability is linked to the non-compliance of the manufacturer with the requirements of special protective laws. There exist special regulations, e.g. in connection with the production of food, pharmaceuticals (*Arzneimittelgesetz*, AMG) and many others.

C. Product Liability Act

I. Overview

The Product Liability Act (*Produkthaftungsgesetz, ProdHG*) operates on the basis of strict liability, i. e. there will be product liability regardless of whether the manufacturer was responsible for the damages caused by his products, as long as the products have to be considered as being unsafe. Similar to Sec. 823 (1) BGB, a liability according to the ProdHG requires that the defective product has caused damage to life, health of human beings or to property other than the hazardous product itself. Damage to property is only covered in case it is intended for private use, Sec. 1 ProdHG, and the damage exceeds a deductible of EUR 500.00, cf. Sec. 11 ProdHG. This is the reason why claims under the ProdHG are of no use when considering how to take recourse for defective products in the supply chain. The liability for personal injuries is limited to a maximum amount of EUR 85 million, Sec. 10 ProdHG. The liability according to the ProdHG cannot be waived in advance, Sec. 14 ProdHG. Since 2004 the liability under the ProdHG extends also to damages for pain and sufferings.

Products in terms of the ProdHG are all kinds of movable objects, even if they are part of another object. Also under the ProdHG a product is considered to be defective if it does not provide that level of safety that the general public, particularly with regard to the relevant purpose of use, may expect at the time of bringing the product into the market. As a consequence of the afore-said, there is no liability according to the ProdHG if formerly unknown risks become known because of new insights after bringing the product onto the market: there is only an obligation to observe whether the products show risks that the manufacturer was not aware of before, Sec. 823 (1) BGB.

II. Persons Liable

According to Sec. 4 ProdHG, the liability according to Sec. 1 ProdHG falls upon:

The manufacturer of the end product; the suppliers (who manufacture parts for the end products or raw materials); the so-called "quasi manufacturer"; the importer into the EWR; under certain circumstances also the distributor (if no other liability can be construed).

If there is more than one person liable who faces liability, they are all considered to be liable as joint and several debtors (*Gesamtschuldner*).

III. Statute of Limitation

Claims for compensation based on the ProdHG become time-barred within three years from the moment when the claimant became aware or should have become aware of the damage, defect and the person responsible for the damage, Sec. 12 ProdHG. Claims based on Sec. 1 ProdHG expire 10 years after the moment of bringing the product onto the market, at the latest.

IV. Burden of Proof

Product liability claims are often particularly dependent on whether difficult technical issues can be proven in court. German procedural law does not provide for a discovery procedure. The outcome of a law suit, therefore, often depends on the question, which of the parties bears the burden of proof. Generally, the claimant has to prove all requirements of its claim, e.g. for contractual warranty as well as for claims under the law of torts or the Product Liability Act, the defectiveness of the product or its inherent hazards at the moment of passing of the risk. As the injured person typically is not able to see behind the curtain of the manufacturing process, the burden of proof is shifted to some extent: in principle, the injured person only has to prove that its damage has been caused by a defect of the product or by an unsafe product. From then on it is presumed that the manufacturer is responsible because of non-compliance with the afore-mentioned obligations, unless the manufacturer can demonstrate that he acted neither intentionally nor negligently. Under the law of torts it is, therefore, up to the manufacturer to prove that the suffered loss has other reasons and is not attributable to him. Furthermore, in the case of a consumer product purchase, it is assumed that the product was already defective at the moment of passing of the risk if a defect appears within six months from the passing of the risk (see above).

V. Amount of Claims for Damages

Contrary to the USA, for example, German law does not provide for punitive damages – only the concrete and proven loss has to be compensated. Even though the amounts of compensation for pain and suffering awarded by German courts have increased during recent years, they cannot be compared to the level of some awards which have been made in the USA.

D. Criminal Law Implications

Whether a manufacturer of hazardous products is obliged to recall its products – as opposed to giving a mere warning to users – depends on whether the hazardous products only endanger other property or whether they endanger life or health of human beings with a certain likelihood. If the latter is the case the relevant manufacturer or even distributor may be obliged to recall the product. According to the landmark "leather spray"-decision of the German Federal High Court (*Bundesgerichtshof*, BGH) the manufacturer/distributor will not only be liable for payment of damages to injured persons, but its management is also subject to criminal prosecution, if it does not comply with a statutory obligation to recall the products in the individual case. In this case, all managing directors of a manufacturing company were convicted under criminal law – partly resulting in imprisonment – for not properly addressing health risks emanating from the company's products when these risks became known after bringing the products onto the market.

However, it has to be noted that according to the German Federal High Court[14] this does not necessarily entail an obligation to recall the products, i. e. to replace the hazardous products by safe products for free, in cases where the warranty period for the relevant product has expired. Depending on the circumstances of the individual case, and in particular the foreseen behavior of the users, it may be sufficient to simply issue a clear warning to the customers and users, even if the hazardous products endanger life or health of the users of these products.

E. Product Safety Act

Based on the EU-directive 2001/95/EC, special regulations apply for consumer products and work equipment according to the Product Safety Act (*Geräte- und Produktsicherheitsgesetz*, GPSG) since 2004. The Product Safety Act confers additional powers on the regulatory authorities such as ordering the recall of unsafe products from the market. Furthermore, it establishes a duty to notify the national authorities when a product carries serious risks to consumers. Besides, it strengthens the existing obligations of manufacturers and distributors such as to carry out sample testing of marketed products, maintain proper screening of customer complaints and recall products

14 BGH NJW 2009, 1080, 1081.

to protect consumer health. What is more, it entitles and encourages the relevant national authorities throughout the EU to actively exchange all information obtained from manufacturers with each other and with the public, using modern information technology.[15] Starting 1st December 2011 a new law on product safety (*Produktsicherheitsgesetz, ProdSG*) applies. This confers additional powers to the relevant national authorities, imposes additional penalties (up to EUR 100,000.00) on manufacturers, importers or dealers and – in general – seeks to strengthen the market surveillance.

Volker Steimle
volker.steimle@luther-lawfirm.com

15 cf. EU Rapid Alert System (RAPEX) under www.ec.europa.eu

CHAPTER 25
PUBLIC PRIVATE PARTNERSHIP

DR. HANS-GEORG HAHN
DR. OLIVER KAIRIES

The impacts of the financial crisis which we are currently undergoing are complex and in most parts serious. That applies also and in particular for the public sector. Due to the occurred and the expected massive losses of the public authorities, the exigency to privatize or merge costly public institutions or publicly owned undertakings with a commercial partner will increase. Therefore, the following article is of significant importance.

A. General Aspects

The still empty coffers of the public sector in Germany are increasingly forcing federal, state and local authorities to partly or fully sell their amenities and business operations or to transfer their functions of state wholly or partially to the private sector under other cooperation models. In terms of investment activities, it is the local municipalities in particular which are facing the challenge of clearing the investment backlog to the tune of several hundred billion Euros over the next five years. This is unlikely to be possible without the engagement of the private sector.

The legal framework and general conditions for the involvement of private investors are in place in many areas in Germany. Key markets such as the electricity and gas, telecommunications and water markets have been deregulated. Other traditionally public services, e.g. health services, local public transportation and sewage works, are being sold or run more efficiently with the support of private companies and investors.

This situation offers immense business opportunities for private investors. The public enterprises that are up for sale frequently operate inefficiently compared with private sector companies. Yet private investors can unleash considerable profit potential, by taking optimization and restructuring measures, improving management structures, tapping into new business areas and markets which were off bounds to the public sector under public law and other synergy effects. This especially applies to enterprises whose potential the public sector was unable to realize for legal and/or political reasons. Public authorities are also often under considerable financial and political (once privatization proceedings have been initiated) pressure to sell.

Foreign investors in particular often overestimate the resistance of the local population to privatization and underestimate the legal and practical means of reducing personnel expenses. Performance-based compensation, the conclusion of collective wage agreements applicable only to the company in question, reasonable periods during which notice of termination may not be given and withdrawal from the public collective bargaining system are legally possible and increasingly (politically) accepted, a situation which employees are having to accept more and more. Numerous privatizations in Germany have been a great success for both the public sector and the private investor. The "wave of privatization" and "privatization friendliness" is set to grow in many areas in the future, especially due to the current financial crisis also affecting the public sector.

B. "Privatization" and Forms of "Privatization"

The term "privatization" is not used uniformly, nor is it defined by law. A distinction can be made between the following privatization forms:

I. Formal Privatization

The reorganization of a public service or a public organization or legal form (e.g. public-law institution (*Anstalt des öffentlichen Rechts*), municipal enterprise operated by an administrative agency (*Regiebetrieb*), owner-operated municipal enterprise (*Eigenbetrieb*), etc.) into a company with a private legal form (e.g. *Gesellschaft mit beschränkter Haftung* (limited liability company), *Aktiengesellschaft* (stock corporation), etc.) is known as formal privatization.

Example: *Deutsche Bundesbahn* (federal railways), a special asset of the federal government, was reorganized into *Deutsche Bahn Aktiengesellschaft* (a stock corporation).

Following formal privatization, the public authority remains the sole owner/shareholder of the company reorganized into a private legal form.

The most important reasons for formal privatization are:

The expectation that the enterprise can be run more efficiently in a private legal form, e.g. as a result of the decrease in political influence; the creation of the possibility of (subsequent) investment in the company by private investors, as public-law organizations and legal forms do not permit investment.

II. Regular Privatization

The partial or full sale of a public enterprise by way of an asset deal or the (partial) privatization of a private company wholly owned by a public authority in an asset or share deal is referred to as regular privatization or, simply, privatization.

Example: the Federal Republic of Germany, the State of Lower Saxony and DB Regio AG sold 82,96 % of the shares in the railway company *Osthannoversche Eisenbahnen Aktiengesellschaft* to a private transportation company.

III. Contracting Out

Contracting out means subcontracting functions of state while retaining the responsibility for such services.

Example: the City of Dresden, while remaining responsible for performance of the service, transferred the function of state of sewage disposal to *Stadtentwässerung Dresden GmbH.*

Contracting out and regular privatization can be conducted simultaneously.

Example: a private strategic partner acquired a 49.9 % participation in *Stadtentwässerung Dresden GmbH.*

C. Market Assessment of Key Privatization Areas in Germany

The key public companies undergoing privatization include in particular:

I. Public Utilities

Up until the end of the 1990s, there was a true wave of privatization among public utilities companies. A lot of German and foreign investors competed to invest in public utilities companies, which generally provided electricity, gas, district heating (sometimes including electricity generation) and in some cases, water.

It remains commonplace for private investors to hold minority interests (up to 49.9 % of shares), although the legal arrangements in the investment agreements generally treat the private investor as if it held 50 % of the shares. In many cases, the public seller was also granted a put option enabling it to sell further shares within a specific period of time at a price calculated in accordance with an agreed formula. Only a few individual investments in public utilities have been up for sale in Germany in the past one or two years. The market is largely consolidated.

II. Local Public Transportation

The German local public transportation market has opened up during the last couple of years as a result of public transportation companies being privatized, rather than by local public transportation services being put out for tender. Both public and private transportation service providers from Germany and abroad took their chances in this competition. For the owner, strategic partnerships of this kind offer a way of mitigating the increasing market risks. For the organization responsible for the service, the separation of supply and demand creates an organizational structure in line with competition law, enabling transportation services to be put out to tender in the future without discrimination and without conflicts of interest under EU law.

However, local municipalities can still preserve much of their influence by retaining the majority of voting and/or veto rights. Their objective is to fix the municipal subsidies payable in long-term agreements and thereby limit the financial risks. This requires negotiation of an employment package that includes employees' acquired rights in order to make the sale of shares possible in the first place.

For international investors in particular, municipal transportation companies make interesting acquisition targets due to their long-term operating licenses. More municipalities are expected to decide on a sale, and the consolidation process in Germany is expected to accelerate. Experts estimate that between five and ten large operator companies will remain in the medium term.

III. Hospitals

The German hospital market has been undergoing fundamental change during the last few years. The introduction of flat fees per case (Diagnosis Related Groups, DRG), budget capping and the limitation of subsidies from the states, combined with an investment backlog, in particular lead to incalculable financial risks for municipal hospital operators. Especially during the last year, the hospital market in Germany has had to cope with looming insolvencies affecting small municipal as well as large county hospitals. Moreover, after an action brought by a private hospital operator, the European Court of Justice has to resolve whether the common practice among public hospitals of having their accumulated operating losses funded by tax revenues from their supporting public authority represents aid that is not compatible with Art. 86 et seq. of the EU Treaty.

Against this background and to safeguard both the future and competitiveness of their hospitals while avoiding future financing obligations, an increasing number of municipal hospital operators have decided to sell their hospitals. As a result of this slowly but steadily rising wave of privatization, the hospital market has been transformed into a buyer's market, in which buyers are increasingly able to influence the terms of the transaction. Thus, for example, investors often want to acquire a majority shareholding in a hospital company or buy the hospital outright to ensure that they can exercise decisive influence over the running of the hospital. Following privatization, municipalities only hold a "golden share", i. e. a nominal interest in the hospital company, if any at all. This gives them certain rights of codetermination under corporate law.

Large private hospital operators with activities nationwide or medium-sized private hospital operators with regional activities have been the main parties interested to date in the privatization of German hospitals. Surprisingly, foreign investors have yet to invest in German hospitals. One alternative to the full or partial sale of a hospital to a private operator is to establish a municipal hospital group. In this case, several municipalities and sometimes also a private hospital operator invest in a holding company that is the sole shareholder of several hospital companies and provides central services for these companies.

Hospital privatization in whatever form offers the opportunity to pool expertise and exploit synergies, thus considerably improving efficiency in the hospital sector. During the last two years, these circumstances have motivated many German states to think about putting forward privatizations of their large University hospitals. These privatization processes are quite complex and require not only high quality legal, tax and financial advice, but also the cooperation of the legislative body of the state, as several state bills need to be altered. The first privatization of a University hospital (Giessen and Marburg) in 2006, a role model of a successful privatization, inspired many other German states – there are still University hospitals all over Germany that are on the brink of a privatization. Quite often large private hospital operators can trigger such privatization processes by tailor-made concepts guaranteeing better financial performance and a strong support of academic research.

Example: the state of Hessen sold 95 % of the shares in *Universitätsklinikum Giessen und Marburg GmbH* to a private hospital operator.

IV. Sewage Disposal

Current ecological, economic and political conditions call for a strategic realignment of municipal sewage companies. In particular, the public sector is struggling with the high backlog of investments required in the sewerage system and sewage works. Recently the private sector has made inroads into the sewage disposal market in Germany. The first significant privatizations in the area of sewage disposal (*Berliner Was-*

serbetriebe, *Abwasserversorgungsbetriebe in Bremerhaven or Hansewasser*) have only recently gone ahead.

The reason why public sewage disposal companies have jumped on the privatization bandwagon relatively late in comparison to other utilities, is this area's special link to the public sector. In Germany, sewage disposal is defined by law as a "function of state" incumbent on municipalities. This means that municipalities are unable to fully shed sewage disposal services, unlike energy supply, for example. Although this does not prevent the privatization of municipal sewage disposal facilities, it must be taken into consideration in the legal structure of a privatization of this kind. In this case, contracting out and regular privatization must be combined.

If it has not already done so, the municipality whose sewage disposal is carried out by an owner-operated municipal enterprise or a municipal enterprise operated by an administrative agency, should found a private-law company, e.g. a limited liability company (*GmbH*). Protected by an agreement with the municipality, this private-law company then provides sewage disposal services for the municipality, while the municipality retains responsibility for this function of state. A private investor can then have a stake in the private-law company.

This "gradual" privatization requires the various interests of all parties involved to be covered by a complex agreement. Its content can be characterized as the combination of an asset deal (transfer of the assets required to conduct sewage disposal services to the private-law company and sometimes provision of the necessary specialist personnel from the owner-operated municipal enterprise to the private-law company) and a share deal (sale of an interest in the private-law company to a private investor as a strategic partner of the municipality) as well as the compliance with the regulations governing the charges for the services at hand. In Germany, sewage disposal by multi-utility groups is still in its infancy. It is water supply rather than sewage disposal that is currently the focus of attention. Global groups operating in the area of sewage disposal, especially from France, are attempting to gain a further foothold in Germany. Thus, the German sewage disposal market still could be carved up and offers numerous opportunities for private investors to take their share of the cake.

Example: the City of Dresden, while remaining responsible for the provision of sewage disposal, transferred the corresponding function to *Stadtentwässerung Dresden GmbH*, followed by a 49.9 % investment by a private strategic partner in *Stadtentwässerung Dresden GmbH*.

V. Municipal Housing

Only a comparatively small number of housing companies have been privatized to date. It may be assumed that larger portfolios will be put on the market in the coming years. There have only been a few examples of the privatization of public housing companies since the sale of *Deutschbau* in 1997. However, a growing interest on the part of German (e.g. Viterra (E.On Group), IVG, etc.) and foreign investors – in particular financial investors – in former welfare housing in Germany has since become evident. A number of investors (investor groups) have now appeared in a market which, up until a few years ago, had not been concerned with the acquisition of housing portfolios. These investor groups have recognized that considerable value-added potential can be exploited by increasing efficiency. Optimizing maintenance and modernization through economies of scale achieved by consolidating existing portfolios is leading to a significant reduction in costs and an increase in value. Investors are also benefiting from the margin that can be generated through the individual sale of residential units to tenants.

This trend is being driven by the low interest rates which provide an attractive return on capital employed for the acquirer as a result of low borrowing costs with a corresponding debt/equity ratio and also allow tenants to buy their apartments at favorable conditions.

A number of standards for mitigating the social impact have evolved in recent years in connection with the privatization of public housing companies. These standards comprise specific arrangements which must be included in the purchase agreement with the acquirer to cushion the social impact of the change in ownership, e. g. clauses to protect tenants, employees, the housing company as a going concern and the interests of minority shareholders. However, the enforcement of such standards conflicts with the anticipated proceeds from the transaction.

VI. Other Areas

The general budget constraints of the public sector are also forcing federal, state and local authorities to examine all other areas in which services are performed for citizens to determine whether they can be transferred to private-law companies. Even functions of state involving force (e. g. prisons) may be outsourced to private companies.

These other areas cover a wide spectrum of economic activities from cemetery maintenance, waste disposal, housing of the mentally ill, detention of convicted criminals, certification and audit firms, to the privatization of casinos. Without expanding on the specific features of each area, the following applies: the public authority must always ensure that privatization is more economical than the previous form of providing the service. The bidder must be able to demonstrate that this is the case when preparing its determination of a purchase price for a company or the price of a service to be provided for the public authority at a later date; due to the requirement to identify the most economical form of privatization, a competitive bidding process is almost always carried out. The regulations governing such processes are generally fairly identical; the closer the subject of privatization is to the core functions of state, the more likely the investor will find itself subject to the de facto and/or legal control of the public authority, even after the privatization, due to laws, directives, etc. (which are often only enacted in connection with the privatization). Such control may relate to both the supervision of casinos by law and inspections by the health authorities to ensure that patients are properly cared for. If there is any scope for contractual arrangements, public-law agreements may be an appropriate complement to private law agreements. In this manner, the private investor can exercise a certain degree of influence over subsequent actions by the authorities in relation to the investment.

> *A detailed due diligence review remains the safest way for the investor to gain a clear understanding of the legal, tax and economic conditions of the investment and the associated risks. The investor has a right to insist on adherence to private sector standards even if a business has previously been publicly run.*

D. Regular Privatization (Tender Procedure)

The sale of shares in a company by the public sector is only subject to procurement law if construction, service or supply agreements subject to compulsory tendering are concluded in connection with the sale of the shares.

Regular privatization is subject to the stringent and extremely formal rules of procurement law, which tends to be an overall hindrance to smooth privatization. This opens up a range of opportunities for investors to have the procedure and decision reviewed by the responsible public procurement tribunals or by the courts. However, observance of the provisions of procurement law is not only important for the public sector. Frequently, dealing with this complex area is also relatively difficult for the private bidder. It may therefore be worthwhile for a private investor to consult a recognized expert in procurement law.

E. Regular Privatization (Discretionary Sale)

If procurement law is not applicable, privatization is carried out by way of a discretionary sale, i. e. the procedure can be organized at the discretion of the public seller. However, budgetary law provisions require that the "best value" (not necessarily the highest purchase price) be attained for the asset sold. Generally a fair and transparent bidding process is conducted by an investment bank. The intention to sell is announced publicly. Interested parties have the opportunity to submit an indicative offer on the basis of an information memorandum. The best (normally some 4 to 6) bidders in this phase are then allowed to conduct a due diligence review and, on the basis of an agreement drafted by the seller, to make a so-called binding offer, which is not actually legally binding. By this time, the number of bidders may have been reduced, and negotiations are held until one or more bidders makes a legally binding offer. Often this "final offer" may not be subject to approval by the executive body of the bidder, although it is subject to acceptance on the part of the seller and approval by the seller's supervisory authority.

F. Privatization Agreements

Privatization is a special form of a company sale, as is reflected in the related agreements. The agreements that are normally negotiated are the following:

I. Purchase Agreement

An integral component of the purchase agreement are the warranties provided by the municipality. The statutory warranty laws are normally contracted out in their entirety and replaced by a self-contained contractual warranty system. For the municipality, it is important to limit the cases of liability as far as possible and to cap the amount of liability. Ideally, from the municipality's point of view this will be a mere fraction of the purchase price. Quite apart from the purely economic consideration that the municipality has no interest in subsequently "repaying" the purchase price due to warranties, unlimited liability on the part of the municipality is also problematic in terms of public law, since municipalities cannot assume unlimited liability under the municipal charters of the federal states. In order to identify potential liability risks to the municipality at an early stage and to provide contractual cover for such risks, a detailed due diligence review by experienced lawyers and tax advisors is highly recommended, prior to privatization.

II. Redrafting of the Articles of Association

As part of (partial) privatization of a municipal company, it will also be necessary to redraft the articles of association, since private partners will also demand that they be granted appropriate shareholder rights.

Numerous federal states require that the municipality has appropriate influence, in particular over the supervisory board or a relevant supervisory body. This influence should also be ensured, for example, by means of appropriate provisions in the articles of incorporation. The influence of the municipality should ordinarily be determined according to the amount of the investment in the capital stock and/or according to the voting rights. The appropriateness is determined according to the purpose and amount of the investment. A controlling influence is not required, such that a minority interest on the part of the public authority is also permitted provided that appropriate influence is otherwise ensured. It is not clearly regulated as to how the public authority can ensure its influence if a supervisory board or other supervisory body does not exist. In practice, however, this question hardly ever arises because municipalities mostly call for the creation of a supervisory board even if this is not legally required, so as to create a means of influence by establishing transactions requiring approval. In the case of a facultative, i. e. voluntarily established supervisory board, it is legally possible if required – at least with a German limited liability company – to individually define the rights of the supervisory board and thus to place considerable restrictions on it.

III. Syndicate Agreement

In the syndicate agreement, the municipality and the private-sector partner set out the main business objectives and the future strategy of the company through which these objectives are to be attained. At this point, the private-sector partner is called on to put forward ideas and suggestions on how to secure and underpin the long-term success of the company. Since the "best partner" cannot just be identified on the basis of the bid price – and strategy also plays a decisive role – this gives the private-sector partner the opportunity to make its mark and set itself apart from the competition. In this context, the private-sector partner may be asked to agree to contractual obligations to invest in specific company projects. However, the municipality must ensure that these obligations are actually enforceable with penalties for failure to comply and are not merely declarations of intent. Special rights for the partners may also be stipulated in the syndicate agreement to supplement the provisions of the company's articles of incorporation, e. g. rights to appoint members to the management or supervisory board or rights to veto key shareholder resolutions.

An important aspect that is decisive for the political success of the privatization is the labor law framework, in particular the protection against dismissal, vocational training support and continuing education. It is recommended that the long-term commitment of the private-sector partner to the joint venture be secured by means of suitable provisions, e.g. restriction on sale for a specific period.

The private-sector partner may also be interested in acquiring additional shares in the joint venture at a later date, in particular to become the majority shareholder. In this case, the syndicate agreement may provide for a put option, whereby the private-sector partner offers to purchase additional shares from the municipality at a specific purchase price or at a purchase price to be determined on the sale date and which the municipality may accept by an agreed date.

The content of all agreements must be coordinated and take account of the individual features of the specific case as well as do justice to the interests of each partner. The above information can only provide a rough overview of the typical content of agreements without going into detail. The extremely complex contractual framework of any privatization is always unique.

G. Privatization Expertise

As discussed above, the privatization of public-sector enterprises has become an independent transaction market with relatively rigid ground rules, even though each case is unique.

Foreign investors looking to acquire a formerly publicly run enterprise or to manage a company as a joint venture with public authorities in Germany would be well advised to seek professional support for this investment from the outset. This can be assured by a multidisciplinary team of lawyers, tax advisors and, if required, a corporate finance firm well versed in the typical rules followed in a competitive bidding process. These advisors should also have the proven competence in the relevant industry sector that is indispensable to the success of the acquisition.

In many cases, the procedural rules are affected by European competition law. The special features of German budgetary law and the political implications of the procedures must also be taken into account in the selection of an advisor. It is therefore recommendable to work with law firms in Germany. Personal references are crucial in the selection of advisors in order to demonstrate to the public authorities from the outset that they are dealing with proven and reliable contact partners – a success factor not to be underestimated. The authors have reported on a few of their own projects in this chapter. They belong to a group of some 25 lawyers specialized in public-sector transactions in various areas.

H. PPP – an Investment Culture for the Future

A powerful infrastructure is more than just an important geographic advantage: it is a prerequisite for an economy's growth and efficiency. Due to the tight financial situation of public budgets, investments in German infrastructure have decreased since 1992 – resulting in an immense investment backlog. According to a study compiled by the German Urban Development Institute (*Deutsches Institut für Urbanistik, Difu*) in 2008, the greatest need for investment exists in road construction (EUR 162 billion), schools (EUR 73 billion), and wastewater disposal (EUR 58 billion). Other areas requiring massive investment are the healthcare industry and general public building construction. Against this background, the cooperation of the public and private sectors (public private partnership) has become increasingly more important for the provision of public services. With a view to ensuring the efficient use of its scarce financial means, the state is compelled to limit its activities more and more to its core duties, having recourse to private capital and know-how in the planning, construction, financing, and operation of properties.

I. Fair Allocation of Risks and Long Term Cooperation

PPP models are characterized by a partnership-based approach. The objective is to enhance efficiency by involving a private investor over the entire lifecycle of the project. An assessment of 30 PPP projects by the Difu, carried out on behalf of the PPP task force of the Federal Ministry of Traffic, Construction and Urban Development (*Bundesministerium für Verkehr, Bau und Stadtentwicklung, BMVBS*) in 2008, has shown that the PPP procurement channel was between 3 % and 19 % – according to the responsible Parliamentary State Secretary at the Federal Ministry, on average 16 % – more efficient than the traditional realization by the public sector. In such projects, the public sector acts with a view to obtaining the relevant service either at the same cost with an increase in quality or at a lower cost with constant quality as compared to traditional realization. PPPs are therefore long-term, contractually agreed forms of cooperation over the lifecycle of a property (normally between 15 and 25 years). The projects generally comprise the stages of planning, constructing or rehabilitating, financing and operating as well as maintaining a property. As a consequence, the state ceases to be a producer and provider of public infrastructure, becoming instead a purchaser of complex services. The long-term nature of the contractual relationships opens up reliable and profitable fields of work to private companies.

II. Widespread Applications

A restriction on PPP projects to particular sectors or industries does not generally exist, so the realization of public private partnerships is conceivable in all areas of infrastructure. The possible fields of application comprise:

- Public building construction (inter alia, in administration, health care and education);
- Traffic industry (construction of roads, railways and waterways, harbours);
- Public utility infrastructure (water and waste industries);
- Defence sector; and science, research, IT projects.

III. Realized Projects

The number of PPP projects carried out in Germany has risen continuously in the past years and numerous successful models have been implemented. In autumn 2008, the contracts for the 100th and 101st building construction projects within the framework of a public private partnership were signed during a ceremony organized at the Federal Ministry of Traffic, Construction and Urban Development. Some 90 projects with an investment volume of approximately EUR 1.4 billion have been completed in the area of building construction. Luther Rechtsanwaltsgesellschaft mbH has been, and still is, involved in a large number of PPP projects, particularly pilot projects, and has provided material advice. Among these projects are, for example, the construction contract of the new Berlin-based seat of the Federal Ministry for Education and Research (*Bundesministerium für Bildung und Forschung – "BMBF"*), which has an investment volume of EUR 310 million andwas awarded in 2011 to a private bidding consortium, and the first penitentiary established in Germany in the form of a PPP (JVA Burg, Sachsen-Anhalt) with an investment volume of approximately EUR 100 million.

IV. Facilitation and Acceleration Through New General Framework

Based on a state initiative, the "Partnerschaften Deutschland AG", a federal PPP competence center, was established in 2008 and took up work at the beginning of 2009. By the end of the subscription period, 10 federal states, 82 municipalities and 33 other public sponsors had signed a framework agreement. Private-sector companies (finance, construction, service providers as well as advisors and planners) may also acquire shares. The purpose of the *Partnerschaften Deutschland* is to provide specific project-related advice to the public sector at an early stage, as well as advice on the basic work required to improve the general conditions for PPPs (e.g. standardization of contracts, transfer of knowhow, etc.). Now that a clear political intention can be observed to realize PPP projects on a larger scale where this offers economic advantages, the plan is for PPP models to become even more established. The immediate target the state wishes to achieve with its initiative is to triple the PPP share in public building construction, which means a rise from 4.5 % at present, to about 15 %.

Important steps have already been taken to achieve this target, for example, the adoption of the "Law regarding the acceleration of the implementation of PPPs" to remove fiscal disadvantages with respect to real-estate tax and real-estate transfer tax and to clarify certain ambiguities in public procurement law. The Federal States of North Rhine-Westphalia and Hessen, too, have struck new paths in PPP projects in the hospital sector: Hessen makes it possible for construction work carried out within the framework of public private partnerships to be subsidized by the Federal State of Hessen after economic efficiency has been proven. In the Federal State of North

Rhine-Westphalia, the new University Medicine Act stipulates an obligation with regard to projects having an investment volume of more than € 15 million to examine whether their realization through a PPP is more economical than traditional realization by the public sector itself.

V. Great Potential for Future Projects

About 60 % of public investment in construction is generated in the area of municipal infrastructure under the responsibility of towns and municipalities. The Difu predicts a need for investment in the amount of EUR 704 billion until the year 2020. Traffic investments planned by the German state amount to approximately EUR 10 billion annually, until 2012. Moreover, there still is a clearly noticeable need to develop the new federal states. While 6 % of the need for investment in the Western part of Germany results from an investment backlog, the figure is 24 % in the Eastern part of Germany. The investment promotion resolved within the framework of the current "2nd Economic Stimulus Package" by the German government and current reforms in public procurement law offer further incentives for more investment especially by medium-sized businesses. According to a Difu study, medium-sized businesses are currently involved in the realization of up to 80 % of the PPP projects in building construction. The Federal Ministry of Construction states that the investment volume of the ongoing projects is EUR 3.5 billion, while another 120 projects with an investment volume of approximately EUR 6 billion are being prepared. These figures suggest that PPPs have established themselves as an alternative to classic public procurement.

Dr. Hans-Georg Hahn
hans-georg.hahn@luther-lawfirm.com

Dr. Oliver Kairies
oliver.kairies@luther-lawfirm.com

CHAPTER 26
PUBLIC PROCUREMENT

ACHIM MEIER
ULF-DIETER PAPE

German public procurement law contains comprehensive regulations governing the legal relationship between public authorities and private entrepreneurs in relation to the provision of works, goods and services. The intention of public procurement law is to achieve a balance between economically reasonable procurement by public authorities on the one hand and the legal protection of private entrepreneurs on the other.

A. Introduction

Pursuant to the federal, state and local public budget laws and the German Act Against Restraints of Competition (*Gesetz gegen Wettbewerbsbeschränkungen, GWB*), all public procurement contracts must generally be put out to tender. The Ordinance on Awards of Public Orders (*Vergabeverordnung, VgV*) and three other bylaws (VOB/A for works, VOL/A for deliveries and services and VOF for special services such as services from architects, auditors or consultants) constitute the legal framework for the award of public contracts in addition to the GWB. Since the federal, state and local budget laws, to the extent they apply to public procurement, are somewhat vague and do not provide legal protection for the tenderer, public procurement law underwent a significant change at the time of the amendment of the GWB in 1998, which involved the incorporation of most of the European Directives on the coordination of the procedures for the award of public contracts into the legislation. However, the incomplete implementation of the European Directives unfortunately makes it necessary to carefully check both the national regulations and the European Directives.

The EU's policy on public procurement is found mainly in the free movement provisions of the Treaty on the Functioning of the European Union (TFEU) and in a series of legislative measures that take the form of directives. The main public procurement directives are the following:

- Directive 2004/18/EC – the Public Sector Directive (Directive 2004/18/EC of the European Parliament and of the Council of 31st March 2004 on the coordination of procedures for the award of public works contracts, public supply contracts and public service contracts [2004] OJ L134/114). This regulates the procedures for awarding most major contracts of public bodies (government departments, local authorities etc). For example, it requires major contracts to be advertised through the EU's Official Journal so that they are publicized to all interested parties and regulates the criteria that can be used for selecting firms to tender and awarding contracts.

- Directive 2004/17/EC – the Utilities Directive (Directive 2004/17/EC of the European Parliament and of the Council of 31st March 2004 coordinating the procurement procedures of entities operating in the water, energy, transport and postal services sectors [2004] OJ L134/1). This regulates the procedures for awarding major contracts for bodies engaged in certain activities in the sectors of water, transport, energy and postal services ("utility activities"). It contains similar kinds of obligations to those in the Public Sector Directive.
- Directive 89/665/EEC – the Public Sector Remedies Directive (Directive 89/665/EEC of 21.12.1989 on the coordination of the laws, regulations and administrative provisions relating to the application of review procedures to the award of public supply and public works contracts [1989] O.J. L395/33). This deals with remedies for firms to enforce the EU procurement rules applying to contracts governed by the Public Sector Directive.
- Directive 2009/81/EC – the Directive on the award of contracts in the fields of defense and security. The Directive 2009/81/EC is applicable to the award of certain contracts in the fields of defense and security by contracting authorities and entities. The definition of the contracts covered by the Directive is based on a twofold approach: In the area of defense, the scope of the Directive is based on that of Article 346 TFEU and covers, in principle, all contracts for the procurement of military equipment, works and services. Moreover, the Directive also applies to all sensitive purchases which have a security purpose and involve classified information.

B. Legislation in the EU

For public contracts above the EU-threshold values, chapter 4 of the GWB, the procurement regulation for public supplies and services, the procurement regulations for the award of independent contractor services (*Verdingungsordnung für freiberufliche Leistungen-VOF*), the procurement regulation for public works (*Vergabe- und Vertragsordnung für Bauleistungen-VOB/A*) and the VgV are applicable.

For all other contracts below the EU-threshold values, the budgetary laws of the federal, state and local governments as well as the first sections of the VOB/A and the VOL/A have to be executed by the contracting entities bound by such rules. Hence, the applicable law is set together in a "cascade-system", which could be pictured as follows:

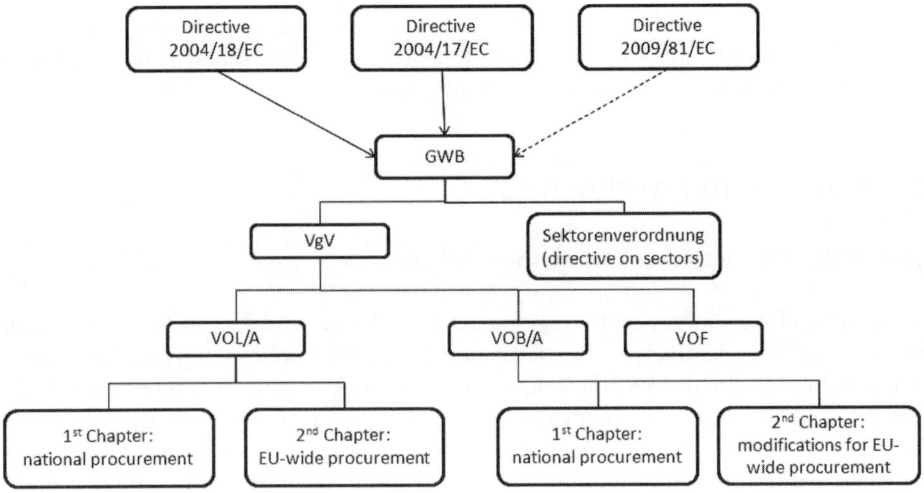

C. Thresholds

Chapter IV of the GWB regulates the award of public contracts that exceed certain thresholds which are fixed by public ordinances. These are EUR 4.845 million for works and EUR 193,000.00 for goods and services. A threshold of EUR 387,000.00 applies to the utilities sector. Contracts on goods and services concluded by the Ministries of the Federal Government are also included within the scope of the GWB to the extent they exceed EUR 133,000.00. For contracts in the fields of defense and security a threshold of EUR 378,000.00 is applicable.

Most of the public contracts in Germany do not reach the value of the relevant threshold. Especially in the field of construction, nearly 95 % of our public contracts do not fall within the scope of the Directive 2004/18/EC and the corresponding national law.[1]

D. Public Contracts

A public contract is defined as a contract for pecuniary interest concluded between a supplier and a contracting authority, the subject matter of which is supplies, works

1 Public Procurement in Europe, Cost and Effectiveness, A study on procurement regulation, prepared for the European Commission, March 2011.

or services. Contracts relating to public works concessions are also governed by the same rules as those contracts for a direct pecuniary interest, although no legislation has yet been passed with regard to service concessions.

I. Contracting Authority

Contracting authorities set forth in the GWB are:

the Federal Government, State, regional and local authorities, as well as the special funds of each, respectively; other legal entities under public or private law which were established for the specific purpose of meeting the general interest, which do not have an industrial or commercial character, and which are for the most part financed or controlled by public authorities; associations of public authorities governed by public law; and natural or legal entities under private law which operate in the fields of drinking water, energy, transportation or telecommunications if such activities are exercised on the basis of special or exclusive rights granted by a public authority.

E. General Principles

The general principles underlying the national legislation on public procurement under transparency, competition, non-discrimination and equal treatment are set out below:

I. Equal Treatment Principle

In their communications on procurement, the Commission put the view forward that there is a general equal treatment principle under the TFEU that is similar to the Directive and applies to all discriminatory treatment, not just discrimination on grounds of nationality.[2] The equal treatment principle requires that comparable situations must not be treated differently and that different situations must not be treated in the same way, unless such treatment is objectively justified.[3]

---

2 European Commission, Commission Communication on the Community Law applicable to contract awards not or not fully subject to the provision of the public procurement directives, June 23, 2006.

3 Joint Cases C-21/03 and C-34/03, Fabricom [2005].

II. Transparency

Although there is not yet a general definition of the principle of transparency, it could be stated that the principle contains four main dimensions, mainly:

- Publicity for contracts;
- Publicity for the rules of the process;
- Limits on discretion and
- Provision for verification and enforcement.[4]

F. Types of Procedures

Public supply, works and service contracts are awarded through one of four different types of procedures, namely: (i) an open procedure; (ii) a restricted procedure; (iii) a negotiated procedure; and (iv) a "competitive dialogue" procedure. The open procedure has priority over the restricted procedure, the negotiated procedure and the "competitive dialogue" procedure.

Although stricter than required by the underlying EU directives, the restricted procedure generally ranks above a negotiated procedure. Only those contracting authorities which operate in the fields of drinking water, energy, transportation or telecommunications may freely choose from the four procedures provided by the GWB.

I. Open Procedure

Open procedures are those procedures in which an unlimited number of undertakings are invited to submit a tender following a public announcement. The rules on the time limit for the receipt of tenders are strict. The tenders cannot be negotiated after their submission.

II. Competition

Competition is important to achieve an economic result. Only a competitive process carried out in an open, objective and transparent manner can achieve best value for money in public procurement.

---

4 Arrowsmith, The law of public and utilities procurement, 2nd edition, 2005.

III. Restricted Procedure

This is a two-stage-process where only those parties who meet minimum requirements in regard to professional or technical capability, experience and expertise and financial capacity to carry out a project are invited to tender. As a first step, the requirements of the contracting authority are set out through a contract notice in the OJEU and expressions of interest are invited from potential tenderers. The second step involves issuing the complete specifications and tender documents with an invitation to submit tenders only to those who process the minimum level of professional, technical and financial expertise and capacity. It is important to note that only the criteria relating to personnel situation, financial capacity, technical capacity, relevant experience, expertise and competency of candidates set out in the Directive 2004/18/EC are permissible.

IV. Negotiated Procedure

Negotiated procedures involve a public invitation to participate as a rule. A limited number of selected undertakings are then invited to submit a tender. There are no further rules set out regarding the regulation of the rest of the negotiated procedure. Nevertheless the contracting authorities are obliged to follow the general principles as the "principle of competition," the "principle of transparency" and the "principle of equal treatment" as laid down in Sec. 97 GWB. Contracting authorities are allowed to negotiate the terms of the contract directly with one or more parties without advertising in some named cases. This is a departure from the general principles and a very exceptional procedure. The main instances, where the procedure may be used are:

- In cases of extreme urgency;
- When, for technical or artistic reasons or due to the existence of special or exclusive rights, there is only one possible supplier or service provider;
- When an open or restricted procedure has not attracted appropriate tenders;
- Extension of existing contracts and repeat contracts subject to certain conditions.

Contracting authorities should ensure that the precise circumstances to justify negotiations exist before deciding on the use of this procedure. Definitions of "exceptions" and "urgency" are strictly interpreted by the Commission and the courts.

V. Competitive Dialogue Procedure

The new "competitive dialogue" is an attractive alternative to the negotiated procedure for certain particularly complex projects. The objective of the procedure is to provide a flexible procedure which preserves not only competition between economic operators but also the need for the contracting authorities to discuss all aspects of the contract with each candidate.

VI. Suitability of Firms (Qualification and Eligibility)

In any public procurement, procuring entities will generally exclude suppliers who are not considered capable of performing the contract reliably or who do not meet other relevant conditions for a procurement.[5] Suppliers could be excluded from the proceeding by grounds relating to four main categories:

- Economic and financial standing,
- Technical and professional ability,
- Enrolment of a trade or professional register and possession of a licence,
- Professional honesty, solvency and reliability.

As a general principle, contracting authorities can only exclude firms because of the failure to fulfill obligations required in the announcement.

Practically, the choice of bidders in restricted or negotiated procedures is mainly based on the firm's experience.

VII. Award Criteria

A contract must be awarded on the basis of one of two criteria:

- Lowest price or
- Economically advantageous tender.

Under the lowest price principle, the award goes to the lowest tenderer. Many authorities use this for simple purchases, where the nature and quality of items offered does not vary much between different suppliers.

Under the most economically advantageous tender principle, the authority may award the contract to the firm whose tender has the most advantages, taking into account all relevant factors. The Directives list various factors which could be used, such as running costs, servicing costs, level of after-sales services, technical assistance, technical merit, environmental characteristics.

Selection criteria may not be used as award criteria.

5 Arrowsmith, EU Public Procurement Law, An Introduction.

VIII. Time for Tendering

In open procedures, firms must be given 52 days to bid. This time limit may be reduced if there has previously been publication of advance information referring to the contracts. Furthermore, the 52-days-period could be reduced by publishing the announcement electronically. In restricted procedures and negotiated procedures, firms must be given 37 days to respond after dispatch of the contract notice. Also, this time limit may be reduced to 30 days when the notice is drawn up and transmitted by designated electronic means. In restricted procedures, the invited firms must be given 40 days to bid. A reduction of this time limit is possible if there has previously been publication of an advance notice. Even in cases of urgency, the time limit must be not less than 10 days. For the restricted procedure there is no written time limit for the bid. However, the time limit must be adequate to prepare the bid as well as being in the interest of the contracting authority.

G. Individual Rights of the Tenderer and Legal Protection

One of the great achievements of the comprehensive 1998 amendment of the German law on public procurement was the establishment of basic legal rules to protect the individual rights of tenderers. This amendment was included to harmonize German public procurement law with standards established in European law. The GWB provides that undertakings have a right to bring a claim to ensure that the provisions concerning award procedures are complied with by the contracting entity.

H. Structure of the Jurisdiction

Public procurement awards are subject to review by Public Procurement Tribunals upon application by a tenderer. These tribunals, which have been established both by the Federal Government as well as by State authorities, may also institute preliminary remedies if certain of the applicant's rights are jeopardized during the award procedure. Decisions of a Public Procurement Tribunal can be sent to the Court of Appeal which has jurisdiction over the relevant Public Procurement Tribunal.

I. Legal Remedies to Get the Award

While the EU directives on public procurement do not prescribe any structure for legal remedies, the German public procurement law has developed an effective and detailed system of legal remedies in favor of applicants as well as of tenderers. Each legal remedy is conditional upon a complaint having been made by the applicant or the tenderer. This complaint has to be filed with the contracting authority instantly after a mistake is identified in the tender documents or following the misconduct of the contracting authority. "Instantly" means normally "within three days". However, if the applicant or tenderer needs legal advice in order to recognize the fault, the limit may be extended up to 15 days. If the applicant/tenderer fails to comply with the obligation to immediately file a formal complaint, he will be barred from filing a later complaint in respect of the alleged infringement. The contracting authority has to inform the unsuccessful tenderers about the outcome of the selection 15 days (in case of transmission per facsimile or e-mail 10 days) before giving the award to the tenderer with the best offer. The unsuccessful tenderers have to be informed about the name of the successful tenderer and the reasons why their tenders have not been selected. If the contracting authority does not inform the tenderers as prescribed or makes the award before the end of the 15 days period, any contract with the preferred tenderer would be void. German jurisprudence has extended this provision in favor of the tenderers to state that any public contract which is concluded contrary to any public procurement procedure is generally regarded as void. The unsuccessful tenderer then has to file his claim at the latest within the 15-day prior-notice period. Otherwise the contracting authority could conclude the procurement procedure, giving the award to the selected tenderer. Any contract concluded after the 15-day-period cannot be revoked by any later court decision. However, if a claim has been filed with the competent court, the contracting authority may (with limited exceptions) be restricted from finalizing the contract with its preferred bidder during court proceedings. Any legal transaction carried out contrary to this prohibition is automatically deemed to be void.

J. Legal Remedies to Receive Compensation

If the contracting authority has accepted the tender and concluded the contract with the tenderer before the competitor has filed his or her complaint before the Public Procurement Tribunal, and this complaint was served on the contracting authority, neither said tribunal nor the Court of Appeal can revoke the contract. A tenderer may subsequently demand compensation in a second proceeding before a civil court for the costs of preparing its tender or of its participation to the extent the contracting entity violates a provision intended to protect undertakings, provided the applicant would have had a realistic chance of being awarded the contract. If the tenderer can submit evidence that his tender was the most economically advantageous and that the contracting authority would have been obligated to conclude a contract with him, the tenderer can demand compensation for the profit he would have earned upon acceptance of the tender.

K. Current Developments

I. Legislation

The German Government has decided to implement the EU directives in the "old" complex system of GWB, VgV and the existing three bylaws (VOB/A, VOL/A and VOF) within the so-called *Gesetz zur Modernisierung des Vergaberechts* in February 2009. An all-embracing reform intended to reduce the complexity of the German public procurement law by unifying the provisions of the existing three bylaws to one single body of regulations has been postponed for the time being. The Directive 2009/81/EC has to be implemented into German law by now. Since 21st August 2011 the Directive is effective. It is planned to issue a certain chapter in the VOB/A. The more relevant part of the provision of deliveries and services in the fields of defense and security are likely to be included in the VgV. The Directive introduces formal proceedings for the procurement of all goods not specified in the so-called 1958 list, particularly dual-use goods, construction contracts, delivery orders for sensitive equipment and other military equipment and service contracts coming under the Directive. In the past, arms contracts have often been awarded to undertakings from the awarder's country. This could hardly be maintained for the future against the background of the rules of the new Directive. Explicitly, it has to be noted that the new rules on defense procurement include special rules relating to the need of confidentiality and security.

II. Privatization

The growing trend of privatization of public functions by selling public enterprises (especially public transport companies and public utilities) or subcontracting public services to private companies (recently especially planning, establishing and running public buildings for a long period) is reflected in numerous law suits which have been brought by unsuccessful tenderers. The court decisions have changed the previous patterns of privatization. According to the EU directives and also the GWB, a "public contract" involves the delivery of works, goods and services. The law does not refer to the sale of public enterprises. However, where the public enterprises deliver works, goods or services to any contracting authority, the deal can be governed by public procurement law. In the leading case, the contracting authority established an enterprise, awarded the municipal waste disposal contract to this enterprise, and sold all shares of this enterprise to a private company directly afterwards. The Public Procurement Tribunal examined the case from an economic perspective and decided that the sale of the shares of this public enterprise had to be regarded as an award of a public contract. As an exception to the so-called "in-house privilege", the Directive coordinating procedures for the award of public supply contracts and also the GWB are not applicable, provided that the local authority exercises over the institution concerned (and to which it wishes to award a contract) a degree of control similar to that which it exercises over its own departments and, at the same time, that institution carries out the essential part of its activities with the controlling local authority or authorities (ECJ, Case C-107/98 – Teckal). The participation however, even as a minority, of a private undertaking in the capital of a company in which the contracting public authority is also a participant excludes in any event the possibility of such aforementioned public control over the institution (ECJ, Case C-26/03 – Stadt Halle). It can be regarded as a rule that the sale of public enterprises is governed by strict procurement laws in relation to when the deal is intended to avoid a regular public procurement procedure. As described above, unsuccessful companies, or companies simply not properly informed by the public institution, can claim that such a privatization is void and has to be retendered. Furthermore, the privatization (especially of public transport companies) could be regarded as an unlawful subsidy if the contracting authority has disregarded the public procurement laws. This is also important for the successful bidder as in such a situation, he could be forced to pay back the "economic advantage" received from the transaction.

Achim Meier
achim.meier@luther-lawfirm.com

Ulf-Dieter Pape
ulf-dieter.pape@luther-lawfirm.com

CHAPTER 27
RESTRUCTURING AND INSOLVENCY LAW

REINHARD WILLEMSEN

The German insolvency law (hereinafter "InsO") significantly restricts a creditor's options and course of action shortly before and during the insolvency/bankruptcy of the debtor. Therefore, it is essential to focus on German insolvency law, in order to avoid risks and to agree on contracts, loans and other investments in Germany in such a way that they will be excluded from becoming an estate in the case of bankruptcy. The following legal remarks concentrate on the options available to ensure investments are protected against insolvency risks, including how to reduce losses in case of insolvency of a debtor, what are the legal obligations which apply on the insolvency of a company and how insolvency proceedings operate.

A. Obligation to File for Insolvency

The company's representative or even its shareholders are obliged to file for insolvency if a reason for filing occurs: a limited company has to file for insolvency immediately (not later than three weeks) after the occurrence of over-indebtedness (1) or the inability to pay its due liabilities (illiquidity) (2). The petition for insolvency must be filed, first of all, by the company's legal representative(s) (executive director, directors). If the director fails to file for insolvency immediately after becoming aware of the over-indebtedness/illiquidity he will be personally liable for all further obligations of the company and may, in addition, be prosecuted. Where the company no longer has a legal representative, the shareholders/stockholders are liable in the second degree to file the insolvency petition.[1] This subsidiary liability is excluded only if the shareholders/stockholders did not have knowledge of the company's over-indebtedness or inability to pay. It is important to emphasize that the obligation to file for insolvency under the German Insolvency Code is applicable to all kinds of companies with limited liability, including foreign companies (e.g. Ltd.) that have an administrative seat in Germany. Companies which have no limited liability such as partnerships or individual persons (merchants) are not obliged by the German Insolvency Code to file for insolvency even when a reason for insolvency has occurred.

---

1 Sec. 15a (3) InsO.

I. Over-Indebtedness

According to Sec. 19 (2) InsO a company is over-indebted if the debtor's assets no longer cover its existing liabilities, unless the continuation of the company is likely in the circumstances (so-called "positive continuation prognosis" – *positive Fortführungsprognose*). In principle, the continuation prognosis constitutes a liquidity prognosis and has to be assessed by a liquidity plan, which should cover the current and the subsequent fiscal year. If there is a positive continuation prognosis, the debtor is not facing over-indebtedness and consequently is not obliged to file an insolvency petition. Usually, an impending illiquidity[2] indicates a negative continuation prognosis. If there is a negative continuation prognosis, over-indebtedness has to be determined by a special "status of over-indebtedness" (*Überschuldungsstatus*). Therein, assets must be stated at liquidation value (net asset value). A shareholder's loan, given to its company under condition of subsequent ranking,[3] must not be included in the status of over-indebtedness.[4] Furthermore, the status of over-indebtedness must consider accounting rules as applicable under insolvency law, which only comply in part with accounting rules under commercial and tax law. If the result shows that the debtor's assets do not cover its existing liabilities, over-indebtedness has occurred.

II. Illiquidity

Usually the majority of insolvency petitions in Germany arise because of illiquidity. A company is obliged to file for insolvency proceedings, if it is illiquid e.g. if it is unable to honor payment obligations when they are due (Sec. 17 InsO). Not every non-payment leads to illiquidity in this sense. Illiquidity as ruled in Sec. 17 InsO occurs if the debtor cannot pay more than 90 % of the due liabilities within 21 days (statutory definition for illiquidity). Despite this, illiquidity can be excluded if the closure of the liquidity gap is considered to be of the utmost probability. In order to emphasize the importance, we repeat that a delay in filing for insolvency proceedings – which is usually after more than three weeks after the occurrence of the obligate insolvency reason (illiquidity or over-indebtedness) is an criminal offence which results in civil as well as criminal liability of the respective representatives (see above). Liability cannot be excluded by the argument that the company has not one representative but several; in such a case, the German courts have held in various decisions that every individual participant of the board of directors or the management is responsible for the financial review of the company and for ensuring an organizational structure which enables the occurrence of an obligate insolvency reason to be recognized.

2 Sec. 18 InsO, see below.
3 Sec. 39 (2) InsO.
4 Sec. 19 (2) InsO.

B. Facultative Insolvency Reason, Competence to File for Insolvency

For companies, impending illiquidity does not lead to the obligation to file for insolvency, though in order to start early restructuring the insolvency code provides this insolvency reason as a facultative one. Consequently, where impending illiquidity occurs, a company can (but is not obliged to) file for insolvency (Sec. 18 InsO). Impending illiquidity is deemed to have occurred if it can be presumed that the debtor will not be able to honor existing payment obligations when they become due. As stated above, an impending illiquidity indicates a negative continuation prognosis which is an indicator of over-indebtedness and therefore in most cases creates an obligation to file for insolvency. As mentioned above, partnerships of natural persons, merchants or private individuals are not obliged to file for insolvency in the case of the occurrence of an insolvency reason. However, this can happen in cases where recovering from the debts is from an economical prognosis perspective very unlikely, or in order to start a restructuring processes.

C. Commencement Proceedings

Upon receipt of the petition for insolvency, the locally competent first instance court (*Amtsgericht*) will (usually within one day) appoint an interim insolvency administrator/expert and will order interim measures to avoid any further reductions of the insolvency's estate by the debtor. The competent court depends on the debtor's place of residence or center of main interest. Normally, all transfers by the debtor subsequent to the commencement of proceedings will only be effective with the consent of the interim administrator (after his appointment). Nevertheless, any contract partner will remain contractually bound to the company and not to the interim administrator. On the other hand, creditors fear – in case they have pending contracts and are obliged to deliver or act first (duty to act first – *Vorleistungspflicht*) – that they will not get payment for executed services. In such a situation, the creditor has two main options: First of all, he may, pursuant to Sec. 321 German Civil Code, claim payment first from the debtor and refuse execution of its services until receiving such payments. The second option would be to contact the preliminary administrator and claim a so-called "confirmation of claim/cost-coverage" (*Deckungszusage*). The German High Court has decided that such a confirmation of the preliminary administrator results in a privileged position of the respective creditor for claims, which occur within the preliminary insolvency period. Nevertheless, it is strongly recommended to have such a confirmation by the administrator in written form and to have it checked by a legal expert in order to avoid that any additional clause or interpretation of the wording could lead to a loss of the creditor's privileged position. If it seems that the debtor's assets will be sufficient to cover the costs of the insolvency proceedings (for court and administration) the insolvency court will commence insolvency proceedings and appoint a (final) insolvency administrator. As a result of the commencement of the insolvency proceedings, the right of the debtor to manage and transfer assets that constitute part of the insolvent estate shall pass to the insolvency administrator. Until this order of commencement, the debtor may withdraw its petition without any reason. In the order of commencement, the court shall set dates for: the first creditor's assembly; not less than six weeks and not more than three months after the order of commencement; a creditors assembly in which registered claims shall be examined; application for debtor in possession (self-administration).

After commencement of the insolvency proceedings, the administrator has three possible ways for further action: (a) liquidation of the company by selling out all of the company's assets and terminating its business; (b) insolvency plan; (c) a so-called "transferring restructuring".

I. General Winding-up Option

When the assets are not sufficient to continue the business, the insolvency administrator will wind up the debtor-company. In such a situation, creditors often ask if there are special termination rights for the administrator and whether some claims are secured within the insolvency procedure. The German insolvency law recognizes three categories of creditors (in case of inclusion of subordinated creditors, such as shareholders, etc one can speak also of five categories): the general insolvency creditor and two kinds of privileged creditors. The latter are creditors which have some security or mortgage over some insolvency assets that entitles them in the case of a property rights to claim segregation;[5] in the case of special securities (such as pledge, fiduciaries, etc.) the creditor is not entitled to claim segregation but he will get approximately 90 percent of his claim because the administrator is obliged to wind-up secured assets and may retain 9 percent of the achieved value (so-called "winding-up charge" = *Verwertungspauschale*). The remaining revenue of the respective sold asset has to be paid to the secured by this asset creditor. Such privileged positions of creditors are consequently important to know in situations of contract negotiations and in order to achieve an insolvency-risk-free agreement with business partners. Therefore, we strongly recommend that investments agreements or delivery contracts be reviewed with regard to insolvency risks and privileged creditor positions. Furthermore, details of this will be set out in this chapter below.

5 Right for segregation, Sec. 47 InsO.

II. Insolvency Plan

This is a special insolvency proceeding, comparable with Chapter 11 of the U.S. Insolvency Act. Despite liquidation or asset stripping, the debtor is given the chance to restructure his company. Therefore, he (or the insolvency administrator) is entitled to prepare and file an insolvency plan with the insolvency court. The plan contains a description and a creative part. The creative part sets out the options for the creditors in order to receive satisfaction of their outstanding debts and a plan as to how the position of the company can be changed. The creditors have to give their consent and the insolvency plan needs to be authorized by a resolution of the creditors and by the insolvency court. If an insolvency plan can be implemented in that way, the insolvency administration will be suspended. At the moment of printing the present document, the insolvency plan procedure as well as other aspects of the German insolvency law were under reconstruction and the respective draft-law under discussion in the German Parliament. A brief overview of this may be found at the end of the present chapter.

III. "Transferring Restructuring" and "Acquisition out of Bankruptcy"

Transferring Restructuring means that a part or all of the assets of the insolvent debtor-company will be transferred to a new company (the administrator gets an equivalent purchase price). The rest of the company will be liquidated. The restructuring of an insolvent company is widespread and common in practice. This involves a part or all of the assets being transferred to a new company (the administrator gets an equivalent purchase price). The rest of the company will be liquidated. Transferring restructuring has several advantages: trade and business of the insolvent company can be continued; creditors are satisfied on a higher quota than by insolvency; and the involvement of the insolvency administrator can be reduced. There are no special insolvency-related implications for an acquisition out of bankruptcy. It should be emphasized, however – with reference to the voidability rules of German Insolvency Law – that any vendee involved with an asset deal or an acquisition before insolvency (during the companies crisis) should await the commencement of the insolvency proceedings. The purchase of a business-critical company (or a part of it) is risky, especially if only some assets are sold whilst the remaining company is filing for insolvency: this is because any insolvency administrator will be entitled to contest an asset deal which took place a few months before filing for insolvency. To avoid this risk, an acquisition out of a bankruptcy is usually preferable.

D. Voidability Rules of German Insolvency Law

Due to the fact that Insolvency Law seeks to ensure an equal treatment of creditors in the case of the insolvency of a debtor, some legal acts of the debtor and the creditors before and after the petition of insolvency can be contested and may be rescinded by the insolvency administrator. There are long-term voidability risks (Sec. 133 and Sec. 135 (1) InsO) as well as short term voidability risks.[6]

E. Long-term Voidability Risks

A very broad option to void is contained in Sec. 133 (1) InsO. Pursuant to this regulation the administrator may void any transfer of assets which was executed within 10 years prior to the date of commencement for proceedings from the debtor to the creditor. Such voidability requires that the debtor was – at the time of the asset-transfers – at least in a situation of at least impending illiquidity but paid anyway in full knowledge of this and hereby caused disadvantages to the claims of other creditors. Furthermore, the creditor had to be aware of the debtor's pending illiquidity and the disadvantages which would occur for other creditors by fulfillment of the respective claim of one or a few creditors. Such preconditions have to be proved by the administrator – especially concerning the individual debtor's and creditor´s intent and knowledge about the aforesaid. However, sentence 2 of Sec. 133 (1) InsO contains a facilitation in favor of the administrator for proving those issues. Pursuant to that sentence, it is sufficient to prove circumstances and facts from which the creditor should have known or obviously should have been able to be aware of (i) the pending illiquidity of the debtor and (ii) the negative consequences for other creditors occurring in case of payment by the debtor. This sentence was subject to several High Court decisions within the last five years, by which the Courts even made the requirements for the quality of those proofs even lower by judging that already proven tendencies of certain matters (*Beweisanzeichen*) are sufficient. At first sight, the aforementioned might support the impression of a very high risk for any business in Germany as it is hard to predict whether a contract partner will fall into insolvency within the next ten years and a appointed administrator start to claim back any payment. In order to avoid that broad risk impression, it has to emphasized that such a voidability option is usually used by administrator to claim back payments or asset transfers executed within two or three years prior to the commencement of insolvency proceedings. For a period of ten years prior to insolvency proceedings it is usually difficult for the administrator to prove the existence of impending illiquidity because after three years, usually less documentation exists for former periods. Documentation and communication play an important part in regard to

6 Sects. 130, 131, 132 InsO.

voidability risks. After the administrator has been appointed, he usually first of all reviews financial matters, payments, transfers of assets and communications, looking for hints and issues that give him reason to void those transactions. Therefore, it is always important to have sufficient information about the financial status of a contract partner and/or to have contracts executed within a short period and at arm's length because this provides a privilege to the creditor.[7] In the case of such a privilege, voidability is excluded. In order to avoid either voidability by Sec. 133 InsO on the whole or to ensure that preconditions of the privilege of Sec. 142 InsO are fulfilled, it is strongly recommended to have legal advice especially in the case of agreements with business partners in financial difficult or risky state.

Furthermore, in cases where an insolvency has occurred, it is strongly recommended to be careful in communications with a (preliminary) administrator, in order to avoid any – unintended – provision of a proof of awareness or knowledge. The proofs of the administrator will also depend largely upon the reporting/documentation policy of the relevant business, especially concerning the pre- and present-crisis communication and documentation between creditor and debtor. Business partners should therefore pay close attention to the communication and especially should try to avoid pressure. Such pressure is regarded as a sign of knowledge of the impending illiquidity as well as of the awareness of discrimination against other creditors in the case of payments by the debtor. The preferable strategy always should be to enforce and execute the claim by the legal authorities after fruitless reminders of payment obligations. Any act of enforcement and execution of a claim by legal authorities (*Gerichtsvollzieher*) will only be invalid if they were performed one month prior to the commencement of insolvency proceedings. The authority's execution and enforcement – provided they lead to fulfillment of the claim – cannot be voided by the administrator by Sec. 133 InsO. It has to be highlighted that neither the creditor nor the enforcing authority should agree on than often offered voluntary fulfillment by the debtor because this is regarded as "acting of the debtor" and therefore by Sec. 133 InsO covered behavior of the debtor. Further avoidable legal acts are related to shareholder-positions: pursuant to Sec. 135 (1) no. 2 InsO any return of loans given by shareholders of the debtor within one year before the insolvency petition was filed can be voided by the administrator. Consequently, shareholders often try to have third parties (very often bank institutes or investors) give the loans, accompanied by a security/mortgage of the shareholder. Such a construction is even more risky because it entitles the administrator to void such securities for ten years prior to the date of the insolvency petition (whereas the provision of the respective security is of relevance), Sec. 135 (1) no. 1 InsO. It is strongly recommended to shareholders, not to provide loans or securities for third-party-loans but – as far as is feasible – to invest in missing equipment and let/rent the technology. Despite former voidability, such "provision for usage" is not voidable since several reforms of corporate and in-

7 Sec. 142 InsO, *Bargeschäftsprivileg*, see below.

solvency law took place in 2008 in Germany. Voidability might only occur in case of periodical rental claims which are far beyond arm's length. However, the existing broad space for calculation may be used by the lessee. In the case of the insolvency of the respective subsidiary or company, the shareholder may claim transfer of his property and will not lose its – otherwise provided – loan return claim. In any case, for all of such long-term-voidability risks, it is strongly recommended to have support from specialists, concerning communication with administrators. Very often, there can be reached – even in obvious cases – a settlement between administrator and creditor, due to the fact that the administrator will have less effort in getting the voided payments or assets (he does not have to check any lawsuit risks which are usually related to the parallel liability risk of the administrator towards the creditors). Though, on the other hand, the administrator may face personal liability if he did not consider the interest of the remaining creditors assembly, which might be more interested in voiding the whole amounts instead of reaching fast decisions. In any case, special attention to the wording in communications with administrators is very important.

F. Short-term Voidability Risks

Next to the aformentioned main long-term contestation rules, there are some (more or less) "short-term" contestable legal acts: any satisfaction of claims by the debtor which has not been agreed upon before (e.g. the payment of a purchase price has been agreed, but an asset or a real estate is given) can be contested if this has taken place up to three months before the petition for insolvency. In this case, if the creditor had knowledge of the debtor's illiquidity, any payment or satisfying act in favor of this creditor made within a three month prior to the filing for insolvency will be contestable. Contestation in the latter case as well as in the case of the above mentioned Sec. 133 InsO is excluded if the satisfying act was an immediate counter performance to the creditor's goods or services. Therefore, ordinary cash transactions or payments for services or goods within up to two weeks are privileged and not contestable, provided they are at arm's length.

G. Voidability Risk (*Aufrechnungsverbote*) and Assignment in Advance (*Vorausabtretungen*)

In many situations, some creditors avoid becoming a general insolvency creditor with a low expectation for its claim by using set-up options. Unfortunately, there are several risks that such set-ups may be regarded as invalid and the creditor has to pay the full claim of the debtor/insolvency administrator, while on the other hand he only can file his claim to the insolvency schedule. The general rule for a valid set-up without insolvency related risks concerns claim and counterclaim, as far as they both occurred and became due either before commencement of the insolvency proceedings or after it. In cases where the claim occurred before but the counterclaim after opening of insolvency proceedings, a set-up is legally invalid and not possible. Although, pursuant to Sec. 96 no. 3 InsO rules that in cases where a creditor creates together with the debtor a counter claim counterclaim in a voidable way, such a set-up of the claims is invalid even if both claims occurred before commencement of the insolvency proceedings. Such situations are e.g. if the debtor sells the creditor some assets and the creditor declares a set-up for the purchase price with his own counterclaim. Consequently, any contract or business with a company that is in a financially critical situation which is supposed to create a set-up option should be reviewed also with regard to the aforesaid invalidity of set-ups. Furthermore, in recent times creditors often try to secure their claims – especially in cases of high rental payments in business areas or loan return – by way of assignment in advance of future claims (*Vorausabtretung*). Unfortunately, in many cases the High Court decided in 2010 and 2011 that almost any kind of assignment in advance is invalid after the date of opening of insolvency proceedings. There exist a few exclusions, such as with regard to assignment of salaries and rental agreements. Nevertheless, a precautionary and professional review of any supposed assignment in advance with business partners in financially critical circumstances is strongly recommended.

H. Shareholder's Loans

Where a shareholder loans money to the company on terms which mean that the credit/loan is of subsequent ranking and the company subsequently falls into insolvency (Sec. 39 para. 1 no. 5 InsO), it is likely that the lending shareholder will get very little of the loan back, if anything. Furthermore, loans by third persons which are secured by a shareholder's guarantee will be treated in the same way as direct shareholder loans (Sec. 44a InsO). In addition, every repayment of a loan within a period of up to one year before the date of filing for insolvency can be contested and rescinded by the insolvency administrator. Even worse, security which has been granted for a loan can be contested and nullified by the administrator if given up to ten years before the date of the insolvency petition. The German Insolvency Law states that there are two exceptions to this rule: (i) loans to "small stakeholders" (small stakeholder's privilege, *Kleinbeteiligungsprivileg*) or (ii) "privileged restructuring loans" (*Sanierungsprivileg*).

If a shareholder's stake is less than 10 % and he is not participating in the management of the company, his loans or the return of a loan cannot be contested by the insolvency administrator.[8] Where a creditor provides an insolvent company

8 Sec. 35 (5) InsO, small stakeholder's privilege.

with a loan as part of the restructuring of the company, the creditor's claims or returns of those loans are free from the risk of becoming part of the insolvency's estate (Sec. 39 (4) InsO), as long as he or she takes a share in the company at the same time.

I. Cash-Pooling

Substantial progress has been made by the latest legislative reform, which now gives cash-pooling[9] an official legal basis which has been absent until now. Nevertheless, cash-pooling loans and accounting (upstream loans as well as downstream loans) still face a high risk of being included in an insolvency's estates, because every return of a shareholder's loan during the last year before filing for insolvency can be contested by the insolvency administrator. Due to the fact that cash-pooling accountings (in the customary way of zero or conditional balancing) are legally defined as shareholder loans, no cash-pooling agreement with a German subsidiary should be contracted under German Civil Law without specific legal advice. Only by considering these insolvency risks and the individual structure of a planned cash-pooling can the financial responsibilities of a foreign investor in the bankruptcy of a German subsidiary be avoided or at least reduced. To avoid extensive liability in relation to a cash-pool created as a result of participation in a German subsidiary, legal advice concerning the company's structure and the basic agreements is essential.

J. Managing Insolvency Risks and Possibilities of Financial Reorganization

Foreign investors can realize high profits from investments in companies which are temporarily in the middle of a financial reorganization. However, it is important to take legal advice regarding the efficiency of the financial reorganization and potentially higher insolvency risk. Secondly, investors must secure their investments against insolvency risks. This is relevant for every investment in Germany. As from October 2008, the German insolvency law and the Company Code have been reformed (the so-called German Act to Modernize the Law Governing Private Limited

9 Willemsen/Rechel, *Erweiterte Geschäftsführerhaftung beim Cash-Pooling*, (Extended Liability of Managing Directors concerning Cash-Pooling), GmbHR 2010. Willemsen/Rechel, "*Cash-Pooling und die insolvenzrechtliche Anfechtbarkeit absteigender Darlehen – Unterschätzte Risiken und mögliche Vermeidungsstrategien*" (Cash-Pooling and insolvency voidability risks for downstair-loans – underestimated risks and possible strategies of their avoidance), BB 2009, 2215 pp.

Companies and to Combat Abuses, MoMiG). Advantageously for investments, this reform sets its focus on increasing the protection of creditors. At the same time, the risk of a shareholder's investments becoming an estate of bankruptcy of an affiliated German company has also been increased.

Investments can be protected against insolvency risk by collateral securities which provide in the case of the debtor's or affiliated company's bankruptcy prior rights of segregation (*Aussonderungsrecht*) or pre-ferential rights (*Absonderungsrecht*) to the creditor. A right of segregation means that the creditor has a property right in relation to a movable good or claim which he is able to separate from the insolvency's estate in case of bankruptcy. In the case of the insolvency of the business partner, property rights will entitle the owner to claim his assets directly back without participating in the insolvency proceedings. Therefore, investments in business assets should not be implemented by pure loans or payments but always in connection with collaterals and property rights.

Furthermore, an investment alternative is a (financial) leasing agreement – this is because the investor will remain the owner of the leased assets and has a right for prior segregation in the case of the bankruptcy of his business partner. Another right for segregation is created by the assignment of claims, especially found in factoring agreements. It must be highlighted that a specific characteristic of German civil law means that a payment itself will not lead to a change of ownership. Under German law, change of ownership (only) takes place with an effective transfer of goods and an agreement to do this. Therefore, in order to avoid the loss of rights in the case of the insolvency of a business partner (e.g. purchaser), contracts should be prepared with a retention of title in relation to the sold assets. The retention of title gives the vendor "privileged property-rights" (right of segregation) in the assets if the insolvency administrator should decide against fulfillment of the contract. If the insolvency administrator decides that following the execution of the contract the investor has no right of segregation, the investor can still claim full payment of the purchase price prior to other creditors.

Problems can occur if the investor financing the (noncurrent) assets is also a shareholder in the company in which he had made the investments. Although the shareholder has a right of segregation, the insolvency administrator can refuse the return of the asset within a period of one year following the commencement of insolvency proceedings. This is justified by the interests of the insolvent company in continuing production and trade. However, if the administrator decides to use the goods during this period he is obliged to pay the rental, which was paid during the last year prior to the filing for insolvency proceedings. Agreements regarding chattel mortgages do not give rise to a right of segregation, only preferential rights of the creditors in relation to the realization's revenue (Sec. 51 no. 1 German Insolvency Code). The same preferential rights without a right of segregation apply to pledges (Sec. 50 InsO) and rights in immovable goods (Sec. 49 InsO, real estates, mortgage, land charge).

The best approach in order to avoid insolvency risks for German subsidiaries or to protect general investments in risky companies is to implement an "early warning and reporting system" and/or a "crisis-avoidance system" within a group of affiliated companies or within the supply chain. Furthermore, Managing Directors are permanently obliged to keep control of the company's cash-flow development, reporting of negative development (e.g. the loss of half of the company's registered capital) and discuss possibilities of restructuring. Options that can be taken in order to avoid the status of insolvency can be: factoring; selling of inventories; an increase of the (basic) capital; restructuring reduction of capital (Sec. 58a–f GmbHG); the admission of a personally liable shareholder or a dormant shareholder; a "strong" letter of comfort; and/or a letter/statement of subordination of creditors who have a claim against the insolvent company; etc.

K. Liability Risks of Managing Directors

Next to the general liability of Managing Directors concerning the failure to file for insolvency proceedings in legal due time or in case they reduce stock capital of a company below a certain level, there exists an additional risk to be liable with private property for payments or assets transfers of the company after the occurrence of illiquidity. Such risk does especially exist in the case of cash-pooling but also in general financial structures and has its origin in Sec. 64 German Limited Liability Law (GmbHG).[10] After the occurrence of illiquidity the Managing Director may only allow such payments which are necessary in order to continue business (such as wages or electricity etc.). Any other payment will be claimed by a later appointed administrator directly from the MD personally.

L. Liability Risks of the Insolvency Administrator

Sometimes, negotiations between creditors and insolvency administrators can be influenced by remarks or reminders of the administrator's liability. Although the insolvency administrator still has a strong position in German insolvency law and will very likely retain this, there exist a few regulations concerning his liability towards the creditors which are important to know in order to avoid that the administrator represents only the partial interests and claims of the main creditors. As main creditors usually are bank institutions, administrators often try to serve their interests in order to be – directly or indirectly – proposed or recommended as an administra-

10 Willemsen/Rechel, *Erweiterte Geschäftsführerhaftung bei Cash-Pooling*, GmbHR 2010, 349.

tor in other insolvency proceedings. First of all, the administrator is obliged to treat the insolvency creditors equally. Pursuant to Sec. 60 InsO the administrator will be personally liable in cases of breach of his legal obligations, of which equal treatment of all insolvency creditors is an important principle.

Furthermore, the administrator has to guarantee financial reporting and proper transparent winding-up. Especially, concerning very big insolvency proceedings, administrators usually either provide a business audit service or mandate audit firms to ensure this. In such cases, the administrator usually can exclude any liability as far as he maintains and monitors the audit process. Smaller insolvency cases usually are audited by the administrator and his personal staff.

Very often, creditors complain about late payment or missing interim reports about the insolvency procedure. Unfortunately, such cannot be enforced under German insolvency law, as long as the administrator provides at the end of the insolvency proceedings a proper final report, containing all financial and asset-related matters. However, in case of a breach of those obligations, creditors can enroll their objections (in best cases, together with respective proving material or documents) in the insolvency court which has the general supervision of insolvency proceedings and the administrator. Such is especially recommended in case of the administrator's final invoice, charging for his services.

M. Pending Reform of German Insolvency Law

German insolvency law often is criticized for unpredictability as well as for missing restructuring incentives, especially in the business sphere. In order to change and improve this, a draft law is currently under discussion in the German parliament (*Bundestag*).[11] Hereinafter is a brief overview of the proposed modifications, in case the draft law should be enacted and come into force within the publication period of the present book.

The announced changes are important from the creditor's point of view, as they will allow more influence of the creditors concerning the appointment of the insolvency administrator as well as containing an improvement to influence restructuring decisions. Furthermore, the rules of the insolvency plan will be simplified and tightened. Especially shareholders, who were not willing to invest into the debtor-company but

---

11 Willemsen/Rechel, Insolvenzrecht im Umbruch – ein Überblick über RegE-ESUG [German insolvency law changing – overview about the reform proposals of the governmental draft law], BB 2011, 834 pp. Willemsen/Rechel, Die Reform des Insolvenzplanverfahrens – ein Zwischenstandsbericht (Reform of the insolvency plan procedure – preliminary results, BB 2010, 2059 et seq.

aimed at getting satisfaction in case of a successful restructuring, can be excluded partially from the restructuring process without indemnification claims. This will also improve from an economical point of view the interest of investors in participating at debt-equity-swaps and insolvency plans.

Reinhard Willemsen
reinhard.willemsen@luther-lawfirm.com

CHAPTER 28
INSURANCE LAW

DR. ALEXANDER MÖNNIG

The first insurance company of the world was founded 1676 in Hamburg, Germany. Today, after 336 years, over 600 German and more than 1000 foreign insurance companies are conducting insurance business in Germany. The German insurance sector is a specially regulated market supervised by the Federal Financial Supervisory Authority ("Bundesanstalt für Finanzdienstleistungsaufsicht" or "BaFin"). In recent years the regulatory framework of the insurance business underwent permanent and fundamental changes, such as several amendments of the German Insurance Supervision Act (Versicherungsaufsichtsgesetz), a profound reform of the German Insurance Contract Act (Versicherungsvertragsgesetz) and the creation of the first set of rules for insurance intermediaries.

A. Direct Insurance Business

There are different ways to build up a direct insurance business in Germany:

A person or company located in a state outside Germany may establish a German stock corporation (*Aktiengesellschaft* or AG), European company (*Europäische Gesellschaft* or *SE*) or a mutual insurance company (*Versicherungsverein auf Gegenseitigkeit* or *VVaG*). Insurance undertakings located in a non-EU/EEA state may establish a branch in Germany. Insurance undertakings located in an EU/EEA state outside Germany may conduct insurance business in Germany on the freedom of establishment basis, i. e. via a branch (*Niederlassungsfreiheit*) or on the freedom of services basis (*Dienstleistungsfreiheit*).

I. Establishment of a Company in Germany

Besides the general incorporation rules that apply to the formation of a company, there are additional rules that apply to the establishment of an insurance undertaking. These rules are stipulated in the German Insurance Supervision Act (*Versicherungsaufsichtsgesetz*, hereinafter referred to as "VAG").

According to Sec. 5 (1) VAG the company requires a license granted by the competent supervisory authority in order to be allowed to carry out insurance business in

Germany. The competent authority for a company that is acting not only locally but nationwide in Germany is the Federal Financial Supervisory Authority (*Bundesanstalt für Finanzdienstleistungsaufsicht* or *BaFin*).

In order to obtain the license, the company has to file an application with a business plan (*Geschäftsplan*) attached (Sec. 5 (2) VAG). The business plan has to contain a description of the purpose and organization of the company, the area of the intended business operations and in particular has to state clearly the conditions which shall ensure that the future liabilities of the company can permanently be met.

Furthermore, the business plan has to contain the following (Sec. 5 (3) VAG):[1]

The Articles of Association in so far as they do not refer to General Terms and Conditions of insurance; information about the classes of insurance that are intended to be carried out and which risks of a class of insurance are intended to be covered; affiliation agreements (*Unternehmensverträge*) as specified under Sects. 291 and 292 of the German Stock Corporation Act (*Aktiengesetz* or *AktG*) as well as outsourcing agreements.

The business plan shall also give evidence of the existence of own funds in the amount of the minimum guarantee fund and the composition of those funds. In addition, estimates have to be submitted for the first three financial years with respect to the expenses for commissions and other current operating expenses, the expected premiums, the expected expenses for claims incurred and the expected liquidity situation. It has to be stated what financial means are expected to be available to meet the liabilities under the insurance contracts and the requirements with respect to the financial resources (Sec. 5 (4) VAG).

In addition, the following information has to be submitted (Sec. 5 (5) VAG):[2]

In the case of substitutive health insurance (*substitutive Krankenversicherung*) and compulsory insurances (*Pflichtversicherungen*) the General Terms and Conditions of insurance; in the case of substitutive health insurance the principles for the calculation of the premiums and mathematical provisions including the calculation bases, mathematical formulas, imputed derivations and statistical evidence used; information about the intended reinsurance arrangements; an estimate of the expenses for setting up the administrative services and the organization for intermediaries as well as a proof that the necessary funds for this purpose (*Organisationsfonds*) are available; the information necessary to assess the reliability and qualification of the managers and directors (detailed requirements are stipulated in Sec. 7a (1) VAG); information

1 For further details see Präve in: Prölss, VAG-Kommentar, 12th ed. 2005, Sec. 5 VAG, 13 et seq.

2 For further details see Präve in: Prölss, VAG-Kommentar, 12th ed. 2005, Sec. 5 VAG, 104 et seq.

about holders of 10 % of the capital or voting rights in the company (detailed requirements are stipulated in Sec. 7a (2) VAG) and about any other close relationship between the company and another natural or legal person (*enge Verbindung*, a definition is given in Sec. 8 (1) no. 4 VAG); data required for assessing the good repute and professional qualification of the responsible actuary (*Verantwortlicher Aktuar*) for life insurances, accident insurances, liability insurances and substitutive health insurances; in case of automobile liability insurance, the name and address of the claims settlement agent (*Schadensregulierungsbeauftragter*, detailed requirements are stipulated in Sec. 7b VAG); the information necessary to assess the reliability and qualification of the members of the supervisory board (detailed requirements are stipulated in Sec. 7a (4) VAG).

The head office of the company must be located in Germany (Sec. 7 (1a) VAG).

Besides the insurance business, the company is not permitted to carry out another business that is not directly related to the insurance business whereas, in principle, such a direct relation is only assumed if the other business is not associated with an extra financial risk (*Verbot des Betreibens versicherungsfremder Geschäfte*, Sec. 7 (2) VAG).

On the basis of this information the competent supervisory authority decides whether the license will be granted – wholly or only for some classes of insurance – or refused. If the company is a subsidiary or sister company of an insurance company or bank that is located in an EU/EEA state the German supervisory authority has to ask the competent authority in this EU/EEA state for a statement.

If the license is granted, it will be granted separately for each class of insurance applied for. If the license to carry out life insurance is granted the company is not allowed to carry out any other class of insurance; the same applies if the company is granted the license to carry out substitutive health insurance, Sec. 8 (1a) VAG (*Spartentrennungsgebot*).

II. Business of an Insurer Located in a Non-EU/EEA State

Insurance undertakings located in a non-EU/EEA state that do not establish a German insurance company (see above) have to establish a German branch instead in order to carry out insurance business in Germany, except where only home-foreign insurance business (*Korrespondenzversicherung*) is conducted.

Besides the general rules that apply to the establishment of a branch in Germany, in principle, the same rules of the VAG apply as with regard to the establishment of a German insurance company (see above). However, some special rules are stipulated in Sec. 105–110 VAG:

According to Sects. 105 (2), 106b (1) VAG, an insurance undertaking located in a non-EU/EEA state requires a license to operate via a German branch. The license is granted by the Ministry of Finance (*Bundesministerium der Finanzen* or *BMF*).

In order to obtain the license the insurance undertaking has to file an application with a business plan (*Geschäftsplan*) attached and has to submit the information according to Sec. 5 (4) sentence 3 and sentence 4 and (5) VAG (see above). In addition,[3] the following information has to be submitted (Sec. 106b (1) VAG):

The Articles of Association of the insurance undertaking; the name of the members of the management and the supervisory board of the insurance undertaking; a certificate of the competent supervisory authority in the home state of the insurance undertaking which states (i) that the insurance undertaking can, in its home country, under its own name, acquire rights and incur liabilities, sue and be sued in court, and (ii) which classes of insurance the insurance undertaking is allowed to carry out and which types of risks it actually covers; the balance sheet and the profit and loss account for each of the past three financial years.

With regard to the capitalization of the insurance undertaking, the following applies: the financial resources have to be sufficient in a way that the interests of the insured are adequately safeguarded and it can be deemed that the liabilities under the insurance contracts will be permanently fulfilled (Sec. 106b (2) VAG which contains more detailed requirements).

According to Sec. 106 (3) VAG, an authorized agent (*Hauptbevollmächtigter*) has to be appointed for the German branch who has to have his domicile and permanent residence in Germany. He must meet the same obligations and personal requirements the VAG requires for the board of directors of a German insurance company (i. e. the requirements under Sec. 7a (1) VAG, see above). He is deemed to have the power of representation for the insurance undertaking. The authorized agent has to be filed for registration with the German commercial register.

On the basis of this information, the Ministry of Finance decides whether the license will be granted – wholly or only for some classes of insurance – or refused.

If the license is granted, it will be granted separately for each class of insurance applied for. The *Spartentrennungsgebot* (Sec. 8 (1a) VAG, see above) also applies here and is extended in view of the insurance undertaking's business, i. e. if the insurance undertaking is operating life insurance together with other classes of insurance, the license will not be granted in Germany for life insurance business. The same applies if the insurance undertaking is operating substitutive health insurance together with other classes of insurance (Sec. 106c VAG).

---

3 For further details see Kollhosser in: Prölss, VAG-Kommentar, 12th ed. 2005, Sec. 106b VAG, 4.

If the license is granted, the insurance undertaking has to conduct business via its German branch only and is not allowed to operate via the home foreign insurance business (*Korrespondenzversicherung*, Sec. 107 VAG).

III. Business of an Insurer Located in an EU/EEA State

Insurance undertakings located in a EU/EEA state outside Germany that do not establish a German insurance company (see above) may, according to Sec. 110a et seqq. VAG, conduct insurance business in Germany either on the freedom of establishment basis, i. e. via a branch (*Niederlassungsfreiheit*), or on the freedom of services basis (*Dienstleistungsfreiheit*). The rules of Sec. 110a et seq. VAG do not apply if the insurance undertaking only carries out the home-foreign insurance business.

If the insurance undertaking intends to operate via a German branch, the general German rules for the establishment of a branch apply. In addition, the insurance undertaking has to notify the competent supervisory authority of its home state – according to the rules of this state – about the intention to conduct insurance business via a branch in Germany.

According to Sec. 110a (2) VAG, the supervisory authority of the home state has to forward certain information about the insurance undertaking (according to Art. 32 of the Directive 92/49/EC and Art. 40 (2) and (3) sub para. 2 of the Directive 2002/83/EC) to the BaFin and has to notify the insurance undertaking accordingly. The branch is allowed to start business after a period of two months from the date of notification, unless the BaFin informs the insurance undertaking of an earlier date. In the case of substitutive health insurance the insurance undertaking has to submit the General Terms and Conditions of insurance before the start of business is allowed (Sec. 110a (2b) VAG).

The insurance undertaking has to appoint an authorized agent (*Hauptbevollmächtigter*) for the German branch who has to be registered with the German commercial register.

If the insurance undertaking intends to operate on the freedom of services basis the insurance undertaking has to notify the competent supervisory authority of its home state – according to the rules of this state – about the intention to conduct insurance business via a branch in Germany.

According to Sec. 110a (2a) VAG the insurance undertaking is allowed to start business when the supervisory authority of the home state has forwarded certain information about the insurance undertaking (according to Art. 35 and Art. 36 of the Directive 92/49/EC and Art. 42 (1) or Art. 43 of the Directive 2002/83/EC) to the BaFin and has notified the insurance undertaking accordingly. In case of substitutive health insurance the insurance undertaking has to submit the General Terms and Conditions of insurance before the start of business is allowed (Sec. 110a (2b) VAG).

IV. General Terms and Conditions

Regardless of how the direct insurance business in Germany is operated the insurance undertaking's General Terms and Conditions have to contain full information about (Sec. 10 VAG):[4]

The events which trigger the insurer's obligation to pay benefits and the special cases where this obligation is excluded or suspended; the nature and size of the benefits of the insurer and when they become due; the date when the premium becomes due and the legal consequences of a delay in premium payment; the policyholder's and the insurer's unilateral rights to influence the content of the insurance contract (e.g. revocation, rescission and termination rights) as well as the conditions (*Obliegenheiten*) and duties to give notice before and after the insured event has occurred (*Anzeigepflichten*); the forfeiture of an insurance claim in the event of failure to observe time limits; the domestic places of venue; the principles and standards of profit participation (*Überschussbeteiligung*), if applicable.

Sec. 10 VAG does not apply to "large risks" in terms of Sec. 210 German Insurance Contract Act (*Versicherungsvertragsgesetz*, hereinafter referred to as "VVG").

V. Information and Advice

According to Sec. 6 VVG, the insurance undertaking is obliged to specify, in particular on the basis of information provided by the customer, the demands and the needs of that customer as well as the underlying reasons for any advice given to the customer on an insurance product.

The insurance undertaking has to produce a record on this according to the complexity of the insurance contract being proposed and has to provide the customer with this record in textual form (*Textform*, i. e. on paper or on any other durable medium available and accessible to the customer) prior to the conclusion of any specific contract. However, the customer may waive his right to be provided with the record by signing a separate waiver, provided that he has been informed by the insurance undertaking that the waiver may be disadvantageous for the customer if he wants to

---

4 For further details see Präve in: Prölss, VAG-Kommentar, 12th ed. 2005, Sec. 10 VAG, 3 et seq.

claim compensation in case of a violation of duties by the insurance undertaking. The insurance undertaking may delegate these duties to its insurance agent (see below).

The aforementioned duties do not apply where:

The insurance contract is mediated by an insurance broker (*Versicherungsmakler*, see below); or the insurance contract is concluded via distant selling (*Fernabsatz*); or the insurance contract covers only "large risks" in terms of Sec. 210 VVG.

According to Sec. 7 VVG, the insurance undertaking has to provide the customer with the policy provisions including the General Terms and Conditions and further information in textual form before the customer has applied for the insurance.

The details about what further information the insurance undertaking has to provide to the customer are contained in a by law to the German Insurance Contract Act which is the Versicherungsvertragsgesetz-Informationspflichtenverordnung or VVG-InfoV.[5]

B. Reinsurance Business

The special rules stipulated in Sec. 119 et seq. VAG apply to the reinsurance business of reinsurance undertakings. The rules of the VVG do not apply to reinsurance contracts.

C. Insurance Intermediary Business

The insurance mediation business in Germany has been regulated in accordance with the Insurance Mediation Directive 2002/92/EC. The Directive has been implemented into German law in the German Trade, Commerce and Industry Regulation Act (*Gewerbeordnung*, hereinafter referred to as "GewO"), the VVG and a bylaw (*Versicherungsvermittlungsverordnung*, hereinafter referred to as "VersVermV"). The rules apply to all persons and companies that want to carry out the insurance mediation business in Germany.

The regulatory requirements for carrying out the insurance intermediary business and the obligations for insurance intermediaries in Germany are as follows:

---

5 For detailed information on the content of the VVG-InfoV see Knappmann in: Prölss/Martin, VVG-Kommentar, 28th ed. 2010, page 1182 et seq.

I. License

According to Sec. 34d (1) GewO, the intermediary has to obtain a license from the Chamber of Commerce and Industry (*Industrie- und Handelskammer* or *IHK*) in order to be allowed to carry out the insurance intermediary business in Germany. To obtain the license the intermediary has to meet the following requirements.[6]

Knowledge and abilities: the intermediary must pass a test to prove that he possesses appropriate knowledge and ability to conduct insurance mediation. Persons who have acted as intermediaries continuously since 31st August 2000 or who have already passed an equivalent test, e.g. insurance/financial salesman (*Versicherungskaufmann/ Fachwirt für Finanzberatung*), are exempted from this test. Good repute/reliability (*Zuverlässigkeit*): the intermediary must have a clean police record with regard to any crimes and offences against property within the last five years prior to application. Proper financial circumstances: the intermediary must have proper financial circumstances, i. e. must not have become bankrupt. Professional indemnity insurance: the intermediary must have professional indemnity insurance. The insurance must be taken out from an insurer that is allowed to carry out the insurance business in Germany. The insurance has to cover the EU/EEA area and the insurance sums must amount to at least EUR 1,13 million per claim and EUR 1,7 million in aggregate per year. First on 15th January 2013 and then every five years the insurance sums will be adapted according to the changes in the European consumer price index.

Exceptions from the license requirement are made in the following cases:

Sec. 34d (3) GewO: an insurance agent can apply for an exemption from the license requirement if the insurance mediation is a supplementary business to his main business (*produktakzessorischer Vermittler*). However, certain requirements also apply to this agent (e.g. he has to take out a professional indemnity insurance, see above). Sec. 34d (4) GewO: an insurance agent does not need a license if he works for only one insurer exclusively or for several insurers, provided that their insurance products do not compete with each other (*gebundener Vermittler* or *Ausschließlichkeitsvertreter*) and at least one of the insurers assumes full responsibility for the agent's actions. Sec. 34d (5) GewO: no license is required if the intermediary is located (or has a branch) in an EU/EEA state and is registered in a register that has been established in accordance with the rules of the Insurance Mediation Directive 2002/92/EC. Sec. 34d (11) GewO clarifies that the German authorities are not competent for issuing a license for EU/EEA insurance intermediaries, i. e. an EU/EEA insurance intermediary would not get a German license even if he would apply for one. Instead – according to the rules in the EU/EEA state where he is located – the intermediary

6 For further details see Schönleiter in: Landmann/Rohmer, GewO-Kommentar, 57th ed. 2010, Sec. 34d GewO, 65 et seqq.

has to inform his regulator that he wants to carry out the insurance intermediary business in Germany, and the regulator then informs the German Chamber of Commerce and Industry accordingly. Sec. 34d (9) GewO: the license requirements do not apply to persons

1: if all the following conditions are met:

- The principal professional activity of the person is not insurance mediation, i. e. insurance mediation is only a sideline business for this person;
- The person exclusively mediates insurance contracts that only require knowledge of the insurance cover that is provided;
- The person does not mediate life assurance contracts or insurance contracts that cover liability risks;
- The insurance is complementary to the product or service supplied by any provider, and the insurance either covers the risk of breakdown, loss of or damage to goods supplied by that provider; or it covers damage to or loss of baggage and other risks linked to the travel booked with the person, including accident and liability insurance, provided that the cover is ancillary to the main cover for the risks linked to that travel;
- The amount of the annual premium does not exceed the amount of € 500.00; and
- The total duration of the insurance contract, including any renewals, does not exceed five years.

2: who mediate insurances in connection with building loan agreements.

3: who mediate creditor insurances for loans that finance goods/services the intermediary has sold/rendered to the policyholder.

II. Employees

Intermediaries according to Sec. 34d (1), (3) or (4) GewO (see above) are obliged to ensure that their employees who are involved in the intermediary business are reliable and adequately qualified (which can be achieved by regular training; a formal test is not required).

III. Registration

Intermediaries according to Sec. 34d (1), (3) or (4) GewO (see above) must be registered in the electronic intermediary register[7] with the competent chamber of commerce and trade.

7 http://www.vermittlerregister.info

No registration is required in case of Sec. 34d (5) and (9) GewO (see above).

In general, the application for registration has to be filed by the intermediaries, however, in the case of an intermediary according to 34d (4) GewO (see above) the insurer that assumes unrestricted liability for the intermediary's business is responsible for the application.

IV. Information and Advice

1. Sec. 11 VersVermV

The intermediary has to provide the customer with the following information at the first business contact:[8]

His name, company name and address; his status, i. e. broker (*Versicherungsmakler*) or agent (*Versicherungsvertreter*) according to Sec. 34d (1), (3) or (4) GewO and the register in which he has been included and the means of verifying that he has been registered; the address, telephone number and internet address of the German Chamber of Commerce and Industry (*Deutscher Industrie- und Handelskammertag e.V.* or *DIHK*) which is the body that administers the intermediary register; any direct or indirect holding of more than 10 % the intermediary holds in an insurance company or an insurance company holds in the intermediary; the address of the German Ombudsmanservice (*Versicherungsombudsmann e.V.*) which is the competent arbitration board a policyholder can turn to in case of disputes with the intermediary.

The information has to be provided in textual form. Many intermediaries print the information on the back of their business cards.

2. Sects. 60, 62 VVG

An insurance agent (i. e. an intermediary who is under a contractual obligation to conduct insurance mediation business with insurance undertakings; *Versicherungsvertreter*) has to inform the customer on which market and information basis he conducts the mediation services. In addition the insurance agent has to provide the customer with the names of the insurers he mediates insurances for and has to inform the customer if he mediates insurances for one insurer exclusively. An insurance broker (i. e. an intermediary who is not under a contractual obligation to conduct insurance mediation business with insurance undertakings; *Versicherungsmakler*) is obliged to give advice on the basis of an analysis of a sufficiently large number of insurance contracts available on the market, to enable him to make a recommendation in accordance with professional criteria regarding which insurance contract

8 For further details see Dörner in: Prölss/ Martin, VVG-Kommentar, 28th ed. 2010, Sec. 11 VersVermV, 1 et seq.

would be adequate to meet the customer's needs ("fair analysis"). This obligation does not apply if the broker informs the customer that he does not give advice on the aforementioned basis. In this case he has to inform the customer on which market and information basis he conducts the mediation services and provide the names of the insurers he bases his advice on. The aforementioned information has to be provided in textual form before the customer has applied for the insurance. However, the customer may waive his right to receive the aforementioned information by signing a separate waiver.

3. *Sects. 61, 62 VVG*

The insurance intermediary is obliged to ask the customer about his demands and needs for insurance cover. On this basis he has to render advice to the customer and inform the customer about the underlying reasons for his advice given to the customer on a given insurance product.

The intermediary has to produce a record of this according to the complexity of the insurance contract being proposed and has to provide the customer with this record in textual form prior to the conclusion of any specific contract. However, the customer may waive his right to receive the record by signing a separate waiver, provided that he has been informed by the intermediary that the waiver may be disadvantageous for the customer if he wants to claim compensation in case of a violation of duties by the intermediary.

The aforementioned requirements of Sec. 11 et seq. VersVermV and Sects. 60–62 VVG are not applicable if and as far as:

The intermediary mediates reinsurance contracts (Sec. 17 VersVermV and Sec. 209 VVG); the intermediary mediates "large risks" in terms of Sec. 210 VVG (see Sec. 17 VersVermV and Sec. 65 VVG); Sec. 34d (9) no. 1 GewO applies (see above) (Sec. 66 VVG).

V. Protection of Monies

An insurance agent is deemed to be authorized for the receipt of payments by the policyholder on behalf of the insurer, unless the policyholder knows or would be grossly negligent not to know that the insurer did not authorize the intermediary for to receive payments. This rule does not apply to insurance brokers, however, an insurance broker can also be authorized by the insurer for the receipt of payments. Where the intermediary is not (deemed to be) authorized to receive payments from the policyholder on behalf of the insurer, he must only receive payments from policyholders if he has provided sufficient security (e.g. via bank guarantee) or has taken out a sufficient insurance for those payments (4 % of the premiums collected annually, minimum EUR 17,000.00). First on 15th January 2013 and then every five years, the minimum insurance sum will be adapted according to the changes in the European consumer price index.

The intermediary is not authorized to receive payments by the insurer on behalf of the policyholder unless he has been authorized by the policyholder in writing. In cases where the intermediary is not authorized by the policyholder, he must only receive payments by the insurer if he has provided sufficient security (e.g. via bank guarantee) or has taken out a sufficient insurance for those payments (4 % of the premiums collected annually, minimum EUR 17,000.00). First on 15th January 2013 and then every five years the minimum insurance sum will be adapted according to the changes in the European consumer price index.

If the intermediary is located in another EU/EEA state he is exempted from the aforementioned obligations to provide security or take out insurance if the protection of monies is secured according to Art. 4 (4) of the Insurance Mediation Directive 2002/92/EC.

In cases when the intermediary is obliged to provide security or take out insurance he has to prove it to the policyholder on request and has to keep a copy in his files.

The intermediary has to record any payments he has received in connection with insurance contracts. The records must contain the following information (if applicable):[9]

Name and address of the policyholder; if and to what extent the intermediary is authorized to receive payments from the policyholder and the insurer;

Kind and amount of monies the intermediary has received from the policyholder for transfer to the insurer; kind, amount and scope of security/insurance that has to be taken out by the intermediary, name of the security/insurance provider; assignment of the policyholder's monies.

However, no record has to be produced when the intermediary has to fulfill a comparable duty due to bookkeeping regulations.

The aforementioned provisions are not applicable if and as far as:

9 For further details see Stenger in: Landmann/Rohmer, GewO-Kommentar, 57th ed. 2010, Sec. 14 VersVermV, 1 et seq.

The intermediary mediates reinsurance contracts (Sec. 17 VersVermV and Sec. 209 VVG); the intermediary mediates "large risks" in terms of Sec. 210 VVG (Sec. 17 VersVermV and Sec. 65 VVG); Sec. 34d para. 9 no. 1 GewO applies (see above) (Sec. 66 VVG).

Dr. Alexander Mönnig, LL.M. (Manchester), E.M.L.E.
alexander.moennig@luther-lawfirm.com

AUTHORS

Ackermann, Hans Christian
Hans-Christian Ackermann, lawyer, certified specialist in employment law. He provides advice on all aspects of individual and collective employment law, particularly concerning acquisitions, restructuring and outsourcing, as well as company pension schemes. This includes the respective negotiations with works councils and trade unions. He also provides assistance to board members, managing directors and executive employees. Hans-Christian Ackermann also lectures regularly on the topic of employment law at various seminars and training programs.

Dr. Altenschmidt, Stefan
Dr. Stefan Altenschmidt, lawyer, focuses on energy law and on environmental, planning and regulatory issues. He advises companies and trade associations, in particular on environmental law, climate protection and emissions trading law, and planning law. He also represents his clients at national administrative and constitutional courts and at the European Court of Justice. Dr. Altenschmidt regularly holds seminars and publishes articles relating to environmental and energy law issues.

Bauer, Silvia
Silvia C. Bauer, lawyer, focuses on data protection-, IT- and e-Commerce. She conducts data privacy audits and advises national and international companies in all questions related to data protection, in particular regarding the worldwide exchange of data and data protection management. Furthermore, she acts as an external data protection officer for several German companies and regularly lectures on data protection and IT law.

Bonnmann, Rüdiger

Rüdiger Bonnmann, lawyer, specializes in administrative law. The focus of his advisory services is real estate law. He provides assistance to project developers, insurance companies, retail companies, and construction companies in construction and real estate law; he provides advice on contractual issues and zoning law, among other things, and also offers on-going advice during construction projects. He also specialises in commercial landlord and tenant law.

Erberich, Ingo

Ingo Erberich, lawyer, specializes in real estate law. He advises on the drafting of contracts, especially for the purchase of real estate, commercial tenancies, and construction contracts. His work also includes advice on project developments, real estate transactions and the related due diligence reviews. He specializes in litigation proceedings concerning commercial tenancy rights and private construction. He mainly advises foreign real estate investors, project developers, sporting venue operators, insurance companies, retailers, industrial companies, and companies from the construction industry.

Dr. Freigang, Ulrike

Dr. Ulrike Freigang, lawyer, focuses on real estate law and litigation. This includes in particular advice to national and international clients on real estate transactions (due diligence, drafting purchase agreements and conducting negotiations), tenancy law (lease agreements and other utilisation contracts), private construction law, and judicial and extrajudicial support during litigation proceedings.

Dr. Fritzsche, Michael

Dr. Michael Fritzsche, lawyer, specializes in real estate transactions (due diligence, purchase agreements, advice on negotiations, structuring of acquisitions and financing), facility management, property law (in particular lease agreements), construction and tendering law, developing projects and structuring contracts for PPP/PFI models, advice on business activities and infrastructure projects of the public sector and public law entities.

Gross, Franz-Rudolf

Franz-Rudolf Gross (LL.M.), lawyer, specializes in energy and anti-trust law. He advises national and international undertakings on all regulatory as well as on contractual issues including network access, unbundling, concessions, network regulation and energy supply agreements. He also focuses on competition law including German and European merger control, antitrust proceedings, contractual issues and the abuse of dominant positions.

Dr. Hahn, Hans-Georg

Dr. Hans-Georg Hahn, lawyer, provides legal assistance in national and international acquisitions and corporate sales, complex due diligences, so-called post-merger integrations, as well as MBOs/MBIs. He also specializes in restructuring privately owned companies and public organizations. In dealing with public authorities, he mainly assists in drafting complex competitive bidding procedures and in accompanying privatizations and the formation of strategic partnerships.

Dr. Happ, Richard

Dr. Richard Happ, lawyer, specializes in corporate law/ M&A, international arbitration and litigation. He advises and represents both German and foreign clients in national and international arbitration proceedings. He has acted as counsel or arbitrator in cases under DIS, ICC, SCC, UNCITRAL, ad-hoc and ICSID rules. A particular focus is on the energy sector. He also specialises in the legal protection of investments made abroad. Dr. Richard Happ has provided advice and represented German States and companies and has acted as a legal expert during several foreign arbitration proceedings.

Dr. Hellmich, Stefanie

Dr. Stefanie Hellmich, lawyer, specializes in data privacy law, and electronic business dealings. She also specialises in IT and licensing law, in particular drafting distribution, outsourcing, cooperation, maintenance and support agreements. She offers assistance during business transactions and provides legal advice to both providers and users.

Dr. Janssen, Helmut

Dr. Helmut Janssen, lawyer, specializes in European and German antitrust law, commercial and distribution law and public law. He has defended companies against anti-trust allegations raised by the European Commission, the German Federal Cartel Office and the US Department of Justice Antitrust Division. Dr. Janssen has assisted numerous clients in foreign and domestic merger control proceedings, in designing and defending distribution systems. He consults on cooperation agreements between competitors and on compliance measures. Dr. Helmut Janssen also assists in a wide range of public grants cases (EU state aid). A further area of expertise is international trade law (WTO as well as EU anti-subvention/anti-dumping policy).

Dr. Kapp, Thomas

Dr. Thomas Kapp, lawyer, specializes in antitrust law. He deals with all issues relating to national and international antitrust law, in particular, cartel damage claims, administrative fine proceedings in connection with breaches of antitrust law, merger control, distribution law, and compliance. He is regularly representing clients before national and European courts (e.g. paper/wholesale company – FCJ, case KRB 12/07, bathroom fixtures wholesale company – CFI, case T-386/10). He is author/co-author of many books and articles related to antitrust law. He is a well-known speaker at seminars and symposia.

Dr. Kobabe, Rolf

Dr. Rolf Kobabe, lawyer, specializes in capital market law, funds, and regulatory law. He focuses on structuring funds (financial instruments and investments), mezzanine capital and other types of structured finance, private placements and companies' own issue of shares, as well as regulatory issues in the field of financial services. Dr. Kobabe has in the past accompanied and advised more than 250 issued funds and other investment products regarding all types of assets (including ships, real estate, and green bonds). He also represents clients when it comes to defending against or enforcing claims in connection with failed capital investments. Dr. Kobabe has published numerous books, brochures, and articles on current capital market developments.

Dr. Kobes, Stefan

Dr. Stefan Kobes, lawyer, specializes in administrative law. He provides advice on all matters relating to construction planning law, particularly drafting site development plans, obtaining permits for construction projects and emissions, the decontamination of contaminated sites, obtaining permits for emissions trading, and monitoring greenhouse gas emissions. Dr. Kobes advises companies from the energy industry, ceramic industry, paper industry, and wood material industry. He also advises real estate developers and businesses nationwide. Dr. Stefan Kobes has published numerous articles on contamination and emissions trading law. He regularly speaks on current topics relating to environmental law.

Dr. Kuhnle, Thomas

Dr. Thomas Kuhnle, lawyer, specializes in corporate law. He focuses on buying and selling companies. His advice ranges from structuring transactions and due diligence inquiries to contract negotiations and post-acquisition integration. His clients are strategic investors from various fields (in particular commerce, machine construction, and the automotive industry), private equity institutions, and banks.

Leyendecker, Claudia

Claudia Leyendecker, lawyer and tax advisor, specializes in banking and insurance law matters, financing, and the mergers and acquisitions of banks and insurance companies. In addition to advising large companies, banks, and insurance companies in all banking and insurance supervisory matters, international projects as well as assisting in financial matters, she liaises between banking law and corporate law, in particular mergers and acquisitions. Furthermore, she advises investment companies with regard to the management of investment funds in accordance with the regulatory requirements for pension funds and insurers.

Dr. Mäder, Detlef

Dr. Detlef Mäder, lawyer, focuses on competition and trademark law as well as other related areas of intellectual property law (e.g. design law and product piracy law). Dr. Detlef Mäder advises numerous nationally active companies in issues regarding the configuration and protection of marketing measures as well as in disputes over intellectual property rights. Dr. Mäder also provides assistance to national and international clients with their demands for trademark and design rights or their defense thereof.

Meier, Achim

Achim Meier, lawyer, provides legal advice during the construction process (with a focus on civil and plant construction) and the structuring of PPP projects and real estate transactions (for both the buyer and the seller). In addition, he has in-depth knowledge and a wealth of experience in the area of infrastructure and large building projects. Achim Meier advises his clients in all matters relating to public procurement law and private building law, both within the scope of PPP projects and within the scope of conventional implementation models, as well as in court and arbitration proceedings. He also specializes in the defence against and enforcement of additional claims.

Dr. Mönnig, Alexander

Dr. Alexander Mönnig, lawyer, focuses on corporate law/ M&A and insurance law. He provides comprehensive advice to domestic and foreign insurance companies in all matters pertaining to insurance supervision, insurance contract law, and insurance intermediary law including product design and the development of distribution channels. Dr. Mönnig has special expertise in the areas of residual debt insurance, payment protection, and property insurance in the form of protection against coincidental damages and warranty extensions (e.g. for entertainment electronics), together with related products.

Pape, Ulf-Dieter
Ulf-Dieter Pape, lawyer, focuses on public procurement law, real estate law, and public private partnerships. He mainly advises public authorities and private companies on all aspects of public procurement law. He has extensive experience in accompanying procedures for procurement by tender and in structuring privatization proceedings on behalf of both the contractor and the bidder. Additionally, he advises both public contractors and bidders in review proceedings.

Dr. Rath, Michael
Dr. Michael Rath, lawyer, certified specialist in IT law, specializes in IT, data protection and copyright law. Dr. Rath is a member of the German Society for Law and Computer Science (DGRI) and an accredited mediator for IT disputes with the arbitration board of DGRI. He advises national and international companies on all matters relating to IT, data protection, e-discovery, IT procurement, IT outsourcing, and (IT) compliance requirements. He is also author of various IT publications and give lectures concerning these fields of law.

Dr. Schmidt, Wulff-Axel
Dr. Wulff-Axel Schmidt, lawyer, specializes in all issues relating to competition, trademark, copyright, and IT law. He focuses on implementing strategies for sourcing and protection law (for example in acquisitions, mergers, and sales) as well as drafting license, cooperation, and IT project agreements. He focuses on the realization of intellectual property strategies (for example in the context of acquisitions, mergers, and sales) as well as on drafting license, cooperation, and IT project agreements.

Dr. Schneider, Volker
Dr. Volker Schneider, certified specialist in employment law. He focuses on employment law and provides comprehensive advice in matters pertaining to collective labor law and individual employment law as well as restructuring and corporate transactions, corporate constitution law, employee dismissal protection, bankruptcy labour law and labour law for management board members.

Siegemund, Ulrich
Ulrich Siegemund, lawyer and tax advisor, specializes in national and international tax law. He has worked for two of the Big Four and has advised numerous multinational groups of companies from different industries. His main focus lies on international tax law (inbound and outbound), acquisitions, tax-optimized structuring and restructuring, and real estate transactions. He is co-author of commentaries on the German Corporate Income Tax Act and has published several articles in professional magazines.

Dr. Stappert, Holger
Dr. Holger Stappert, lawyer, specializes in antitrust law. He provides advice to clients during high-level merger control, abuse of dominance and administrative fine proceedings at both German and European levels. Dr. Holger Stappert also is an experienced specialist for energy law and energy contract law. Dr. Stappert regularly releases publications on current issues on antitrust and energy law and is a regular speaker at seminars and professional symposia.

Steimle, Volker
Volker Steimle, lawyer, specializes in the law of national and international distribution of goods, including product liability and product safety. A particular focus of his work is litigation in matters of supply and distribution contracts, both in State courts as well as in national and international arbitration proceedings. Volker Steimle is a member of the German Institution of Arbitration (DIS). He has an industry focus on the Automotive industry and on industrial products.

Stoecker, Detlev
Detlev Stoecker, lawyer and notary, specializes in advising national and international investors on real estate transactions in various different forms (asset/share deals), acting on behalf of both the purchaser and the seller from the initial structuring of the acquisition, on due diligences, drafting contracts and conducting negotiations and providing finance advice up to and including providing contract management advice following the completion of the transaction. He deals with investment properties and portfolios as well as real estate projects.

Weidlich, Thomas (LL.M.)
Thomas Weidlich, attorney-at-law, specializes in corporate and capital markets law. He has extensive experience in initial and secondary offerings, capital raisings and other capital measures (rights issues, capital reductions, dept-to-equity-swaps and contributions in kind) as well as group restructurings (mergers, spin-offs and change of legal form, intercompany agreements). He also has a strong focus on cross-border acquisitions and joint ventures. This includes advising on the whole transaction process from the structuring stage through complex due diligence reviews to contract negotiations. He is a member of the International Bar Association (IBA) and the Inter-Pacific Bar Association (IPBA).

Willemsen, Reinhard
Reinhard Willemsen, lawyer, focuses on providing commercial law advice. In addition he is head of the restructuring and insolvency department and advises on recapitalisation and bankruptcyinsolvency law (not only on the side of the debtor, but also for creditors); he deals with all legal aspects relating to trade law (such as negotiations of trade agreements, agent contracts, product liability etc.). He is also dedicated to assisting German businesses in Russia and Russian businesses in Germany.

Wittler, Jutta
Jutta Wittler, lawyer, mediator and arbitrator, specializes in building and architectural law. Her services include providing legal advice and litigation and arbitration advice during the construction process including international plant engineering and construction projects. She also lectures at seminars on training specialist lawyers and also on the Code of Architects' and Engineers' Fees 2009 (HOAI 2009). She is one of the editors and co-authors of the Handbook of Construction and Architectural Law.

Dr. Yates, Angelika
Dr. Angelika Yates, lawyer, focuses on complex domestic and international M&A transactions and joint ventures. She mainly provides legal advice in connection with European investment projects in the Asia-Pacific region (with an emphasis on Australia, India, Singapore, and Malaysia). She is also actively involved in capital market law, especially with regard to initial public offerings by German corporations abroad or by foreign corporations in Germany.

LUTHER

Profile

Luther Rechtsanwaltsgesellschaft mbH is one of the top addresses among German commercial law firms. From our eleven German offices and seven international offices, our lawyers and tax advisors advise their clients both in legal disputes and in organisational issues. We focus on providing efficient and far-sighted advice which leads to the desired commercial results. This, together with the sensible allocation of time and personnel resources, provides the basis for our innovative advice.

Luther provides legal and tax advice in all areas relevant to companies, investors and the public sector. Knowledge of the market in which our clients are active is a prerequisite for providing successful advice.

Luther is located at seven important finance and investment centres in Europe and Asia. In addition, we have long-standing, close relationships with business law firms in all relevant jurisdictions around the world. Furthermore, we are the German member firm of Taxand, a worldwide organisation of independent tax advisory firms. More than 2,000 tax specialists from approx. 50 countries are presently part of the Taxand network.

Areas of Practice

- Antitrust Law
- Banking, Finance & Capital Markets
- Business Succession and Private Clients
- Commercial and Distribution Law
- Corporate Criminal and Criminal Tax Law
- Corporate Law / M&A
- Dispute Resolution
- Employment Law
- Energy Law
- Environment Planning Regulatory
- Foreign Trade Law
- Insurance Law
- Protection of Intellectual Property and Copyright Law
- Public Private Partnership

- Public Procurement Law
- Real Estate
- Restructuring and Insolvency Consulting
- Tax Advice
- Technology, Media and Telecommunications